Topics in Practical Halacha
Vol. 2

Selected topics of practical Halacha from the four sections of Shulchan Aruch in accordance to the rulings of Shulchan Aruch Harav, Chabad Custom, and other Halachic authorities

Compiled by: Rabbi Yaakov Goldstein

..

Topics in Practical Halacha Vol. 2

Published and copyrighted © by
Yaakov Goldstein
Bar Yochaiy Safed, Israel
For orders, questions, comments, contact:
Tel: 050-695-2866
E-mail: rabbiygoldstein@gmail.com
www.shulchanaruchharav.com
Available on Amazon.com

5781 • 2020

ISBN-13: 978-1984119483

Cover Design by Ron Isaiah

Approbations for the Authors previous work of "A Semicha Aid for Learning the Laws of Shabbos"
Reprinted with the explicit permission of the Rabbanim

ב"ה

RABBI MENACHEM M. GLUCKOWSKY
CHABAD RECHOVOT
12 HAGANA ST. RECHOVOT ISRAEL
Tel: 08-9493176 Fax:08-9457620 Cel: 050-4145770

מנחם מענדל גלוכובסקי
רב קהילת חב"ד ברחובות
מען : רח' ההגנה 12/1 רחובות 76214
משרד 08-9493176 פקס. 08-9457620 נייד 050-4145770

Elul 577

I have seen the valuable Sefer "A Semicha Aid for Learning The Laws of Shabbos" written by Rabbi Yaakov Goldstein. The purpose of this Sefer is to assist students learning Semicha in learning the material from the Alter Rebbe's Shulchan Aruch, as well as for them to come out with a valuable and large database of knowledge in practical Halachic questions dealt with in contemporary authorities. It excels in its clear presentation, concise language and thorough summaries in all the relevant laws covered in the Shulchan Aruch of Admur.

It can also serve the general English public in giving them the opportunity to learn the Laws of Shabbos faithful to the opinion of the Alter Rebbe.

Mention must be made, as writes the author in his foreword, that one is not to use this Sefer, amongst all Sefarim of Melaktim, to Pasken for himself. One must rather address all matters which require clarification to a qualified Rav.

I bless the author for his work and wish him much success.

Menachem Mendel Gluckowsky.

Approbations for the Authors previous work of "A Semicha Aid for Learning the Laws of Shabbos"
Reprinted with the explicit permission of the Rabbanim

בס"ד

RABBI B. YURKOWICZ

CHABAD LOD

ברוך בועז יורקוביץ

רב ומד"א דשיכון חב"ד לוד

אה"ק ת"ו

The book "The laws of Shabbos" written by Rabbi Yaakov Goldstein is a comprehensive compilation of the laws and customs of Shabbos, up until the many Poskim of today's time, which discuss the practical applications of the laws. Sefarim of this nature are very important and will certainly strengthen the proper observance of Shabbos.

I thus come here with words of blessing and praise to my dear acquaintance, the author, who brings merits to the masses through this important work.

As the author himself has mentioned in his foreword I reiterate that which is known that the layman cannot use this Sefer to Pasken for himself even after learning it in whole, but must rather address all their questions to a qualified Rav.

I am confident that in the merit of this spreading of the laws of Shabbos, on which the Sages state "If the Jews guarded Shabbos they would be redeemed", it will hasten the coming of our righteous Moshiach speedily in our days.

Rabbi Baruch Jurkavitch

הרב ב... בועז יורקוביץ'

רב מרא דאתרא שיכון חב"ד לוד

08-9256070, 054-7977042

Important Notice

The Halachas provided in this book are intended to serve as an aid in understanding Halacha and as a resource of practical Halachic questions and sources for the English reader. It is not meant at all to take the place of a competent Rav, Moreh Horaah or one's own personal research of a Halacha.

Foreword

Acknowledgement:

First and foremost, I give thanks to the Almighty which has blessed me to be able to compile this work. I thank my wife, My Eishes Chayil, Shayna, which if not for her support this book would have been impossible to accomplish. I thank all the Rabbanim and Rosheiy Yeshivas which have given me advice and support regarding the project, and of course my students in which through teaching them many insights have been added to the laws written here, following the dictum of the Sages "And from my students more than all". A special thanks to Rabbi Roberto Szerer and his wife who have graciously given their support throughout the course of the writing of this Sefer, The merit of the masses rests on their shoulders. I also thank Rabbi/Dr. Kenneth Trestman and his wife for their monthly support throughout the course of the writing of this Sefer.

The importance of learning Halacha:

It is known and evident the importance that the study and knowledge of Halacha plays in the role of the life of a Jewish man and woman. As is known, the Rebbe lived and preached that one must be a Shulchan Aruch Yid, a Jew which every movement of his life is dictated by the directives of the Shulchan Aruch. To such extent was the knowledge of Halacha in the forefront of the Rebbe's eyes, that he pleaded and suggested in a talk of Yud Shvat 1955 that in today's times the Yeshivas are not to begin the accustomed deep analytical studies in Talmud until the students have been taught the fundamental principles of Jewish belief and the laws which are written in Shulchan Aruch. The Rebbe continued, "If the situation continues the way it is, then in a number of years from now there will not be a Rabbi which will know a simple law regarding a Jew's daily life, such as a law in the laws of Muktzah. Yes, he will know maybe a law in Nezikin or Choshen Mishpat from the Talmud which he learned, but he will be ignorant of the simplest of laws brought down in Shulchan Aruch".

Ruling of Shulchan Aruch:[1] In the laws of Talmud Torah the following ruling is given: The learning of practical Halacha takes precedence over learning other fields of Torah. Only after one is clearly well versed in practical Halacha, and knows the detailed laws relevant to his daily life, is he to study other parts of Torah in depth. One is to learn majority of Orach Chaim and selected sections of Yoreh Deah, Even Haezer and Choshen Mishpat.

The opinion of the Chassidic Rabbeim: The Baal Shem Tov and Maggid state that the evil inclination tries to persuade a Jew not to learn practical Halacha and tells him to spend all of his days learning the Talmud and its commentaries. This is done in order so the person does not serve G-d properly according to His will.[2] The Alter Rebbe distanced people from learning Torah simply for the sake of Pilpul and emphasized the necessity of learning in depth for the sake of practical Halacha.[3] The Mittler Rebbe decreed that every community is to set a study session to learn the entire Alter Rebbe's Shulchan Aruch on the section of Orach Chaim.[4] The Rebbe Rashab writes that every Chassid is obligated to learn the Alter Rebbe's Shulchan Aruch Orach Chaim from beginning to end and that every person is to establish a daily learning session to learn and review these Halachos.[5] In today's generations one must especially have Mesirus Nefesh not to swerve from even one letter of Shulchan Aruch.[6] The Rebbe Rayatz reiterates this by saying that every Jew must establish a daily Torah session in Halacha, each person on his level; Shulchan Aruch or Kitzur Shulchan Aruch.[7]

---

[1] Hilchos Talmud Torah 2:9-10; Shach Yoreh Deah 246; Hakdama of Mishneh Berurah; Toras Menachem 13 p. 236
[2] Tzivas Harivash 117; Or Torah of the Maggid 221
[3] Beis Rebbe p. 32
[4] Hakdama of Mittler Rebbe in Shulchan Aruch Harav
[5] Kuntrus Hatefilah 17
[6] Sefer Hamamarim "Ein Hakadosh Baruch Hu Ba Betrunya" 1888
[7] Sefer Hamamarim 1926 p. 263

The directives of the Rebbe:[8]

Learning Halacha as part of the Yeshiva schedule: The Rebbe stated that a revolution is to be made in the learning curriculum of the Yeshivas, for it to include the section of Orach Chaim and practical Halacha. The Rebbe stated that if the Yeshivas don't desire to change the curriculum of the regular study hours, it should at least be encouraged when the students are on break.[9] The Yeshivas are not to begin the accustomed deep analytical studies in Talmud until the students have been taught the fundamental principles of Jewish belief and the laws which are written in Shulchan Aruch.[10] This applies even to the Yeshivos Gedolos, as we see that the knowledge of the Yeshiva students is very minute amongst the laws found in Orach Chaim.[11] If I had the power I would establish that every Mosad, beginning from the kindergartens and through the Yeshivos and Kolalim, establish a Shiur in these practical laws.[12]

The importance of being an expert on the laws in Orach Chaim: Elsewhere the Rebbe stated: Unfortunately, we see amongst many students that the more they expand their knowledge in Talmud and its commentaries the less they know the laws relevant to their practical life. The laws in Orach Chaim are extremely necessary for one to be constantly well versed in them, as the questions that arise in these subjects in many instances do not give one the time to ask a Rabbi or look in a Sefer for the answer.[13] This especially applies to the laws of Birchas Hanehnin; Hefsek in Tefilah; Muktzah and laws of the like of which the ignorance in these topics is appalling.[14]

Establishing Shiurim in practical Halacha in all communities: If I had the power I would establish that every community has a Shiur in these practical laws.[15] These Shiurim should take place in the local Shul.[16] Thus each community, and even each individual, is to include within his Torah Shiurim a set time for learning and reviewing practical Halacha.[17] One is to have a Shiur in these Halachas every single day, even for a few minutes.[18] For this purpose it is not necessary to learn specifically from the Shulchan Aruch [which can take much time] but rather to learn from compilations of Halachas such as those found in Derech Hachaim, Kitzur Shulchan Aruch and other compilations.[19] The Rav giving the Shiur is to then give over any extra information that the listeners need to know, that is not included in the compiled Halachas.[20]

Summary:
Every Jew is to have a set learning session every day in practical Halacha, even for a few minutes a day. One is to use this time to learn practical laws from available Halacha compilations, and not necessarily from the actual Shulchan Aruch.

The goal of this Sefer:

This Sefer comes in continuation of our series of Sefarim catered to the English-speaking public on the Shulchan Aruch. Our goal is to cover all the sections of Orach Chaim and the practical sections of Yoreh Deah, Even Haezer and Choshen Mishpat, in faith to the Alter Rebbe's rulings and customs of Chabad Lubavitch. Our previous Sefarim covered specific topics in Halacha, giving our readers a full and complete treatise on the subject topic. This Sefer however is the start of a new series within our general

---

[8] See Shulchan Menachem 4 p. 238-244 for a compilation of letters and Sichos on this topic.
[9] Sichas Tzav 13th Nissan found in Toras Menachem 13 p. 236
[10] Sichas Yud Shvat 1955
[11] Igros Kodesh 16 p. 116
[12] Igros Kodesh 10 p. 270
[13] Igros Kodesh 10 p. 130
[14] Igros Kodesh 10 p. p. 130; p. 192; p. 270; p. 355
[15] Igros Kodesh 10 p. 143
[16] Igros Kodesh ibid based on the saying of Chazal [Brachos 8a] "Hashem loves the gates of Jewish law more than the Shul and Batei Midrash."
[17] Igros Kodesh 7 p. 238
[18] Toras Menachem 7 p. 114; Learning the Halachas every single day will help one remember also the Halachas he learned the day before. [ibid]
[19] Igros Kodesh 7 p. 238; Igros Kodesh 10 p. 144; Igros Kodesh 11 p. 281; Igros Kodesh 13 p. 24; Toras Menachem 7 p. 114; "This does not refer to Tur and Beis Yosef, but rather to Shulchan Aruch and Beir Heiytiv. However one who has time for more is praised." [ibid]
[20] Igros Kodesh 13 p. 24

Halacha series, and does not cover any one specific subject in Halacha but rather encompasses various practical Halachic topics throughout all sections of Shulchan Aruch. It is meant to provide the reader with a clear summary of practical subjects in Orach Chaim, Yoreh Deah, Even Haezer, Choshen Mishpat. It provides a clear, and concise, organized essay on Jewish law. In addition, it contains a wealth of practical Q&A that is not dealt with in Shulchan Aruch and gives the reader a clear background of the Rabbinical opinions on the subject. In addition, it provides a wealth of information in the footnotes, which include sources, reasons, overview of the rulings of other Poskim, and clarifications. Thus, the goal of this Sefer is on the one hand to give the English-speaking public clear guidance of answers to Halachic questions, and at the same time hand him vast background knowledge of the subject at hand, thus fulfilling the Rebbe's instructions that every Jew is to be wealthy in knowledge of Torah. Many of the Halachos printed in this Sefer have featured on our Daily Halacha email and Whatsapp messages in written and audio format.

Understanding the format of the Halachas provided within this Sefer and the Poskim they are based on:
The rulings provided in the Sefer are faithful to the rulings of the Shulchan Aruch Harav, otherwise known as the Alter Rebbe's Shulchan Aruch, in all cases of conflict with other Poskim. The Chabad customs are mentioned in their relevant places. The other opinions applicable, such as the opinion of the Michaber, Mishneh Berurah, Kaf Hachaim and other opinions, are mentioned in the footnotes. The above only applies to those areas of Halacha in which we merited to have the writings of the Alter Rebbe, which is Orach Chaim and a minority of Yoreh Deah and Choshen Mishpat. However, the majority of Yoreh Deah, Choshen Misphat, and the entirety of Even Haezer we did not merit to receive the writings of the Alter Rebbe, and therefore in these Halachas we followed the rulings of all the classical Poskim who voiced an opinion, and in cases of dispute the dispute is mentioned. The Halachas provided are split into three sections:

1. The Halacha Section: The Halacha section is the main section written in the non-boxed area. In general, only those rulings recorded in the Shulchan Aruch of Admur or Michbaer/Rama/Shach/Taz are brought and summarized within this section. Many times, there are additional explanations, stipulations and clarifications of a Halacha which is brought in other Poskim. All these additions are brought in brackets or footnotes. This allows the reader to maintain an understanding of the Halacha as written by the Shulchan Aruch without the additional comments of later authorities, but at the same time gain from their necessary additions.
2. The footnotes: The footnotes provide the reader with a number of different points of information. They provide the sources for each statement written, as well as additional explanations and opinions of a given Halacha. Many footnotes serve to delve into the wording of the Shulchan Aruch in a given Halacha, his intent and the background of his rulings.
3. The boxed area: The boxed area which follows each Halacha serve to provide a concise summary of the Halacha and additional practical Q&A that have been dealt with in contemporary Poskim and relate to the given subject. The Q&A section does not include Halachas that are explicitly ruled in the Shulchan Aruch, as these Halachas have already been written in the Halacha section of the book. The Q&A section lends the learner a greatly needed base knowledge for practical application of the resulting law learned within a topic. Many times, even after one has sifted and comprehended the final ruling of Admur, its influence within practical cases remain obscure. This is besides for the fact that researching a question amongst the sea of Poskim is both time comprising as well as not always practical. We therefore have compiled many major practical Halachic questions which connect with a given Halacha that was learned. The answers given have been compiled from various sources, as noted in the footnotes. In cases where a dispute amongst Poskim is recorded we have not given final rulings, being that we are not in a position to rule for the public like which Posek one is to follow. In these cases one is to consult with his personal Rav and receive guidance for what he is to do. **It is of importance to note that the ruling of one's personal Rav takes precedence over any dissenting opinion brought in the book, whether or**

not this opinion is known to the Rav. Furthermore, even those which are in Rabbinical position of giving rulings are not to base their rulings on opinions brought in this book without first studying and verifying its source. As is known, one may not base a ruling on summarized Halachas [Melaktim, a compiler of opinions] but is rather to discern this for himself in the sources that are brought. [See Piskeiy Teshuvos Vo. 3 in the approbations of Gedolei Yisrael, and the introduction there.]

Historical background of Shulchan Aruch Harav:[21]

The Shulchan Aruch Harav, also known as the Alter Rebbe's Shulchan Aruch, or Shulchan Aruch Admur Hazakein; was written by Rav Schneur Zalman of Liadi.

Its initiation: The Maggid of Mezritch was encouraged by the heavenly courts to search amongst his students for a proper candidate to compile a new Shulchan Aruch.[22] The Maggid of Mezritch chose the Alter Rebbe to write this compilation.[23]

When was it written: It was written anywhere between the years 1765-1775.[24] Some[25] prove that the section of Orach Chaim was written in the years 1771-1772. The Rebbe Rayatz writes[26] that the Maggid asked Admur to write the Shulchan Aruch when he was 21 years old.[27] The other sections of the Shulchan Aruch were written at a later time. An exact date has not been historically proven.[28]

The laws of Tzitzis-Amongst the first sections to be written:[29] Amongst the first subjects to be compiled by the Alter Rebbe were the laws of **Tzitzis** and the laws of Pesach, which were written while he was in Mezritch, prior to the arrival of the brothers Rav Shmelka of Nickelsberg and Rav Pinchas Horowitz. When the holy brothers saw the work of the Alter Rebbe on these two subjects, they praised it tremendously and blessed him to merit completing his work.

How long did it take to write?[30] The section of Orach Chaim was written by Admur in a span of two years.

When was it printed? The Shulchan Aruch was first printed in its entirety after the Alter Rebbe passed away, in the year 1816.[31] Certain sections of the Shulchan Aruch were printed beforehand. Hilchos Talmud Torah was printed in Shklov in the year 1794.[32]

The name "Shulchan Aruch Harav": The source for this name "Shulchan Aruch Harav" is seemingly based on the title of "Rav" that was given to Admur by the students of the Maggid and the Maggid himself. The following is the story related to the giving of this title:[33] The Maggid once told Reb Zusha "write to our Gaon Reb Zalmana Litvak to come here". Upon the students hearing that the Maggid referred to the Alter Rebbe as our Gaon, they gave him the title "Rav". When Reb Avraham Hamalach

---

[21] See the following resources for historical background of the Shulchan Aruch Harav: Hakdama of Shulchan Aruch Harav, written by the children of Admur; Sifrei Halacha Shel Admur Hazakein; Sefer Hatoldos.

[22] To note that the Gr"a also intended on writing a Shulchan Aruch with all of his final rulings, bringing only one opinion. However this did not come into fruition being the Gr"a testified that he did not have heavenly permission to do so. [Hakdama of Biur Hagr"a written by his children] However the Maggid received Divine consent and motivation to write a new Shulchan Aruch. [Sifrei Halacha Shel Admur Hazakein p. 7 footnote 1; Talpiyos 4:1-2 p. 184 in name of the Admur of Radzin]

[23] Igros Kodesh Admur Hazakein [printed in Maggid Dvarav Leyaakov Hosafos p.47]; Hakdama on Shulchan Aruch Harav, written by the children of Admur. The Maggid stated that the four cubits of Halacha are dependent on the Alter Rebbe and that even the first thought of the Alter Rebbe in a given topic is a glimmer of Divine spirit [Ruach Hakodesh]. [Letter of Maggid printed in Sefer Hatoldos p. 36]

[24] It is unclear as to exactly which year Admur began writing the Shulchan Aruch. The above years are the estimated years of when it was written. [See Sifrei Halacha Shel Admur Hazakein p. 9] Many say that the writing of the Shulchan Aruch was begun by Admur at the age of 25. Accordingly, the beginning of the writing of the Shulchan Aruch would have been in 1770. This is five years after the Alter Rebbe arrived in Mezritch. [He arrived in Mezritch for the first time at the age of 20 -Hakdama of Shulchan Aruch written by the children of Admur; Igros Kodesh Admur Hazakein 2:32; See also Beis Rebbe 2:1; Likkutei Dibburim 3:483.] The year that the Alter Rebbe arrived in Mezritch was 1764. [Rebbe in Haggadah Shel Pesach "Bedikas Chameitz"]

[25] Footnote 16-17 in Hakdama of new Kehos printing.

[26] Sefer Hasichos 1929 Sukkos brought in Sefer Hatoldos 3 p. 161

[27] Accordingly it was written in the year 1765-1767. Vetzaruch Iyun

[28] See Sifrei Halacha Shel Admur Hazakein p. 9-10

[29] Hakdama of Shulchan Aruch written by the children of Admur

[30] Hakdama of Shulchan Aruch Harav, written by the children of Admur.

[31] Prior to that time the Chassidim had many hand written copies of the Shulchan Aruch. However it was not printed in a formal book. [Piskeiy Hasiddur introduction]

[32] Sefer Hatoldos p. 33

[33] Likkutei Dibburim 1 p. 100-101

told this over to his father the Maggid, the Maggid replied "The Chevraya Kadisha have projected the truth in this statement. A name has meaning, and the Halacha is like Rav. The **Shulchan Aruch of the Rav** will be accepted within all of Jewry."

Following the rulings of Shulchan Aruch Harav versus other Poskim:[34]
Chabad Chassidim have accepted the rulings of the Shulchan Aruch Harav for all matters, whether for leniency or stringency. This applies even if majority of codifiers argue on his opinion. This is similar to those who follow the opinion of the Rambam [or Michaber] and do not divert from his opinion. The Maggid stated that the four cubits of Halacha are dependent on the Alter Rebbe and that even the first thought of the Alter Rebbe in a given topic is a glimmer of Divine spirit [Ruach Hakodesh].[35] His rulings and arbitrations are considered as if they were given on Sinai.[36] The Tzaddik, Reb Levi Yitzchak of Berditchev writes[37] as follows: I testify heaven and earth that if the Alter Rebbe were alive in the times of the Rif and Rambam he would be considered like one of their contemporaries etc. His "words of gold" is literally like the words of the Rif and Rambam of blessed memory."

---

[34] Hakdama of Ketzos Hashulchan; See Divrei Nechemia Yoreh Deah 1
[35] Letter of Maggid printed in Sefer Hatoldos p. 36
[36] Letter of Maggid printed in Maggid Dvarav Leyaakov Hosafos p. 100
[37] Brought in Piskeiy Hasiddur ibid

About the author:

Rabbi Yaakov Goldstein currently lives with his wife Shayna, and eleven children K"H, in Tzfas, Israel. Rabbi Goldstein received Semicha from Rabbi Schneur Zalman Labkowski of the Tomchei Temimim headquarters in 2005 and served as a chaplain in the Lotar/Kalatz and K9 unit of the IDF from years 2005-2008. He is also a certified Shochet, and has performed Hashgacha work in slaughterhouses. Rabbi Goldstein is the director of Shulchanaruchharav.com, the world's leading web-based Halacha database, and is the director of the Home Study Semicha Program, a self-study web-based Semicha program. He is a prolific author of over 30 Sefarim studied by a wide range of readers throughout the world, which is used regularly in Semicha programs around the globe. He is a world renowned Posek, answering questions to a web-based market, and serves as a local Posek, Rav, and Lecturer, in the Tzemach Tzedek community Shul in Tzefas, Israel. His many classes can be heard both from his website, Vimeo and YouTube channel. Students can join live to classes given in the Tzemach Tzedek Shul, through the " בית חבד צפת Chabad Tsfat" YouTube channel.

Other works by the Author

The present author has written books on various subjects in Shulchan Aruch. Some of these sections are not yet available to the public in a published format although all currently available **free of charge** on our website Shulchanaruchharav.com. In order for these subjects to become available on the bookshelf, and in order to add more subjects to the website, we are in need of funding. If you or anyone you know would like to sponsor a Halachic section to become available in print or on the web, please contact the author and the merit of spreading Halacha, and the merit of the Alter Rebbe, will certainly stand in your favor!

The following is a list of other subjects currently available in print:

*All books are available for purchase on Shulchanaruchharav.com & Amazon.com

1. *The Chassidishe Parsha-Torah Or-Likkutei Torah*
2. *The Weekly Parsha Summary*
3. *The Tanach summary series-Sefer Yehoshua-Shoftim*
4. *Topics in Practical Halacha Vol. 1*
5. *Topics in Practical Halacha Vol. 2*
6. *Topics in Practical Halacha Vol. 3*
7. *Topics in Practical Halacha Vol. 4*
8. *Awaking like a Jew*
9. *The Laws of Tzitzis*
10. *The Laws of Tefillin*
11. *The Laws of Tefillin-Summary Edition*
12. *The Laws & Customs of Kerias Hatorah*
13. *Kedushas Habayis-A comprehensive guide on Siman Reish Mem*
14. *The laws & Customs of Rosh Chodesh*
15. *The laws & Customs of Pesach*
16. *The Pesach Seder*
17. *The Pesach Seder--Summary Edition*
18. *Between Pesach & Shavuos*
19. *The laws & Customs of Shavuos*
20. *The Laws & Customs of the Three Weeks*
21. *The Laws of Rosh Hashanah*
22. *The Laws & Customs of Yom Kippur*
23. *The Laws of Sukkos-Summary edition*
24. *The Laws & Customs of Chanukah*
25. *The Laws of Purim*
26. *A Semicha Aid for Learning the Laws of Shabbos Vol. 1*
27. *A Semicha Aid for Learning the Laws of Shabbos Vol. 2*
28. *The Laws of Shabbos Volume 3*
29. *The Practical Laws of Meat & Milk*
30. *The Laws and Customs of Erev Shabbos and Motzei Shabbos*
    - *The laws of Shabbos-Workbook*
31. *A Semicha aid for learning the laws of Basar Bechalav*
    - *Basar Bechalav-Workbook*
32. *A Semicha aid for learning the laws of Taaruvos*
    - *Taaruvos-Workbook*
33. *A Semicha aid for learning the laws of Melicha*
    - *Melicha-Workbook*
34. *The Laws & Customs of Mourning Vol. 1*
35. *The Laws & Customs of Mourning Vol. 2*
36. *The Laws & Customs of Mourning-Summary Edition*

Daily Halacha Subscription:

To subscribe to our websites mailing list please visit www.shulchanaruchharav.com **on your desktop** or tablet [not available on phone webpage] and look for the subscription bar on the right side of the page to enter your email to subscribe.

The subscription is free and includes a daily Halacha topic sent to you via email and/or WhatsApp, and a weekly Parsha email with a Parsha summary, Chassidic insights, and more. Likewise, you will be kept updated on all of our future publications.

Online Home Study Semicha Program
Under the Auspices of
Rabbi Yaakov Goldstein, Director of Shulchanaruchharav.com & Author of the "Semicha Aid" and
"Halacha Aid" series

Semicha Program

Shulchanaruchharav.com runs an international Home Study Semicha Program, H.S.S.P., catered for those who desire to study the Semicha curriculum and receive Semicha certification although do not have the ability to do so in a Yeshiva setting. A home study program is hence available for students of all ages to become efficient in Halacha and receive Semicha certification from the comfort of their home, in accordance to their time and leisure. For more information on this program please see our website shulchanaruchharav.com.

The purpose of our Semicha program:

The purpose of our Semicha program is to provide Jewish men throughout the world the opportunity of learning practical Halacha within a Semicha curriculum. The entire idea behind today's Semicha is, as explained by the Lubavitcher Rebbe, to increase one's knowledge of practical Halacha in order to be aware of possible Halachic issues involving day to day occurrences. At many times one is unable to turn to a Rav to verify the answer for a Shaala and hence prior knowledge is necessary. Through this program one will gain knowledge in various topics of practical Halacha. The student will be tested and receive certification for his accomplishments. We provide learning text books for each subject. These textbooks are meant to accompany the student throughout his home learning and afterwards whenever a question comes up. This allows students who are unable to learn in an actual Semicha institute to also learn the curriculum, gain the knowledge, and receive certification.

What is the difference between your Semicha program and other online Semicha programs that already exist?

Baruch Hashem we have seen the sprout of many different Semicha programs which cater to different types of students and a variety of settings. Some online Semicha programs currently available, offers the student an online Yeshiva setting of learning Semicha with live online classes. Other programs do not provide set online classes by a teacher, but rather allow the student to learn the material on his own or with a Chavrusa at his own pace, with assistance from the Rabbinical staff. Our program offers both tracks. One can choose the **self-study track**, in which he follows the course module and completes the study of material, and assignments on his own, using the literature that we provide. A second track, the **Yeshiva track**, allows students to join an online classroom platform which includes live Shiurim by Rabbi Goldstein, who will escort the student in his learning throughout the course. Another aspect of our program which has not yet been seen in other Semicha programs is that we offer a large variety of practical Halachic topics for study within the Semicha curriculum. Another novelty of our program is that it caters also to those who do not have background in Hebrew and are unable to learn from the original text. We offer our own Semicha text which is made available in English.

For further details visit shulchanaruchharav.com!

.

Table of Contents

Table of Contents

Orach Chaim

---------------**Hashkamas Haboker**-------------

1. Saying Modeh Ani:[1]
This Halacha is an excerpt from our Sefer "Awaking like a Jew"

Immediately upon awakening, even prior to washing one's hands[2], it is proper[3] to [accustom oneself[4] to] recite Modeh Ani.[5] [It is said as a reminder that Hashem is standing over him, in order to motivate him to get up with alacrity.[6] Alternatively, it is said in order to thank Hashem, immediately upon awakening, for the pleasure received in having one's soul returned.[7]]

In what position is it to be recited? One should say it while still sitting, or lying, on his bed.[8] [One who sits up on his bed, is to do so without placing his feet on the ground.[9] One is to place one hand against the other, and lower his head upon reciting Modeh Ani.[10]]

---

[1] Admur in Siddur; Basra 1:6; Kama 1:5; Beir Heiytiv 1:5; M"B 1:8 based on Seder Hayom; Siddur Yaavetz Hashkamas Haboker 3; Siddur Haarizal; Ateres Zikeinim. Not mentioned in Tur, Shulchan Aruch, Taz or Magen Avraham.
When did the recital of Modeh Ani begin? In Talmudic times, Modeh Ani was not recited. The reason for this is because they were able to recite the entire blessing of Elokaiy Neshama upon awakening, due to lack of [heavy] impurity. There was thus no need to recite Modeh Ani, as in Modeh Ani there is nothing new or additional to the blessing of Elokaiy Neshama. Saying Modeh Ani is only required in our times being we cannot recite Elokaiy Neshama due to the impurity, and it is thus said in order that the thanks be given immediately upon awakening from sleep. ["On the Essence of Chassidus" p. 58 based on Rabbeinu Yonah in Brachos 60b; Shulchan Menachem 1:1] There is likewise no mention of Modeh Ani in the Rambam as he simply records [Hilchos Tefilah 7:3] that as soon as one awakes he should say Elokaiy Neshama.
The first source: The first source which records the custom to recite Modeh Ani is the Seder Hayom. [Authored by Moshe Makir Tzfas 1600] To note from Siddur Yaavetz 3 "The sect of later Chassidim has added, on their own accord, to say Modeh Ani upon awakening". This implies that even in the 1700's the idea of saying Modeh Ani was not yet widespread.
[2] Admur Kama 1:5, Basra 1:66, and Siddur state that it may be said prior to washing hands; Hayom Yom 11th Shvat and Rebbe in Igros Kodesh 10:23 [28th Tishreiy 5715] state that it is specifically to be said prior to washing. So is also implied from the term "immediately" used in Admur and from fact that Admur in both SH"A and Siddur explains why this can be said prior to washing. This is also understood from the fact Admur in his Siddur placed the saying of Modeh Ani prior to Netilas Yadayim. [ibid]
The reason Modeh Ani is allowed to be said prior to washing hands: There is no prohibition in saying Modeh Ani prior to washing hands, despite that in general it is forbidden to bless G-d before washing, as there is no mention of one of the seven names of G-d in this statement [Kama 1:5; Basra 1:6; and Siddur] and therefore this statement is not considered to contain the holiness required for clean hands. [Kama ibid] This allowance to recite Modeh Ani before washing hands applies even if one slept without clothing and hence most probably touched areas of his body that are normally covered. [Basra 1:6]
Other Opinions: Some Poskim rule one is to only say Modeh Ani after washing hands. [Yaavetz in his Siddur Hashkamas Haboker 4; opinion in Chida in Kesher Gadol 1:1; Rechev Eliyahu and Minchas Aron brought in Igros Kodesh 10:23] Practically, we rule as above that Modeh Ani precedes washing of the hands as so is the ruling of most Poskim. [Igros Kodesh ibid; Kaf Hachaim 1:4; Piskeiy Teshuvos 1 footnote 28 writes that the Yaavetz is the sole opinion who holds that Modeh Ani is to be said after washing, however as brought above, there are other Poskim who agree to his ruling.]
[3] Lit. Tov [Siddur, and Shulchan Aruch in both versions]
[4] Admur Basra 1:6 and Siddur
[5] Other Verses: Some write that one is to also say the verse of "Baruch Shenasan Torah Liamo Yisrael" [Siddur Yaavetz; Siddur Daas Kedoshim] and the prayer of "Yehi Ratzon Milifanecha Sheyihei Libi Nachon…" [Siddur Yaavetz] This is not our custom.
[6] Admur in Siddur and Basra 1:6
[7] Shulchan Menachem 1:1; It is necessary to thank Hashem immediately upon awakening being that every blessing needs to be said in close proximity to the pleasure received. In "The essence of Chassidus" chapter 10 [p. 58-60] the Rebbe explains this to be the level of Pshat of the meaning behind Modeh Ani.
The level of Remez: The recital of Modeh Ani alludes to the resurrection, as just like we see that after sleeping our soul is returned, so too the dead will eventually have their soul returned. This then is the Remez meaning of Modeh Ani "That you have returned my soul [and hence] I believe [in the resurrection]". [See Midrash Eicha 3:23]
The level of Drush: The message that Modeh Ani teaches a Jew is with regards to returning collateral of a debt to its owner. Just like Hashem returns our soul which he could choose to "collect" due to our many "debts" so too we should act accordingly to others and return collaterals that they gave us in exchange for loans. [See Midrash Eicha 3:23]
The level of Sod: According to the "esoteric" part of Torah, Modeh Ani is explained in the following manner: the words "living and eternal King" refer to the Divine attribute of Malchus as it is united with the attribute of Yesod. The word *melech*, King, indicates G-d's attribute of Malchus, and "living and eternal" His attribute of Yesod. "Living and eternal King who has restored my soul within me" means, then, that the restoration of the soul comes from the level of Malchus as it unites with the level of Yesod. [See Shaar Hakavanos Drushei Halayla]
The level of Chassidus: See "Sparks of Chassidus." For a thorough explanation of the Chassidic addition to all previous four explanations, see "On The essence of Chassidus" chapters 12-15.
[8] Admur Basra 1:6
The reason not to stand: The reason why one should not stand, is because Modeh Ani is to be said immediately upon awakening and one should not suddenly stand up on his feet immediately upon awakening. [Admur Basra and Kama 1:6] The reason for this is because one who does so is closer to death than life. [Admur Kama ibid]
[9] It is our custom not to place our feet on the ground until after washing hands, as explained in our Sefer "Awaking like a Jew" Chapter 4 Halacha 3 Q&A!
[10] Sefer Haminhagim p. 3 [English Edition] based on Sichas Chag Hashavuos 2nd day 1949 chapter 13 printed in Sefer Hamamarim 5750 p. 244; See Hiskashrus 623 p. 16
Background:

Summary:
Immediately upon awakening, prior to washing one's hands, one is to place one hand against the other, lower his head, and say Modeh Ani. One should say it while still sitting or lying on his bed, and not while standing. One who sits up on his bed, is to do so without placing his feet on the ground.

Q&A
In what position are the hands to be held while reciting Modeh Ani?[11]
There are different customs followed amongst Chassidim with regards to the positioning of the hands while saying Modeh Ani. Some[12] are accustomed to place the hands over each other [right over left] in an overlapping position, near the heart, as some people do during Shemoneh Esrei.[13] [Exhibit A] Others[14] lock the hands together in an embrace. [Exhibit B] The most common custom is to place the fingers and palm of the hands next to each other and hold them forward, away from the body.[15] It is told that the Rebbe Rayatz demonstrated the positioning of the hands upon revealing this custom and his hands were positioned like the third custom mentioned.[16] [Exhibit C]

Where is the Nekuda [stop] to be made within the sentence of Modeh Ani?[17]
One is to make a slight break between the words Bichemla and Raba Emunasecha.

How are women to pronounce the word; Modeh or Modah?[18]
There are those[19] who say that women should say "Modah" rather than Modeh. Practically, one should follow the custom of their community.[20]

May one say Modeh Ani if he has feces on his body or within four cubits of it?
Some[21] write that it may not be said.[22] However, other Poskim[23] rule it is allowed.[24]

The Rebbe Rayatz stated the following during a gathering on the 2nd day of Shavuos 1949: When they educated me to say Modeh Ani they told me to place one hand over the other and to nod my head downwards while saying it. When I was a bit older, although still a child, I asked my father for the reason behind this custom. He answered me: In truth, you must fulfill without asking why, although since I told you to ask me all your questions [I will thereby give you an explanation]. My father then called into his study the beadle Yosef Mordechai who was 80 years old at the time. He asked him how he says Modeh Ani, and he answered that he approximates his two hands together and lowers his head. He then asked him why he does so, and he answered "I don't know but that is how I was taught to do it since I was a child. My father than replied: You see he does it because his father taught him to do it that way and so on and so forth all the way back to Moshe Rabbeinu and Avraham Avinu who was the first Jew. A Jew must comply by his tradition without asking why he must do so. [ibid] Rabbi Leibel Groner stated that when he compiled Sefer Haminhagim, he was in doubt whether to enter this custom into the Sefer and the Rebbe answered him to do so, as it is a directive that is pertinent to the public. [Hiskashrus 623 p. 16]

[11] See Hiskashrus 623 p. 16; 711 p. 15
[12] Rav Tzvi Hirsh Ganzburg states that this is the custom he received.
[13] See Admur 95:4
[14] Rav Yitzchak Goldberg, Rosh Hayeshiva of Migdal Eimeik states that this is the custom of his family and of Anash that he knew in France.
[15] The Rebbe was asked how this position does not reflect the grace the Christians practice prior to meals and sleep. The Rebbe answered: The Rabbeim knew of this and nevertheless placed their hands in this position. The Christians prior to sleep prostrate themselves on their knees, which we do not do, and it is hence not similar. [Rav Leibel Groner, printed in Hiskashrus 623 p. 17]
[16] The correctness of this latter position is also to be understood from the fact the Rebbe answered why it is not forbidden due to being similar to the Christians, and it is only this latter position which contains a similarity.
[17] Shaareiy Teshuvah 1:5 based on Yad Efraim 4; Kitzur SHU"A 1:2; M"B 1:28; Kaf Hachaim 1:5; Siddur Im Dach and Siddur Tehilas Hashem both place the Nekuda after Bichemla.
[18] Likkutei Sichos 24:410
[19] In Halichos Shlomo [2 footnote 17] Rav SZ"A is brought to rule that women are to say Modah and not Modeh.
[20] Seemingly this refers to the sect of Jewry that one is affiliated with and not ones living community.
[21] Piskeiy Teshuvos 1:5
[22] As one may not think of Torah and Mitzvos while he has feces on him. [See Admur 85:1] The same prohibition applies with regards to thinking about Hashem [Rebbe in Hisvadyos Naso 1983 p. 1601; Lehoros Nasan 1:1; Tzitz Eliezer 13; Levushei Mordechai 171; See Vayivarech David 15; This is also implied from the fact that in 85:1, the Halacha dealing with what one should think about in a bathroom, no mention is made of thinking about G-dliness.]
Analysis on above: Vetzaruch Iyun from the fact that it is permitted to mention Hashem in a bathhouse so long as one does not mention one of His seven names, and hence one may say Chanun or Rachum [the merciful one]. [85:2] Thus seemingly the same would apply here, that it is permitted to say Modeh Ani in an impure area [near feces], being that one is not mentioning any of Hashem's Divine names. [Accordingly, the above Poskim only forbade contemplating about Hashem in an impure area, while simply mentioning Him they would allow.] On the other hand, however, there are Poskim who rule that even Chanun and Rachum may only be said if it does not refer to Hashem himself, and one is using it to

May one say Modeh Ani if he smells feces, such as from the diaper of a child?[25]
<u>Child can eat grains</u>: If the child is old enough to consume a Kezayis [27 grams] of grains, such as porridge, then it has the same ruling as explained in the previous Q&A.
<u>Child cannot eat grains</u>: If the child is not yet old enough to consume a Kezayis of grains, then it is permitted to say Modeh Ani in his presence.

Sparks of Chassidus
The Chassidic Meaning of Modeh Ani:[26]
<u>The five levels of the soul and their corresponding method of service of G-d</u>: A Jews G-dly soul contains five levels. Nefesh, Ruach, Neshama, Chaya, and Yechida. Each level of the soul represents a different ability of the soul. For example, the Neshama level refers to one's intellectual abilities, while the Ruach refers to one's emotions. Regarding ones G-dly soul[27], these levels are all in relation to one's service of G-d. Thus, ones Neshama level of his G-dly soul refers to one's comprehension and understanding of G-d's greatness, while ones Ruach level refers to one's love and fear of G-d. The lowest level of the soul is Nefesh. This level does not represent service of G-d out of love for Him or due to one's comprehension of His greatness, but rather it is done simply because G-d is his King, despite lack of feeling or comprehension. This level although being the lowest, is a prerequisite for revealing the levels above it. As first and foremost, one must accept upon himself an eternal attachment to G-d. irrelevant of what he may or may not feel or comprehend. In other words, his attachment to G-d is not based on feeling or understanding but rather an essential connection which rides above feeling and understanding. Throughout a Jews day he serves G-d using each one of these soul powers. However, the beginning of his service must commence with his Nefesh, accepting the yoke of heaven despite lack of feeling or understanding. This is referred to as Kabalas Ol.
<u>The inner meaning of Modeh Ani</u>: The inner meaning behind saying Modeh Ani as soon as one awakens, is to emphasize the lower service of Nefesh. That even before one has had the ability to think about G-d's greatness and feel love for Him, he first accepts G-d as his eternal King.
<u>The greatness of Kabalas Ol</u>: In truth, although this is the lowest level of service, being that it doesn't involve any of one's emotions and intellect, nevertheless, for this same reason, it is rooted higher than the other levels of service, as it is an expression of his soul's essence which cannot be separated from G-d under any circumstances, irrelevant to if he feels burning love for G-d or understanding of His greatness. Thus, the reciting of Modeh Ani expresses the essence of the soul, the Yechidah.[28]
<u>The inner reason for why Modeh Ani is recited before washing hands</u>:[29] It is for this reason (from a Chassidic perspective) that one says Modeh Ani even before purifying his hands through washing. As all of the impurities in the world cannot contaminate the Yechidah of a Jew. Certainly, a person may

---

refer to another person. [Kaf Hachaim 85:12 in name of Gur Aryeh] Likewise the Peri Megadim [85 A"A 3] rules that one may not pray in a bathroom using the names Rachum Vechanun. Vetzaruch Iyun as to the opinion of Admur [based on his wording in 85:2] in all this.
[23] Eretz Tzevi 1:52
[24] His reasoning is because it is permitted to mention Rachum Vechanun in a bathroom being that one is not explicitly mentioning Hashem's name. Hence, we see one may think about Hashem. The same would then apply with Modeh Ani of which one thinks about Hashem but does not mention any of His names. He explains the reason it is permitted to think about Hashem is because one's body figuratively covers the words and it is as if the feces is covered. This is not similar to thinking words of Torah near feces which is forbidden being that when thinking Torah, one's entire body becomes like a vessel for Torah as is learned from a verse in the Talmud. [ibid; see there in which he bases some of his logics on Tanya]
[25] Based on Admur 81:1
[26] Based on "On the Essence of Chassidus" chapter 11
[27] As explained in Tanya chapter 2, every Jew has two souls, a G-dly soul and an animal soul. The G-dly soul is "a part of G-d above". Meaning it is a revelation of G-d and thus its entire existence is only for G-dliness.
[28] In Sichas Parshas Toldos 1992 the Rebbe explains that before one says Modeh Ani, immediately upon awaking is when his actual soul's essence, which is even above Yechidah, is revealed. As the Yechidah, although being the highest level, is only a revelation of the essence, but not the essence itself. It is the highest level of expression of the soul, but is not the soul itself. Thus, as soon as one awakens is when his actual essence is revealed without expression, without even the expression of Yechidah. The Rebbe concludes that according to this, as soon as one awakens he should feel the spirit of Moshiach, which is the essence of Moshiach.
[29] Hayom Yom 11th Shvat

be lacking in one respect or another, but his or her Yechidah always remains perfect, and thus is not considered to be impure. Therefore, the Modeh Ani prayer which expresses the Yechidah can be said despite that the persons lower soul levels may be considered impure.

Stretching the Modeh Ani throughout the day:
The Rebbe Rashab stated that the dot after the word Bichemla in Modeh Ani needs to be spread throughout the entire day. The meaning of this statement is that at every moment of the day, one is required to infuse the service of Modeh Ani [Kabalas Ol] within his service of G-d.

Exhibit A

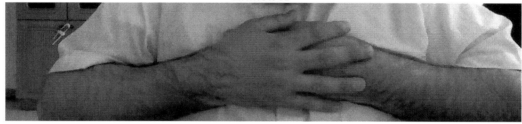

Exhibit B

Exhibit C[30]

---

[30] Rav Yosef Goldstein O.B.M. of San Diego, California, demonstrates the way he himself saw the Rebbe Rayatz during the Sicha of the 2nd night of Shavuos demonstrate to the congregation how to position the hands while saying Modeh Ani.

Birchas Hashachar
2. Does one recite the morning blessing of Elokaiy Neshama if he did not sleep at night?

A. Background:[31]

It is disputed amongst the Poskim[32] whether the fifteen morning blessings starting from Hanosein Lasechvi Vina, are to be said even if one did not sleep at night, and did not receive the benefit for which the blessing was established. Practically, we rule that one is to recite all fifteen morning blessings even if he did not sleep at night, and hence did not receive their corresponding benefits, as they were established based on the normal daily routine benefits and not based on personal benefits.[33] The question, however, is raised regarding whether this custom likewise applies to the blessing of Elokaiy Neshama, which is said prior to these 15 blessings, thanking Hashem for the return of the soul. Perhaps it should be said even if one did not sleep at night, due to the custom of thanking Hashem for the normal daily routine benefits. On the other hand, perhaps this blessing was never established in this manner and hence requires one to actually receive the benefit of waking from sleep in order for it to be said. Practically, this matter is debated amongst the Poskim based on different ways of learning the Peri Eitz Chaim, and the practical ruling of the Siddur differs from the accepted Chabad custom today. The following are the details of this matter:

B. The Law:

Some Poskim[34] rule Elokaiy Neshama is to be recited in the morning even if one did not sleep at night, just as is customarily done regarding the other morning blessings, and so is the widespread Sephardi custom. Other Poskim[35], however, rule that if one did not sleep at night, or slept for less than 60 breaths

---

[31] See Admur 46:7

[32] First opinion-Rambam: Some Poskim rule that if one did not receive the corresponding pleasure of a particular blessings then he may not recite that blessing. Hence if one did not hear the rooster crow, or did not walk or did not get dressed or did not wear a belt, (or stayed awake the entire night and hence did not need to remove the slumber from his eyes) then he may not say the blessings that correspond to these pleasures. [1st opinion in Admur ibid; Michaber 46:8; Rambam Tefila 7:7-9]

Second Opinion-Rosh: Other Poskim rule that all blessings said over the natural order [and public benefit] of the world, such as "Hanosein Lasechvy Bina" and "Roka Haaretz Al Hamayim" may be recited even if one did not receive their pleasure. However, those blessings which are said for a person's personal benefits, such as "Malbish Arumim" and "Hameichin Mitzadeiy Gaver" and "Ozer Yisrael Begevura" and Oter Yisrael", then if he did not receive their corresponding pleasure, such as if he is still lying unclothed in his bed, then they may not be said at all. [2nd opinion in Admur ibid; Tur 46; Rosh 9:23; See Tosafus Brachos 60b; Rabbeinu Yona in Sefer Hayirah; Levush 46:8]

Third Opinion-Ramban: Other Poskim rule one can say all the morning blessings even if he did not receive any of the corresponding pleasures at all. The reason for this is because the blessings are not only being said for his personal benefits but rather as a blessing that Hashem created the needs of man which the general populace receive benefit from, irrelevant of whether or not he received this benefit. [3rd opinion in Admur ibid; Rama 46:8; Ramban Pesachim 7b; Shut Min Hashamayim 12; Sefer Heshkol Birchas Hashachar; Sefer Hamichtam Brachos 60 in name of Rav Nytraiy Gaon, Rav Amram Gaon]

[33] Admur 46:7 *"The widespread custom is like the third opinions and one may not swerve from it."*; Siddur Admur; Rama ibid; Peri Chadash 46:8; Birkeiy Yosef 46:12; Rav Poalim 2:8; Kaf Hachaim 46:49 in name of many Poskim; Ketzos Hashulchan 5:6; Piskeiy Teshuvos 46:14

Ruling of Sephardim: Although the Michaber 46:8 rules like the Rambam, nevertheless even the Sefaradim follow the Rama in this regard to recite the blessings even if they did not receive its benefit. [Peri Chadash 46:8; Birkeiy Yosef 46:12; Rav Poalim 2:8; Kaf Hachaim 46:49 in name of many Poskim; Piskeiy Teshuvos 46:14]

Gra and Chazon Ish: The Chazon Ish rules that according to the Gr"a one may not recite the blessings of any pleasure that one did not receive. He would direct people to follow this opinion. [See Piskeiy Teshuvos 46 footnote 147]

The blessing of Hamaavir Sheiyna until Hagomel Chassadim Tovim: Some Poskim rule that if one did not sleep the night before he is not to say the blessing of Hamaavir Sheiyna, being that it is said for removing the slumbers of sleep from one's eyes [see Admur 46:7 in parentheses]. [Ateres Zahav 46:6; Elya Raba brought in M"B 46:24] Other Poskim however rule it is to be recited. [Shaareiy Teshuvah 46:12 in name of Arizal; Birkeiy Yosef 46:12; Kaf Hachaim 46:49; Shulchan Hatahor 46:8; Aruch Hashulchan 46:13; Ben Ish Chaiy Bracha 3; Oar Letziyon 2:4-9] Other Poskim arbitrate that one is to hear the blessing from another person. [Peri Megadim 46 A"A 2; Shaareiy Teshuvah 46:12; M"B ibid; Siddur Yaavetz; Chayeh Adam 8:9; Derech Chaim; Birchas Habayis 35:2; Likkutei Mahrich; Toras Chaim Sofer 7] According to the Siddur of Admur and Admur 46:7 one is to recite the blessing of Hamaavir Sheiyna even if he did not sleep the night before. [Ketzos Hashulchan 5:6] Regarding why according to the Siddur one does not recite Elokaiy Neshama but does recite Hamaavir Sheiyna-see Ketzos Hashulchan 5 footnote 8 and Shaar Hakolel 1:10

[34] Implication of Admur 46:7 and 494:3; Shaareiy Teshuvah 46:12 in accordance to his understanding of the Arizal in Peri Eitz Chaim; Birkeiy Yosef 46:12; Ben Ish Chaiy Bracha 3; Shulchan Hatahor 46:8; Aruch Hashulchan 46:13; Kaf Hachaim 46:49; Or Letziyon 2:4-9

Ruling of Admur in Shulchan Aruch: Admur does not explicitly state in the Shulchan Aruch whether one is to say the blessing of Elokaiy Neshama if he did not sleep at night. However, it is implied from 46:7 and 494:3 that it is to be said. See glosses of Rav Raskin on Siddur p. 8

[35] Admur in Siddur based on Peri Eitz Chaim Shaar Habrachos 4, as explained in Shaar Hakolel 1:10 [unlike understanding of Shaareiy Teshuvah 46:12 in Peri Eitz Chaim]; Hagahos Ateres Zahav 46:6; M"B 46:24 in name of Elya Raba; Ketzos Hashulchan 5:5; Piskeiy Teshuvos 46:15; See Ketzos Hashulchan 5 footnote 8; Shaar Hakolel 1:10 and Rav Raskin on Siddur p. 8 for the proofs against the understanding of the Shaareiy Teshuvah in the Peri Eitz Chaim; See also Yagdil Torah Jerusalem 5:40.

worth [i.e. thirty minutes[36]], then the blessing of Elokaiy Neshama **may not** be recited.[37] [According to this opinion, if one is in doubt whether he slept for 60 breaths, then he is to recite the blessing without Hashem's name.[38]] Other Poskim[39] conclude that due to doubt, one is to hear the blessing from another person, and so is the widespread Ashkenazi custom.

The Chabad custom:[40] Admur in his Siddur [unlike his implied ruling from the Shulchan Aruch] holds of the latter opinion that the blessing is not to be recited [and that there is no need to even hear it from someone else], and seemingly so was the Chabad custom in previous times.[41] The public directive from the Rebbe Rayatz likewise follows this ruling, although emphasizing one may hear it from another person who did sleep. However, the private directive of the Rebbe Rayatz is that one should say the blessing, as rules the first opinion above.[42] It is implied from the above directives that unless one received a private directive from the Rebbe otherwise, then he is not to say the blessing, as is the public directive. Nonetheless, the accepted, widespread, custom amongst Chabad Chassidim today is to follow the private directive and recite the blessing of Elokaiy Neshama even if one did not sleep the night before.[43] [The blessing is to be said after Alos[44], immediately after washing hands with a blessing.[45]]

Summary:
The widespread Sephardi custom, and the widespread Chabad custom of today, is to recite the blessing of Elokaiy Neshama in the morning even if one did not sleep at night. The widespread Ashkenazi custom is to hear this blessing recited from another.

------------------Tzitzis------------------

3. The purpose of the Mitzvah of Tzitzis:
This Halacha is an excerpt from our Sefer "The laws of Tzitzis"

The purpose of the Mitzvah of Tzitzis is stated explicitly in the verse[46] "And you will see it and remember all the Mitzvos of Hashem, and you will do them, and you will not stray after your hearts and your eyes". The Tzitzis serve as a constant reminder of the Mitzvos of Hashem. Upon seeing the Tzitzis, one is reminded of the Mitzvos of Hashem and consequently fulfills them. This also helps a person avoid the temptation of sin that is aroused through the eyes and heart, as written explicitly in the verse above.

How the Tzitzis reminds one of the Mitzvos:[47] A certain individual was warned by a friend regarding a certain matter. The individual went ahead and made a knot around the area of his belt in order to constantly remember the warning. The knots of the Tzitzis serve a similar purpose; to remind us of the Mitzvos of Hashem at all moments. It is for this reason that the Tzitzis contains five knots, as they

---

[36] See our Sefer "Awaking like a Jew" Chapter 4 Halacha 17 Q&A
[37] The reason: This blessing of Elokaiy Neshama refers to one's personal benefit of awakening and not the general pleasure that the world receives. Therefore, it may not be said if one did not receive this personal benefit. [Ketzos Hashulchan 5 footnote 8; Peri Megadim 46 A"A 2]
[38] Ketzos Hashulchan 5:5
[39] Peri Megadim 46 A"A 2; Shaareiy Teshuvah 46:12; Siddur Yaavetz; Chayeh Adam 8:9; Derech Chaim; M"B ibid; Birchas Habayis 35:2; Likkutei Maharich; Toras Chaim Sofer 7; See Rebbe in Likkutei Sichos 9 p. 276
[40] See Likkutei Sichos 9 p. 276; Shulchan Menachem 1:6; Shaareiy Halacha Uminhag vol. 1 page 25; Heichal Menachem 2:213; Hiskashrus 931; Shevach Hamoadim p. 240 footnote 7 in name of Rabbanei Anash; Rav Raskin in footnotes on Siddur p. 8
[41] As is evident from the rulings of the Shaar Hakolel 1:10 and Ketzos Hashulchan 5:5 to follow this ruling of Admur in the Siddur
[42] Background: In a letter dated on the 9th of Tishreiy 1949 the Rebbe responded as follows to the question of whether one is to recite the blessing of Al Netilas Yadayim and Elokaiy Neshama in a case that he did not sleep at night: "The public directive follows the ruling in the Siddur of Admur that it is not to be said, although one may hear it from another person who did sleep. (However, the private directive is to say it. This is what I heard from my father in law the Rebbe Rayatz)."
[43] Shevach Hamoadim p. 240 footnote 7 in name of Rabbanei Anash that although from this letter it remains unclear as to whether a Chassid is to follow the private or public directive, in actuality, the custom has become to follow the private directive and so rule Rabbanei Anash; See also Heichal Menachem ibid for a Yechidus recorded in which the Rebbe told a Chassid that one is to follow the private directive.
[44] Based on Siddur and 47:7 that the other blessings of Birchas Hashachar may only be said after Alos [in a case that one did not sleep] as this is the time that people wake up.
[45] See our Sefer "Awaking like a Jew" Chapter 4 Halacha 16
[46] Bamidbar 15:39; brought in 11:27
[47] Admur 24:1; Tur 24; Michaber 24:1

correspond to the five books of the Torah. We tie the Tzitzis to every corner in order so whatever corner we turn to, we will remember the Mitzvos.[48] Likewise, the Tzitzis themselves represent the number 613 which corresponds to the 613 Mitzvos, as when the five knots are added to the 8 strings and to the Gematria of 600 of the word Tzitzis, it equals 613, hence helping one remember all the Mitzvos.[49] [Likewise, the ל"ב/32 strings of the Tzitzis correspond to the first and last letter of the Torah, as the first letter of the Torah begins with a Beis and the last letter of the Torah ends with a Lamed.[50]]

The greatness of the Mitzvah

Weighs against all Mitzvos:[51]

The Mitzvah of Tzitzis is so great that it weighs against all the other Mitzvos in the Torah.[52] Thus, anyone who fulfills the Mitzvah of Tzitzis is considered as if he had fulfilled all the Mitzvos of the Torah.[53] It is for this reason that Moshe Rabbeinu could not make the Jewish people swear with the wording "keep all the Mitzvos" as it could be interpreted as referring to only the Mitzvah of Tzitzis.[54] Although idol worship is also weighed against all the other Mitzvos, nevertheless, people commonly understand the word Mitzvah to refer specifically to Tzitzis.[55]

Guards one from sin:[56]

The Mitzvah of Tzitzis is unique amongst all the Mitzvos in that it has a Segula to save a person from sin[57], as related in the following fascinating story in the Gemara in Menachos:[58]

There is not even a light Mitzvah in the Torah which does not have a reward in this world and the next world. Go and learn from the incident that occurred to a certain individual and the Mitzvah of Tzitzis. There was once a Jew that was very scrupulous in the Mitzvah of Tzitzis. He heard that there is a harlot on a certain island that takes 400 gold coins as her wage. He sent her the 400 gold coins and set up a time to meet with her. When the set time arrived, he came and sat by the entrance of her home. The maidservant came out [and saw him, and then told her master] "The man who sent you 400 gold coins has arrived and is sitting by the threshold of the entrance." She told him to enter, and he entered. She prepared for him seven beds; six of silver and one of gold [one higher than the other in the form of bunk beds]. Between each bed there was a silver ladder, with exception to the ladder that reached the top bed, which was made of gold. She sat on the seventh bed unclothed. He proceeded to ascend the ladders unclothed, and sat opposite her. His four Tzitzis began to [miraculously[59]] hit him on the face and he [changed his mind], descended [from the beds] and sat on the ground. She also proceeded to descend and sit on the ground. She said to him "In the name Gapah, [the king[60]] of Rome, [I swear[61]] that I will not leave you until you tell me what blemish you see on me?" He said to her "I agree that I have not seen a beautiful woman as you, however there is one Mitzvah that Hashem our G-d has commanded us, and its name is Tzitzis. Regarding this command the verse states "I am Hashem your G-d" twice; one time to teach us that He is the one that

---

[48] Admur ibid; Michaber ibid; Tur ibid

[49] Admur 11:27; Michaber 11:14

[50] Chayeh Avraham in name of Tashbatz 261; Kaf Hachaim 8:63

[51] Gemara Nedarim 25a; Shavuos 29a; Menachos 43b

[52] Gemaras ibid; This is learned from the verse which states "And you shall remember all the Mitzvos of Hashem" regarding looking at the Tzitzis. [Rashi ibid] Likewise, the Tzitzis correspond to 613, as explained above. [Kaf Hachaim 8:31

[53] Sifri Shelach 15:39; Pardeis of Rashi Hilchos Tzitzis; Shivlei Haleket

[54] Nedarim ibid; Shavuos ibid

[55] Tosafos Shavuos ibid "Mitzvas Tzitzis"; See Tanya chapter 37 that throughout the Talmud Yerushalmi, Stam Mitzvah refers to the Mitzvah of Tzedaka.

[56] Elya Raba 24:4; Shaareiy Teshuvah 24:4; M"B 24:5; Kaf Hachaim 24:25

[57] Although in general we say that Mitzvos do not save one from the Yetzer Hara [See Rava Sotah 21a], nevertheless, the Mitzvah of Tzitzis has ability to do so. [Elya Raba ibid]

[58] Menachos 44a

[59] Rashi ibid; Iyun Yaakov ibid

[60] Rashi ibid

[61] Rashi ibid

will punish in the future, and one time to teach us that He is the one that will reward in the future. Now, the [four sets of strings] appeared to me like four witnesses [and prevented me from sinning]." She then said to him "I will not leave you until you tell me your name, the name of your city and the name of the Yeshiva that you learn Torah in." He proceeded to hand her a letter [with all the requested information, and then parted from her]. This woman got up [to travel to the Yeshiva in order to convert, and prior to traveling she] distributed a third of her wealth to the kingdom [so they permit her to convert[62]*], a third to paupers, and a third she took with her. In addition, she took with her the bedding of the seven beds from the above incident. She arrived at the Beis Midrash of [a certain*[63]*] Rebbe Chiyah and told him "Command me [the laws] and make me a convert." He said to her "My daughter, perhaps you have [come to convert] due to your desire to marry one of my students?" She proceeded to remove the letter [that she had received from the student, and told the Rabbi the entire miraculous story*[64]*]. He then said to her "Go acquire what you had purchased." Those beddings that she had offered [the student in a forbidden fashion] she now offered them to him in a permitted fashion [i.e. she married him]. This is the reward that one receives in this world [i.e. the man married her, received a third of her wealth, and the gold and silver bedding].*

Surrounded by Mitzvos:[65]
Rebbe Eliezer Ben Yaakov stated: Whoever has Tefillin on his head and Tefillin on his arm and Tzitzis on his garment, and a Mezuzah on his door, is guaranteed not to sin, as the verse states "Vehachut Hameshulash Lo Bemiheira Yinatek," as well as the verse states "The angel of Hashem rests around those who fear Him, and it saves him from sin".

The jealousy of the angel Michael:[66]
The Baal Shem Tov stated that even the angel Michael, which is the greatest of the angels, would give up all of his Divine service, and experience of G-dliness, for the sake of fulfilling even one Mitzvah of Tzitzis from amongst the four Tzitzis that every Jew wears.

---

4. May one wear a cotton Tallis Katan?
This Halacha has been adapted based on our Sefer "The laws of Tzitzis"

A. The issues of concern:
Wearing a cotton Tallis Katan touches upon two Halachic issues 1) Is the material Biblically obligated in Tzitzis, and hence is one Biblically fulfilling the Mitzvah upon wearing it? 2) If the cotton garment has wool material Tzitzis tied to it [which is the case today], is it Kosher?

Issue 1: What materials are Biblically obligated in Tzitzis?[67] A wool garment is Biblically obligated to have Tzitzis according to all opinions.[68] If a Tallis is made of material other than wool or linen, it is disputed as to whether it is Biblically obligated in the Mitzvah of Tzitzis, or only Rabbinically.[69] Practically, the main opinion follows those who rule that all materials are Biblically obligated.[70] Nevertheless, being there are opinions who argue, those who desire to fulfill the Mitzvah of Tzitzis on its highest standard[71] [i.e. according to all opinions[72]] are to be careful to wear a pair of Tallis Gadol/Katan

---

[62] Rashi ibid

[63] Tosafos ibid

[64] Rashi ibid

[65] Menachos 43b

[66] Sefer Hasichos 1988 p. 308

[67] Admur 9:4; Michaber 9:1 and 6

[68] Admur 9:4; Michaber 9:1 and 6; Ketzos Hashulchan 6:1

[69] Some Poskim rule it is only Rabbinically obligated in Tzitzis. [Michaber 9:1; Rif; Rambam 3:2; Gemara Menachos 39b] Others rule all materials are Biblically obligated in Tzitzis. [Rama 9:1; Tosafos; Rosh; Smag; Mordechai]

[70] Rama 9:1; Admur in Kuntrus Acharon 9:1 "and so is the main opinion"; Admur in 9:1 learns the verses in a way that shows all garments are Biblically obligated

[71] Lit. Mitzvah Min Hamuvchar. However, the Michaber ibid writes "Every G-d fearing Jew is to…" Vetzaruch Iyun as to what the difference is between the wording of Admur and that of the Michaber. The wording of the Michaber suggests that every G-d fearing Jew must do so, while the wording of Admur suggests that this matter is optional to each person. Perhaps the explanation is that in truth we [Ashkenazim] hold mainly like

that is entirely made from sheep wool, meaning that both the garment and fringes are made from sheep wool, and by doing so one fulfills the Mitzvah of Tzitzis without any question.[73]

Issue 2: The material of the fringes:[74] Some Poskim[75] rule that wool or linen fringes may be used as Tzitzis for a garment of any material.[76] Other Poskim[77] rule that the material of the fringes must be similar to the material of the garment. Accordingly, a cotton Tallis Katan must have cotton material strings tied to it, and if wool material fringes are attached, the Tzitzis is invalid. Practically, although the custom is not like this opinion[78], nevertheless, it is proper for every G-d fearing Jew to be stringent upon himself like this opinion, and hence tie cotton material Tzitzis onto a cotton Tallis.[79] Likewise, even those who are lenient like the first opinion, to tie wool strings to a cotton garment, it is proper not to recite a blessing upon wearing such Tzitzis. Thus, a blessing should not be recited over a cotton garment that has wool fringes. Rather, one is to recite a blessing over a different Tallis and have in mind to exempt also this Tallis.[80] [Nevertheless, from the letter of the law, one may say a blessing over this Tallis, if he so chooses.[81]]

B. The final ruling:

From the letter of the law, one may be lenient to wear a cotton Tallis, even if it contains wool fringes.[82] Nevertheless, those who desire to fulfill the Mitzvah of Tzitzis on its highest standard are to avoid wearing a cotton Tallis [whether of a Tallis Katan or Tallis Gadol, if a wool Tallis is available] even if the fringes are made from cotton.[83] [This applies even in the summer.[84]] If however the fringes are made from wool [which is the case today being that cotton fringes are not manufactured], then although the custom is to be lenient, every G-d fearing Jew is to be stringent upon himself to avoid wearing it [whether it is a Tallis Katan or Gadol] and if he does wear it, it is proper that a blessing not be recited.[85] Practically, the Chassidic custom is to be particular to only wear wool Taleisim.[86]

---

the opinions that rule that all materials are a Biblical obligation, as rules Rama 9:1 unlike the Michaber 9:1, and hence Admur does not use the same wording as the Michaber and rather uses a more lenient wording.

[72] Michaber ibid

[73] Admur ibid; Michaber 9:6 in name of Igur and Rabbeinu Yeshaya and Maharil; M"B 9:5; Kitzur SHU"A 9:12; Ben Ish Chaiy Noach 1; Kaf Hachaim 9:5; Halichos Shlomo 3 footnote 25; Or Letziyon 2:2 footnote 3; Igros Moshe 1:2; 2:1; 3:1; Yoreh Deah 3:52

[74] 9:1; Michaber 9:2

[75] Stam opinion in Admur and Michaber ibid

[76] The reason: One verse states "Venasnu Al Tzitzis Hakenaf Pesil Techeiles", while a previous verse states "Veasu Lachem Tzitzis Al Kanfei Bigdeihem". What was the necessity of repeating the word "Kenaf:corner" in the latter verse? This is coming to teach us that the Tzitzis must be made of the same material as the corners of the garment. Another verse however states that "Lo Silbash Shatnez Tzemer Upishtim Yachdav, Gedilim Taaseh Lecha Al Arba." This verse seems to imply that the fringes may be made of only wool or linen, and not of any other material. Hence the two verses seem contradictory. The explanation is as follows: Strings of wool or linen are valid to be used for garments of any material, whether of wool, linen or any other material, and on this it says "Tzemer Upishtim Gedilim Taaseh Lecha". However, strings of other materials are only valid for garments made of that same material. [Admur ibid]

[77] Maharam 444; Hagahos Maimanis 3:6

[78] As is seen from the fact we allow tying wool strings to a silk garment. [Admur ibid; Terumos Hasdeshen 44]

[79] Admur ibid; M"A 9:3

Other opinions: Some Poskim rule it is better to attach wool strings to a silk garment. [Beir Heiytiv 9:1 in his understanding of M"A 9:4; Admur in Kuntrus Acharon 9:2 negates his understanding of the M"A.] Some Poskim are lenient to even initially allow one to wear a cotton Tallis Katan, even if the fringes are made from wool. [Gr"a in Maaseh Rav 17 and in M"B 9:6; Chazon Ish brought in Orchos Rabbeinu 1:18]

[80] Admur 9:5; M"A 9:3 in name of Bach and M"A 8:16 as explained in Kuntrus Acharon 9:2

Is one to say the blessing if he does not have another Tallis available? Tzaruch Iyun if according to Admur even in such a case one should not say a blessing, or only when he in any event has another Tallis available is he not to say a blessing.

Other opinions: See Beir Heiytiv 9:1 brought in previous footnote who implies a blessing is recited on a silk Tallis with wool Tzitzis!

[81] As we do not apply the rule of Safek Brachos Lihakel against a Minhag, and the custom is like the first opinion, as stated above in Rama and Admur ibid; Likewise, Admur only writes that it is proper not to say a blessing, and does not prohibit doing so.

[82] As according to all, cotton material is at least Rabbinically obligated in Tzitzis, and it is only a Mitzvah Min Hamuvchar to wear wool. [Admur 9:4] Likewise, even if the fringes are made of wool, the custom is to be lenient to tie even wool strings to a cotton pair of Tzitzis, and only a G-d fearing Jew is to be stringent. [Admur 9:4]

[83] Admur 9:4; Michaber 9:6; M"B 9:5; Kitzur SHU"A 9:12; Ben Ish Chaiy Noach 1; Kaf Hachaim 9:5; Halichos Shlomo 3 footnote 25; Or Letziyon 2:2 footnote 3; Igros Moshe 1:2; 2:1; 3:1; Yoreh Deah 3:52

[84] Igros Moshe brought in previous footnote

[85] Admur 9:5 as brought in Halacha 2A!

The reason: If the fringes of the cotton Tallis is made of wool [as is the commonly sold material of all Tzitzis today] then some Poskim [Maharam Merothenberg] rule that the Tzitzis is invalid, and it is as if one is wearing a four-cornered garment without Tzitzis. Now, although in conclusion we rule that the custom is to be lenient, nevertheless every G-d fearing Jew is to be stringent. [9:4]

Summary:
It is permitted to wear a cotton Tallis Katan, and those who choose may even say a blessing over it. Nevertheless, every G-d fearing Jew is to avoid wearing a cotton Tallis, and is to rather wear a wool Tallis, and so is the Chassidic custom. Likewise, in the event that one needs to wear a cotton Tallis, it is proper that a blessing not be recited over it.

Q&A
May one who is particular to wear a wool Tallis, wear a cotton Tallis during the nighttime?
Some[87] learn that one may be lenient to wear cotton Tzitzis at night even if he is generally particular to only wear a wool Tallis, as stated above. The Chassidic custom is to be particular to wear wool Taleisim even at night.[88]

------------------Tefillin----------------
5. Is one obligated to wear Tefillin upon reciting Shema before Davening Shacharis?
If one is reciting Shema prior to sunrise, prior to Davening, he may read Shema even if he is not yet wearing Tefillin.[89] If however one is reciting Shema after sunrise, he is not to say it until he puts on Tefillin.[90] [Nevertheless, the custom amongst most Chassidim is not to wear Tefillin when saying Shema prior to Davening, even after sunrise.[91] However, some Chassidim are accustomed to wear Tefillin upon reciting Shema prior to Davening[92], and so was the directive of the Rebbe Rashab and Rebbe Rayatz.[93] This is not the widespread Chabad custom.]

Other opinions: Some Poskim are lenient to even initially allow one to wear a cotton Tallis Katan, even if the fringes are made from wool. [Gr"a in Maaseh Rav 17 and in M"B 9:6; Chazon Ish brought in Orchos Rabbeinu 1:18]

[86] See Igros Kodesh 14:229 [brought in Shulchan Menachem 1:44 footnote 14]

[87] Piskeiy Teshuvos 9:2, based on Ashel Avraham 21 that states "I was accustomed to wear a Tallis Katan of linen at night" and hence certainly he would allow one to wear cotton, of which from the letter of the law is obligated in Tzitzis at least Rabbinically. However, Tzaruch Iyun as how one can learn from this anything, as he himself writes that he is disturbed if this is proper, being that perhaps this makes it appear like Baal Tosif.

[88] Heard from Rav Eliyahu Landau Shlita

[89] Admur 58:4 "One is to read at least the first Parsha before sunrise even if he did not yet wear Tallis and Tefillin Shema without Tefillin before sunrise" 58:5 "However if one is reading it after sunrise…"; Based on Levush 58:2

The reason: As it is a Mitzvah to read Shema in its proper time before sunrise, and is hence similar to the ruling in 66:11 that one may say Shema without Tefillin if he does not have Tefillin and is worried that the time will pass. Vetzaruch Iyun if one must wear Tefillin if he has much time until sunrise and is able to do so, as in 66:11 Admur forbids reading the Shema without Tefillin unless one suspects the time will pass. Thus, perhaps this entire law of Admur refers to one who does not have time or ability or desire to wear them before sunrise, although ideally he should do so. Vetzaruch Iyun!

Other opinions: Some Poskim rule one is not to read Shema prior to sunrise without Tefillin. He is rather to read only the first verse and Baruch Sheim. [Kaf Hachaim 58:8]

[90] Admur 66:11; Siddur Admur [Letter 22]; M"A 66:12; Degul Merivava and Rav Akiva Eiger, brought in M"B 46:33; Kaf Hachaim 25:27

The reason and explanation: Admur in the Siddur and 66:11, based on M"A ibid, rules that it is better to Daven in private with Tefillin than to Daven with a Minyan but without Tefillin due to Eidus Sheker. Likewise, he implies that one is not to say Shema without Tefillin unless the time of Shema is passing. From here we learn that saying Shema without Tefillin is Eidus Sheker even if he plans to wear Tefillin later on and say Shema again while wearing them. So is also proven from Torah Or Vayakhel in that one cannot draw down the Penimi without first having worn Tefillin and drawing down the Makif. Now, Admur 58:4-5 makes it evident that this refers only when reading Shema after sunrise, as in 58:4 he permits reading Shema before sunrise without Tefillin while in 58:5 he writes that if it is after sunrise one is to read Shema as soon as possible with Tallis and Tefillin. Vetzaruch Iyun as to the difference between before and after sunrise, that before sunrise it may be said without Tefillin and after sunrise it may not! Perhaps then one must say this entire law of Admur refers to one who does not have time or ability or desire to wear them before sunrise, although ideally he should do so. Vetzaruch Iyun!

[91] Chozeh Melublin [brought in all the following Sefarim]; Beis Yitzchak 17; Os Chaim Veshalom 25:6; Rebbe in Toras Menachem 28th Sivan 1952; See Rameh in Alfasi Zuta Brachos ibid; Miasef Lechol Hamachanos 25:31; Ashel Avraham Buchach 25 that a proof can be brought from Tisha Beav; Minchas Yitzchak 2:108; Yabia Omer 1:4 in name of many Poskim; Piskeiy Teshuvos 25:8

The reason: As it is only considered false testimony to say the morning Shema without Tefillin if one does not plan to wear Tefillin at all that day, and hence plans to nullify the Mitzvah that he read in Shema. If, however, one plans to wear Tefillin later on, then it is not considered false testimony at all. [Rebbe in Toras Menachem 28th Sivan 1952] A proof for this can be brought from the fact that the Gemara [Brachos 14b] compares saying Shema without Tefillin to bringing a Karban without Nesachim, now just as one can bring the Nesachim after the Karban, so too he can wear Tefillin after Shema. [Chozeh Melublin brought in Sefarim ibid] Furthermore, one is to specifically say Shema before wearing the Tefillin as the Tefillin are higher than the saying of Shema and one is hence to follow the order of Maalin Bakodesh to fist say Shema and then wear Tefillin. [Os Chaim Veshalom ibid; Rebbe ibid]

[92] Os Chaim Veshalom ibid that so is the custom of some and that doing so is a Hiddur Mitzvah

---

Q&A

Is one to wear Tefillin when reciting Shema as part of Karbanos?
If one is not fulfilling his obligation of Shema with this recital, then even according to the stringent opinion brought above, he is not required to wear the Tefillin while reciting it.[94] If however, one is planning to fulfill his obligation with this reading, then this enters the same discussion as above.

According to the stringent opinion brought above, may one say the first verse of Shema for the sake of fulfilling one's obligation without wearing Tefillin?[95]
Even according to the stringent opinion brought above, one may recite the first verse of Shema without Tefillin.

Is one required to wear Tefillin when reading Shema after Davening, such as by Shnayim Mikra and the like?
No. The above obligation only applies when one is reciting Shema for the purpose of fulfilling his obligation. If, however, one is simply reciting it to read from the Torah, then there is no obligation to wear Tefillin.[96] However some[97] were stringent even in such a case.

---

6. Covering the Tefillin Shel Yad:[98]

There is no need to be particular to cover the Tefillin Shel Yad [i.e. hand Tefillin], such as with one's sleeve, and one can choose to wear it either revealed [with his sleeves rolled up on top of the Shel Yad] or concealed [under a sleeve].[99] [Thus, although often one's sleeve automatically covers the Shel Yad, there

---

[93] Directive of Rebbe Rashab in Kuntrus Eitz Chaim 25 "After wearing Tefillin and Kerias Shema, and after drinking tea, they are to learn for two consecutive hours"; Igros Kodesh of Rebbe Rayatz letter 3302 "Certainly they are careful to say Kerias Shema Ketana with Tefillin"; Sichas Shelach 1952 "The Rebbe Rayatz told me that his father the Rebbe Rashab would read Shema in the morning with Tefillin

[94] Degul Merivava and Rav Akiva Eiger, brought in M"B 46:33; Binyan Olam 7; Kaf Hachaim 25:27

[95] As Admur 25:1 rules that the false testimony is due to the verse of Ukeshartam, and hence if one is not reading it there is no false testimony; Kaf Hachaim 25:27 according to Tosafos and Ran
Other opinions: Some Poskim rule that even the first verse of Shema is not to be said without Tefillin, if one intends to fulfill his obligation. [Kaf Hachaim 25:27 based on Rashi and Maadnei Yom Tov]

[96] Degul Merivava and Rav Akiva Eiger, brought in M"B 46:33; Binyan Olam 7; Kaf Hachaim 25:27; Os Chaim Veshalom 25:6; Rebbe in Toras Menachem 28th Sivan 1952; So is also proven from Admur 34:5 and Siddur Admur that allows saying Shema while wearing Tefillin of Rabbeinu Tam and considers it a Hiddur.

[97] Minhag Hageonim to wear Tefillin during Shema of Maariv, brought in Hagahos Maimanis on Rambam Tefillin 4 in name of Baal Haittur, brought in Beis Yosef 25; Custom of Chasam Sofer to not way Shema while wearing Rabbeinu Tam Tefillin, recorded in Likkutei Chaver Ben Chaim, brought in Os Chaim Veshalom ibid; Minhagei Chasam Sofer 1:22 that he would not say Shnayim Mikra of Shema without Tefillin.
The reason: As the Biblical Mitzvah of wearing Tefillin applies throughout the entire day, and hence whenever one reads Shema without Tefillin he is testifying falsely. [Os Chaim Veshalom ibid; Rebbe ibid]

[98] Admur 27:8 *"The obligation to cover the Shel Yad is only in a case when the Shel Yad is being worn over an item which is never usually covered, such as a cloth or bandage, however when it is worn on the actual skin, there is no need to cover it."*; Rama 27:11 *"By the Tefillin Shel Yad there is no need to be particular in whether they are revealed or concealed"*; Mordechai p. 96; Menachos 37b *"A Mumar questioned Rav Ashi who had his Shel Yad revealed, don't you hold that the Shel Yad must be a personal sign that is not for others, and he replied it refers to an area which is a personal sign"*; M"A 27:21; Machatzis Hashekel ibid; See also Admur 27:23 regarding not covering the head Tefillin and Admur 45:2 regarding entering a cemetery. This law is omitted from Ketzos Hashulchan 8; See Piskeiy Teshuvos 27:23; There is a picture of the Chofetz Chaim in which his Shel Yad is not covered. [See Heroes of Modern Jewish Thought p. 47]

[99] The reason: One who is wearing his Tefillin Shel Yad over his clothing due to an injury must beware to cover the Shel Yad so it is not revealed, as the verse [Shemos 13:9] states "Vehaya Lecha Leos Al Yadecha" which means to say that the Shel Yad is to be for you a sign, and not a sign for others. However, the obligation to cover the Shel Yad is only in a case when the Shel Yad is being worn over an item which is never usually covered, such as a cloth or bandage, however when it is worn on the actual skin, there is no need to cover it. This applies even if his shirt, and all his clothing, tears in the area opposite the Tefillin Shel Yad. Now, although the Shel Yad can be seen by others, this does not pose any issue, as the Torah was not particular to require the Tefillin Shel Yad to specifically be covered, and rather it may be worn even if revealed, so long as it is placed on an area that is normally covered, which is the bicep. [Admur ibid; See M"A ibid Machatzis Hashekel ibid] This means to say as follows: From the words "Lecha Leos" we learn that the purpose of the Shel Yad is to serve as a sign for oneself and not for others. However, this does not mean to say that the Shel Yad must be covered so others don't see, but rather that it must be placed on an area that is normally covered, such as the bicep. The fact that it is placed on a normally covered area, suffices to emphasize that it is a personal sign "Lecha Leos", even if in truth others can see it, due to a torn shirt. In other words, from this Drasha of the Gemara we learn that one may not have a Chatzitza between the arm and the Tefillin. Likewise, when it is placed over a sleeve due to an injury due to lack of choice, it must be covered, as only then does one fulfill the personal sign of "Lecha Leos", as otherwise, it is placed on an area that is seen by others.

is no need to be particular in this matter.[100] However, some Poskim[101] rule that one must be particular that the Tefillin Shel Yad is always covered, such as under the sleeve.[102] Likewise, according to Chassidus and Kabala, the Tefillin is to remain covered throughout the time it is worn.[103] Furthermore, some people, based on Kabala, are accustomed to cover the bicep using their Tallis [or jacket] even upon putting on the Tefillin Shel Yad.[104] The custom of the Rebbe Rashab was to cover the Tefillin Shel Yad with his sleeve, and he would do so even prior to putting on the Shel Rosh.[105] So was also done by other Gedolei Yisrael, to immediately cover the Shel Yad, prior to wearing the Shel Rosh.[106] The Rebbe's was often witnessed to have his Shel Yad covered with his sleeve, although on occasion, it was seen to be uncovered.[107] Practically, the widespread Chabad custom of previous generations was to be particular to always cover the Shel Yad[108], although today, for some reason, some Chassidim are particular in this while others are not.[109] It is however a widespread Chabad custom to cover the Shel Yad while saying the blessing, as brought above from the Poskim.]

---

[100] See Admur ibid *"This applies even if his shirt, and all his clothing, tears in the area opposite the Tefillin Shel Yad."* Which implies that usually it is covered by his clothing; See also Admur 45:2 that *"It is permitted to enter a cemetery with only the Tefillin Shel Yad, being that it is covered"*, thus implying that it is normally covered.

[101] Orchos Chaim Tefillin 17 and Mordechai Menachos 12 in name of Shimusha Raba, brought in Beis Yosef in end of 27; Levush 27, brought in Birkeiy Yosef 27:5, Shaareiy Teshuvah 27:17, Kaf Hachaim 27:56; See Admur 45:2 that "It is permitted to enter a cemetery with only the Tefillin Shel Yad, **being that it is covered**", thus implying that it is to be covered. However, in truth, this is just saying that the Shel Yad is commonly covered by one's clothing, and not that one must be particular to do so.

[102] The reason: This is due to the literal understanding of "Lecha Leos", that the Tefillin is to be only a personal sign and not a sign for others. [Orchos Chaim Ibid; Shimusha Raba ibid; Beis Yosef ibid; Levush ibid]

[103] Implication of all sources in next footnote who hold of the reason of "Lecha Leos" [see Ishkavta Derebbe p. 36 that they all hold it must be covered even when putting it on and certainly upon wearing it]; Siddur Im Dach p. 18 [Said by the Alter Rebbe, written by the Mittler Rebbe, and edited by the Tzemach Tzedek] *"By the Tefillin Shel Yad it says Lecha Leos and not to others as an Os, from which we learn that the Shel Yad must be covered and not revealed, as is known."*
The reason: As the Tefillin Shel Yad represents the investment of the Divine light into the vessels, in which the light is concealed and not revealed. [Siddur Im Dach ibid]

[104] Birkeiy Yosef 27:4 in name of his grandfather Rav Avraham Azulaiy [the Chesed Leavraham], based on the teachings of the Arizal, brought in Shaareiy Teshuvah ibid; Shaar Hakavanos Derush 5; Peri Eitz Chaim Shaar Hatefillin 10; Olas Tamid p. 34; Elya Raba 27:5; Shalmei Tzibur p. 39; Zechor Leavraham 1 Os Taf; Beis Oved Tefillin 28; Kisei Eliyahu 25:2; Chesed Lealafim 25:12; Kaf Hachaim [Falagi] 10:18; Ben Ish Chaiy Vayeira 15; Shulchan Hatahor 27:1; Kaf Hachaim 25:32
The reason: As the Tefillin are to be put on privately. [Poskim ibid] Alternatively, this is due to the Drasha of Lecha Leos. [Maharikash, brought in Ben Ish Chaiy ibid; Kaf Hachaim ibid] Due to the first reason, some of the Poskim ibid write that even the Shel Rosh is to be covered while putting it on. [Gloss in Peri Eitz Chaim ibid; Birkeiy Yosef ibid in name of Rav Avraham Azulaiy; Shalmei Tzibur ibid; Kaf Hachaim ibid]

[105] Ishkavta Derebbe p. 32; Rabbi Leibel Groner related to me that the Rebbe was accustomed to place the plastic box on prior to the Shel Rosh. See coming footnotes for possible explanation.
The reason: Although it is forbidden to make any interval between the wearing of the Shel Yad and Shel Rosh, nevertheless, since we hold of the Drasha of Lecha Leos Velo Leacheirim Leos, therefore covering the Shel Yad is included as part of the Mitzvah of wearing it, and is hence not considered an interval. [Ishkavta Derebbe ibid]

[106] See Orchos Rabbeinu; Kovetz Shefa Kodesh; Zechor Leavraham; Piskeiy Teshuvos ibid

[107] From a look in videos and pictures, it appears covered by the sleeve in many of the shots. Rabbi Leibel Groner however stated to me that while this was case in many instances, not always did the Rebbe's sleeve cover his Shel Yad. It is strange that there are those who say that the Rebbe never covered his Shel Yad. In any event, it is unclear if in general the Rebbe was particular to cover the Shel Yad and only on occasion did it slip out, or if the Rebbe was not particular in this matter at all, and let the sleeve make the decision. [When wearing short sleeves, it often on its own can cover the Shel Yad.] Vetzaruch Iyun; However, see next footnotes!

[108] Ishkavta DeRebbe ibid; See also Toldos Levi Yitzchak 1 p. 138

[109] Perhaps one can suggest that the widespread custom of today to place a box on top of the Shel Yad [which was not followed in previous times, and was not done by the Rebbe Rashab-see Ishkavta Derebbe footnote 23] itself suffices in place of covering the Shel Yad, and hence we no longer need to be particular to also cover it with the sleeve, as did the Rebbe Rashab. This can also explain why the Rebbe was accustomed to cover his Shel Yad with the box prior to putting on the Shel Rosh [heard from Rav Leibel Groner], as the box fulfilled this necessity, and thus does not serve as an interval between the Shel Yad and Shel Rosh. [unlike the ruling in Piskeiy Teshuvos 27:23] Likewise, perhaps the Rebbe was not particular to always cover the Shel Yad also with a sleeve, being it was already fulfilled with the box.

Summary:

According to final ruling in Halacha, there is no need to be particular that the Shel Yad remains covered, and one can choose to wear it either revealed, with the sleeve rolled up above it, or concealed under his sleeve. However, based on Chassidus and Kabala, the Shel Yad is to be covered upon saying the blessing, and remain covered throughout the time it is worn. Practically, the widespread Chabad custom of previous times was to cover the Shel Yad with the sleeve, and so was the custom of the Rebbe Rashab, and so is the custom of many Chassidim even today. Others, however, are not particular today to cover the Shel Yad with the sleeve, perhaps due to the fact the Shel Yad is in any event covered by the box. Nonetheless, those who do not wear the box over the Shel Yad, are to be particular to cover it with the sleeve, based on the Chassidic custom.

Q&A

When is one to cover the Shel Yad, before or after putting on the Shel Rosh?

The Rebbe Rashab was particular to cover the Shel Yad before putting on the Shel Rosh[110], and the Rebbe was witnessed to put on the plastic box prior to the Shel Rosh.[111]

------------------*Amen*----------------

7. How to answer Amen:[112]

Answering Amen to a blessing contains a number of laws and restrictions. The proper answering of Amen is so severe, that Ben Azaiy states in the Talmud[113] that the longevity of one's life is dependent on it.[114] These laws apply both towards Amen after a blessing, or of Kaddish. [These laws however do not apply towards Amen of a blessing that does not include Hashem's name, such as a Mi Shebeirach, or Harachaman, or a personal blessing given by a friend and the like.[115]]

A. The vowelization and timing-Amen Chatufa:[116]

One is not to answer an Amen Chatufa.[117] This includes two regulations:

1.   One is not to pronounce the Alef of the Amen with a Chataf Kamatz or Kamatz Chataf but rather with a Kamatz Gadol.[118] [One is likewise not to overemphasize the Mem of the word Amen, as this causes the Nun to sound as if it has the vowelization of a Tzeirei.[119]]
2.   One is not to hurry and answer Amen prior to the blessing being concluded.[120] [This includes the entire last word of the blessing, and thus one is not to answer Amen until it is concluded. This applies even if the Chazan is lengthening the concluding word of the blessing with a melody.[121]]

B. The Pronunciation-Amen Ketufa:[122]

One is not to answer an Amen Ketufa.[123] This includes two regulations:

---

[110] Ishkavta Derebbe ibid

The reason: See previous footnotes!

Other opinions: Some write one is not to cover the Shel Yad prior to putting on the Shel Rosh, due to it being an interval. [Piskeiy Teshuvos 27:23]

[111] Heard from Rav Leibel Groner; unlike Piskeiy Teshuvos 27:23

The reason: See previous footnotes!

[112] Admur 124:1

[113] Regarding that the law of Amen Yesoma applies by Kaddish so rules: Admur 56:4; 124:11; M"A 56:6; M"B 56:10; Igros Moshe 4:1

[114] Brachos 47a

[115] Chavas Daas Y.D. Kuntrus Beis Hasafek 110:20; Piskeiy Teshuvos 124:14

[116] Admur ibid; Michaber 124:8; Brachos 47a

[117] The severity: Ben Azaiy stated that whoever answers an Amen Chatufa his years will be snatched r"l. [Brachos ibid]

[118] Admur ibid; Michaber ibid

[119] Kaf Hachaim 124:45

[120] Admur ibid; Aruch "Amen"; M"B 124:35

[121] M"B 124:35; See Rivivos Efraim 1:88; Piskeiy Teshuvos 124 footnote 129

[122] Admur ibid; Michaber ibid; Brachos ibid

[123] The severity: Ben Azaiy stated that whoever answers an Amen Ketufa his years will be cut r"l. [Brachos ibid]

1. One is not to skip the Nun of the Amen. Skipping is defined as one who does not verbalize it strongly enough to be recognizable.[124] [The same applies for the Alef of the Amen.]
2. One is not to split the Amen into two.[125]

C. The Approximation-Amen Yesoma:[126]
One is not to answer an Amen Yesoma.[127] This includes two regulations:
1. *Not to delay the Amen*:[128] One is not to delay the Amen. Rather, immediately upon one hearing the conclusion of the blessing, he is to answer Amen. [The Amen must be answered within Kdei Dibbur of the conclusion of the blessing[129], which is approximately 2 seconds.[130]]
   Chazan concludes Kaddish with melody:[131] If the Chazan is lengthening in melody the recital of the concluding words of Kaddish "Veimru Amen", then if he is lengthening a lot, the congregation is to recite the Amen immediately [upon him beginning the words Veimru].[132] [This applies for any blessing that concludes with the words Veimru Amen.[133]]
   In proximity of Amen of a congregation:[134] If a blessing is said in public and the people hearing it answer Amen, then it is permitted to answer Amen so long as majority of the congregation have not yet finished their Amen, [and one knows which blessing was said, as will be explained in another Halacha].[135] If however the majority of the listeners have already answered Amen, then one may not answer Amen, even if there is still a minority of people answering Amen.[136] However, there is an opinion[137] who rules that one may answer Amen immediately after the Amen of the congregation, even if the majority of the congregation (or even all the congregation) have already completed their Amen, and if he answers immediately afterwards, it is considered as if he is answering Amen after the blessing.[138] Practically, it is all dependent on how close in proximity one's start of his Amen is to the conclusion of the blessing. Thus, if he heard an individual answer Amen for another person's blessing, and he knows what blessing it is, he may answer Amen after the conclusion of the first Amen, if the first Amen was said without being lengthened. However, by a congregation, in general their Amen is lengthened and drawn-out as it is not possible for everyone to begin and end at the same exact time, and hence if majority of the congregation has answered, it is usually too distanced from the concluding blessing for one to

---

[124] Admur ibid; Michaber ibid

[125] Admur ibid; Rama ibid; Aruch ibid

[126] Admur ibid; Michaber ibid; Brachos ibid

[127] The severity: Ben Azaiy stated that whoever answers an Amen Yesoma his children will be Yesomim r"l. [Brachos ibid]

[128] Admur ibid; Rama ibid; Abudarham ibid

[129] M"B 124:34 based on P"M 124; See Biur Halacha 124:8 "Miyad"

[130] Piskeiy Teshuvos 124:14

[131] Admur ibid; M"A 124:14; M"B 124:35

[132] The reason: As the great lengthening of a Niggun is considered an interval. [Admur ibid]

[133] See Piskeiy Teshuvos 124 footnote 129

[134] Admur 124:11

[135] The reason: Even though many people in the congregation have already finished answering Amen, such as is the case if one finished Shemoneh Esrei as the Chazan concluded a blessing, and many people in the congregation have already answered Amen, nevertheless, so long as majority of the congregation have not yet completed the Amen, he may answer with them. (Now, although there is delay between the conclusion of the blessing and the start of his Amen, nevertheless) so long as majority of the congregation have not completed their Amen, it is still considered that the aspect of this blessing has not been fully completed, as the answering of Amen is also part of the blessing, as explained in 167:3. [Admur ibid, parentheses in original]

[136] The reason: (As one does not answer Amen after an Amen but rather after the blessing, and one is required to answer Amen immediately after the conclusion of the blessing, otherwise it is considered an Amen Yesoma.) Now, although there is a minority of people who are still reciting Amen, nevertheless this is due to the fact that they lengthen the Amen, and therefore their Amen is meaningless in this regard, as one who lengthens in Amen too much is making a mistake. Accordingly, the aspect of the blessing has been fully completed upon majority of the congregation completing their Amen. (If one were to now answer Amen it would be considered an Amen Yesoma, being that it has a long delay between the conclusion of the blessing and the start of his answer. Now, although the Amen of the congregation is also part of the blessing, nevertheless, one may not answer Amen after them, as one does not answer Amen after an Amen but rather after the person saying the blessing.) [Admur ibid, parentheses in original]
Other opinions: Some Poskim rule that one may answer Amen even after majority of the congregation has completed their Amen, so long as its Kdei Dibbur of the Amen of the majority. [Biur Halacha 124:8 "Miyad"; Piskeiy Teshuvos 124:14]

[137] 2nd opinion in Admur ibid; Taz 124:6

[138] The reason: As the entire congregation began their Amen immediately after the conclusion of the blessing, [and there is hence no interval involved]. [Admur ibid]

answer Amen. However, in the event that the Amen of the majority, or entire, congregation was said quickly, and hence its conclusion is in close proximity to the conclusion of the blessing, then one may still answer Amen.

Kaddish/Kedusha and Barchu:[139] The same laws apply towards answering for Kaddish/Kedusha/Barchu, that so long as majority of the congregation have not yet completed their answering, one may still answer. This applies even if one did not hear the words of the Kaddish/Kedusha/Barchu of the Chazan, as will be explained in another Halacha. (Furthermore, according to the latter opinion brought above, even if majority of the congregation has completed their recital, so long as there are still nine people remaining [who are still answering] it is permitted to answer.[140])

2. *Not to answer an Amen if did not hear blessing*: One is not to answer Amen to a blessing that one did not hear and does not know its identity, as will be explained in another Halacha.

Q&A

May one answer Amen to a blessing if he spoke after its conclusion?[141]
No.

May one answer Amen to a blessing if the Chazan already began the next blessing?[142]
No.

The Baal Korei answering Amen:
The Baal Korei must answer Amen to the blessing of the Olah, just like the congregation.[143] The Amen must be answered in close approximation to its conclusion.[144] Nevertheless, the custom is for the Baal Korei to drag out the Amen more than the rest of the congregation, in order to summon their attention to the start of the reading.[145] [It is however forbidden for the Baal Korei to delay beginning the Amen until the congregation concludes its Amen, as it must be in approximation to the conclusion of the blessing, as stated above. Those Baal Koreis who are accustomed to answer Amen only after the conclusion of the congregation, are saying an Amen Yesoma, of which the Sages severely warned against.[146]]

May one answer Amen, Kaddish, Kedusha through a Telephone, radio, live video/audio internet hookup?[147]
Some Poskim[148] rule one is not to answer Amen or Kedusha in such circumstances.[149] Other Poskim[150] rule one is to answer Amen and for Kaddish/Kedusha.[151] Practically, one may be lenient in this

---

[139] Admur ibid; Rama 124:11

[140] Admur ibid, parentheses in original
The reason: The reason one requires nine people remaining is because a Davar Shebakedusha may not be said with less than ten people, and the nine people join the Chazan for a Minyan. [Admur ibid]

[141] Rav Akiva Eiger, brought in Biur Halacha 124:11 "Vekodem"

[142] Magen Giborim, brought in Biur Halacha 124:11 "Vekodem"

[143] See M"B 141:17 in name of Elya Raba and Shaar Efraim

[144] Admur 124:1; Michaber 124:8; Brachos 47a

[145] M"B ibid

[146] See Admur ibid; Brachos ibid; Piskeiy Teshuvos 139 footnote 70

[147] The Halachic issues regarding this question are 1) Is this considered an Amen Yesoma? [Admur 124:11] 2) Must one suspect that there are feces interfering between the answerer and the person saying the blessing? [Admur 55:22]

[148] Piskeiy Teshuvah 167; Rav SZ"A in Minchas Shlomo 9:1; Moadim Uzmanim 6:105; Mishpitei Uziel 1:5 [brought in Igros Kodesh 13:221as opinion of Sefaradim]; Beir Moshe 3:166-168; See Mishneh Sachir 30; Tzitz Eliezer 20:19; Ratz Katzevi 2:10; Piskeiy Teshuvos 56:3

[149] The reason: Being that there may be feces or idols that intervene between him and the area that the blessing or Minyan is taking place. [See Admur 55:22; Koveitz Ohalei Sheim 5:104] Alternatively, this is because it is defined as an Amen Yesoma since the person is not in the same room as the person saying the blessing. [Piskeiy Teshuvah ibid; Minchas Shlomo ibid; Moadim Uzmanim ibid] Vetzaruch Iyun Gadol as to why being in a different area would make it an Amen Yesoma, contrary to the explicit ruling in Admur 55:22 based on the Gemara and Poskim

matter.[152] [If however there is a number of seconds of delay between the "live" hookup and the actual events taking place then according to all opinions one may not answer Amen to a blessing or to Kaddish/Kedusha.[153] In many live broadcasts, there are several seconds of delay between the events and the broadcast, and hence in such a case one may not answer Amen to the blessings or Kaddish.[154]] Answering Amen to a recording:[155] One may not answer Amen to a blessing said in a recording.[156]

D. The length-Amen Ketzara:[157]

One may not answer a short Amen.[158] This means that the Amen [may not be said quickly and rather] is to be slightly lengthened. It is to be lengthened to the amount of time it takes to say the words Keil Melech Neman.[159] One however is not to lengthen the Amen too much, as the word is not expressed properly when it is over extended.

E. The loudness:[160]

One who answers Amen is not to raise his voice louder than the person who said the blessing.[161] [However, if one is doing so in order to motivate the public to answer Amen, then it is permitted to raise one's voice.[162]]

Q&A

Do the above regulations of Amen [Yesoma/Ketzara/Chatufa etc] apply when answering Amen to a non-blessing?[163]

These laws do not apply towards Amen of a blessing that does not include Hashem's name, such as a Mi Shebeirach, or Harachaman, or a personal blessing given by a friend and the like. The concept of Amen Yesoma and the like were only applied towards an Amen of a blessing that is obligated for one to answer Amen towards.[164]

Do the above regulations of Amen [Yesoma/Ketzara/Chatufa etc] apply when answering Amen to Kaddish?[165]
Yes.

---

[150] Minchas Elazar 2:72; Igros Moshe 2:108; 4:91; Yechaveh Daas 2:68; See Igros Kodesh 13:179 and 13:221 and Likkutei Sichos 21:497 [printed in Shulchan Menachem 1:81] that the Ashkenazim [i.e. Minchas Elazar of Hungary] are lenient in this, thus implying that the Rebbe rules like the opinion.

[151] The reason: This is permitted as a) There is no need to be in the same room as a person in order to answer Amen, [Admur 55:22] Now, although most certainly there are feces or idol worship in-between, nevertheless we are lenient being that the phone wires that carry the voice bypass the feces and idols. This is in addition to that the wires are in the air, higher than ten Tefachim and is thus considered a different Reshus. [Minchas Elazar ibid; See Admur 345:17]b) There is no need to hear the actual voice of the person saying the blessing so long as one knows what blessing he is answering for. [Admur 124:11]

[152] So seems to be the leaning opinion of the Rebbe ibid; See Piskeiy Teshuvos 56:3 that one may be lenient regarding Amen of a blessing [however not obligatory] however not regarding Kaddish and Kedusha

[153] Admur 124:11

[154] Heard from a media technician; Verified through sampling various live broadcasts and seeing a delay between different channels.

[155] See Admur 124:11 regarding the definition of an Amen Yesoma; Mishpitei Uziel ibid; Piskeiy Teshuvos 215:3

[156] The reason: If it is not live then there is no greater Amen Yesoma than this. [See Admur ibid]

[157] Admur 124:12; Michaber ibid; Brachos ibid; Rashi on Rif 35

[158] The severity: Ben Azaiy stated that whoever answers an Amen Ketzara his years will be shortened r"l. Whoever lengthens his Amen, his years are likewise lengthened [Brachos ibid] The reason for this is because one who hastily says his Amen appears as if the Amen is a burden that he wishes to cast off of him. [M"B 124:36; Beis Yosef 124]

[159] The reason: As Keil Melech Neman is the Roshei Teivos of the word Amen. [Admur ibid and 61:4; Levush 124:4]

[160] Admur 124:13; Michaber 124:12; Brachos 45a and 47a according to Nussach of many Rishonim

[161] The reason: As the verse [Tehillim 34:4] states "Gadlu LaHashem Iti Uneromima Shemo Yachdav." [Admur ibid]

[162] M"B 124:47

[163] Chavas Daas Y.D. Kuntrus Beis Hasafek 110:20; Piskeiy Teshuvos 124:14

[164] Although it is a Mitzvah to answer Amen to one who hears someone blessing a Jew, nevertheless, seemingly it is not an obligation to do so. [Admur 189:6 "It is a Mitzvah to answer Amen"; However, some Poskim rule it is an obligation to answer Amen to a prayer or blessing, such as Harachaman. [M"A 215:3 in name of Midrash; Chesed Lealafim 215:4; Kaf Hachaim 215:11]

[165] Regarding that the law of Amen Yesoma applies by Kaddish so rules: Admur 56:4; 124:11; M"A 56:6; M"B 56:10; Igros Moshe 4:1

> **May one say the word Amen for no reason?**
> Some Poskim[166] rule one may not do so. Other Poskim[167] however rule it is permitted to recite Amen for no need.

----------------Davening-General----------------

8. Speaking/Hefsek for the sake of Davening:

The subject of speaking [i.e. Hefsek/interval] during Davening carries many laws and details, regarding the cases in which it is permitted to be done. It is beyond the scope of this article to summarize all these detailed laws, and its focus is solely on the general subject of talking for the sake of Davening.

A. The general law of Hefsek for the sake of a Mitzvah:

Hefsek for the sake of a Mitzvah:[168] It is forbidden to make an interval between Baruch Sheamar [and Yishtabach, and between Birchas Shema] and Shemoneh Esrei even for the sake of a Mitzvah [with exception to those cases explicitly recorded in the Poskim[169]].

Between Yishtabach and Yotzer Or:[170] Some Poskim[171] rule that between Yishtabach and Yotzer Or, one may even initially speak for the sake of a Mitzvah. [However, other Poskim[172] rule one may not speak for the sake of a Mitzvah even between Yishtabach and Yotzer Or.] Practically, the custom and final ruling follow the former opinion.[173] [However, some Poskim[174] rule that today the custom is to no longer make an interval in-between Yishtabach and Yotzer Or, even for the sake of a Mitzvah.]

B. Speaking [i.e. Hefsek] for the sake of the Davening:

Some Poskim[175] rule that the above prohibition against making a Hefsek even for the sake of a Mitzvah only refers to a Mitzvah that does not involve the Davening. However, one may speak for the sake of Davening [such as in the examples to be explained] whether in Pesukei Dezimra or Birchas Shema.[176] Other Poskim[177] however rule one may not speak even for the sake of Davening, [with exception to the cases to be explained], and so is the ruling of Admur.[178] Practically, in a time of need one may be lenient during Pesukei Dezimra, as will be explained.[179]

---

[166] Derisha 127:1 "It is forbidden to answer Amen for no reason"; Se also M"B 215:21; Biur Halacha 215:4 "Veassur"

[167] Chavas Daas Y.D. Kuntrus Beis Hasafek 110:20

[168] Admur 51:4 and 53:3; Rama 51:4; Levush 51:5

[169] For example, Mitzvos that will be lost if delayed, such as the blessing over thunder, may be said in Birchas Shema. [Admur 66:4; M"B 66:19]

[170] Admur 51:4; 53:3 [regarding blessing on Tallis]; 54:3; Michaber and Rama 54:1

[171] Tur in name of Seder Rav Amram Gaon; Kol Bo 4

[172] Rif; Rosh, brought in Kaf Hachaim 54:11; See Darkei Moshe 54:

[173] See Admur 51:4; 53:3 [regarding blessing on Tallis]; 54:3-4; Rama 51:4; 54:1

[174] Implication of Michaber 51:4; Aruch Hashulchan 54:4; Kaf Hachaim 54:11; Shulchan Hatahor 53:1; See M"A 54:2 regarding saying Shir Hamaalos between Yishtabach and Yotzer; Igros Kodesh 8:99; Piskeiy Teshuvos 54:3 in name of Darkei Moshe; Hefesk B'Tefillah 2:10 footnote 15 [p. 39] based on M"B 53:7 who prohibits initially stopping for a Mitzvah between Yishtabach and Yotzer

[175] So rule regarding Yaaleh Veyavo before Shemoneh Esrei of Maariv: Michaber 236:2 based on Rashba 293; Bach 236 [see Machatzis Hashekel ibid]; Levush Abudarham; M"A 236/1; M"B 236/7; 422/1; Derech Hachaim 33/81; See Peri Hasadeh 2:15; Hisorerus Teshuvah 4:4 regarding getting a Minyan

[176] The reason: As an interval which is done for the need of the prayer is not included in the prohibition against making a Hefsek. [Implication of Michaber ibid; Igros Moshe ibid regarding Pesukei Dezimra] Now, although the Rashba writes that it is allowed due to the fact that the Shemoneh Esrei of Maariv is voluntary [see M"A ibid in name of Rashba] nonetheless, this is not the main reason in the Rashba, and the main reason is as explained above, that the allowance is due to that it is being done for the sake of the prayer. [Machatzis Hashekel ibid that Bach argues and learns the main reason of Rashba is due to that it is for the need of prayer]

[177] So rule regarding Yaaleh Veyavo: Siddur Admur; Sefer Haminhagim p. 69 [English]; Rashal brought in M"A 236:1; Kaf Hachaim 236/16; Ketzos Hashulchan 27/5; Igros Moshe 1:22

[178] The reason: As the main reason of the Rashba ibid for permitting to announce Yaaleh Veyavo is due to that Shemoneh Esrei is a voluntary prayer. [M"A ibid in name of Rashba; Rashal ibid, explained in Machatzis Hashekel; Igros Moshe 1:22]

[179] Igros Moshe 1:22

The reason: Although some Poskim learn that the allowance by Maariv is only due to the fact that the Shemoneh Esrei of Maariv is voluntary [see M"A ibid in name of Rashba; Rashal and Siddur Admur, brought in previous footnote; However, see Machatzis Hashekel ibid that Bach argues and learns the main reason of Rashba is due to that it is for the need of prayer] nevertheless, Pesukei Dezimra is more lenient in this regard, as the prohibition of Hefsek is due to the Hefsek in middle of the blessings, and just like one may make a Hefsek after a blessing, before the Mitzvah, for the sake of the Mitzvah, so too here. [Igros Moshe ibid]

Summary:
It is forbidden to speak for the sake of a Mitzvah, unless one is between Yishtabach and Yotzer Or, in which case some Poskim rule that one may be lenient. However, if the matter is for the sake of Davening, one may be lenient in Pesukei Dezimra.

Q&A

May one ask someone to join the Minyan?[180]
Yes. It is permitted to do so even if one is in Birchas Shema.[181] However, one should only do so if he cannot communicate through writing [i.e. SMS messaging, whatsapp etc].[182]

May one announce the page number for the congregants of the Minyan?
Some Poskim[183] rule that one may do so between the Perakim of Pesukei Dezimra, however not in Birchas Shema.[184] Initially, however, one is to prepare cards with the page numbers and raise them upon reaching the place, for the congregation to see. One may not announce the page numbers in Birchas Shema, even if it means that he will have to Daven in private at home.[185] [Nonetheless, some Poskim[186] are lenient even in such a case.]

May one announce that there are feces in the area, and it is therefore forbidden to Daven?[187]
Yes.

May one correct the Baal Korei if he is in middle of Pesukei Dezimra?[188]
Yes. [However, only if this is a correction that is due to a pronunciation which invalidates the words.[189]]

If one remembered in middle of Davening that he did not recite Birchas Hatorah what is he to do?
Pesukei Dezimra:[190] If one remembers in middle of Pesukei Dezimra, or between Yishtabach and Barchu, then he is to stop and recite all three blessings of Birchas Hatorah, including the verses of Birchas Kohanim.
Birchas Shema: If, however, he already began Birchas Shema, then he may no longer stop to say it.[191] Some Poskim[192] rule he is to intend not to fulfill his obligation with Ahavas Olam and then recite Birchas Hatorah after Davening. Others[193] however rule that one is to specifically intend to fulfill his

---

[180] Hisorerus Teshuvah 4:4; Peri Hasadeh 2:15

[181] The reason: As it is permitted to even transgress a Biblical command of freeing a slave for the sake of having a Minyan [see Admur 90:17], thus certainly one may transgress the laws of Hefsek for the sake of having a Minyan. Likewise, Bein Haperakim is no worse than asking Shalom due to Kavod. [Hisorerus Teshuvah ibid]

[182] Hisorerus Teshuvah ibid

[183] Igros Moshe 1:22

[184] The reason: Although some Poskim learn that the allowance by Maariv is only due to the fact that the Shemoneh Esrei of Maariv is voluntary [see M"A ibid in name of Rashba; Rashal and Siddur Admur, brought in previous footnote; However, see Machatzis Hashekel ibid that Bach argues and learns the main reason of Rashba is due to that it is for the need of prayer] nevertheless, Pesukei Dezimra is more lenient in this regard, as the prohibition of Hefsek is due to the Hefsek in middle of the blessings, and just like one may make a Hefsek after a blessing, before the Mitzvah, for the sake of the Mitzvah, so too here. [Igros Moshe ibid]

[185] Igros Moshe ibid based on the stringent opinion above

[186] All Poskim in 1st Q&A who permit announcing Yaaleh Veyavo; as well as Hisorerus Teshuvah ibid

[187] Piskeiy Teshuvos 51:7

[188] Lev Chaim 3:5

[189] See Michaber 142:1

[190] M"B 51:10; as there are opinions who say it is forbidden to recite the verses in Pesukei Dezimra prior to Birchas Hatorah.

[191] M"B 51:10

[192] Peri Megadim 52; However, there are Poskim who argue on this advice, and state it does not help even if one has this in mind. [See Biur Halacha 52 "Umikol Makom"; Tehilah Ledavid 47:6]

[193] M"B 52:9; Biur Halacha "Umikol Makom"

obligation with Ahavas Olam and is to then learn Torah immediately after Davening. Practically, one is to follow the latter opinion.[194]

May one wear Tallis and Tefillin with a blessing in middle of Davening?
See our Sefer "The Laws of Tzitzis" chapter 1 Halacha 8, and our future Sefer on "The laws of Tefillin" where this matter is discussed in length.

9. Drinking during Davening:[195]

Once one has begun Baruch Sheamar, it is forbidden to drink until after Shemoneh Esrei [and Tachanun[196]].[197] This prohibition applies even between the paragraphs [i.e. Bein Haperakim]. However, prior to Baruch Sheamar, and after Shemoneh Esrei [and Tachanun], it is permitted to recite a blessing over a drink.

Eating during Shacharis: It is forbidden to eat even before Davening, as explained in 89:5. Even those who are accustomed to eat a snack before Davening in order to have strength to Daven [see 89:5] may not eat beginning from Baruch Sheamar until after Shemoneh Esrei [and Tachanun], as stated above regarding drinking during Davening.

Q&A

If one is very thirsty, or feels sick, and is having trouble concentrating in Davening, may he take a drink past Baruch Sheamar?
Some[198] write that it is permitted to say a blessing on a drink, and drink it, in the event that one is very thirsty, or is sick, and as a result is experiencing difficulty in concentration.[199] In such a case, it is best to delay the drinking until he is between the paragraphs [Bein Haperakim].[200] This especially applies between Yishtabach and Yotzer Or.

If one had a drink before Davening and did not yet recite an after blessing, may he drink during Davening, past Baruch Sheamar?
If one consciously had in mind not to conclude his drinking session upon beginning to Daven, and thus the Bracha Rishona that he said on the drink carries over[201], then seemingly it is permitted to drink even past Baruch Sheamar, being that he is not required to say a new blessing.[202] However,

---

[194] As explains Biur Halacha ibid and Tehilah Ledavid ibid the reasons not to rely on the advice of the Peri Megadim, and so is also implied from Admur in 47:6

[195] Admur 493:17 regarding Besamim, that one may not say a blessing over it in Davening; So also rules regarding Besamim: M"A 494:9; Shelah Miseches Shavuos; Elya Raba 494:12; P"M 494 A"A 5; Kaf Hachaim 494:57

Other opinions: Some Poskim rule it is permitted to recite a blessing over Besamim, in between the Perakim of Pesukei Dezimra. [Chok Yaakov 494:7]

[196] As one is meant to recite Tachanun immediately after Shemoneh Esrei without making an interval. [Admur 131:1] Now, although in 493:17 Admur mentions between Baruch Sheamar and Shemoneh Esrei, and does not mention Tachanun, this is because it is dealing with the day of Shavuos in which Tachanun is not recited.

[197] The reason: As it is forbidden to make a speech interval and recite a blessing over the drink during Davening.

[198] Piskeiy Teshuvos 51:9; See Revivos Efraim 6:29 who brings Rabbanim who rule this way, although he does not give any conclusion of his own; See Vayivarech David 1:14

[199] The reasons behind this ruling: 1) We find regarding other intervals, that they are permitted to be made for the sake of concentration in Davening. 2) Admur ibid states regarding Besamim that since one is able to avoid intending to smell the smell of the Besamim, therefore, the blessing is not an obligation. Perhaps one can learn from here that if one cannot avoid the drink, such as due to being very thirsty, then since he may drink, he may also say a blessing over it.

[200] As in this event one also gains the opinion of the Chok Yaakov ibid who permits reciting a blessing over Besamim during Davening.

[201] However, in the event that one simply forgot to recite an after blessing prior to starting Baruch Sheamar, then seemingly it is considered Hesech Hadaas from the Bracha Rishona, as people are not accustomed to drink during Davening, and it is hence similar to one who said Shir Hamaalos before Bentching. Vetzaruch Iyun, as Shir Hamaalos concludes the meal while starting to Daven does not conclude the meal, as one may Daven in middle of a meal.

[202] So is implied from Admur and Poskim ibid regarding Besamim that only the actual blessing is an interval and not the act of taking the Besamim and smelling it and so would apply also to drinking.

some[203] write that the actual act of drinking is itself an interval. This especially applies after one begins the blessing of Yotzer Or. Practically, this should not be done unless one is very thirsty, as stated above. In such a time of real need, one may drink during Davening, past Baruch Sheamar[204] [so long as he is not in the midst of the first paragraph of Shema[205], or in Shemoneh Esrei[206], or between Gaol Yisrael and Shemoneh Esrei[207]].

If one ate or drank before Davening and forgot to recite an after blessing, may he say it if he is past Baruch Sheamar?[208]
Yes, as if he waits until after Davening, the time for which he can recite the after blessing may expire [Shiur Ikkul[209]].[210] One is to recite the after blessing between the paragraphs [Bein Haperakim].[211]

10. Men Davening/learning in face of a female child, or relative, whose body is not properly covered:[212]
It is forbidden for a man to Daven or learn Torah in the view of an immodestly dressed woman, as explained in detail in Shulchan Aruch chapter 75. In this Halacha we will discuss the age from which this prohibition begins, and whether it applies to relatives.

A. From what age girl does view of an uncovered area prohibit Davening and learning in its presence?
Some Poskim[213] rule it is forbidden for a man to Daven or learn Torah in presence of a not modestly dressed girl who is age three and onwards. Other Poskim[214] however rule the prohibition of learning Torah and Davening in presence of uncovered area does not begin at age three but rather at a later age, when the girl's body is developed enough to cause men to have attraction to her [i.e. age 6-7[215]]. Nevertheless, even in their opinion, it is proper to educate a girl to dress modestly from age three, especially if she is coming to Shul.[216] Practically, the Rebbe[217] concludes like the former opinion that according to Halacha girls must be educated from age three in the laws of modesty.

---

[203] Piskeiy Teshuvos 51 footnote 86; Heard from Harav Yaakov Yosef Zatzal; See Beis Oved 51:3; Makor Chaim 51; Kaf Hachaim 51:17 that initially, one is not to make any interval during Davening, even if it does not involve speech, just as is the law regarding Shema.

[204] <u>The reason</u>: As the main prohibition of Hefsek is specifically regarding speech. [See Admur 51:4] And thus we rule that one may stop to make non-speech intervals even during Kerias Shema, after the first Parsha, if it is for the sake of a Mitzvah [Admur 63:7] even though one may never make an interval for speech even if it is for the sake of a Mitzvah, even in Pesukei Dezimra. [Admur 51:4] Certainly, then this applies during Pesukei Dezimra. [Beis Oveid ibid] Likewise, this allowance also applies in a time of need. [Poskim ibid]

[205] Admur 63:7; Vetzaruch Iyun if the Heter of a need applies to the 2nd paragraph of Shema or only if it contains a slight Mitzvah, as rules Admur there.

[206] See Admur 96-97; 104

[207] Admur 111:1

[208] Piskeiy Teshuvos 51:10

[209] See Admur 184:3 and Ketzos Hashulchan 60 footnote 20 that one must recite an after blessing immediately after an un-filling meal due to suspicion that Shiur Ikkul would already pass.

[210] This is similar to any Mitzvah Overes, of which its blessing is permitted during Davening, until Shemoneh Esrei. [See Admur 66:4]

[211] As in this event one also gains the opinion of the Chok Yaakov ibid which permits reciting a blessing over Besamim during Davening.

[212] Admur 75:1; Rav Chisda in Brachos 24a

[213] Biur Halacha 75:1 "Tefach Megula" in name of Shulchan Shlomo; Ketzos Hashulchan Vol 1, Haaros Page 90 in name of Chayeh Adam [that from 3 years old a girl is considered an Ervah regarding Shema and Torah learning]; Shut Daas Sofer 1:11; Ben Ish Chaiy Bo 8 brought in Kaf Hachaim 75:10 [concludes to be stringent when possible]; Halichos Shlomo 20:9 in name of Rav SZ"A; Az Nidbaru 13:1; Likkutei Sichos [18 p 448] and other prominent Rabbis of this generation; See letter of Rav Farkash in "The Jewel of our Crown" page 79; Chesed Lealafim 75:8, brought in Kaf Hachaim 75:10, leaves this matter in question regarding any Ketana; Ashel Avraham of Buchach 75 brings sides to be stringent and lenient in this matter. See Piskeiy Teshuvos 75:8 footnote 82aa

[214] Yifei Laleiv 75:2 [brings up question and leans to be lenient]; Maharam Brisk 2:70; Chelek Levi 36; Salmas Chaim 76; The Chazon Ish [16:9] famously ruled that the laws of modesty for a girl do not begin from age 3 but rather from a later age from when their bodies are developed enough to cause men to have desire for them; Chesed Lealafim 75:8, brought in Kaf Hachaim 75:10, leaves this matter in question regarding any Ketana; Ashel Avraham of Buchach 75 brings sides to be stringent and lenient in this matter. See Piskeiy Teshuvos 75:8 footnote 81;

[215] See Az Nidbaru 12:49; Or Letziyon 2:6-12; Piskeiy Teshuvos 75:8 footnote 87

[216] Salmas Chaim 67; Orchos Rabbeinu 2:204 that this applies even according to Chazon Ish ibid; See Maharam Brisk 2/70 that even though in his opinion it is permitted to Daven in their presence, nevertheless, they are not to be brought to Shul when dressed immodestly.

[217] The Rebbe in a letter in Likkutei Sichos [18 p 448] writes that according to Shulchan Aruch the age of Tznius needs to begin at three years old and a day, although one should not be oppressive about this and should speak in a pleasant way. [For a translation of the letter see "Beautiful within" page 39]

B. May a man Daven or learn within sight of his daughter, sister or mother who is not fully dressed?

Adult relatives:[218] The prohibition against a man learning or Davening in view of uncovered areas of a woman's body, applies even to female relatives. Thus, it is forbidden for a man to learn Torah, or pray, or say a blessing, within sight of an adult relative who has part of her body uncovered, if this area of the body is required to be covered according to the laws of Tznius. This includes all relatives, whether it be one's mother, daughter, sister or wife. A girl is considered an adult in this regard when any of the following three signs of adulthood are present, which include 1) age [11 years old][219], 2) puberty [pubic hair][220], or c) maturity [shame to be naked in front of the relative].[221] [Thus, if the legs/feet[222], upper arm[223], or chest of these women are viewable, he may not Daven or learn until he turns his head away.[224]]

Children relatives: Some Poskim[225] rule it is permitted to learn Torah and Daven in view of a daughter [granddaughter, sister[226]] who is not modestly dressed, if the girl is below the age of adulthood, as defined above [i.e. below age 11 and has not reached puberty or maturity].[227] Other Poskim[228] however argue and rule it is forbidden to Daven and learn in view of the improperly clothed female relative just like any other girl.[229] [Accordingly, once a daughter or sister have reached the age of three and above[230] one may no longer Daven or learn in their view when they are not properly covered.]

---

[218] So is evident from all Poskim who discuss the law regarding children relatives, as explained next.

[219] Girsa/interpretation of Rosh in Keddushin ibid; Tur 21; Bach 21; M"A 73:2; M"B 72:3; See Chelkas Mechokeik 21:12 that Michaber E.H. 21:7 is being more stringent than Bach, not more lenient, however Bach ibid understands Michaber to rule like Rif

[220] Michaber E.H. 21:7

From what age do signs of puberty count: Some Poskim rule it applies at any age, even prior to 11/12 years of age. [Implication of Michaber ibid; Chelkas Mechokeik 21:12; Beis Shmuel 21:15] Other Poskim rule it only applies once the child reaches the age of 11 for a girl and 12 for a boy and has grown two pubic hairs. [Michaber 73:3-4 and Admur 73:3 regarding Shema and implies that may co-sleep even past this age, and on this the M"A ibid asked his question]

[221] Michaber E.H. 21:7

Background: There is general confusion in Poskim regarding the exact age of adulthood due to various opinions, and contradictory statements, as well as various versions of text: See Kiddushin 81b for two opinions in name of Rav Assi; See Rishonim [Rif; Rashi; Rosh] brought in Beis Yosef E.H. 21 "Keitzad" for different versions of the second opinion of Rav Assi; See Michaber 73:3-4 and Admur 73:3 who give one definition [i.e. age] regarding Shema; See Michaber E.H. 21:7 who gives a second definition [i.e. puberty and maturity] regarding co-sleeping without clothing; See Tur O.C. 73 and E.H. 21 who gives slightly different definitions between Shema and co-sleeping; See M"A 73:2 who questions the seeming contradiction in both the Michaber and Tur between the ruling in O.C. regarding Shema and the ruling in E.H. regarding co-sleeping; See also M"B 73:11; For possible answers of contradiction: See Perisha E.H. 21 [i.e. in O.C. refers to case that other people are in room, in E.H. refers to Yichud with child]; Elya Raba 73:5 [O.C. refers to father/son, mother/daughter; E.H. refers to Mother/son, father/daughter] See P"M 73 A"A 2; Machatzis Hashekel 73:2; Kaf Hachaim 73:11

Opinion of Admur: Admur 73:3 defines adulthood regarding Shema as 12:13 or 11:12 with puberty, and implies that it remains permitted to sleep together unclothed even passed this age and the issue is only regarding Shema, which is in clear contradiction to Kiddushin ibid and Tur/Michaber E.H. ibid, of which Admur certainly does not argue on. This is the same question the M"A ibid asks on Michaber O.C. ibid. Vetzaruch Iyun Gadol on Admur ibid who saw the words of the M"A and most certainly the answer of the Elya Raba ibid or Perisha ibid but offered no hint in the text to an answer for this great contradiction; Furthermore, it is quite clearly implicit from the wording of Admur ibid that he refers also to a case of father/daughter and hence the answer of Elya Raba is negated. The only option is to say Admur holds like Perisha. If correct, the ages given by Admur in 75:3 only relate to when other people are around and in regard to Shema. Vetzaruch Iyun Gadol, as concludes the M"A ibid! In conclusion, it is completely unclear to me as how Admur rules regarding co-sleeping irrelevant of Shema and hence we cannot use the age given by Admur ibid to also learn regarding age for co-sleeping.

[222] See Admur 75:1 that this applies even when there is less than a Tefach of revealed skin

[223] See Admur 75:1 that this applies only when there is a Tefach of revealed skin

[224] Admur 75:1

[225] Biur Halacha 75:1 "Tefach" in name of Shulchan Shlomo; See M"A 74:9 towards end who suggests that seeing an Erva has the same law as touching

[226] Piskeiy Teshuvos 75:9 in name of Birur Halacha

[227] The reason: The above Poskim compare the law of learning in front of a Erva [brought in chapter 75] to the law of sleeping together with family [Chapter 73], and just like relatives may sleep together and say Shema even unclothed until the age of adulthood, so too he may Daven and learn in view of her, until the age of adulthood. [See also M"A 74:9 towards end who also suggests such a connection]

[228] Chazon Ish 16:9; Neziros Shimshon; Or Letziyon 2:6; See Piskeiy Teshuvos 75:9; See Birur Halacha

[229] The reason: As the allowance of 73:3 is only regarding learning and Davening while skin is touching and not regarding seeing the unclothed part. [ibid]

[230] See A regarding the age of Tznius, and Issur of learning/Davening for a Ketana

11. Standing for Kaddish and Barchu:[231]

Some Poskim[232] rule it is not necessary [for the listeners] to stand during the recital of Kaddish and Barchu. Other Poskim[233] rule one is required to stand upon answering Kaddish or any Davar Shebakedusha [i.e. a matter that requires a Minyan].[234] Practically, it is proper to suspect for their words.[235] [The Ashkenazi custom is to stand for Kaddish. The custom of Sephardic Jewry is not to stand.[236] Regarding the Chabad custom: The Rebbe was witnessed to stand for most of the Davening, including the Kaddeishim. In those times that the Rebbe was sitting, he would stand when the Chazan reached Yehei Shmei Rabba.[237]]

If one was already standing, may one sit down?[238] Even according to the lenient opinion, in the event that one was already standing prior to the recital of Kaddish, such as after Hallel [or after Yishtabach, Tachanun, Aleinu, and the like], it is good/proper[239] to remain standing, and not sit down, until after answering Amen Yehei Shmei Rabba. According to the stringent opinion, one must remain standing.

The Chazan:[240] The Chazan, [or other person reciting Kaddish, according to all opinions] is required to stand for the recital of Kaddish, Barchu, and any other Davar Shebakedusha.

Summary:
It is proper for one to stand during Kaddish, Barchu and any other Davar Shebakedusha. This especially applies in a case that one was already standing, in which case he is not to sit down during Kaddish, until at least after Amen Yehei Shmei Rabba. [However, the custom is to remain standing until the end of Kaddish-see Q&A!]

Q&A

Until where in the Kaddish is one to remain standing?[241]
Some Poskim[242] rule that one is to stand until the conclusion of Amen Yehei Shmei Rabba. Other Poskim[243] rule one is to stand until after the Amen of Deamiran Bealma. [Practically, the widespread custom is to stand throughout the entire Kaddish, and so should be followed.[244] When the Rebbe would stand for Kaddish, he would remain standing until the conclusion of the entire Kaddish.]

---

[231] Admur 56:5; See Kaf Hachaim 56:20-22; Piskeiy Teshuvos 56:4; Admur ibid concludes in parentheses: (See Chapter 146:4 for a similar discussion regarding if one must stand for Kerias Hatorah.)

[232] 1st opinion in Admur ibid, brought also in 53:1; Maharil Tefila 3, brought in Darkei Moshe 56:5; Arizal Shaar Hakavanos Kaddish; Peri Eitz Chaim Shaar Hakadeishim 6; brought in M"A 56:4 and Taz 53:1 and 56:2

[233] 2nd opinion in Admur ibid; Rama 56:1; Hagahos Minhagim in name of Yerushalmi [Arizal ibid claims it is misprint in Yerushalmi]; Shiltei Giborim on Mordechai Birchas Hashachar 5; Reishis Chochmah Shaar Hayirah 15:59

[234] The reason: One can learn this as a Kal Vachomer from Eglon. The verse [Shoftim 3:20] states that Eglon, the king of Moav, stood up on his own from his throne, upon hearing the word of Hashem. [Now, if a gentile got up in honor of Hashem then] certainly we, Hashem's nation, [should stand up in His honor]. [Admur ibid; M"A ibid]

[235] Admur ibid; M"A ibid "one is not to be lenient"; M"B 56:8; Aruch Hashulchan 56:9 that the custom is stand only for the necessary Kaddeishim that must be said during the prayer
Other opinions: Many Poskim conclude like the ruling of the lenient opinion and custom of Arizal. [Kneses Hagedola 55:1; Yad Aaron; Shalmei Tzibur p. 81; Kesher Gudal 8:14; Siddur Beis Oved; Chesed Lealafim 56:7; Kaf Hachaim [Falagi] 13:7; Yifei Laleiv 56:3; Ben Ish Chaiy Vayechi 8; Kaf Hachaim 56:20 that so is custom]

[236] Sephardic Poskim brought under the lenient opinion

[237] Pinat Halacha of Sichat Hashavua, by Harav Yosef Simcha Ginsberg; However, Rabbi Leibel Groner replied to me that the Rebbe sat for Kaddish and only slightly lifted himself for the saying of Amen Yihei Shmei Raba; Rav Eli Landau related to me that he does not know of any specific Chabad custom in this regard other than the ruling of Admur in the Shulchan Aruch.

[238] Admur ibid; M"A ibid; Darkei Moshe 56 that so was custom of Maharil; Shaar Hakavanos ibid that so was custom of Arizal; Chesed Lealafim ibid; Ben Ish Chaiy ibid; Many Achronim brought in footnote under lenient opinion

[239] Admur ibid; M"A ibid does not mention that it is merely "proper" to do so, but simply states that so was the custom of the Maharil; Many of the other Poskim ibid write that one must remain standing and the Kaf Hachaim 56:22 writes it is Mitzvah to remind one who is coming to sit down in middle of Kaddish that he may not sit.

[240] Admur 53:1; Bach 53; Taz 53:1; P"M 53 M"Z 1

[241] M"B 56:7

[242] Admur ibid, M"A ibid, Darkei Moshe 56 in the lenient opinion of Maharil regarding if one was already standing, brought in M"B ibid

[243] Elya Raba, brought in M"B ibid

[244] Halichos Shlomo 6; Piskeiy Teshuvos 56:4

---------------Shema----------------

12. Saying Shema prior to sunrise:[245]

When Davening in a Vaasikin/Neitz Minyan:[246] The initial time for Davening Shemoneh Esrei is by sunrise. It is a Mitzvah Min Hamuvchar to read the Shema slightly prior to sunrise, intending to complete the Shema and its last blessing of Goal Yisrael with sunrise. Immediately upon finishing Goal Yisrael by sunrise, one Davens Shemoneh Esrei, thus accomplishing the approximation of Geula to Tefila, and the Davening of Shemoneh Esrei by its initial time of sunrise.[247] One who is able to do this [finish Goal Yisrael immediately by sunrise and then Daven Shemoneh Esrei] receives great reward and is guaranteed a portion in the world to come.

When not Davening by Neitz:[248] Some Poskim[249] rule one is only required to read the Shema before sunrise if he plans to Daven Shemoneh Esrei with sunrise [Vaasikin]. If however he is unable to Daven Shemoneh Esrei exactly by sunrise, then he is not read the Shema and Daven before sunrise and is rather to read it after sunrise, upon Davening.[250] Other Poskim[251] however rule that Shema is initially required to be recited prior to sunrise, irrelevant as to the time one plans to Daven Shacharis.[252] Hence, one should always say Shema before sunrise even if Shemoneh Esrei will only be Davened after sunrise, and one will be unable to proximate Geula to Tefila. Practically, although the main opinion follows the first opinion, nevertheless it is proper to suspect for the latter opinion and to read at least the first Parsha of Shema prior to sunrise [even if he will only be Davening after sunrise].[253] This applies even if one has not yet worn Tallis or Tefillin.[254] Upon Davening later after sunrise, one is to read the Shema with its Brachos, as is regularly done.

Summary:

It is a Mitzvah Min Hamuvchar to Daven Vaasikin; recite Shema and its blessings slightly before sunrise and then Daven Shemoneh Esrei immediately by sunrise. Even one who is not Davening Vasikin, it is proper for him to recite at least the first paragraph of Shema before sunrise, even though he does not plan to Daven Shemoneh Esrei at sunrise and is not wearing Tallis and Tefillin, and will thus only Daven later on.

---

[245] Admur 58:4; Ketzos Hashulchan 19:12

[246] Admur ibid; Michaber 58:1

[247] The wording here follows the first opinion mentioned next and rules that the reason behind Vaasikin is for the purpose of Davening Shemoneh Esrei at sunrise, and is not due to any obligation of when to recite the Shema.

[248] Admur ibid in parentheses

[249] 1st opinion in Admur; Michaber ibid who rules the Davening of Vasikin is only a Mitzvah Min Hamuvchar; Majority of Rishonim in Brachos 9b; Rashba; Tosafos Yuma 37b; Rosh; See Rashi ibid and 26a; Megillah 23a

[250] The reason: This opinion rules that the purpose of reading the Shema slightly before sunrise is only for the sake of Davening Shemoneh Esrei by sunrise, [after approximating Geula to Tefila], and is not due to any obligation to read Shema before sunrise. Thus, if one in any event does not plan to Daven Shemoneh Esrei at sunrise, then there is no reason for saying Shema before sunrise, as Shema may even initially be recited until the 4th hour of the day. One is not to say Shema and Shemoneh Esrei before sunrise, as one is initially to Daven Shemoneh Esrei from sunrise and onwards and not before hand. [ibid]

[251] 2nd opinion in Admur; Ramban in Milchamos; Rabbeinu Yona Brachos 9b; See Rashi ibid and 26a; Megillah 23a; Rambam Shema 1:11; Peri Chadash; See Birkeiy Yosef 58:2; Vetzaruch Iyun why Admur does not mention the Rambam as one of the sources of this opinion

[252] The reason: This opinion rules that the reason for Davening Neitz is not only to say Shemoneh Esrei with sunrise, but additionally, in order to recite Shema before sunrise. The reason for this is because one is to initially read the Shema at a time that majority of people awaken, as majority of people awaken prior to sunrise, as only the princes aristocrats and the like waken after sunrise. [ibid] The Rambam ibid, and other Rishonim who rule like him, hold that the reading of Shema after sunrise is Bedieved, and the entire Mitzvah is for it to be read before sunrise.

[253] Admur ibid; implication of Beis Yosef; see M"A 58:3; Siddur Yaavetz; Ashel Avraham Buchach 25; See Piskeiy Teshuvos 58:5

[254] Admur ibid; Levush 58:2

Other opinions: Some Poskim rule one is not to read Shema prior to sunrise without Tefillin. He is rather to read only the first verse and Baruch Sheim. [Kaf Hachaim 58:8]

The law if one has time to put on the Tefillin: Admur 58:5 rules that when reading Shema after sunrise one is to read Shema as soon as possible with Tallis and Tefillin. Vetzaruch Iyun as to the difference between before and after sunrise, that before sunrise it may be said without Tefillin and after sunrise it may not! Perhaps then one must say this entire law of Admur refers to one who does not have time or ability or desire to wear them before sunrise, although ideally, he should do so. Vetzaruch Iyun!

-----------------Shemoneh Esrei----------------

13. Wearing gloves during Davening:[255]

One may not wear gloves while Davening [Shemoneh Esrei], as is done by travelers.[256] [If however, one is cold some Poskim[257] rule he may wear gloves to protect him from the cold. Other Poskim[258] however rule it is forbidden to wear gloves even in such a case, and so is implied from Admur.[259] Practically, if one cannot concentrate on his prayers due to the cold, then he may wear it.]

14. Said Vesein Tal Umatar Levracha prior to its allowed time of 7th MarCheshvan or 5th December:[260]

If one said Vesein Tal Umatar Levracha during the summer, outside of its allowed time, which is between Pesach and 7th Cheshvan [in Eretz Yisrael] or 5th December [in the Diaspora], there is a difference in law between Eretz Yisrael and the Diaspora.

Eretz Yisrael:[261] In Eretz Yisrael, if one said Vesein Tal Umatar after Pesach, [during the summer[262], which is any time between Chol Hamoed Pesach and the 7th of MarCheshvan[263]], one is required to go back and repeat from the beginning of Bareich Aleinu. If one already concluded Shemoneh Esrei, then he must repeat it from the beginning.

Diaspora-between Pesach and Shemini Atzeres:[264] In the Diaspora, if one said Vesein Tal Umatar after Pesach, [during the summer[265], which is any time between Chol Hamoed Pesach and Shemini Atzeres], then if one is in a country that as a whole does not need rain during the summer, it follows the same ruling as Eretz Yisrael, and one must go back to Bareich Aleinu or repeat Shemoneh Esrei. If, however, one's country as a whole requires rain even during the summer months, then one who said Vesein Tal Umatar during those months is not required to go back and repeat from the beginning of Bareich Aleinu.[266] Nevertheless, if one wills, he may repeat the Shemoneh Esrei as a Tefilas Nedava.[267]

Diaspora-between Shemini Atzeres and the 7th of Cheshvan: If one asked for rain after Sukkos, prior to the 7th of MarCheshvan, according to Admur and other Poskim, Shemoneh Esrei is to be repeated. See Q&A!

Diaspora-between 7th of Cheshvan and 5th of December:[268] In those countries [that in general need rain after Sukkos[269] and that's when their rain season begins[270]], if one said Vesein Tal Umatar after the 7th of Cheshvan, prior to the 5th of December, he is not required to go back, or repeat Shemoneh Esrei. [This applies even if his country is not currently in need of rain, such as it already rained plenty, so long as it is

---

[255] Admur 91:5; M"A 91:5; Olas Tamid 91:3; Elya Raba 91:6; Bach 91; Kaf Hachaim 91:22; M"B 91:11; Ketzos Hashulchan 12:4

[256] The reason: From M"A and Admur ibid "like travelers" it is implied that the issue is because one appears like a traveler and not like a person appearing before the king. However, the Bach ibid makes no mention of this and simply writes that one who wear gloves during Davening, on him the verse says "Al Tvoeini Regel Gava, Veyad Reshaim Al Tinideini" [Bach ibid] This implies that wearing gloves is an act of haughtiness.

[257] Conclusion of Beir Moshe 4:39; Piskeiy Teshuvos 91:5

[258] Neta Shurak 6, brought in Beir Moshe ibid; See there that according to him it is better to Daven alone at home without gloves than to Daven in Shul with gloves.

[259] As M"A and Admur ibid writes the reason is because one appears like a traveler, and makes no mention of "Gava", thus implying that even when the wearing does not involve Gava, but simply to prevent the cold, one is not to wear it. Vetzaruch Iyun.

[260] Admur 117:1 and 3; Michaber 117:2-3

[261] Admur 117:3; Michaber 117:3; Rambam 10:8 and Taanis 3a regarding Morid Hageshem

[262] Michaber ibid

[263] See Q&A that according to Admur and other Poskim this applies even after Sukkos, before the 7th of Cheshvan, although other Poskim argue.

[264] Admur 117:1; Michaber 117:2; Rama 117:2; Rosh 4:10

[265] Michaber ibid

[266] The reason: As some Poskim rule that such lands may ask for rain in Bareich Aleinu, even in the summer. [2nd opinion in Admur ibid; Rashi Taanis 10a; Machzor Vitri 24; Ravaya Taanis 848]

[267] Admur ibid; Michaber ibid

[268] Admur 117:1; Mateh Moshe 1:141; Elya Raba 117:3; Radbaz 6:2; Olas Tamid 117:3; Kneses Hagedola 117:4; Soles Belula 117:1; Birkeiy Yosef 117:3; Beir Heiytiv 117:6; Tehilah Ledavid 117:1-2; Biur Halacha 117:1 "Hatzerichim"; Kaf Hachaim 117:8; Ketzos Hashulchan 21:8; Poskim in Piskeiy Teshuvos 117:4 footnote 33

Other opinions: Some Poskim rule that all countries in the Diaspora are to repeat Shemoneh Esrei prior to the 5th of December. [Maharikash, brought in Birkeiy Yosef ibid and Kaf Hachaim ibid, in argument against the Radbaz]

[269] Admur 117:1 "these lands whose planting season is in Tishreiy, need rain after Sukkos otherwise the seeds that were planted will be destroyed"; Peri Chadash 117, brought in Beir Heiytiv 117:6; Mamar Mordechai 117:8; Biur Halacha 117 "Hatzerichim"; Tehilah Ledavid 117:1-2; Kaf Hachaim 117:8 that so is implication of all Poskim ibid, unlike Beir Heiytiv

[270] Ketzos Hashulchan 21:8

a general time that the country needs rain.[271] If, however, the country is not yet in need of rain, then Shemoneh Esrei is to be repeated if rain was mentioned prior to the 5th of December.[272]] Nevertheless, if one wills he may repeat the Shemoneh Esrei as a Tefilas Nedava.[273]

If one mistakenly said Vesein Tal Umatar between Shemini Atzeres and the 7th of Marcheshvan, is he to repeat Shemoneh Esrei?

Some Poskim[274] rule that one who said Vesein Tal Umatar after Sukkos, prior to the 7th of Marcheshvan in Eretz Yisrael, or prior to the 5th of December in the Diaspora, is not required to repeat Shemoneh Esrei.[275] This applies whether in Eretz Yisrael or the Diaspora.[276] From majority of Poskim[277], however, it is evident that one must repeat the prayer if Vesein Tal Umatar was recited prior to the 7th of Cheshvan, whether in Eretz Yisrael, and certainly in other lands, and so practically rule some of today's Poskim[278].[279] Practically, according to Admur, the prayer is to be repeated.[280]

---

[271] Ketzos Hashulchan 21:8 footnote 21 in implication of Admur ibid who does not make any such differentiation; Implication of Rosh, brought in M"A 117:4 and Machatzis Hashekel ibid; Biur Halacha 117:1 "Hatzerichin"; Piskeiy Teshuvos 117:4

Other opinions: Some Poskim question that perhaps the above law that one does not have to repeat only applies if there is currently a drought in the country, and it is in need of rain, otherwise, he must repeat Shemoneh Esrei, even though it is currently the rain season in his country. [M"A 117:4 in implication of Michaber 117:2]

[272] Implication of Admur ibid who writes the ruling of not repeating Shemoneh Esrei to only "these countries" and these countries refer to "these lands whose planting season is in Tishreiy, need rain after Sukkos, otherwise the seeds that were planted will be destroyed", hence implying that countries that do not need rain after Sukkos, one must repeat Shemoneh Esrei prior to the 5th of December; See also Ketzos Hashulchan 21:8 "a country whose rain season is at that time"; Peri Chadash 117, brought in Beir Heiytiv 117:6; Mamar Mordechai 117:8; Biur Halacha 117 "Hatzerichim"; Tehilah Ledavid 117:1-2; Kaf Hachaim 117:8 that so is implication of all Poskim ibid, unlike Beir Heiytiv;

Other opinions: Some Poskim rule that all countries are exempt from repeating Shemoneh Esrei between the 7th of Cheshvan and the 5th of December. [Beir Heiytiv 117:6 that so is implication of Mateh Moshe 1:141; Radbaz 6:2-58; Olas Tamid 117:3, Kneses Hagedola 117, [However see Mamar Mordechai 117:8 and Kaf Hachaim 117:8 who argues on Beir Heiytiv]; Toras Chaim 3:3 [Maharchash-Rav Chaim Shabsi of Salunki, Greece 1600] brought in Rav Akiva Eiger 117; Toras Chaim Sofer 117:6; Piskeiy Teshuvos 117:4]

[273] Admur ibid; Rama 117:2

[274] Toras Chaim 3:3 [Maharchash-Rav Chaim Shabsi of Salunki, Greece 1600] brought in Rav Akiva Eiger 117; Tehilah Ledavid 117:1-2; Toras Chaim Sofer 117:6; Orchos Chaim Spinka 117:1; Rav SZ"A in Halichos Shlomo 8:18; Or Letziyon 2:7-31; Yabia Omer 5:15; 10:10; The following Rishonim rule that one may even initially ask for rain in Eretz Yisrael from after Sukkos: Ritva.

[275] The reason: As after Sukkos it is no longer a Siman Kelala to have rain, and thus we begin saying Mashiv Haruach, and only when it's a Siman Kelala do we make one repeat Shemoneh Esrei. [Toras Chaim ibid; Tehilah Ledavid ibid; Toras Chaim Sofer ibid]

[276] Poskim ibid

Does this apply in all countries that don't need rain before the 7th of Marcheshvan? Some of the Poskim ibid imply that their ruling applies in all countries, as there is no country in which rain is a Siman Kelala after Sukkos. This is also implied from the fact they plainly state that in all the Diaspora there is no need to repeat Shemoneh Esrei without making any differentiation. [See Toras Chaim and Toras Chaim Sofer ibid] However, the Tehilah Ledavid ibid implies that this ruling only applies to lands that need rain after Sukkos, and not to all lands.

[277] See Michaber 117:1 and 117:3; Admur 117:1; Mateh Moshe 1:141; Elya Raba 117:3; Radbaz 6:2; Olas Tamid 117:3; Kneses Hagedola 117; Beir Heiytiv 117:6; Biur Halacha 117:1 "Hatzerichim"; Ketzos Hashulchan 21:8

Background: So is implied from Setimas Haposkim who do not state that after Sukkos, before 7th of Cheshvan, has a different status: See Michaber 117:1 "In the rain season one must say Visein Tal Umatar and in...Eretz Yisrael one begins from the 7th of Cheshvan." Then in Michaber 117:3 "If one asked for rain in the summer months he must repeat"; So also rules without making a differentiation all other Poskim who record this Halacha. In addition, it is clearly evident from the following Poskim that prior to the 7th of Cheshvan one must repeat Shemoneh Esrei, as they rule that in the Diaspora Bedieved one need not repeat Shemoneh Esrei if he said Visein Tal Umatar prior to the 5th of December. However, they stipulate that this only applies after the 7th of Cheshvan, hence implying that if it was said before the 7th of Cheshvan then it needs to be repeated: So rules: Admur 117:1; Mateh Moshe 1:141; Olas Tamid 117:3; Kneses Hagedola 117; Elya Raba 117:3; Beir Heiytiv 117:6; Biur Halacha 117:1 "Hatzerichim"; Ketzos Hashulchan 21:8

[278] Chazon Ish in Dinim Vehanhagos 4:26; Lehoros Nasan 7:5; Avnei Yashpei 1:16; Koveitz Mibeis Levi 17:99 in name of Rav Wozner

[279] The reason: Possibly the reason is as follows: a) Once the Sages made their Takana not to say Visein Tal Umatar before the 7th of Cheshvan, Shemoneh Esrei must be repeated if one made a mistake, as although it is not a Siman Kelala, since in majority of the summer it is a Siman Kelala, therefore they did not differentiate in their decree. [See Admur 114:5 for a similar ruling regarding one who said Mashiv Haruach after Pesach when it is still the rain season] b) Perhaps it is a Siman Kelala to have rain fall on the pilgrims returning from Jerusalem! Now, although we said before that if an entire country needs rain in the summer, then Bedieved if one requested in the summer he does not need to repeat, and the same should seemingly apply here, that if the country needs rain after Sukkos they should not need to repeat, seemingly that was only said regarding countries with a summer rain season, while those with a winter rain season, must wait until the 7th of Cheshvan. Vetzaruch Iyun!

[280] See Admur 117:1; Unedited Sicha of 7th of Cheshvan 1986 [printed in Hisvadyus 1986 1 p. 509] "It is forbidden to ask for rain prior to the 7th of Cheshvan and if one does so he does not fulfill his obligation and must repeat the prayer"; However, in the tape of this Sicha the Rebbe stated that there is a question in what to do if one did so, and did not give a final ruling on the subject.

Background: See Admur 117:1 "The same applies if in these lands an individual made a mistake and asked for rain from the 7th of Cheshvan and onwards he is not required to repeat" Thus, clearly implying that before the 7th he must repeat, unlike the ruling of the former Poskim who say no one has to repeat starting from after Sukkos. This is furthermore implied from the fact Admur ibid limits the ruling of the Mateh Moshe to only "these lands", hence proving that not being a Siman Kelala is not enough and there has to actually be in need for rain. This defies the entire reason of logic of the lenient Poskim.

Kedusha

15. Lifting the eyes during Kedusha:[281]

It is customary to lift one's eyes upwards [towards heaven] upon saying the words Kadosh Kadosh Kadosh[282] [during Kedusha of Chazaras Hashatz].[283] It is proper for the eyes to be closed while they are raised.[284]

The greatness of this custom:[285] A support for this custom is found in Sefer Heichalos[286] "Blessed are you to Hashem, the Heavens and those that descend on the Divine chariot[287], if you will say and relate to my children that which I do at the time that they sanctify and say "Kadosh Kadosh Kadosh". Teach them that [at this time] their eyes are to be raised to the Heavens, to their prayer houses, and they should lift themselves above. There is no pleasure in the world like that moment when their eyes are raised and meet with my eyes, and my eyes with their eyes[288], and at that moment I grasp my Kisei Hakovod, which contains a resemblance of Yaakov, and I hug it and kiss it and remember their exile, and quicken their redemption.

16. Talking and learning Torah during Kedusha:[289]

It is forbidden to speak in middle of Kedusha.[290] This applies even if there is a Minyan present aside for him.[291] It is even forbidden to learn Torah during Kedusha [even in one's thought[292]].

Where in Kedusha is it forbidden to speak/learn: It is permitted [to speak and learn Torah] while the Chazan is singing a Niggun [with exception to between Kadosh and Baruch, as will be explained], although not during the time that the Chazan is saying the words of Kedusha. [The words of Kedusha in

---

[281] Admur 125:3; Rama 125:1; Tur in name of Minhag Ashkenaz and France; Shivlei Haleket based on Sefer Heichalos; Ketzos Hashulchan 22:8

[282] So is the wording in Admur and in the Sefer Heichalos brought by Taz 125:2 and Admur ibid, however the Rama ibid simply writes Kedusha.
Other opinions and Sephardic custom: Some Poskim write one is only to lift the eyes upwards for the first word of Kadosh. [Ateres Zekeinim 125] Other Poskim write that one is to lift the eyes for Nakdishach, and lower them for Kadosh Kadosh Kadosh. [Makor Chaim of Chavos Yair 125:2;] The Sephardic custom is to place the eyes downwards upon reciting Kadosh Kadosh Kadosh. [P"M 125 M"Z 2] Practically, we lift the eyes for all three words of Kadosh, as so is implied from the majority of Poskim. [Elya Raba 125:3]
Custom of Rebbe and Chabad: In reply to the question regarding the Chabad custom, and custom of the Rebbe, regarding lifting the eyes towards heaven during Kedusha, Rav Groner responded "We never saw the Rebbe lifting his eyes at that time. Neither did the Altere Chassidim" Rav Eli Landa responded that indeed the Rebbe recited it from within the Siddur and did not raise his eyes, although he was hesitant to deduce from here that so should be the public practice.

[283] Admur ibid; Rama ibid

[284] Admur ibid; Taz 125:2; Soles Belula 125:2; Shalmei Tzibur brought in Kaf Hachaim 125:9; Arizal, as brought in all the following Poskim; Chida in Machazik Bracha 125:3 and Kesher Gudal 18:18; Shaareiy Teshuvah 125:3; Ben Ish Chaiy Teruma 4; Kitzur SHU"A 20:4; Aruch Hashulchan 125:3; Kaf Hachaim 125:9
The reason: As it is not proper to have revealed eyes facing upwards, as during prayer one's eyes are meant to point below, while ones heart is to be directed above. [Taz ibid]
Other opinions: Some Poskim rule that the eyes are to be open upon saying Kadosh. [Bach 125, brought in P"M 125 M"Z 2; Elya Raba 125:3; Rashal in Yam Shel Shlomo Yevamos 12:21; Magen Giborim; M"B 125:6]

[285] Admur ibid; Taz 125:2; Tur 125; Shivlei Haleket; Elya Raba 125:3; Soles Belula 125:2; Shalmei Tzibur brought in Kaf Hachaim 125:8

[286] Heichalos is a generic name for the journals written by the Sages who traveled through the spiritual worlds called Pardes. One of these Sefarim is known as Heichalos of Rebbe Yishmael Kohen Gadol, which includes thirty chapters of mystical descriptions of occurrences within the spiritual worlds upon the visitation of Rebbe Yishmael.

[287] The term "Yordei Hamerkava" refers to the Tzaddikim who entered into Pardes, and were revealed the above information. Amongst those Sages known to have traveled within Pardes is Rebbe Yishmael Ben Elisha, Rebbe Akiva, Rebbe Nechunya Ben Hakana; Rebbe Nasan, and other Sages mentioned in the Sifrei Heichalos.

[288] This is the end of the wording of the Sefer Heichalos, the remaining wording is brought in the Shivlei Haleket, and mentioned in Taz and Admur ibid

[289] Admur 125:2; M"A 125:1; M"B 56:1; 125:1; Ketzos Hashulchan 22:8

[290] Admur 56:7 and 125:2; Rama 125:1; Mahariy Abuhav; Shivlei Haleket 8 in name of Miseches Derech Eretz Zuta
The severity: Anyone who speak during Kedusha on him the verse [Yeshaya 43:22] states "And not to me did you call Yaakov..", as explained in chapter 56:7. [Admur ibid] This verse emphasizes that Bnei Yisrael are not calling to Hashem in prayer but rather to the foreign G-ds, and hence one who speaks during Kedusha is comparable to not only one who does not pray, but on the contrary, to one who is praying to a foreign G-d. [See Rashi and Radak on verse ibid] One time, Eliyahu Zal was found [by Rav Aacha] and with him were 4000 camels carrying a load. He was asked "What are these camels carrying?" and he replied that they are carrying wrath and anger. They continued to ask, "Why and for what purpose?" He told them, this is to take vengeance with wrath and anger against those who speak between Kaddish and Barchu, Kedusha and Kedusha, Kadosh and Baruch, between a Bracha and a Bracha, between a chapter and a chapter, and between Amen Yihei Shmei Raba and Yisbarech." [Admur 56:7; Manhig Tefillah 4 in name of Midrash; Shivalei Haleket 15; M"B 56:1]

[291] Admur 125:2; M"A 125:1; Hagahos Yeish Nochlin [Yeish Nochlin is of the father of Shelah, and the Hagahos is of his son Yaakov, the brother of the Shelah]

[292] M"B 125:1
The reason: As one must listen to the words being said by the Chazan. [M"B ibid]

which it is forbidden to speak or learn, include the sentence of Nakdishach, Kadosh, Baruch and Yimloch[293]] however, the dialect that is added on Shabbos [and Yom Tov] is not considered part of Kedusha [and hence there is no prohibition to speak[294] or learn while it is recited, and certainly one may think words of Torah at this time[295]].[296] Nevertheless, it is forbidden to speak between Kadosh and Baruch [even during the additional dialect added on Shabbos, and even if the Chazan is singing].[297] Furthermore, it is good not to speak at all [even of Torah[298]] throughout the entire Kedusha until after the Amen of Hakeil Hakadosh.[299] [This applies even if one already Davened and is answering Kedusha a second time.[300]]

Summary:
It is forbidden to speak, or even learn Torah in one's mind, while the sentences of Nakdishach/Kadosh/Baruch/Yimloch are recited by the Chazan. However, when the Chazan is in midst of singing [and is not saying the above words] it is permitted to think words of Torah in one's mind. Likewise, it is permitted to think words of Torah in one's mind during the recital of the dialect that is added on Shabbos/Yom Tov. Nevertheless, one should not to speak at all even during these parts [even of Torah], until after Amen of Hakeil Hakadosh. This especially applies between Kadosh and Baruch in which it is forbidden to speak.

Q&A
May one verbalize words of Torah while the Chazan is singing, or by the added Nusach of Shabbos/Yom Tov?
One is not to do so throughout the Kedusha, until after Amen of Hakeil Hakadosh.[301] It is forbidden to do so between Kadosh and Baruch.

Is it proper to learn words of Torah in one's mind while the Chazan is singing etc?
Yes. It is proper for each person to have a Sefer to learn from in his mind during the singing, and he thus accomplishes having Torah and Tefila in one place.[302] Nevertheless, it is improper to do so on the expense of the Chazan, leaving him to sing a solo when he desires the help of the congregation.[303]

May one who is in middle of Davening continue to Daven during the singing and added dialect of Kedusha?[304]
Although from the letter of the law he may Daven during the singing and added dialect of Shabbos, it is proper not to continue Davening until after Amen of Hakeil Hakadosh.

---

[293] See Admur 125:1; M"A 125:1; M"B 125:1

[294] So is implied from Admur ibid that even speaking is permitted [after Baruch, during the Niggun or added Nussach], and certainly verbalizing words of Torah, and on this is the novelty of the Maharil [brought next] that it is best not to speak at all, even during this time. However, from M"B ibid it is implied that speaking is forbidden by all parts, and only thinking words of Torah is permitted. See Piskeiy Teshuvos 125:3 footnote 20 that although so is implied from Admur and others, it is implied from the source of M"A ibid in Yeish Nochlin that speaking is forbidden, and so explicitly rules the Makor Chaim 124:4 that it is forbidden to speak at all, even of a Mitzvah, until after Amen of Hakeil Hakadosh. Afterwards, I saw that so is explicitly written in Yeish Nochlin and the Hagahos that only learning in one's thought is permitted and not to verbalize. However, from Admur ibid it is clearly implied that even verbalizing is permitted, as otherwise there is no novelty in his continued statements of not speaking between Kadosh and Baruch etc. Vetzaruch Iyun!

[295] M"B ibid that one is not required to listen to its recital.

[296] Admur ibid; M"A ibid; M"B ibid;

[297] Admur 56:7 and 125:2; Manhig Tefila 4 in name of Midrash

[298] Implication of Admur ibid; M"B ibid; Makor Chaim ibid; Piskeiy Teshuvos 125:3 footnote 20

[299] Admur 125:2; Maharil, brought in Darkei Moshe 125:2; Elya Raba 125:5; Kaf Hachaim 125:16

[300] See Kaf Hachaim ibid

[301] See footnote in the Halacha above that from Admur ibid it is implied that it is allowed from the letter of the law, although it is proper not to do so. However other Poskim rule that it is forbidden to do so.

[302] Yeish Nochlin ibid

[303] See Piskeiy Teshuvos 67 footnote 16 and 125 footnote 19 in name of Chassidishe Sefarim that doing so "transgresses" Lo Saamod Al Dam Reiacha, and Hakeim Takim Imo.

[304] Implication of Admur ibid; Piskeiy Teshuvos 125:3 based on Makor Chaim, unlike Rav SZ"A in Halichos Shlomo 8:38 who says one may continue Davening

17. What is the Chazan to do if he accidently skipped Kedusha and said the blessing of Ata Kadosh?[305]

Did not yet say Hashem's name in the blessing of Hakeil Hakadosh: If the Chazan did not yet say Hashem's name in the concluding blessing in Ata Kadosh, he is to go back and say Kedusha.

Said Hashem's name in the blessing of Hakeil Hakadosh: If the Chazan already recited the concluding blessing of Hakeil Hakadosh [or said Hashem's name in which case he must conclude the blessing of Hakeil Hakadosh] but has not yet begun the next blessing of Ata Chonen then it is disputed in Poskim as how he is to follow: Some Poskim[306] rule he is to recite Kedusha in that area and then continue with the blessing of Ata Chonen. Other Poskim[307] rule he is to return to the beginning of the prayer. Other Poskim[308] rule he is to continue his prayer as usual, [and after its completion, say Shemoneh Esrei again with Kedusha].[309]

Began the blessing of Ata Chonen: Some Poskim[310] rule he is to return to the beginning of the prayer. Other Poskim[311] rule he is to recite Kedusha in that area and then retract and repeat the blessing of Ata Kadosh.[312] Other Poskim[313] rule he is to continue his prayer as usual [and after its completion say Shemoneh Esrei again with Kedusha].[314]

-----------------Tachanun----------------
18. Using a Tallis or Tefillin straps to cover the face during Tachanun:[315]

The custom is to cover the face with a garment upon performing Nefilas Apayim during Tachanun.[316] It does not suffice to cover one's face using his bare arm.[317] [The custom is to use a Tallis to cover the face during Nefilas Apayim.[318] Those that don't have a Tallis are to use another garment.[319]]

Q&A
May one use his Tefillin straps to perform Nefilas Apayim?
Some Bochurim [single men who do not wear a Tallis for Davening until marriage] are accustomed to place the Tefillin straps of the Shel Rosh by their forehead to recite Tachanun. Due to various reasons, it is improper to do so.[320] Likewise, this was never the custom in Lubavitch, as testified by revered Chabad Rabbanim and Mashpiim of the previous generations.[321] Practically, Bochurim are not to use their Tefillin straps for Tachanun but rather are to use the sleeve of their jacket or another cloth.

---

[305] Piskeiy Teshuvos 126:2

[306] Shevet Halevi 9:134; Eretz Tzevi 2:1; Yechaveh Daas 5:13; Rivivos Efraim 5:58

[307] Minchas Shlomo 1:2

[308] Divrei Yatziv 1:70

[309] The reason: As Kedusha is not considered an integral part of the repetition to require Shemoneh Esrei to be repeated, as the main reason for the repetition is to fulfill the obligation of those who do not know to Daven. [ibid]

[310] Minchas Shlomo 1:2; Meat Mayim 44; Rivivos Efraim 2:185 in name of Rav Moshe Feinstein; Piskiey Teshuvos ibid in name of Poskim ibid

[311] Tzitz Eliezer 12:10 based on Kol Bo and Shoel Umeishiv Tinyana 1:66; 119:4 and Kama 3:171; Toras Chaim 114:10

[312] The reason: As Kedusha is an integral part of the repetition, as it is for it that the repetition is recited. [Kol Bo, brought in Beis Yosef 126] It hence follows the laws of all integral matters omitted by the Chazan which require him to retract. Now, one is not required to retract to the beginning of Davening, as it is no worse than one who spoke in middle of the three blessings, in which we do not require him to retract to the first blessing. [Shoel Umeishiv ibid]

[313] Divrei Yatziv 1:70

[314] The reason: As Kedusha is not considered an integral part of the repetition to require Shemoneh Esrei to be repeated, as the main reason for the repetition is to fulfill the obligation of those who do not know to Daven. [ibid]

[315] Admur 131:1; M"A 131:2; M"B 131:3; Aruch Hashulchan 131:7; Rama 131:2

[316] The reason: As one needs to have an interval between his head and the floor upon prostrating on a stone floor, and hence since Nefilas Apayim of today is an extension of the original prostration, we hence cover our faces. [implication of Admur and M"A ibid; See Piskeiy Teshuvos 131:7] Some Poskim however question this reason. [P"M 131 A"A 2] Alternatively, this is in order to avoid placing one's head on his palm on which is written the sins of a person. [Kneses Hagedola 131:10; Elya Raba 131:2 in name of Manhig; Kaf Hachaim 131:47]

[317] The reason: As the hand and the face is part of the same body, and a body cannot be used to cover itself. [ibid; 74:3; 91:4]

[318] Kneses Hagedola 131:10; Elya Raba 131:2 in name of Manhig; Kaf Hachaim 131:47
The reason: Seemingly this is done in order to merit the Tallis with the performance of another Mitzvah.

[319] Kneses Hagedola 131:10; Elya Raba 131:2 in name of Manhig; Kaf Hachaim 131:47

[320] As it only covers a very minute area of one's face, and does not necessarily prevent one from falling on his palm, as brought above. Furthermore, it is not respectful towards the Tefillin, as ruled in Admur 131:1 that for this reason during Shacharis one is to rest his head on the arm that does not have Tefillin. [See Koveitz Haaros 814]

[321] Rav Eli Landau inquired on this matter from his father Harav Yaakov Landau OBM, and from the noted Mashpia Rav Chaim Sholom Kesselman and both stated that such a custom never existed in Lubavitch.

19. How to say "Va'anachnu Lo Neida"

Standing at the end of Tachanun: In the paragraph of "Va'anachnu Lo Neida," which is said in the end of Tachanun, some Poskim[322] rule it is proper to recite the words "Va'anachnu Lo Neida" while sitting and then stand and recite the continuation from "Mah Naaseh". Other Poskim[323] however make no mention of this. [Practically, the custom of the Rebbe was to stand upon saying Mah Naaseh, and so is the widespread custom amongst Chassidim.[324]]

Aloud: Some Poskim[325] rule the above words of "Va'anachnu Lo Neida" and the continuation of "Mah Naaseh" are to be said aloud. Other Poskim[326] however make no mention of this.

20. What is a Minyan to do if the Chazan accidently recited Kaddish after Shemoneh Esrei on a day that Tachanun is recited?

In the event that the Chazan began to recite Kaddish immediately after Shemoneh Esrei, instead of reciting Tachanun, some Poskim[327] rule that Tachanun is nevertheless to be recited after the Kaddish.[328] Others[329] however rule that Tachanun is to be omitted and one thus continues with Ashreiy, or Kerias Hatorah.[330] If the Chazan has not yet completed the Kaddish, then if he has not yet reached the middle of the second stanza of the Kaddish, he is to be stopped, and Tachanun is to be recited.[331]

21. Is Tachanun recited if there is a Chasan in Shul who is getting married that day?[332]

It is customary not to recite Tachanun in the presence of a Chasan[333] on the day that he enters the Chuppah.[334] Tachanun is omitted for the entire day, during all that day's prayers [Shacharis and Mincha], on the day he enters the Chuppah.[335] [Some Poskim[336] however rule that the above only applies if the Chasan is getting married during the day. If, however, the Chasan is getting married at night, then some Poskim[337] rule that Tachanun is to be recited even by Mincha, even if he is present in Shul, while other

---

[322] M"A 131:4; Shelah; Derech Hachaim 38:11

[323] See Admur 131:2 who completely omits this addition; It is also omitted from the Siddur and Ketzos Hashulchan 24:3; I did not find it mention in Kaf Hachaim 131; See Al Minhagim Umikoroseihem [Rav Tuvia Bloy] p. 151-152

[324] Heard from Rav Leibel Groner that so was Rebbe's custom; See Haaros Ubiurim 1062 p. 63 that so was the Rebbe's custom and that the Rebbe mentioned in a Maaneh that not every law omitted by Admur means that he does not hold of it; New Tehilas Hashem wrote this directive as custom of Rebbe, as well as the annotated Siddur of Rav Raskin

[325] M"A 131:4; Shelah

[326] See Admur 131:2 who completely omits this addition; It is also omitted from the Siddur and Ketzos Hashulchan 24:3

[327] Lehoros Nasan 6:7; Halichos Shlomo 11:2; Rivivos Efraim 1:98; Piskeiy Teshuvos 131:4

[328] The reason: As Kaddish is considered a small interval, and was not Halachically meant to be said, and hence one cannot compare this case to the case of exemption by an Avel.

[329] Directive of Chazon Ish, as brought in Orchos Rabbeinu 3:225

[330] The reason: As Tachanun is meant to be recited immediately after Shemoneh Esrei, and once it has been pushed off from its place, it is no longer said, as is the ruling by the house of an Avel. [See Admur 131:5]

[331] See Birkeiy Yosef 282:11; Shaareiy Efraim 7:33; Igros Moshe 4:70-13

[332] Admur 131:5-6; Michaber and Rama 131:4

[333] Admur 131:5; Michaber ibid

This applies both in the house of the Chasan [when Davening with the Chasan in his house-Admur 131:6] and when the Chasan is in the Shul. [Admur 131:5 and 6; Michaber ibid; Shivlei Haleket 30]

[334] Admur 131:5; Rama 131:4

The reason: As this day is his personal Yom Tov. [Admur ibid; See Mordechai Megillah 808; Rav M.S. Ashkenazi in Teshurah Bakodesh Penima]

Other Poskim: Some Poskim rule that Tachanun is only omitted once he gets married. [M"B 131:21 in name of Derech Hachaim 38:9; Chazon Ish] Other Poskim rule that if it is taking place in the afternoon, Tachanun is omitted by Mincha and is recited by Shacharis. [Birkeiy Yosef ibid; Ketzos Hashulchan 24:6]

[335] Admur 131:6; Rama ibid; Hagahos Maimanis 5; Divrei Nechemia 131 Hashlama

This is in contrast to the law by a Bris Mila, in which Tachanun is only omitted during the prayer directly prior to the Mila, and hence if the Mila is taking place after Shacharis, Tachanun is omitted by Shacharis but recited by Mincha. [Admur 131:6; Rama ibid]

[336] See Poskim brought in next two footnotes; Nitei Gavriel Nissuin 6:4; In truth, the case discussed in the Rama and Admur ibid is referring to a Chuppah taking place during the actual day. [See M"A 131:12 in name of Darkei Moshe and Terumos Hadeshen 80 that this Halacha is referring to a Friday wedding, of which the Chuppah must take place during the day; Rav M.S. Ashkenazi in Teshurah Bakodesh Penima; Rav S.D. Levin in Kuntrus Tanaaim p.118]

[337] Simple implication of Peri Chadash 131:4, brought in Beir Heiytiv 131:14; Radbaz 2:175 brought in Shaareiy Teshuvah 131:14; M"B 131:21 in name of Derech Hachaim 38:9; However, see Birkeiy Yosef 131:5 that possibly even in their opinion Tachanun is to be omitted by the prayer prior to the wedding.

The reason: As so long as he has not yet gotten married he is not called a Chasan. [Peri Chadash ibid; M"B ibid in name of Derech Hachaim 38:9]

Poskim[338] rule Tachanun is to be recited by Shacharis and only by Mincha is it to be omitted in his presence.[339] Furthermore, some Poskim[340] rule that even when the wedding is taking place during the day, if it is taking place in the afternoon, Tachanun is omitted by Mincha and is recited by Shacharis. According to this opinion, Tachanun is only omitted by Shacharis when the Chuppah takes place before midday. However, other Poskim[341] rule that even when the Chuppah is taking place at night, Tachanun is omitted in both Shacharis and Mincha of that day in the presence of the Chasan.[342] Practically, the widespread custom is that if the Chuppah is taking place during the day, Tachanun is not recited even by Shacharis.[343] If the Chuppah is taking place at night, many communities are accustomed to recite Tachanun by Shacharis in such a case.[344] The widespread custom in many Chabad communities is not to recite Tachanun even in Shacharis, even when the Chuppah is taking place at night.[345] Each community is to follow the ruling of their Rav.]

Days prior to day of Chuppah:[346] Tachanun is recited as usual, in the presence of the Chasan, on all days prior to the day he enters the Chuppah.

Avoiding Davening in Shul:[347] It is not necessary for the Chasan to avoid coming to Shul in order to allow the congregation to recite Tachanun, although some communities are accustomed to do so, starting one to two days prior to the wedding.

Summary:

Shacharis: Tachanun is omitted by Shacharis when Davening in the presence of the Chasan, if he is getting married during the day. If he is getting married at night, it is disputed as to whether Tachanun is to be omitted by Shacharis in the Chasan's presence, and practically the widespread custom in many Chabad communities is not to recite Tachanun in Shacharis even when the Chuppah is taking place at night. Each community is to follow the ruling of their Rav.

Mincha: Tachanun is omitted by Mincha when Davening in the presence of the Chasan, even if he is getting married at night.

---

[338] Birkeiy Yosef 131:5 [brought in Shaareiy Teshuvah 131:14] that so is the custom of Eretz Yisrael, and it is a compromise between the opinions; Shalmei Tzibur p. 154; Zechor Leavraham 1:6; Chesed Lealafim 131:14; Yifei Laleiv 131:12; Kaf Hachaim 131:70; Ketzos Hashulchan 24:6 rules like this opinion; see Birkeiy Yosef 131:5 that possibly this applies even according to the Peri Chadash and Radbaz ibid.

[339] The reason: As Tachanun is to be omitted from the prayer which is prayed prior to the Chuppah. [ibid]

[340] Birkeiy Yosef ibid that so is custom of Eretz Yisrael; Ketzos Hashulchan 24:6; Yabia Omer 3:11-12

How the above Poskim argue on Rama/Admur: Although the Rama and Admur ibid explicitly rule that Tachanun is omitted the entire day, the above Poskim perhaps learn that the Rama and Admur refer only to once the Chasan is married that day, as explained in M"B ibid in name of Derech Hachaim 38:9, however see Nesiv Hachaim 38:2 who writes that according to Admur one does not say Tachanun that entire day, unlike the explanation of the Derech Hachaim ibid.] To note that Admur in the Siddur completely omits the day of the Chuppah as a day that Tachanun is not recited. Perhaps this is also a reason that the Ketzos Hashulchan does not rule as is the simple understanding of Admur in the Shulchan Aruch.

[341] Mahriy 80, brought in Peri Chadash 131:4 and in Beir Heiytiv 131:14; M"B 131:21 in name of Shulchan Shlomo and Gr"a; Kneses Hagedola, brought in Kaf Hachaim 131:70, writes that he wanted to nullify this custom until he found it written in Mahariy ibid; Some learn the Levush to also rule this way. [brought Shaareiy Teshuvah 131:14]

[342] The reason: Some suggest that the reason for this is because we are accustomed to write the Kesuba during the day and hence the Simcha has already begun. [Rav M.S. Ashkenazi in Teshurah Bakodesh Penima] Others suggest the reason is because the preparation for the wedding and its Simcha already begins 1-2 days before the Chuppah, and hence one may be lenient at least regarding the day of the Chuppah.

[343] Simple understanding of Admur and Rama ibid; Nesiv Hachaim 38:2; Aruch Hashulchan 131:16; Piskeiy Teshuvos 131:21

[344] Sheveit Halevi 7:18; Sheilas Shaul 19; Piskeiy Teshuvos 131:21

[345] Heard from the following Chabad Rabbanim: Rav M.S. Ashkenazi in Teshurah Bakodesh Penima; Rav Asher Lemel Hakohen; Rav S.D. Levin [see Kuntrus Tanaaim p.118]; Rav Raskin in Siddur footnote 414 in name of Rav Z.S. Dworkin.

Ruling of other Chabad Rabbanim: The following Chabad Rabbanim are stringent that Tachanun is to be recited in Shacharis in the event that the Chuppah is taking place at night: Ketzos Hashulchan 24:6; Rav Ginsberg of Omer.

[346] Admur 131:6; M"A 131:12; Terumos Hadeshen 80; Rama ibid "He is only called a Chasan on the day he enters the Chuppah"

Custom not to come to Shul: Some places are accustomed that the Chasan does not come to Shul for a day or two before his Chuppah in order so the congregation can recite Tachanun, However, in the event that the Chasan entered the Shul Tachanun is recited with exception to the day of the Chuppah. [Admur ibid; M"A ibid; Terumos Hadeshen ibid] This implies that there is room to omit Tachanun even two days before the wedding. [see Rav Levin in kuntrus Tanaaim p.118]

[347] Admur 131:6; M"A 131:12

Q&A
Is Tachanun to be recited during Mincha at the wedding hall?[348]
No. Tachanun is not recited even if the Chasan is not present in the Minyan.[349]

---

22. Tachanun on a day of a Bar Mitzvah:

Some[350] communities are accustomed not to say Tachanun in the presence of a Bar Mitzvah boy on the day of his Bar Mitzvah, and so is the widespread Sephardic custom in Eretz Yisrael. Other[351] communities are accustomed to reciting Tachanun on the day of the Bar Mitzvah, and so is the widespread Ashkenazi custom, and so is the Chabad custom.

------------------Kerias Hatorah----------------

23. How many pages is one to show the congregation during Hagbah?

One is to show [up to[352]] three columns of the Sefer Torah to the congregation upon performing Hagbah.[353] Possibly, one is to show exactly three columns [and not less or more].[354] Some Poskim[355] however rule that it is all dependent on the strength one has, and if he is able to hold the Sefer Torah when it is opened many pages [and hence, if one is unable to open it three columns, he can open it less]. [Practically, one is to try to open at least three columns of the Sefer Torah, and if he is able to, many are accustomed to open even more.[356]]

24. Calling up relatives to Aliyos:[357]

From the letter of the law, it is permitted to call two relatives to the Torah for an Aliyah, one after the other. This applies whether they are brothers, or father and son. However, the custom is to avoid doing so, due to Ayin Hara.[358] If, however, one does not call the two relatives by name, then it is allowed.[359] [Practically, however, the custom is not to call up relatives one after the other even if they are not called to the Torah by names.[360] This prohibition applies even if the relatives claim they are not particular about Ayin Hara.[361] It is however permitted to call up relatives for Aliyos, if there is a break of an Aliyah in between in which a relative was not called up.[362]]

---

[348] Piskeiy Teshuvos 131:21

[349] The reason: As this has the same status as the house of the Chasan in which Tachanun is omitted. However see Admur 131:6 "when Davening with the Chasan"

[350] Custom of Egyptian Jewry, brought in Nehar Mitzrayim, Ketzos Hashulchan 24 footnote 19; Yabia Omer 1:27; 4:14; Yechaveh Daas 2:15; Yaskil Avdi 2:15; Mishpitei Uziel 11; See Piskeiy Teshuvos 131:24 footnote 141

[351] Az Nidbaru 11:40; See Piskeiy Teshuvos ibid
Chassidic custom: Some Chassidic communities do not recite Tachanun on the day of the Bar Mitzvah. [Darkei Chaim Veshalom 192]

[352] Miseches Sofrim 14:14, and 3:5; brought in M"B ibid

[353] M"A 134:3 in name of Chidushei Aguda; Miseches Sofrim 14:14 see also 3:5 that one is to open the Sefer Torah three columns; Elya Raba 134:4; Kitzur Shlah; Kitzur SHU"A 23:25; M"B 134:8; Ketzos Hashulchan 25:13; See Igros Kodesh 18:427

[354] M"A ibid; Implication of Kitzur SHU"A ibid and Ketzos Hashulchan ibid

[355] M"B 134:8

[356] So I heard from Rav Groner Shlita

[357] 141:6; Kol Bo 20; Mordechai
Other opinions: Some Poskim rule it is forbidden from the letter of the law to call two relatives one after the other, being that they are considered invalid witnesses. [Orchos Chaim, brought in Beis Yosef; Ateres Zekeinim 141:3; P"M 141 A"A 8] According to this opinion/reason, all relatives that are invalid to testify for each other are likewise not to be called to the Torah one after the other. [P"M ibid] Practically, we do not rule like this opinion. [Kaf Hachaim 141:25 based on Gr"a who proves from the Gemara that even Pesulei Eidus may receive Aliyos, and so is the final ruling of Michaber ibid who rules the prohibition is only due to Maaras Ayin.]

[358] Michaber ibid;

[359] Rama ibid regarding Shevii and Maftir and M"B 141:21 in name of Achronim applies this also to other Aliyos; Emunas Shmuel 47; Elya Raba 141:7; Chesed Lealafim 141:16; Poskim in Kaf Hachaim 141:26; M"B 141:21 [see there however that this only applies in communities that never call up by name, however to initially not call up by name just for this purpose is forbidden, as this itself serves as a recognition. However, see Shaareiy Efraim 1:32 who writes one may be lenient in a time of great need, brought in Shaar Hatziyon 141:22]

[360] Kisei Eliyahu 141; Poskim in Kaf Hachaim 141:32 and so concludes Kaf Hachaim that so is the custom even in those communities that do not call the Aliyos by name; Yechaveh Daas 3:50
The reason: As nevertheless the name is mentioned by the Mi Shebeirach. [Kisei Eliyahu ibid]

[361] Hagahos Beis Yosef; Elya Raba 141:8; Birkeiy Yosef 141:7; Yosef Ometz 16:4; M"B 141:19; Shaareiy Efraim 1:6; Derech Hachaim 14; Kitzur SHU"A 23:13; M"B 141:19; Poskim in Kaf Hachaim 141:29

Shevii and Maftir:[363] One is not to call two relatives for Shevii and Maftir. [This however only applies by Maftir of Shabbos, in which one reads both Aliyos from the same Sefer Torah, and therefore the Ayin Hara applies. If, however, the Shevii and Maftir are read from two different Sifrei Torah, as occurs on Yom Tov, and whenever there are two Torah's taken out on Shabbos, then the Aliyos may be given to two relatives, one for Shevii and the second for Maftir.[364] However, when three Sifrei Torah are removed, relatives may not be called up for Shishi and Shevii, being that Kaddish is not recited in-between. Likewise, when two Sifrei Torah are removed during the week, relatives may not be called up for Shelishi and Revii, being that Kaddish is not recited in-between.[365] However, in a time of need one may be lenient.[366] In such a case, the relative who received the previous Aliyah is to descend from the Amud before the new Aliyah is begun.[367]]

Summary:
Relatives, such as a father and son, or siblings, are not to be called for an Aliyah one after the other. If there was another Aliyah in between, it is permitted to call a relative up. When two Sifrei Torah are removed, it is permitted to call them up for Shevii and Maftir.

Q&A
What relatives are included in the above prohibition against giving an Aliyah one after the other?
Father son:[368] The prohibition applies to a father and son [whether one calls up the son after the father or the father after the son].
Brothers:[369] The prohibition applies to brothers. [This applies whether they are maternal and paternal brothers, or are only paternal brothers, or are only maternal brothers.[370]]
Grandfather and Grandson: Some Poskim[371] rule it is permitted to call up a grandfather and grandson, or vice versa, one after the other [if they do not have the same name[372]]. Other Poskim[373] rule it is forbidden to call up a grandfather and grandson from his son, or vice versa, one after the other. However, a grandson from his daughter is permitted even according to this opinion.[374] Practically, one is to be stringent in this matter unless the community custom is to be lenient.[375] In a time of need one

---

Other opinions: Some Poskim rule it is permitted for relatives to forgive their particularness on this matter. [Noheig Katzon Yosef, brought in Kaf Hachaim ibid; Aruch Hashulchan 141:8] Practically, we do not rule like this opinion. [Kaf Hachaim ibid]
[362] Implication of Michaber and Rama ibid; Mateh Yehuda 141:7; Machazik Bracha 141:4; Kaf Hachaim 141:30
Other opinions: Some communities are accustomed not to call up relatives for Aliyos even if there is a break of an Aliyah in between. [Brought in Mateh Yehuda ibid] Practically, this is not the widespread custom, and so is the custom in Egypt, Eretz Yisrael, Turkey, and most of the world, although those who have a custom to be stringent even in such a case, are abide by it. [Kaf Hachaim ibid]
[363] Rama ibid; Maharil
Other opinions: Some Poskim rule that one may call two relatives for an Aliyah one after the other for Shevii and Maftir, being that the Kaddish is considered an interval in between. [Maharikash, brought in Kneses Hagedola 1431:5 and Kaf Hachaim 141:33] Practically, we are stringent in this matter as rule majority of Poskim. [Kaf Hachaim ibid] However, some Poskim rule one may be lenient like this opinion in a time of need. [Toras Chaim Sofer 141; Eretz Tzevi 1:39; Piskeiy Teshuvos 141:5]
[364] Kneses Hagedola 141:5; Beir Heiytiv 141:6; Olas Tamid 141:13; Elya Raba 141:7; Poskim in Kaf Hachaim 141:33
Other opinions: Some Poskim rule that even in the case that two Sifrei Torah are taken out, one is not to call two relatives for an Aliyah one after the other. [Mateh Yehuda 141:7, brought in Kaf Hachaim ibid] Practically, we are lenient in this matter, as rule majority of Poskim. [Kaf Hachaim ibid]
[365] Shaareiy Efraim 1:32; Hisorerus Teshuvah 1:67; Piskeiy Teshuvos 141:5
[366] Poskim ibid
[367] Toras Chaim Sofer 141; Hisorerus Teshuvah 1:67
[368] Michaber ibid
[369] Michaber ibid
[370] Kneses Hagedola 141:7; Olas Tamid 141:13; Elya Raba 141:8; Poskim in Kaf Hachaim 141:26
[371] Peri Chadash, brought in P"M 141:8; Machazik Bracha 141:5 that some are accustomed like Peri Chadash
[372] Kaf Hachaim 141:27
[373] Kneses Hagedola 141:8, brought in P"M 141:8; Olas Tamid 141:13; Elya Raba 141:8; Mateh Yehuda 141:7; Poskim in Kaf Hachaim 141:27
[374] Kaf Hachaim ibid
[375] Kaf Hachaim ibid
The reason: As the majority of Poskim prohibit it, and matters of danger is Halachically to be viewed even more strict than an Issur. [Kaf Hachaim ibid]

may be lenient.[376] Likewise, Bedieved, if the grandson/grandfather was already called up, he is to take the Aliyah.[377]

Father/son in-law:[378] It is permitted to call a father and son in-law to the Torah one after the other.

What is one to do if he was accidently called to the Torah after an invalidating relative [father/brother]?

If he already went up to the Bima, then he is to accept the Aliyah.[379] It is proper in such a case for the relative who received the previous Aliyah to descend from the Bima right away, and not wait until after the current Aliyah.[380] If he did not yet go up to the Bima, then he is not to go up and rather another person is to be called up in his stead.[381]

If one called a person for an Aliyah and he was not in Shul, may the previous Aliyos son/relative be called for an Aliyah?

Some Poskim[382] rule it is permitted to do so.[383] Other Poskim[384] rule it remains forbidden.

If one called a person for an Aliyah and he was not in Shul, may his son/relative be called up in his place?[385]

Yes.

May a child who is under Bar Mitzvah receive the Aliyah of Maftir, if his father/relative received Shevii?[386]

Yes.

On Simchas Torah, may relatives be called up one after the other?[387]

The custom is to be lenient in this matter.

May two relatives be called up for Hagbah and Gelilah?[388]

Yes. However, one is not to call them both up by name or give them both a Mi Shebeirach.

---

[376] M"B 141:19

[377] Shaareiy Efraim 1:33

[378] Pesach Hadvir 147; Piskeiy Teshuvos 141:4
Other opinions: Some Poskim are stringent in this matter. [Sefer Hachaim [Falagi] 11] Practically, the custom is to be lenient. [Pesach Hadvir ibid; Piskeiy Teshuvos ibid footnote 24]

[379] Kneses Hagedola 141:4; Hagahos Beis Yosef; Elya Raba 141:8; Peri Chadash 141:6; Mateh Yehuda 141:7; Derech Hachaim 14; Kitzur SHU"A 23:13; Poskim in Kaf Hachaim 141:28

[380] Toras Chaim Sofer 141:4; Piskeiy Teshuvos 141:4

[381] Shaareiy Efraim 1:33; M"B 141:18

[382] Shvus Yaakov 3:10

[383] The reason: As since another person was called after the relative, it is enough of an interval to eliminate any Ayin Hara, even though the person did not actually take the Aliyah. [ibid]

[384] Yosef Ometz 16:4; Poskim in Kaf Hachaim 141:31

[385] Shevet Hakehasi 2:65

[386] Kneses Hagedola 141:6; Olas Tamid 141:13; Elya Raba 141:7; Derech Hachaim 14; M"B 141:20; Poskim in Kaf Hachaim 141:34

[387] Shaareiy Efraim 1:32; Piskeiy Teshuvos 141:4

[388] Shearim Hametzuyanim Behalacha 23:10 in name of Avnei Chefetz 16; Piskeiy Teshuvos 141:5

-----------------Beis Hakeneses-----------------

25. Making use of the Bima:[389]

The Bima onto which the Sefer Torah is placed is considered Tashmishei Kedusha[390], and is therefore forbidden to be used for mundane purposes.[391] If, however, the Sefer Torah is not directly placed onto the Bima, but rather is always placed on a cloth which is spread over the Bima, as is done today, then the Bima has a status of Tashmish Detashmishei Kedusha[392] and may thus be used for mundane purposes.[393] However, in such a case, the cloth which is designated to be placed over the table has the status of Tashmishei Kedusha and may not be used for mundane purposes.[394] In all cases, it is permitted to stipulate on the Tashmishei Kedusha that it may be used for mundane matters.[395] Furthermore, in a case that the custom is to allow using the Bima or its cloth for mundane matters, it is permitted to be done even if this stipulation was not explicitly made.[396] Practically, based on this latter ruling, the custom is to make use of the Bima and its covering for mundane matters.[397] [One may thus place Sefarim on top of the Bima, and may lean on it.[398] However, some[399] are stringent in this matter.] In all cases, it remains forbidden to use the Bima/cloth for a belittling purpose.[400]

---

[389] See Michaber 154:3 and 6; Rama 154:8; M"A 154:6; Beis Yosef 154 and Darkei Moshe 154 in name of Rishonim; Maharam Mintz 81; Kneses Hagedola 141; Olas Tamid 141:3; Elya Raba 141:3; Ledavid Emes 5; Shaareiy Efraim 3:11; M"B 141:4-5; Piskeiy Teshuvos 154:4

[390] Michaber 154:3 and 6 regarding chair of Sefer Torah, which refers to the table which is on the Bima [M"B 154:10]; The Bima in 154:7 which is considered Kedushas Beis Hakenses refers to the elevated area that has the Bima of the Sefer Torah placed on it, and not to the Bima itself.

[391] M"B 154:6; Admur 42:4 regarding Tefillin case; 42:6 regarding all Tashmishei Kedusha items; See Maharam Mintz 81; Kneses Hagedola 141; Olas Tamid 141:3; Elya Raba 141:3; Ledavid Emes 5; Shaareiy Efarim 3:11; M"B 141:4-5

[392] M"A 154:6; Beis Yosef 154 and Darkei Moshe 154 in name of Rishonim; Teshuvas Maharam Mintz 81; Kneses Hagedola 141; Olas Tamid 141:3; Elya Raba 141:3; Ledavid Emes 5; Machatzis Hashekel 154:6; P"M 153 M"Z 15; 154 A"A 6; Shaareiy Efraim 3:11; M"B 141:4-5; Aruch Hashulchan 154:4; Rama 154:6 and M"A 154:13 regarding the Paroches that it has a status of Kedushas Beis Hakenses and not Kedushas Aron being the Sefer Torah is never placed on it; See Olas Tamid 154:4; see Piskeiy Teshuvos ibid footnote 158; Maharshag 1:12; Kaf Hachaim 154:22; Tzedaka Umishpat 15 footnote 45; Piskeiy Teshuvos 154:4; See M"B 141:4 that one may lean on the table of the Bima, however he contradicts himself in 154:10 and Shaar Hatziyon 154:8

If one sometimes places the Sefer Torah directly on the Bima: Then the Bima has a status of Tashmishei Kedusha, even though it is majority of the time used with a cloth. [M"A ibid; M"B 154:10; Shaar Hatziyon 154:8] Some say that if the cloth at times slips off the Bima, and the Sefer Torah is hence placed directly on the Bima, then it has a status of Tashmishei Kedusha. [Shaar Hatziyon 154:8] Others however argue on this statement. [Maharshag 1:12]

[393] Beis Yosef ibid; P"M 153 M"Z 15; Implication of Levush 154:3; M"B 154:6; See other opinions in Piskeiy Teshuvos 154:4

[394] See M"A 154:13; Poskim ibid in previous footnotes

[395] Michaber 154:8; Admur 42:4 and 6

[396] Rama 154:8; Beis Yosef 273; Terumos Hadeshen 273; See Admur 42:6 in parentheses

The reason: As the custom makes it be considered as if a stipulation is made. [Admur ibid] This means as follows: Since the custom is to use it, and it is impossible to beware from doing so, therefore Leiv Beis Din makes an initial stipulation in order so people do not stumble on this matter. Thus, even if a stipulation was not made, it is considered as if it was made. [Rama ibid]

[397] Rama ibid regarding table of the shul which seemingly refers to the Bima for Kerias Hatorah; Beis Yehuda 27; Az Nidbaru 3:49; Piskeiy Teshuvos 154:27; See however M"B 141:4-5

[398] Az Nidbaru 3:49; Piskeiy Teshuvos 154:27; Poskim ibid;

[399] This is based on the many Poskim who rule regarding the Baal Korei leaning on the Bima in a time of need that one is not to lean on the cloth that is on the Bima but on the Bima itself. [Teshuvas Maharam Mintz 81; Kneses Hagedola 141; Olas Tamid 141:3; Elya Raba 141:3; Ledavid Emes 5; Shaareiy Efraim 3:11; M"B 141:4-5, see Piskeiy Teshuvos ibid footnote 15]; However, it is unclear why the Poskim ibid are stringent in this regard if we apply Leiv Beis Din Masneh even to the cloth that is on the Bima. Seemingly, then, one must say that all the above Poskim refer to a case that we are unsure if the Minhag is to use the Bima and hence perhaps the Beis Din Masneh does not apply. If, however, we know for certain that the custom is to be lenient, then we apply the rule of Leiv Beis Din Masneh, and it is permitted even initially. Alternatively, one can suggest that initially we do not rely on Beis Din Masneh, although the implication of the Poskim is unlike this approach. [See Rama ibid]

[400] Admur 42:6

Summary:
In those areas that it is accustomed to make use of the Bima for matters other than holding the Sefer Torah, then it is permitted to use it for mundane activity which is not belittling, such as leaning on it or stacking Sefarim on it. Practically, the widespread custom today is to be lenient in this matter, although some are stringent.

Q&A

May one place a hat or glasses on the Bima?
Seemingly one may do so in those areas accustomed to use the Bima for other purposes, such as to hold Sefarim.[401]

May one bang on the Bima?
Some Poskim[402] rule it is forbidden to do so due to it being considered a belittling activity.

26. Kissing children, friends, and relatives in a Shul:[403]

One is not to kiss his small children in Shul.[404] [This implies that it is however permitted to kiss older children, and other people, in Shul.[405] However, some Poskim[406] rule that in truth this applies to children of any age, and not specifically small children. Furthermore, it applies to any person, even non-relatives, as one is to avoid kissing any person in a Shul, being it is a place of love and worship of G-d. It is however permitted to kiss a person who one is obligated to respect and honor, such as to kiss the hand of a Rav, Torah scholar, one's father, and the like.[407] Likewise, one may kiss another as a sign of admiration or gratitude for something he said or did, and so was done by our Sages.[408] Practically, some Chassidim are accustomed to give a "Chassidic kiss" upon greeting a fellow Chassid or friend, as a welcoming expression of Ahavas Yisrael. This seemingly relies on the implication above that the prohibition only applies towards one's small children. However, there are Rabbanim who negate this.[409]]

Summary:
It is forbidden to kiss one's small children in Shul. It is debated amongst Poskim if this prohibition applies also to kissing older children, relatives and friends. It is however permitted according to all to kiss a person who one is obligated to respect and honor, such as to kiss the hand of a Rav, Torah scholar, one's father, and the like, or to give a kiss to another as a sign of admiration or gratitude. Practically, it is customary amongst many Chassidim to give a "Chassidic kiss" upon greeting a fellow

---

[401] As once the custom is to use it for mundane purposes we say Lev Beis Din Masneh and it hence does not have Kedusha.

[402] Az Nidbaru 3:49; Piskeiy Teshuvos 154:27 footnote 158

[403] Admur 98:1; Rama 98:1; Binyamin Zev 163 in name of Aguda; Sefer Chassidim 255; See Piskeiy Teshuvos 98:7; Pamei Yaakov 68 p. 83-87

[404] The reason: In order so one sets in his heart that there is no love like the love of Hashem. [Admur ibid; Rama ibid; Binyamin Zev ibid]

[405] Admur and Rama ibid write small children, and so writes Binyamin Zev ibid. This implies that it only applies to small children and not anyone else, as if it does apply to all people, then why write a misleading wording when you can simply write the Halacha in all its parameters; However, Sefer Chassidim ibid simply writes not to kiss children. So rules Shemesh Umagen 39 [Rav Mashash] that it only applies to small children.
The reason: As by small children there is a natural love expressed towards them, and on this it states that one must leave the love of his wife and children aside when coming before G-d in prayer, and that since a Shul is the place where we express and work on our natural love for G-d it is not befitting to show natural love to others in such a place. However, the kiss given to other people, is simply done cordially out of respect, or honor, and is actually an act of Ahavas Yisrael, which does not contain that same natural love as does kissing a child. [See Shemesh Umagen ibid]

[406] Ben Ish Chaiy Vayikra 11 "One may not kiss the hands of his relatives"; Orach Mishpat 22 of Rav Kook; Piskeiy Teshuvos 98:7

[407] Ben Ish Chaiy ibid regarding kissing the hand of a Rav, Talmid Chacham, and father; Yechaveh Daas 4:12
The reason: As we see that Moshe kissed Aaron when he met him on the mountain of Har Sinai. This seemingly shows that it is permitted to kiss someone in Shul

[408] Piskeiy Teshuvos ibid that we find in Chazal that a Sage would at times kiss a student or colleague as a sign of gratitude or admiration, after hearing a Torah novelty from that person. See Nedarim 9a; Avos Derebbe Nasan 6; Kallah 1:21; Midrash Koheles 5:17

[409] In my correspondence with Harav Eliyahu Landau Shlita, he replied that this should not be done, as it falls under the above prohibition, and the fact that some people do so is seemingly due to lack of knowledge of the law; Rav Leibel Groner responded that he has no knowledge of whether or not the above custom of some Chassidim is proper or not.

Chassid or friend in Shul.

Q&A

May one kiss a child who got hurt in order to calm him down?[410]
Yes.

May a woman kiss her children in the Ezras Nashim?[411]
No. A mother is to avoid kissing her children in the Ezras Nashim, just as is the law regarding men. The same would apply to kissing any other person in the Ezras Nashim, according to those Poskim who extend the prohibition to all people, as explained above.

May one kiss the hand of a person who received an Aliyah?
Some Poskim[412] rule one is not to kiss the hand of one who got an Aliyah. Other Poskim[413] however rule it is permitted to do so, out of respect of the Torah.

May one kiss his son in Shul after his Aliyah for his Bar Mitzvah?[414]
No.

May one kiss a person in Shul outside of the times of Davening?
No. The prohibition applies anytime in a Shul, being that a Shul is designated for the worship and love of G-d.[415] However, some[416] suggest that perhaps the prohibition only applies during times of Davening.

---

[410] Piskeiy Teshuvos 98 footnote 69

[411] Piskeiy Teshuvos 98 footnote 72; See Pamei Yaakov ibid that majority of Poskim rule that the Ezras Nashim contains holiness, and hence is subject to the above prohibition.
Regarding the Kedusha of an Ezras Nashim: See Peri Megadim 151 A"A 1; Rosh Yosef Megila 28a who rules it has holiness; See also Ashel Avraham Buchach 151; Shoel Umeishiv 2:22; Beis Yitzchak 2 Kuntrus Acharon 1:4; Beis Shlomo 1:28; Avnei Nezer 33; Aruch Hashulchan 154:7; Maharash Engel 3:88; Maharsham 1:10; Teshuras Shay 545; Arugas Bosem 27; Imrei Yosher 2:12; Beis Yisrael 24; Tzur Yaakov 152; Minchas Yitzchak 7:8; Sheivet Halevy 5:21; Tzitz Eliezer ibid; Piskeiy Teshuvos 151:1. Some of these Poskim rule that the Ezras Nashim has the holiness of a Shul. Others rule it contains holiness, but to a lesser degree than the men's section.
Other Opinions: The Chochmas Adam 86:15 rules the Ezras Nashim does not have Kedusha. So also leans to rule Yad Halevy 2:3. Many of the above Poskim negate his opinion. See Tzitz Eliezer ibid.
Ruling of Admur in Shulchan Aruch: See Admur 619:18 who mentions the Ezras Nashim as "Beis Hakneses Shel Nashim". Furthermore, from that Halacha it is proven that it has at least a lower level of holiness than the men's section. Nevertheless, one cannot prove from there that it has no holiness at all.

[412] Ben Ish Chaiy ibid; Yechaveh Daas ibid

[413] Shemesh Umagen ibid that so is the custom of Moroccan Jewry

[414] Piskeiy Teshuvos 98 footnote 72

[415] So is implied from the wording of all Poskim ibid; See Piskeiy Teshuvos 98:7 footnote 73

[416] Birchas Chanoch 3 in name of Rav Moshe Feinstein; Beis Yisrael 1:9; See Biur Hagr"a ibid in name of Zohar; Piskeiy Teshuvos ibid

-------------- *Netilas Yadayim* --------------

27. Washing and Al Netilas Yadayim on less than a Kebeitza of bread:[417]

If one will not be consuming a shiur Kebeitza without its shell[418] [53.8 grams[419]] of bread within two times Kdei Achilas Peras [i.e. within 8 minutes[420]], each Kezayis within Kdei Achilas Peras[421] [i.e. 4 minutes[422]], then one is to wash <u>without</u> a blessing prior to eating this bread.[423] This applies irrelevant of the fact that he will say Hamotzi [on any amount he eats] and Birchas Hamazon [if he eats a Kezayis of the bread within 4 minutes]. One must be particularly careful in this matter by the third Shabbos meal.[424] This applies even if one will be holding in his hand a piece of bread that is larger than a Kebeitza, nevertheless, if he eats less than a Kebeitza, he is to wash his hands without a blessing.[425] This applies no matter how much bread he eats that is less than a Kebeitza, even if it is a very small amount, in all cases, he is to wash without a blessing.[426] If one will be consuming a total of a Kebeitza [within Achilas Peras[427]], then he is to wash with a blessing, even if he will be eating a small amount at a time, even if he eats small crumbs that total a Kebeitza.[428] [Due to the above ruling, it is important that when one begins

---

[417] Admur 158:2 "It is questionable...therefore one is to wash without a blessing"; Seder Netilas Yadayim 18 "If wash but will not eat Kebeitza, don't say a blessing"; Michaber 158:2; Rokeiach 328; Ketzos Hashulchan 36:2; Piskeiy Teshuvos 158:7

Other opinions: Some Poskim rule one may wash with a blessing on a Kezayis of bread. [Shaar Hatziyon 158:9 in name of Gr"a in Biur Hagr"a 158; Igros Moshe 4:41 regarding time of need based on Gr"a; See Vezos Haberacha p. 15 and 347; See Ritva on Sukkah 25a]

[418] Admur 158:2; Omitted in Seder; Degul Merivava 158; M"B 158:9; Kaf Hachaim 158:8; See Rambam Tumas Ochlin 4:1; Eiruvin 83a

[419] Shiureiy Torah 3:9; This is opposed to a Kibeitza with its Kelipa which is a Shiur of 57.6 grams; See Shevet Halevi 6:60; Piskeiy Teshuvos 158:7 who writes 57 grams

[420] See Seder Netilas Yadayim 18 that each Kezayis must be eaten within Achilas Peras, [4 minutes] and see Ketzos Hashulchan 36 footnote 5 and Shiureiy Torah 3:9 in name of Reb Yisrael Noach that the second Kezayis must be eaten immediately after the first Kezayis.

[421] Seder Netilas Yadayim 18; Omitted in 158:2 that one must eat the Kibeitza within 8 minutes [See Seder Netilas Yadayim of Rav Alyashvili footnote 230 who learns according to Admur in the SHU"A there is no need to eat it within Peras]; Tehilah Ledavid 158:1; Ketzos Hashulchan ibid; Shenos Chaim 239; Kaf Hachaim 158:9; Piskeiy Teshuvos 158:7; See Kerisus 13; See Siddur Raskin Miluim p. 720 and footnote 230 in new Seder Netilas Yadayim of Rav Alyashvili

[422] This follows the Shiur that each Peras is 4 minutes:

Four minutes: Shiurei Torah 3:15 [p. 303]; Aruch Hashulchan 202:8; Kaf Hachaim 210:5; Piskeiy Teshuvos 210:1 that so is the widespread custom

Opinion of 6-7 minutes: The Tzemach Tzedek [Shaar Hamiluim 1:8-10] records 6-7 minutes regarding the Shiur of Achilas Peras. [Ketzos Hashulchan 36 footnote 5; 59 footnote 4; Shiureiy Torah ibid footnote 35; Sefer Haminhagim [English] p. 93 regarding Tishe Beav] In Shiureiy Torah ibid footnote 35 he concludes that if one ate 17 grams in the first 4 minutes and completed 28 grams in 8 minutes, he may say Birchas Hamazon.

Three minutes-Chabad custom: See Sefer Haminhagim ibid and footnotes 342-344 for a quote of various opinions of Achilas Peras, and for a tradition from the Tzemach Tzedek, in name of Rav Hillel Miparitch, that differs from the response of the Tzemach Tzedek which placed Achilas Peras as 6-7 minutes and rather places Achilas Peras as minimum 3 minutes and maximum 7 minutes. The Rebbe concludes there in the footnote that one is required to suspect for the above tradition. So also rules Igros Moshe 4:41 that Achilas Peras is 3 minutes regarding Bracha Acharona. Accordingly, one should try to eat the Kezayis within three minutes. However, if one ate it within four minutes, and perhaps even within 6-7 minutes, one can rely on the Tzemach Tzedek's other rulings. Vetzaruch Iyun, as perhaps Safek Brachos Lihakel. In any event one is to be very careful in the above.

Other opinions: See Shiurei Torah 3:15; Sefer Haminhagim ibid and footnotes 342-344; Piskeiy Teshuvos 158:7 and 210:1

[423] The reason: It is questionable as to whether one who eats less than a Kebeitza of bread is required to wash his hands due to the following reason: Less than a Kibeitza is not considered food with regards to Tumas Ochlin, and due to this, if an impure person touches food or liquid that is less than a Kibeitza he does not make it impure. [Yuma 80a] This is learned from the verse [Vayikra 11:34] "Mekol Haochel Asher Yochel", which teaches us that the food must be an amount that is called food [that satiates, which is a Kibeitza]. [Now, perhaps the Rabbinical obligation to wash for bread follows similar rules as] the Sages only required washing hands for Chulin due to Serach Teruma, and this obligation was only made intact when one eats the food and not when one touches it. [We thus see that the entire obligation was on food and] less than a Kibeitza, since it is not considered food regarding Tuma, it is also not considered food regarding washing hands. [However, one can also argue that once the Sages made their decree, they did not differentiate in this matter. Practically, due to this doubt that perhaps the definition of food regarding washing follows the same definition regarding Tuma] therefore one is to wash without a blessing. [Admur ibid; Taz 158:3; Olas Tamid 158:3; Mateh Yehuda 158:3; Beis Yosef 158; See Ketzos Hashulchan 36 footnote 4 and 6 who differentiates between the reason given by the Beis Yosef and that of Admur, and explains how Admur's explanation answers two strong questions applicable in the explanation of the Beis Yosef; See also Machatzis Hashekel 158:3 and P"M 158 A"A]

[424] Seder ibid

[425] Admur 158:2

The reason: As he is not eating an amount of bread that is considered food with regards to Tumas Ochlin. [Admur ibid] The novelty here is that the Sages did not make their decree on the amount of bread one is holding but rather on the amount that one is eating [Ketzos Hashulchan 36 footnote 6]

[426] Admur 158:2; M"A 158:4; Elya Raba 158:3; Divrei Chamudos Chulin 8:72; M"B 158:10

Other opinions: Some Poskim rule that one is not required to wash hands at all when eating less than a Kezayis of bread. [Opinion in Michaber 158:3; Taz 158:3; Poskim in Kaf Hachaim 158:10; Shulchan Hatahor 158:12]

[427] Seder ibid; Poskim ibid; Omitted in 158:2 that one must eat the Kebeitza within 8 minutes [See Seder Netilas Yadayim of Rav Alyashvili footnote 230 who learns according to Admur in the SHU"A there is no need to eat it within Peras.]

[428] Admur 158:2; Kaf Hachaim 158:9

his meal, to focus on eating a Kebeitza of bread within the first eight minutes rather than eat the bread slowly and partake in other foods at the same time.[429]]

Summary:
One is to wash hands prior to eating any amount of bread. However, a blessing is only recited if one plans to eat a total of 53.8 grams of bread within eight minutes.

Q&A

If one washed with a blessing with intent to eat a Kebeitza of bread within eight minutes, may he later change his mind?
Some Poskim[430] rule that one may later decide not to eat a full Kebeitza or even any bread at all.[431] Practically, it is best not to change one's mind and he is to eat a full Kebeitza within 8 minutes in order so his blessing does not become a blessing in vain.[432]

May one wash with a blessing if he is not sure if he will eat a Kebeitza of bread within eight minutes?
No.[433]

------------------ *Birchas Hanehnin* ----------------

28. Drinking during a meal of bread:[434]

Some Poskim[435] rule one is not Biblically obligated to recite Birchas Hamazon after eating [a satiating meal of bread[436]] unless he drank [a liquid[437]] during the meal.[438] This however only applies if one was thirsty during the meal [and nevertheless did not drink; if however one was not thirsty, then he is Biblically obligated to recite Birchas Hamazon according to all opinions, if he is satiated from bread, even if he did not drink at all during the meal].[439] [Furthermore, once one drinks a Revius[440], he is Biblically obligated to recite Birchas Hamazon even if he is still thirsty.[441] Other Poskim[442] however rule one is

---

The reason: As although the crumbs do not join for a size of a Kebeitza regarding impurifying food, nevertheless, since he is entering into his abdomen an amount that is considered food regarding Tuma of food, therefore, his eating is considered food also regarding washing hands. [Admur ibid] This ruling applies only according to the reason offered by Admur, however, according to the reason written by the Beis Yosef, one can argue that a blessing is not said unless one enters a full Kibeitza into his mouth at a time. [Ketzos Hashulchan 36 footnote 6]

[429] See Piskeiy Teshuvos 158:7; Shaar Hatziyon 210:10; Maharsham 8:31; Birchas Shamayim 1:17

[430] Machazik Bracha Kuntrus Achron 1; Shaareiy Teshuvah 158:1; Ritva Chulin 106, brought in Kaf Hachaim ibid regarding one who washed with a blessing and then decided not to eat bread; Ketzos Hashulchan 36 footnote 7; Chazon Ish 25:8; See Piskeiy Teshuvos 158:6 footnote 23

[431] The reason: As when the blessing was recited it was not in vain, since one planned on eating, and whether or not one eats in the end does not affect the blessing. [Poskim ibid]

[432] See Sdei Chemed Mareches Brachos 29, brought in Kaf Hachaim 158:6, regarding one who washed with a blessing and then decided not to eat any bread, and that he rules one is not to do so.

[433] The reason: As one may not enter himself into a doubt. One cannot say that such a case is a Sfek Sfeika, as a) some Poskim rule that even by Sfek Sfeika we rule Lihakel and b) One may never initially enter himself into a Sfek Sfeika [see Taz Y.D. 122:8] See however Shevet Hakehasi 5:39

[434] Admur 197:7; Rama 197:4

[435] Opinion in Admur 197:7; opinion in Rama 197:4; Opinion in Darkei Moshe 197:6; Opinion brought in Beis Yosef 197; Bach 197 [rules like Yireim]; Peri Chadash [rules like Yireim]; Yireim 253; Kol Bo 25; Mordechai Brachos 177; Shivlei Haleket 154; This opinion understands the opinion of Rebbe Meir in Brachos 49b to be Biblical
If one drank but did not eat to the point of satiation: According to the above opinion, if one ate a mere Kezayis and drank after being thirsty then he is Biblically obligated to recite Birchas Hamazon even if he is not satiated from the meal. [Rebbe Meir in Brachos ibid, as also explained in Tosafos Brachos ibid; Evident from Admur ibid towards end and M"A 197:12 and M"B 197:28 that according to this opinion one who drank but did not eat to satisfaction should do the Zimun over one who is satisfied but did not drink]

[436] See Tehilah Ledavid 1:57 that according to this opinion the obligation of drinking is only if he ate bread and not if he ate Mezonos,

[437] See M"A 174:2 that this includes if he drank wine

[438] The reason: As the verse [Devarim 8:10] states "Veachalta Vesavata" and the Sages [Rebbe Meir in Brachos 49b] expound this to mean as follows: "Veachalta" is referring to eating food and "Vesavata" is referring to drinking liquid. [Admur ibid]

[439] Admur ibid; Rama ibid; M"A 174:2; Yireim ibid; Poskim ibid; Olas Tamid 197:4; Elya Raba 197 end; Kaf Hachaim 197:32

[440] Olas Tamid states "Keshiru Shetiya" which seemingly means a Revius. Vetzaruch Iyun

[441] Olas Tamid 197:4; Elya Raba 197:10; Kaf Hachaim 197:32

Biblically required to recite Birchas Hamazon after eating a satiating meal of bread even if he does not drink during the meal, even if he is thirsty.] Practically, we do not rule like the former opinion but rather like the latter opinion that holds that the Biblical obligation of Birchas Hamazon is dependent on eating to the point of satiation and not on drinking.[443] Nevertheless, it is proper to suspect for the words of the former opinion.[444] [Accordingly, if one is thirsty during the meal, he is to be particular to drink during the meal in order to be obligated in Birchas Hamazon according to all opinions.[445] This applies even if he only ate a Kezayis of bread.[446] This applies even if he only has wine available as a drink, and by drinking the wine during the meal, he will not be able to recite Kos Shel Bracha over wine.[447] Nevertheless, if one does not desire to drink during the meal due to health reasons, he may avoid doing so.[448]]

Summary:
During a meal of bread, one who is thirsty is initially to have at least one drink sometime during the meal, prior to Birchas Hamazon. This applies even if one only ate a Kezayis of bread. One may drink any liquid.

Q&A

If one did not drink during the meal and is in doubt if he recited Birchas Hamazon, is he to repeat it?

Even if he is satiated from his meal and is thus required to recite Birchas Hamazon due to doubt, some Poskim[449] rule that [if he is thirsty then] in such a case he is to have a drink and only then repeat Birchas Hamazon.[450] Other Poskim[451], however, rule that if he was thirsty during the meal and did not drink, then he is not to repeat Birchas Hamazon, although if he is able to, he is to eat another Kezayis of bread and recite Birchas Hamazon.

---

[442] Tosafos Brachos ibid; Beis Yosef 197 argues on Yireim based on Tosafos ibid "and so is the ruling of all Poskim and so is the final ruling"; Michaber 197:4 omits former opinion; Erech Hashulchan 197:5

[443] Admur ibid "There words is not the Ikkur..the main ruling follows the…"; Beis Yosef 197; M"A 197:12; M"B 197:28 "The former opinion is a Daas Yachid"; Mamar Mordechai 197:12

The reason: As the above Drasha is a mere Asmachta that the Sages used to support the need to recite Birchas Hamazon after eating a Kezayis of bread, as they interpret the verse "Veachalta" to mean eating food, and the measurement of eating is a Kezayis, whiles Vesavata is drinking. However, in no way was this Drasha intending to uproot the simple meaning of the verse which states that one is not obligated to recite Birchas Hamazon unless he ate and was satisfied, even if he did not drink. [Admur ibid; Tosafos Brachos ibid]

Other opinions: Some Poskim rule like the former opinion, that if one is thirsty, he must drink in order to be required to recite Birchas Hamazon. [Bach ibid; Peri Chadash ibid]

[444] Admur and Rama ibid regarding initially being careful to have one who drank make the Zimun; Mamar Mordechai 197:12; Elya Raba 197 in end; P"M 197 M"Z 4; Kaf Hachaim 197:30

[445] M"A 174:2 based on Rama ibid who suspects for opinion of Yireim; Elya Raba 174; Beir Heiytiv 174:2; M"B 174:5; Ketzos Hashulchan 45 footnote 10; Teshuvos Vehanhagos 2:121; Piskeiy Teshuvos 184 footnote 86 and 197:4; This entire Halacha [of Michaber 174:3 and M"A ibid] is omitted in Admur 174, Vetzaruch Iyun

The reason: If one did not drink during the meal, and already recited Birchas Hamazon, and then drank afterwards, then according to the former opinion he now becomes obligated to recite Birchas Hamazon and was not Yotzei with the recital prior to drinking. To avoid this problem one should therefore always drink before Birchas Hamazon. [Teshuvos Vehanhagos ibid, brought in Piskeiy Teshuvos ibid; See Biur Halacha 184 and Sefas Emes brought in Piskeiy Teshuvos ibid] Alternatively, the reason is because one is to always endeavor to fulfill a Mitzvah on its Biblical level according to all opinions. [See Admur 9:4; Michaber 9:1 and 6 regarding wearing a wool Tallis]

[446] Poskim ibid do not differentiate in this matter

The reason: As according to the stringent opinion one is Biblically obligated to Bentch after eating a Kezayis and drinking, as explained above.

[447] M"A ibid; M"B ibid

Other opinions: Some Poskim rule that one is to always leave the cup of wine for after Birchas Hamazon in order to recite Kos Shel Bracha over it. [Michaber 174:3; Mamar Mordechai 174:3; Kaf Hachaim 174:9] Some Poskim rule that when a Zimun is present of three people, one is to leave the cup of wine for after Birchas Hamazon, as even according to Rama ibid it is only proper to drink during the meal and not required. [P"M 174 A"A 2]

[448] Az Nidbaru 10:22; Piskeiy Teshuvos ibid

[449] Birchas Habayis 17:9

[450] The reason: As according to some opinions he is not obligated to recite Birchas Hamazon if he did not drink, and hence even if he is satiated it is not a Safek Deoraisa in their opinion. [Birchas Habayis ibid footnote 13]

[451] Ben Ish Chaiy Chukas 1:9; Kaf Hachaim 184:26

29. Blessing on Twizzlers:

The ingredients of Twizzlers: The Twizzler candy produced by Hershey corporation contains as main ingredients: Corn syrup, wheat flour, sugar, and cornstarch. As per the information received from the OU, who supervises the Kashrus of this product, the Twizzler contains 25% wheat flour.

The general law by products that contain flour:[452] All flour that is placed in a food product for the sake of adding taste and making it into its final product [of taste], is considered the main ingredient [Ikkur] of the food, even if the flour is a minority ingredient and is simply present to enhance the flavor of the majority food. Such a food receives the blessing of Mezonos.[453] However, if the flour is placed simply for the sake of texture or color [not taste], then the flour is considered the secondary ingredient [Tafel] and therefore the blessing would follow the main ingredient.[454] This, however, only applies if one does not at all intend to eat the flour, if however one also intends to eat the flour, even though his main intent is for the majority ingredient, then the flour is considered the Ikkur and its blessing is Mezonos.[455]

The law regarding Twizzlers: Clarifying the correct blessing to say over the Twizzler requires verification of the purpose of the flour ingredient. If its purpose is simply to act as a binder, and one has no intent to eat the flour, then its Ikkur/Main ingredient is considered to be the corn syrup and its blessing is Shehakol. If, however, the flour also serves to give taste to the product, and that is its intended purpose, then its blessing is Mezonos. Practically, the Hershey company does not divulge the intended purpose of the flour, and whether it is for taste or as a binder. A Kashrus representative of the OU, explained that companies do not really comprehend the difference between a binder and taste, as all binders also give taste, and contribute to the final taste of the product. Practically, Rabbi Yisrael Belsky OBM of the OU thoroughly reviewed the product, its ingredients and formulas and concluded the intended use of the flour is as a binder and not for the purpose of contributing taste, and therefore its blessing is Shehakol. This would be the proper blessing even if we could not factually conclude that the flour is used simply as a binder, due to the fact that Shehakol is Motzi a Mezonos food Bedieved, and therefore, when in doubt, a Shehakol is recited.[456] Certainly one cannot recite a Mezonos over the Twizzlers, as perhaps its use is only as a binder, and the blessing of Mezonos would therefore be a Brach Levatala. Some[457] however maintain that due to the unclarity of the purpose of the flour it is proper for a G-d fearing Jew to say the blessing of Shehakol and Mezonos on two different foods.

Summary:
One is to recite a Shehakol over Twizzlers, and not a Mezonos. Those who desire to be meticulous are to recite a Mezonos and Shehakol on two different foods.

---

[452] Admur Seder 3:2-3
[453] Admur Seder 3:2; Luach 4:2; Admur 168:11; 212:1; Michaber 208:2; M"A 212:1; Rav Kahana Brachos 36b and Rava Brachos 37b
[454] Admur Seder 3:3; Luach 4:3; Admur 169:9; Michaber 208:2; 204:12; M"A 204:25; Taz 204:16; Brachos 39a
[455] Admur Seder 3:4; Luach 4:4; Admur 169:9; M"A 212:5
[456] See Seder 1:4; 7:24
[457] See Vezos Habracha 22; Piskeiy Teshuvos 208:5

30. Blessing on onion rings [i.e. rings of onion coated with breadcrumbs]:[458]

Onion rings are typically made through coating a ring of an onion in a flour-based dip, and then deep frying it. In addition to the flour-based dip, some also coat the ring with dry bread crumbs, hence adding a further layer of Mezonos product to the ring. In both cases, one recites the blessing of Mezonos upon eating onion rings.[459] One recites an Al Hamichya after eating them if he ate at least a Kezayis of the Mezonos coating within within Achilas Peras [i.e. 4 minutes[460]].[461] If he is unsure, then he should eat two other foods, one of Al Hamichya and another of Borei Nefashos, and then say both after blessings.[462]

31. What blessing is to be recited over a Tortilla wrap [i.e. Taco]?

Corn/maize flour tortilla: If the Tortilla is made of corn/maize flour, and does not contain any of the five grain flours[463], then its blessing is Shehakol and requires Borei Nefashos, when eaten plain.[464] When eaten as a Taco, with a Ha'adama/vegetable filling [no meat], then if one's main intent of eating is on the vegetables, he states the blessing of the filling [Ha'adama] and exempts with it the blessing of the Tortilla.[465] If however one's main intent is on the Tortilla [such as if one has a very thin vegetable filling], then its blessing is Shehakol.[466] If one's main intent is on both the vegetables and the Taco, then one recites two blessings; Ha'adama on the vegetables, and after eating some of the vegetables, he recites a

---

[458] Sefer Viten Bracha 4:3 [p. 79]

Other opinions: Some write the blessing over onion rings is Haadama. [Luach Rav Prus] Seemingly, he compares this to chicken or fish Shnitzel, and other crumb coated foods, of which the custom is to say the blessing of Shehakol and not Mezonos. However, in truth, one cannot compare the two, as the coating of onion rings is thick and a main part of the food, and is similar to coated peanuts which is Mezonos. [See Piskeiy Teshuvos 208:6] Thus, his ruling regarding breadcrumbs is inaccurate, and its blessing is Mezonos.

[459] The reason: As all mixtures that contain a Mezonos ingredient for purposes of taste, or satiation, receive the blessing of Mezonos even if they are not the main ingredient. [Admur 208:1; Seder 3:2; Luach 4:2; Michaber 208:2; Brachos 36b] Now, certainly onion rings are coated for purposes of eating and tasting the bread crumbs and not just for the onion.

[460] Four minutes: Shiurei Torah 3:15 [p. 303]; Aruch Hashulchan 202:8; Kaf Hachaim 210:5; Piskeiy Teshuvos 210:1 that so is the widespread custom

Opinion of 6-7 minutes: The Tzemach Tzedek [Shaar Hamiluim 1:8-10] records 6-7 minutes regarding the Shiur of Achilas Peras. [Ketzos Hashulchan 36 footnote 5; 59 footnote 4; Shiureiy Torah ibid footnote 35; Sefer Haminhaghim [English] p. 93 regarding Tishe Beav] In Shiureiy Torah ibid footnote 35 he concludes that if one ate 17 grams in the first 4 minutes and completed 28 grams in 8 minutes, he may say Birchas Hamazon.

Three minutes-Chabad custom: See Sefer Haminhaghim ibid and footnotes 342-344 for a quote of various opinions of Achilas Peras, and for a tradition from the Tzemach Tzedek, in name of Rav Hillel Miparitch, that differs from the responsa of the Tzemach Tzedek which placed Achilas Peras as 6-7 minutes and rather places Achilas Peras as minimum 3 minutes and maximum 7 minutes. The Rebbe concludes there in the footnote that one is required to suspect for the above tradition. So also rules Igros Moshe 4:41 that Achilas Peras is 3 minutes regarding Bracha Achrona. Accordingly, one should try to eat the Kezayis within three minutes. However, if one ate it within four minutes, and perhaps even within 6-7 minutes, one can rely on the Tzemach Tzedek's other rulings. Vetzaruch Iyun, as perhaps Safek Brachos Lihakel. In any event one si to be very careful in the above.

Other opinions: See Shiurei Torah 3:15; Sefer Haminhaghim ibid and footnotes 342-344; Piskeiy Teshuvos 210:1

[461] See Admur in Seder 3:2 and 8:3-4

[462] Admur Seder 3:3; Ketzos Hashulchan 59 footnote 7

[463] See Seder 3:6; 8:3-4; Michaber 208:9; Ketzos Hashulchan 59:3; Kaf Hachaim 208:53

[464] Seder 1:10; Admur 202:17; Michaber 208:8; Rif Brachos 26a; Rambam Brachos 3:10

[465] Ikkur exempts Tafel: Admur Seder 3:1 "If one is the Ikkur and the second is secondary to it, one says the blessing on the Ikkur and exempts the secondary."; Luach 4:1; Admur 212:1; Michaber 212:1; Rambam Brachos 3:5; Mishneh Brachos 44a; Ikkur exempts Tafel even if not mixed together, but eating together: Admur Seder 3:8 "This applies even if the foods are not mixed together, but one simply is eating them together."; Luach 4:6; Admur ibid; Michaber ibid; Rambam Brachos 3:5

[466] Poskim ibid

Ha'adama on the filling.[467] If the Taco contains a meat, chicken, fish, or cheese filling, then its blessing remains Shehakol.

Wheat flour tortilla: If the Tortilla contains wheat, or any of the other five grains, then its blessing is either Mezonos or Hamotzi, depending on how it is made.[468] If the majority[469] liquid that was used to knead the flour, is not water [i.e. one used a majority of oil, eggs, spices, and sugar[470]], then it has the status of Mezonos bread[471].[472] Likewise, if the mixture was spiced to the point that it is uncommon for people to set a meal on such bread, then it has the status as Mezonos bread, [even if it was kneaded with majority water[473]].[474] If, however, the majority liquid is water, and if it is not spiced to the point that people do not set a meal over it, then whether its blessing is Hamotzi and Birchas Hamazon is dependent on the thickness of the tortilla, and whether it is baked or fired, as explained in the footnote.[475] Practically, a typical Tortilla recipe calls for majority water as its kneading liquid, and does not contain a great amount of spices, and is baked thin. Accordingly, it should only be eaten within a meal of Hamotzi over a Kezayis of actual bread.[476] If, however, it was made thick, and baked [not fried with a nice amount of oil] then one may say Hamotzi and Birchas Hamazon on the tortilla itself, as it is just like regular bread.

Does one recite a blessing on the filling of a Mezonos Tortilla: If one's tortilla is Mezonos, due to meeting the conditions explained above, then if one's main intent of eating the Taco is also on the filling [which is usually the case] then one is to recite a blessing first on the Mezonos, eat some of it, and then say a blessing on the filling.[477]

---

[467] Admur Seder 7:19 "If the foods were not cooked but are eaten together..then if one's main intent is on both foods, then we do not follow the majority, and rather one says a blessing over both foods."; Luach 10:19; Admur 202:13; Admur 202:23 "Here that the nut is not mixed.. we only follow majority if they were cooked together"; M"A 168:30 [This is unlike the ruling in Admur Seder 3:1 and the Poskim in previous footnote, who rule that whenever one has two foods that are an Ikkur we follow the majority food, as in truth, that ruling refers to a case that the foods were cooked together, or were mixed together. If, however, the foods were not cooked together, and are not mixed together in a way that they are not individually recognizable, which is the case here, then we do not follow the majority. See Admur 202:23; Glosses of Rav Alyashvili on Seder Birchas Hanehnin 3:1 footnote 8]

[468] Seder 8:3; 3:6; Michaber 208:9; Orchos Chaim; Abudarham

[469] See Seder 2:7 "If it was kneaded with some water, one follows the majority"; Luach 8:4; Admur 168:11; Taz 268:7

[470] See Ketzos Hashulchan 48 footnote 11 that they all join against the water to form a majority

[471] This means that it is Mezonos and Al Hamichya, unless one sets a meal on the Tortilla/taco sandwich [as defined in Seder 2:2] in which case it becomes Hamotzi and Birchas Hamazon. As is the law with all Pas Haba Bekisnin Mezonos bread, a Baal Nefesh is to only eat it within a meal, even if he is Koveia Seuda. [See Admur Seder 2:9]

[472] Seder 2:7 and 9; Luach 8:4; Admur 168:11; Michaber 168:7; Rambam Brachos 3:9

[473] Implication of Admur in Seder ibid who omits wording in Admur 168:11 who requires majority spices; See Ketzos Hashulchan 48 footnote 11 that the main thing is that it is spicy to the point that people do not commonly set a meal on it; Glosses of Rav Elyashvili Seder ibid footnote 85

[474] Seder 2:7; Admur ibid; Michaber ibid; Rambam ibid

[475] Thick versus thin: Thin breads [made of flour and water] are not commonly used to set a meal over, but rather for snacking, and therefore we find in the Talmud and Poskim discussion regarding various types of thin breads and their respective law; whether they are Mezonos or Hamotzi. There is a difference between a Terisa [very thin batter, and very thin baking], Truknin [very thin batter, but not very thin baking] and Lachmaniyos [thin batter, baked thin or thick], and they carry various cases and opinions. [See Seder 2:7; Admur 168:13] In this case, however, that Tortillas are commonly made by forming a regular dough, and only then is it baked thin, then seemingly according to all one is to say Hamotzi on the product, irrelevant of how thin it is. [Implication of Seder 2:5 and all Rishonim and Achronim who describe all the cases to have a thin batter, and not just baked thin; Implication of 1st opinion in Admur 168:15 and opinion in Michaber 168:13; Implication of Admur in Seder who omits case of Ugos Yiveishos; See Piskeiy Teshuvos 168:12] However, we find that the Poskim do not accept this differentiation and maintain that the same laws apply whether the batter is thin or thick, as the main point is regarding how thin the product is after it is baked, and whether people set a meal on it. [Implication of 2nd opinion in Admur 168:15 regarding frying and cooking dough that "everything follows the final product" and Michaber 168:13 [Admur in Seder 2:12 completely omits the 1st opinion who argues]; See M"A 168:40 in name of Shlah regarding Rekikin Dakin; See Admur 168:12 regarding Ugos Yiveishos; Aruch Hashulchan 168:30; Minchas Yitzchak 1:71-6; Teshuvos Vehanhagos 3:73; All Poskim who rule Matzah is Mezonos, which include Chida in Machazik Bracha 158:5; Yechaveh Daas 3:12; Or Letziyon 2:13-3] Accordingly, whether the Tortilla is Hamotzi or Mezonos will depend on whether it is baked very thin [Mezonos], thin [dispute-eat within meal], or thick [Hamotzi], just as is the law regarding Lachmaniyos. [See Piskeiy Teshuvos ibid] Practically, being this matter is inconclusive either way, one should only eat a Tortilla within a meal, unless it is thick, in which case it may have Hamotzi and Birchas Hamazon recited over it.

Baked versus fried: Dough can only become Hamotzi if baked, or fried with little oil so it does not stick to the pan. If, however, it is fried in a nice amount of oil, then its blessing is a dispute even if it is baked thick, and is only to be eaten within a meal. [Seder 2:12; See Admur 268:15]

[476] If baked thin but not very thin then, this possibly follows the same law as Lachmaniyos [as explained in previous footnote] which is disputed when baked thin, but not very thin, if it is Mezonos or Hamotzi. [Seder 2:6] Furthermore, even if baked very thin, it still unclear if it receives the law of a Lachmaniyos, or of actual bread [being it was made into actual dough] as explained in the previous footnote.

Other opinions: Some write that if the Tortilla is very thin its blessing is Mezonos, while if it's not very thin but is also not thick, then it's like Mezonos bread. [Piskeiy Teshuvos ibid]

[477] Admur Seder 7:19 "If the foods were not cooked but are eaten together..then if one's main intent is on both foods, then we do not follow the majority, and rather one says a blessing over both foods." Seder 3:7 and Admur 168:9 that one always says the blessing on the Mezonos even if it is not the Ikkur. However, that is referring to a case that they were baked together. In this case since the wrap and filling are cooked separately,

32. Blessing on lemons:[478]

Lemons that are only mildly sour, and are thus edible, receive the blessing of Shehakol.[479] Lemons that are very sour to the point of inedibility, do not receive a blessing at all prior to consumption.[480]

Lemon peel:[481] The peel of a lemon which is edible, receives the blessing of Shehakol prior to consumption.

*32. Blessing on Esrog:[482]

Esrogim that are only mildly sour, and are thus edible, receive the blessing of Shehakol.[483] Esrogim that are very sour to the point of inedibility, do not receive a blessing at all prior to consumption.[484]

Esrog peel: The raw peel of an Esrog which is edible, receives the blessing of Shehakol prior to consumption.[485] If the peel was turned into marmalade, or a chocolate covered treat, then its blessing is Haeitz.[486]

Shehechiyanu:[487] The blessing of Shehechiyanu is not recited upon eating an Esrog.

---

consequently they each receive their designated blessing as each one is not nullified to the other, as explained in Seder 3:1 and 7:19 regarding when both are an Ikkur. See Piskeiy Teshuvos 212:12 regarding eating Mezonos with meat; 212:14 that when there is a large amount of filling one always recites both blessings;

[478] Ketzos Hashulchan 49:16; Brachos Guide in English Birchas Hanehnin; Brachos guide of Rav Prus; Seder Birchas Hanehnin 6:22 of Rav Elyashvili footnote 130

Other opinions: See Piskeiy Teshuvos 202:35 footnote 208 who states there are three types of lemons: a) Very sour and inedible-no blessing; b) Very sour but still edible-Shehakol. This is majority of lemons today; c) Mildly sour lemon-Haeitz according to Admur 205:1; d) Lemon juice with sugar is Haeitz if majority lemon juice; Vetzaruch Iyun Gadol on many of his points, as a) Admur 205:1 never states that a food that can be eaten "Beshas Hadechak" receives its set blessing; b) Admur explicitly states in many places [see below] that we follow the intent of the planting, if planted to eat in its current state; c) Where do these three types of lemons exist? d) How can one say Haeitz on a juice, in direct contradiction to the ruling in Michaber 202:23! Obviously, one may not rely on his words at all regarding this matter, and the ruling remains as stated above!

[479] The reason: As these fruits are edible in a time of need and thus they receive a blessing. [See Admur 202:4; Seder 6:1; Ketzos Hashulchan ibid and 49:7] However, their blessing is Shehakol, as all fruits that are not commonly planted to be eaten in their current state, but rather for use of seasoning, receive the blessing of Shehakol. [Seder Birchas Hanehnin 6:22; Luach 9:9; Admur 203:6 and 204:3-4 and 205:1; M"A 203:4]

[480] See Admur 202:4; Seder 6:1; Ketzos Hashulchan ibid and 49:7; Michaber 202:2; Birchas Habayis 1:49; Piskeiy Teshuvos 202 footnote 96

[481] See Admur 202:9; Seder 6:4 and 15; Ketzos Hashulchan 51:7 footnote 7

[482] Luach of Rav Prus; So rule regarding lemons: Ketzos Hashulchan 49:16; Brachos Guide in English Birchas Hanehnin; Brachos guide of Rav Prus; Seder Birchas Hanehnin 6:22 of Rav Elyashvili footnote 130 and in his Luach; See Piskeiy Teshuvos 202:35; Also, see Luach of Rav Elyashvili in Seder Birchas Hanehnin that an edible raw Esrog is Haeitz. This contradicts the rules that were taught in Admur and Poskim ibid regarding fruits that are not planted to be eaten in their current state. After correspondence, he told me that this is an error, and it should read Shehakol.

[483] The reason: As these fruits are edible in a time of need and thus they receive a blessing. [See Admur 202:4; Seder 6:1; Ketzos Hashulchan ibid and 49:7] However, their blessing is Shehakol, as all fruits that are not commonly planted to be eaten receive the blessing of Shehakol. [Seder Birchas Hanehnin 6:22; Luach 9:9; Admur 203:6 and 204:3-4 and 205:1; M"A 203:4]

[484] See Admur 202:4; Seder 6:1; Ketzos Hashulchan ibid and 49:7; Michaber 202:2; Birchas Habayis 1:49; Piskeiy Teshuvos 202 footnote 96

[485] See Admur 202:9; Seder 6:4 and 15; Ketzos Hashulchan 51:7 footnote 7

[486] Orchos Chaim 202:9 in name of Minchas Pitim; Piskeiy Teshuvos 202:13 footnote 67; Luach of Rav Prus; Luach of Seder Birchas Hanehnin in English; Luach of Rav Elyashvili in Seder Birchas Hanehnin

The reason: Esrog peels that are in jam or candy or chocolate are Haeitz as a) they are cultivated for their peel, and b) the peel is the main part of the fruit. [Poskim ibid based on Ran Shabbos 108; See Admur 202:9; Seder 6:4 and 15 that the only reason a peel is degraded from its blessing is because it is not the main part of the fruit, and hence by an Esrog, since it is the main part of the fruit its blessing is Haeitz.]

[487] Poskim in Piskeiy Teshuvos 225:17 footnote 124

------------------Mincha----------------
33. Saying Karbanos of Mincha before the time of Mincha Gedola?[488]
The Karbanos for Mincha are not to be recited prior to 6.5 hours into the day, which is 30 minutes after midday, and the earliest legal time in which Mincha may be Davened [i.e. Mincha Gedola].[489] [Accordingly, a Mincha Gedola Minyan who begins at the earliest time possible, is to give some time.]

34. Davening Mincha past sunset:[490]
The prayer of Mincha may be recited until evening.[491] It is disputed amongst Poskim as to the definition of "evening." Some Poskim[492] rule it is permitted [even initially[493]] to Daven Mincha past sunset, up until Tzeis Hakochavim.[494] Other Poskim[495] rule one may not Daven Mincha past sunset.[496] Practically, one is to initially Daven Mincha before sunset, although one is not to protest against those who are lenient to Daven Mincha after sunset, until Tzeis Hakochavim.[497] This applies both on Shabbos and during the

---

[488] Shraga Hameir 7:20; Piskeiy Teshuvos 233:1; See Admur Kama 1:13, 47:9; Basra 1:9 that the Karbanos prior to Shacharis may only be recited after Alos, being that the Karbanos are not offered during the day and the same would apply towards the Karbanos of Mincha.

[489] The reason: As the Karbanos of the afternoon were never offered prior to 6.5 hours after morning, and our recital of Karbanos prior to Mincha corresponds to the afternoon Karbanos. [ibid; See Admur ibid]

[490] See Piskeiy Teshuvos 233:6; Biurim on Seder Hachnasas Shabbbos [Levin] p. 65-67; Halacha Berura [Rav Dovid Yosef] 233

[491] Chachamim in Mishneh Brachos 26a and Michaber 233:1, based on Talmidei Rabbeinu Yona on Rif Brachos ibid, that the custom is like Chachamim; See also Shut Admur 7 "And in these generations, many are stringent to Daven Maariv on time"; See Tzemach Tzedek Chidushim on Brachos ibid

Opinion of Rebbe Yehuda: Rebbe Yehuda in the Mishneh ibid famously ruled that Mincha may only be prayed until Plag Hamincha. Thus, the question of Davening Mincha past sunset is only relevant to the opinion of the Chachamim. Practically, the Michaber concludes that the custom is like Chachamim and so is the widespread custom today.

[492] Implication of Michaber ibid "Until **nighttime** according to Chachamim..And now that the custom is to Daven Mincha **until nighttime**" [so implies Aruch Hashulchan 233:8 and M"B 233:14, unlike his interpretation in 233:8]; Rama ibid "He is Yotzei if he Davens Mincha until nighttime, **which is until Tzeis Hakochavim**"; Shaagas Aryeh 17; P"M 89 M"Z 1 "Bein Hashmashos is also a time of Mincha for Chachamim"; 106 M"Z end of siman "Mincha can also be prayed during Bein Hashmashos" [contradicts P"M 233 A"A 7]; Implication of Gr"a 233 [unlike Gr"a 261, see Shaar Hatziyon 233:18]; Ashel Avraham of Buchach 233 "The time of Mincha is until Tzeis Hakochavim"; Maharam Shick 91; Rav Poalim 2:19 based on Poskim and Mekubalim and that so is custom in Yerushalayim and Chevron; and Ben Ish Chaiy Vayakhel 7 regarding women; Kaf Hachaim 233:4-5; Eretz Tzevi 1:1; Shut Beis Avi that so is custom of Polish Jewry to even initially Daven Mincha past sunset; Minchas Elazar 1:13 and Nimukei Orach Chaim 131:2 that the custom of the Belzer Rav was to delay Mincha until close to Tzeis Hakochavim; Meumei Sadeh on Brachos ibid [of Nesiv]; Divrei Yatziv 98-99 that so was custom of Tzanzer Rebbe, Chasam Sofer and Reb Akiva Eiger and so is agreed to by more than 40 Rishonim and Achronim; See Aruch Hashulchan 233:8; Or Letziyon 1:20; Yechaveh Daas 5:22; Mishneh Halachos 7:32; Halacha Berura [Rav Dovid Yosef] 233 for list of many Rishonim and Achronim

[493] So is implied from wording of Poskim ibid, and so is explicitly written in some Poskim ibid; Now, although the Rama permits only Bedieved and time of need, this is because he was referring to those who follow Rebbe Yehuda on a normal basis, however for those who always follow Chachamim, he too would agree that even initially it is allowed

[494] The reason: Perhaps the reason is because Mincha is Rabbinical, and the Sages permitted reciting it during Bein Hashmashos, due to Safek Derabanan Lihakel. [Aruch Hashulchan ibid; See also Admur in Seder Hachnasas Shabbos] Alternatively, the reason is because Mincha corresponds to the Ketores and not to the afternoon Tamid, and the Ketores was allowed to be offered until Tzeis Hakochavim. [Hagahos Maimanis Tefila 3:3 in name of Rabbeinu Chananel; Aruch Hashulchan ibid; See Biur Hagr"a ibid] Alternatively, in truth the limbs of the afternoon Tamid could be offered until Tzeis Hakochavim. [Pnei Yehoshua Brachos 27a; Shaagas Aryeh ibid] The Talmidei HaBaal Shem Tov would intentionally delay Mincha until close to night, in order to battle the Kelipos of darkness with their prayers. [Nimukei Orach Chaim ibid]

[495] Implication of Rambam Tefila 3:4; Talmidei Rabbeinu Yona on Rif Brachos ibid "Do not interpret evening to mean until nightfall but rather until sunset"; Shiltei Hagiborim on Mordechai; Kneses Hagedola 233; Lechem Chamudos; Levush 233; Gr"a 261 and in Maaseh Rav 64 [unlike Gr"a 233, see Shaar Hatziyon 233:18]; P"M 233 A"A 7 "Until Tzeis Hakochavim is difficult to allow" [contradicts P"M 89 M"Z 1; 106 M"Z end of siman]; Aruch Hashulchan ibid concludes to be stringent like Rambam and not Daven Mincha after sunset and to protest strongly against those who do; M"B 233:7 and 14 interprets Michaber and Rama ibid "until night" and "until Tzeis Hakochavim" to mean "until the beginning of Bein Hashmashos" however he then writes that the simple implication is until Tzeis Hakochavim. The M"B ibid concludes to be stringent like the above Poskim to be very careful to Daven Mincha before sunset and that only Bedieved and in a great time of need may one be lenient, and even then only until 15 minutes before Tzeis Hakochavim; See Halacha Berura [Rav Dovid Yosef] 233 for list of many Rishonim and Achronim

Does the above opinion follow the opinion of Geonim or Rabbeinu Tam? See M"B ibid who is clearly going on the opinion of Rabbeinu Tam, and so can be interpreted in many of the above Poskim. See Piskeiy Teshuvos 233:8 and Halacha Berura ibid. Accordingly, it is possible to learn in many of the above Rishonim and Poskim, that they only argued against Davening Mincha past the sunset of Rabbeinu Tam, however, by the sunset of the Geonim, perhaps they agree that one may Daven past sunset. However, in truth, Admur in the Siddur learns the above Poskim to refer to even sunset of the Geonim, as stated there.

[496] The reason: As the prayer of Mincha was instituted in correspondence to the afternoon Tamid sacrifice, whose blood could only be offered until sunset. [Talmidei Rabbeinu Yona on Rif ibid]

[497] Admur in Seder Hachnasas Shabbos "However regarding Mincha, which is Rabbinical, one is not to protest against those who are lenient whether during the week or on Shabbos, especially in a time of need during the short winter days."; Ketzos Hashulchan 26:1 "Mincha may be prayed until sunset, although Bedieved one is Yotzei until Tzeis Hakochavim"; All Poskim brought in coming footnotes who say in time of need may Daven after sunset.

week.[498] This especially applies, in a time of need, such as in the short winter days, [that one may be lenient to Daven Mincha after sunset, up until nightfall[499]].[500]

Summary:
Initially, one is to Daven Mincha before sunset, although one is not to protest those who are lenient to Daven Mincha after sunset, until Tzeis Hakochavim. This applies both on Shabbos and during the week. In a time of need, such as in the short winter days, one may be lenient to Daven Mincha after sunset, up until nightfall.

Q&A
Is it better to Daven Mincha in private before sunset than to Daven with a Minyan after sunset?
Some Poskim[501] it is better to Daven Mincha in private before sunset than with a Minyan after sunset. Other Poskim[502] however rule it is better to Daven Mincha with a Minyan after sunset, then to Daven in private beforehand. It is unclear from Admur as to his opinion on this matter.[503]

Is one to initially Daven Mincha with enough time to complete Shemoneh Esrei before sunset?[504]
Yes.

May one Daven Mincha past Tzeis Hakochavim?
No.[505] However, there were Tzaddikim who were lenient to Daven Mincha even after nightfall.[506]

---

35. May one Daven Mincha and Maariv within Plag Hamincha on Erev Shabbos or during the week?
It is forbidden to Daven both Mincha and Maariv on a single day within the period of Plag Hamincha.[507] [Some Poskim[508] however are lenient to allow a <u>congregation</u> to Daven both prayers, one after the other, within the period of Plag Hamincha, if it will be difficult to gather the congregation again afterwards for Maariv. Other Poskim[509] however rule one may only be lenient to do so if one will Daven Maariv after sunset. There are communities that follow the former opinion and Daven both Mincha and Maariv within Plag Hamincha.[510] It is never permitted for an individual that is not part of a Minyan, to Daven both Mincha and Maariv within Plag Hamincha, as stated above.]

---

[498] Admur ibid
[499] Poskim in next footnote; Seemingly, the intent of Admur is that even initially one may Daven Mincha during Bein Hashmashos in a time of need, and not that simply one is not to protest those who are lenient in a time of need. VeTzaruch Iyun. See Biurim ibid p. 66
[500] Siddur Admur in Seder Hachnasas Shabbos; Darkei Moshe 233 that Maharil would Daven Mincha close to Tzeis Hakochavim in a time of need, brought in M"A 233:6; Mor Uketzia 233; Shoel Umeishiv Gimmel 247; Kitzur SHU"A 69:2; Ketzos Hashulchan 26:1; Or Letziyon 1:20; Shevet Halevi 9:48; M"B ibid also permits in time of need however he limits this to a case of "great need" and only until 15 minutes before Tzeis [according to Rabbeinu Tam]; Piskeiy Teshuvos ibid
The reason: As we see that the Sages permitted one to perform Rabbinical Melacha during Bein Hashmashos of Friday in a time of need, and for the need of a passing Mitzvah. The same then applies regarding Mincha, which is only a Rabbinical obligation. [Admur ibid; See Admur 261:2]
[501] M"B 233:14
[502] Mor Uketzia 233; Shoel Umeishiv Gimmel 247; Shearim Hametzuyanim Behalacha 69:1; Or Letziyon 1:20; Shevet Halevi 9:48; Eiynayim Lamishpat Brachos 27a; Piskeiy Teshuvos 233:6
[503] Admur does not make clear as to what is defined as a time of need to allow delaying Mincha until after sunset. See Admur 90:11 that Davening within the Zeman is more important than Davening with a Minyan.
[504] M"B 233:14
[505] Pashut! See Michaber 233:1; Admur in Seder ibid
[506] See Taamei Haminhagim in Sefer Zichron Tov; The Rebbe Davened Mincha with a Minyan after nightfall during many of the days between the 19th of Kisleiv 5746 and 8th of Shevat
[507] Admur 267:2; M"A 267:1; M"B 267:3; Biur Halacha 267:2 "Umiplag"; Piskeiy Teshuvos 267:2 footnote 19
The reason: As this is a contradiction in regard to whether one holds the period of Plag as day [Mincha] or as night [Maariv]. [ibid]
[508] Regarding weekdays: M"A 233:6; M"B 233:11; Poskim in Kaf Hachaim 233:12; Regarding Erev Shabbos: Derech Hachaim Arvis 1, brought in M"B 267:3; Biur Halacha ibid; Shraga Hameir 5:21; Kinyan Torah 4:27; See Piskeiy Teshuvos 233:3; 267:2
[509] M"B 267:3; Biur Halacha ibid regarding Erev Shabbos; Vetzaruch Iyun from M"B 233:11 who records the ruling of the M"A without argument.
[510] See Shraga Hameir 5:21; Kinyan Torah 4:27

-------------------Bedtime-----------------
36. How much sleep does a person need at night?

The Rambam[511] writes that one is to sleep at night for one third of the day, which is a period of eight hours. In other Sefarim[512], it states that one is required to sleep four hours. Practically, the Poskim[513] conclude that the amount of sleep one needs varies in each person, and each person is to sleep enough time that he has a clear and calm mind for learning Torah and serving Hashem.[514] The Yaavetz[515] writes that a healthy person can sleep for six hours a night, and this is dependent on one's sleeping habits that he acquired. The older one becomes the less sleep he requires.[516]

-----------------Shabbos Davening-----------------
37. Is Meiyn Sheva recited in a private Minyan that is not taking place in a Shul?[517]

The blessing of Meiyn Sheva is only recited in an established Shul, which is defined as an area in which a Minyan Davens on a constant basis. [This applies even if the Shul does not contain a Sefer Torah.[518]] However, in an area that a Minyan only Davens on mere occasion, such as those that make an occasional Minyan in their home [such as in times of rain], then the blessing of Meiyn Sheva is not to be recited.[519] Nevertheless, those communities who are accustomed to recite Meiyn Sheva even by a Minyan of mere occasion, are not to be protested.[520] [In Yerushalayim, the custom is to recite Meiyn Sheva even by an occasional Minyan taking place in a private home.[521] According to Kabala, every Minyan is to recite Meiyn Sheva, irrelevant to where the Minyan is taking place, even if it is a mere one time location.[522] Practically, one may not follow this custom, unless he practices all of his rulings according to Kabala.[523]]

A Minyan in the house of an Avel or Chasan:[524] The Minyan that is accustomed to take place in the house of an Avel or Chasan is not considered a set Minyan and hence Meiyn Sheva is not to be recited.

A set Minyan that will last a few weeks:[525] If a set Minyan will take place in a certain area for a limited amount of time, such as those who make pilgrimage to certain cities and set up a Minyan for a few weeks, then there is an opinion[526] who rules that Meiyn Sheva is to be recited there.[527]

---

[511] Hilchos Deios 4:4

[512] Ashel Avraham Buchach 1; Mahram Schik 1

[513] M"A 238; M"B 238:2; Taz Even Haezer 25:1

[514] Taz ibid

[515] In his Siddur under the section of the bedtime Shema; See also Maggid Dvarav Leyaakov Hosafos p. 47 for a letter that the Maggid wrote to his son Avraham in which he states to his son that he should sleep not less than six hours per night.

[516] See Tiferes Yisrael Avos 6:83

[517] Admur 268:15; Taz 268:8 based on Michaber 268:10; Mahriy Abuhav; Rivash 40

[518] Noam Megadim Minhagim 9; Birchas Habayis 41:7; Devar Moshe 1:32, brought in Piskeiy Teshuvah; Igros Moshe 4:69; Minchas Yitzchak 10:21

[519] The reason: As since the area does not contain a constant Minyan, the reason behind the recital of Mieyn Sheva, which is to allow the latecomers to finish their prayer [and not return home alone], is not applicable in this scenario. Now, although in today's times this reason is no longer applicable even regarding the town's Shuls, and nevertheless it must be recited, this is because the institution of the Sages does not become nullified even when the reason behind the institution becomes no longer relevant. However, by an area without a set Minyan the Sages never instituted to recite Mieyn Sheva since the reason is not applicable, and hence one is not to do so. [Admur ibid; Taz ibid]

[520] Admur ibid; M"A 268:14; Maharlbach 122; Ridbaz
The reason: (As this matter is not mentioned in the Gemara or the words of the Geonim). [Admur ibid]
Other opinions: Some Poskim rule one is to protest them ,being it is a Safek Bracha Levatala. [P"M brought in M"B 268:25]

[521] Ben Ish Chaiy 2 Vayeira 10; Eretz Yisrael of Rav Tukichinsky 5:3; Har Tzevi 1:152; Minchas Yitzchak 10:21

[522] Menorah Tehorah 268:11; Rav Poalim 3:23; Ben Ish Chaiy 2 Vayeira 10; Kaf Hachaim 268:50; See Likkutei Maharich

[523] Kaneh Bosem 2:48; Or Letziyon 2:19-5

[524] Admur ibid; Michaber 268:10; Mahriy Abuhav; Ruvash 40

[525] Admur ibid

[526] Taz ibid; M"B 268:24 in name of Elya Raba limits this to only if the Minyan has a Sefer Torah in the temporary Shul.

[527] The reason: As also by this Minyan there are people who come late. [ibid]

> ## Q&A
> **Is an established Shabbos only Minyan to recite Meiyn Sheva?[528]**
> Yes. Some Poskim[529] write that this applies even if the set Minyan only takes place on Friday night.
>
> **Is Meiyn Sheva to be recited by a family Minyan taking place in a Simcha hall, or in the house of one of the Mechutanim?[530]**
> No. Some[531] however write that if the hall contains a set Shul which serves a different Minyan each Shabbos, and it contains a Sefer Torah, then it may be recited.
>
> **If a set Minyan has temporarily relocated, is a Meiyn Sheva to be recited in the new temporary location?[532]**
> Yes. This applies even if they are Davening in the street.

38. The Chazan accidently recited Ata Chonantanu in his Shabbos repetition:[533]
If the Chazan accidently began reciting Ata Chonantanu in his Shabbos repetition, and then remembered, he is to stop and immediately continue with the Shabbos blessing.[534]

------------------Kiddush----------------

39. Blessing children on Friday night:
It is an old age custom for parents and Rabbis to bless their children and students with Birchas Kohanim on Friday night.[535] Doing so does not transgress the prohibition[536] against a non-Kohen reciting Birchas Kohanim[537], although it is forbidden for the person to raise his hands like a Kohen upon doing so, and he also may not intend to perform the Mitzvah of Birchas Kohanim upon doing so.[538] The blessing may be said with Hashem's name.[539] The blessing is given after Maariv or upon coming home from Shul. The reason for this is because on Shabbos, there is a special holiness that resides on the hands which can be transferred onto the children and students.[540] Some[541] are no longer accustomed to bless the children on Friday nights and rather do so only on special occasions, such as Yom Kippur and the day of the wedding, and so is the widespread Chabad custom.[542]

Placing the hands on the person's head: Due to the above prohibition against lifting the hands while saying Birchas Kohanim, some[543] are accustomed not to even rest both hands on the head of the person being blessed when blessing him with Birchas Kohanim, and rather rest only one hand on his head. Other

---

[528] Birchas Habayis 41:7; Mishneh Sachir 1:91; Igros Moshe 4:69; Minchas Yitzchak 10:21; Shraga Hameir 6:47

[529] See Poskim ibid

[530] Piskeiy Teshuvos 268:13

[531] Piskeiy Teshuvos ibid footnote 98

[532] Tehilah Ledavid 268:13; Minchas Yitzchak 10:21

[533] Ketzos Hashulchan 78:2 in name of Chikikeiy Lev [Rav Yosef Chazan, Izmor]; Shalmei Chagiga; Zecher Leavraham; Shoel Umeishiv Shetisa 22
Other opinions: Some Poskim imply that the Chazan is required to finish the blessing and then continue with the Shabbos blessing. [Perisha 117; See Ketzos Hashulchan ibid]

[534] The reason: As the Chazan is the messenger of the congregation and the congregation did not make this mistake to require its repetition. [ibid]

[535] Sefer Hachaim [brother of Maharl] 3:6; Maavor Yabok Sifsei Renanos 43; Siddur Yaavetz; Pela Yoeitz Brachos; Kaf Hachaim 262:17; See Piskeiy Teshuvos 271:1

[536] See Admur 128:2; Rama 128:1; Kesubos 24b

[537] See Bach 128; M"B 128:3; Kaf Hachaim 128:39; Biur Halacha 128:1 "Viein Lezar"

[538] See Poskim in previous footnote

[539] See Mahariy Assad O.C. 41; Keren Ledavid; Kapei Aaron 64
Other opinions: Some Poskim rule it is forbidden to say Hashem's name in the blessing due to it being in vain. [Noda Beyehuda Kama 6]

[540] Siddur Yaavetz ibid; Kaf hachaim ibid

[541] Makor Chaim of Chavos Yair 270; Menachem Tziyon in name of Rimnavor in Derushim L'Pesach that he would only do so on special occasions and not every Shabbos; This custom is not recorded in the writings of the Arizal

[542] Rabbi Leibel Groner replied to my question as to what is the Chabad custom: *"In majority of instances, I did not hear of or witness this custom in Chabad homes, however there were some Chabad families I knew of who did follow this custom."*

[543] Custom of Gr"a, brought in Torah Temima Bamidbar 6:23; Siddur Reb Shabsi; Maavor Yabok Sisei Renanos 43; See Piskeiy Teshuvos 128:6

Poskim[544] however rule it is permitted and encouraged for one to rest both hands on the head. Practically, the widespread custom is to be lenient and allow the placing of two hands on the head of the person being blessed[545], and so was the custom of the Chacham Tzvi[546] and Rebbe Rashab on Erev Yom Kippur.[547]

40. May a child eat or drink before Kiddush?[548]

If a child wants[549] or needs[550] to eat or drink, he may do so even before Kiddush. This applies both to the Kiddush of night and day.[551] It is forbidden to oppress a child and make him wait until after Kiddush.[552] This applies even if the child is above the age of Chinuch/education [so long as he is under Bar or Bas Mitzvah[553]]. If, however, the child does not want to eat and does not need to eat at this time, and is simply being fed for the benefit of others[554], then [once he reaches the age of Chinuch[555]] he is to be educated not to eat until he hears Kiddush.[556] Nevertheless, it is permitted to give a child who has reached the age of Chinuch to drink from the Kiddush wine in Shul.[557] [Despite the above ruling, as the child becomes older, one may encourage the child to not eat before Kiddush by stating to him that it is proper for him to

---

[544] Siddur Yaavetz Seder Leil Shabbos; Sheilas Yaavetz 2:15 that so was the custom of his father the Chacham Tzevi

[545] See Daas Sofer 1:14; Beir Moshe 4:25; Tzitz Eliezer 11:8; Yechaveh Daas 5:14

[546] Brought in Sheilas Yaavetz ibid

[547] Otzer Minhagei Chabad p. 194

[548] Admur 269:3 regarding Kiddush in Shul; 343:7; 106:3 regarding eating prior to Shacharis; 471:10; 472:23; M"A 106:3; 269:1; M"B 269:1"It is permitted to feed children food on Shabbos morning prior to Kiddush and it is forbidden to oppress him"
Other rulings of Admur: In 343:6 Admur states "Even though the child can wait to hear Kiddush in the place of a meal, in the house of his father **who is educating him in this**" which implies that ideally a father should educate his child to not eat before Kiddush. Perhaps however this is referring to if the child does not feel a need or will to eat or drink before Kiddush, in which case one would then educate the child to wait. Alternatively, perhaps the father may encourage the child not to eat until Kiddush, and only to force the child not to eat is forbidden.

[549] Wording of Admur in 343:7

[550] So is the wording of Admur in 343:7; 471:10, and Ketzos Hashulchan 147:5 that the allowance only applies if the child needs to eat; See last footnote below.

[551] Admur 269:3

[552] Admur 269:3; 343:7; M"B ibid "It is forbidden to oppress him"
The reason: As the [Sages] only prohibited feeding [Rabbinically] forbidden foods [to a child] when the food is forbidden in it of itself, such as a piece of Treifa [Niveila] and the like. However, if the food is Kosher in it of itself and it is just forbidden to be eaten within a certain time slot, then it is permitted to be fed to a child. A proof for this is the ruling regarding feeding a child on Yom Kippur in which case one may do so even if there is no danger involved for the child to fast. [Admur 269:3; M"A 269:1; Yevamos 114b]

[553] SSH"K 52:18; Piskeiy Teshuvos 343:1; According to this, those who are accustomed to make their older children [over 9] delay eating until they hear Kiddush, not only are doing a matter that is unnecessary but it is even forbidden to do so as stated above.

[554] Such as if an adult asks the child to eat a food for the sake of tasting it to see if it needs spices and the like.

[555] See M"B 269:1 that this is approximately between ages 6-7

[556] Based on Admur in 343:6-7; 471:10; Ketzos Hashulchan 147:5 that the allowance only applies if the child wants or needs to eat, and so is clearly implied from 343:6 which bases the allowance of giving a child to drink from the Shuls Kiddush on the lenient opinion mentioned there [and not on the differentiation between a timely and innate prohibition]. Furthermore, in 343:6 Admur states "Even though the child can wait to hear Kiddush in the place of a meal, in the house of his father **which is educating him in this**" which implies that ideally a father should educate his child to not eat before Kiddush. Seemingly this is referring to if the child does not feel a need to eat or drink before Kiddush in which case one would then educate the child to wait. So is also the implication of Admur 621:4 who forbids giving a child to drink the wine of a Bris on Yom Kippur, even though a child may be fed on Yom Kippur, thus implying that there is a difference between whether something is done for his own need [feeding him] or for the need of others [giving him the Bris wine].
Ruling of Admur in 269:3: In 269:3 [as well as 106:3] no mention is made that it is only allowed if the child wants or needs it, and on the contrary, it is implied from there that even if the child feels no desire to eat he may nevertheless be fed, as the case there is discussing giving a child wine of Kiddush from Shul. Thus, seemingly there is no prohibition at all by such foods even if the child does not need or want to eat. However, perhaps one can answer that the reason why no mention of "need/want" was made in 269:3 is specifically because the case there was referring to giving the child to drink from the Shuls Kiddush, of which in truth there is no need for him to want to drink it, as since it is being done for the sake of a Mitzvah and it is a mere time prohibition, it is allowed according to all. The ramification between the two approaches would be if a parent may feed a child before Kiddush even if the sole purpose of doing so is that the child tastes the food on one's behalf.

[557] Admur 269:3; 343:6; Michaber 269:1; Hagahos Maimanis; Tur; See Kaf Hachaim 269:2 regarding the allowance of giving a child to drink the Kiddush in Shul and the various Answers offered
Background: When making Kiddush in Shul, usually there is no one being Yotzei with the Kiddush, being that they plan to eat at home and make Kiddush again there. Thus, the question is asked as to how one may make Kiddush in Shul if no one is being Yotzei. To this, the Alter Rebbe answers that although an adult may not drink the wine, since he must eat in the place that he made Kiddush, nevertheless, a child who has reached the age of Chinuch may drink from it, after hearing the blessing from the adult and fulfilling his obligation.
The reason: We find in Admur two different [and contradictory] reasons behind the allowance: 1) As children may be fed Kosher foods which are time forbidden. [269:3] 2) Alternatively, although the child does not need to drink this wine [and it should hence be forbidden despite the fact that it is only a time forbidden food], nevertheless, it is permitted to give it to him being that it is for the sake of making Kiddush, and is not done on a steady basis, and is only Rabbinically forbidden. [343:6] See previous footnote! See Kaf Hachaim 269:2 for various reasons mentioned in Poskim

abstain on his own from eating or drinking until after Kiddush, even though if he needs or wants to eat, one may not stop him from doing so.[558]]

Summary:
It is permitted for a child to eat or drink before Kiddush until the age of Bar/Bas Mitzvah, if they desire to eat. It is forbidden to oppress the child by making him wait. Nonetheless, one may encourage the child as he gets older to not eat or drink before Kiddush, even though he may do so from the letter of the law.

Q&A

May children eat candies before Kiddush?[559]
Yes. This applies even if the child has reached the age of Chinuch, until the child is Bar or Bas Mitzvah. Nevertheless, as stated above, it is proper to encourage the child, as the child becomes older, that it is proper for him to refrain on his own from eating candies until after Kiddush. Nonetheless, if the child needs or wants to eat, one may not stop him from doing so.

------------------*Shabbos-Melacha*----------------
41. On Shabbos, may one place hot food onto a plate that contains food or liquid?

Whenever one's plate contains food on it, whether a solid or liquid, and one desires to place on it hot food, the question of Bishul [the prohibition of cooking food on Shabbos] arises. In certain circumstances, the hot food can cook the food that is on the plate. In other circumstances, there is no issue with doing so. This depends on the following matters:

1. Is the hot food Yad Soledes [110 Fahrenheit]
2. Is the hot food being poured from a Keli Rishon or a Keli Sheiyni and onwards?
3. Is the hot food a Davar Gush [a hot solid food without gravy such as hot dry baked potatoes or Kugel or rice]?
4. Is the food that is currently on one's plate wet?
5. Is the food currently on one's plate already cooked?
6. Is the food already on one's plate hot or cold?

The law: All hot Yad Soledes[560] [110 Fahrenheit[561]] food that is being poured from a Keli Rishon has ability to cook other foods.[562] This applies even if one uses a ladle.[563] If the food is being poured from a Keli Sheiyni, and is not a Davar Gush, then it does not have ability to cook other foods.[564] Accordingly, if one pours the food content of the pot into a serving bowl, and then serves the food from the serving bowl, then if the food is not a Davar Gush [i.e. it contains gravy], it cannot cook any food that is on one's plate. If, however, one is serving hot food directly from a pot which is a Keli Rishon, and placing it on the plate, then it can possibly cook any food or liquid that is already on one's plate, as will be explained. If the food

---

[558] See Admur 343:6 "Even though the child can wait to hear Kiddush in the place of a meal, in the house of his father **which is educating him in this.**" One must establish that this refers to the father encouraging the child not to eat until Kiddush, as to force the child not to eat is forbidden as stated above, and thus from here we can conclude that one may educate the child through encouragement [Perhaps however this is referring to educating the child not to eat in a case that he does not feel a need or will to eat or drink before Kiddush and is being given to eat for other purposes-Vetzaruch Iyun]; See also Admur 343:7 "Therefore it is permitted to feed him before Kiddush **if he wants to eat**" which implies the child does not have to be educated to eat if he does not want to; So also rules: Or Letziyon 2:47-6; Piskeiy Teshuvos 269:2; See Likkutei Dibburim, vol. 4, p. 1418 that Rabbi Yosef Yitzchak of Lubavitch related: *When I was seven years old, my father [Rabbi Shalom Dov Ber of Lubavitch] said to me on the eve of **Yom Kippur**: "In the evening and all night it is forbidden for you to eat. Tomorrow in the morning until noon you do not need to eat. From then on it depends on your will." My father explained to me the gravity of eating on **Yom Kippur**, and concluded: "If you want to eat, do not ask anybody, only come to me. I have prepared food, water, and juice for you. If I am in the middle of the **Amida** prayer, wait for me; just be careful not to ask for food from anyone else." That year I completed the fast for the first time in my life, and the year after that it was already an easy matter.*
[559] Or Letziyon 2:47-6; Piskeiy Teshuvos 269:2
[560] Admur 318:9;11;24;29 s
[561] Igros Moshe 4:74 ; Minchas Yitzchak Likkutei Teshuvos 29; Rav SZ"A in Minchas Shlomo 1:91; SSH"K 1 footnote 3
[562] Admur 318:19
[563] See Admur 451:28; Shach Y.D. 107:7; Taz Y.D. 92:30; M"B 318:87; Shabbos Kehalacha Vol. 1 p. 84-86;
[564] Admur 318:11; Michaber 318:4

is a Davar Gush [solid hot food without gravy, such as Kugel or rice] then according to some Poskim[565] it retains the status of a Keli Rishon even if it is being served from a Keli Sheiyni and onwards. Whether the Keli Rishon food will cook the food on one's plate is dependent on the type of food that is on it: If the food that is on the plate is a precooked [in liquid] dry solid, such as a hardboiled egg, then it is permitted to place Keli Rishon or Davar Gush food on it.[566] If, however, the food on one's plate is raw, or not fully cooked, or was baked without liquid, or contains moisture that is not cooked, then placing Keli Rishon food on it poses a cooking prohibition.[567] In such a case, one would need to use a new plate, or make sure to transfer the food to a Keli Sheiyni and only then serve from it. If the plate contains precooked liquid that has cooled down [but not congealed], then it is permitted from the letter of the law to pour liquid onto it from a Keli Rishon, but not a hot Davar Gush.[568] Nonetheless, even in such a case it is best to be stringent.[569]

Summary:
Whenever one places hot Yad Soledes food onto one's plate, he is to make sure that the plate is clean from other uncooked foods, and is dry of any cold liquid or moisture. Alternatively, he is to make sure that the hot food is being poured from a Keli Sheiyni and is not a Davar Gush.

Examples:
> Salad, Cold cuts, meat or chicken on one's plate: Its common to serve certain cold foods during the main course, or fish course, such as salad, cold cuts that contain moisture, cold meat or chicken that has congealed gravy, and the like. Placing hot Keli Rishon food on top of these foods is prohibited.

> Plate still wet from drain: One may not serve a hot food directly from the pot [either with or without a serving spoon] onto a wet plate, as it will cook the liquid. Thus, one must make sure the plate is dry. The same applies regarding a hot Davar Gush, that it may not be placed onto a wet plate.

> Plate has spillage from previous course: When setting a table with two plates, for the first and meat course, it is common that the lower plate of the main course, catches crumbs and other leftovers from the first course. The law is as follows: One may not serve a hot food directly from the pot [either with or without a serving spoon] onto the plate if it contains uncooked

---

[565] The Shach in Yorah Deah 105:8 rules that a Davar Gush has the ability to absorb taste into other foods even when in a Keli Sheiyni. So brings Magen Avraham 318:45, although the Tzemach Tzedek explains that the Magen Avraham himself does not hold of this opinion as the final Halacha. Nevertheless, the Peri Megadim seems to rule to be stringent in this Lechatchilah and so rules the M"B 318:45 and 65 and 118 and Ketzos Hashulchan 124 footnote 15 and 39, and so appears to be the opinion of the Igros Moshe regarding practicality. The following Poskim rule leniently regarding a Davar Gush: Rama 94:7; Peri Megadim; Chovas Daas; Chasam Sofer; Aruch Hashulchan; Igros Moshe seems to be lenient from the letter of the law; Tzemach Tzedek Yoreh Deah 65, and so seems to be the opinion of Admur from the fact that in Halacha 31 he omit's the novelty of the Magen Avraham which is that even in a Keli Sheiyni the roast may not have garlic placed on it, and Admur omit's the Keli Sheiyni ruling.

[566] See Admur 318:12 that there is no Bishul Achar Bishul by a dry solid that was cooked. If, however, it was baked, then pouring a liquid onto it from a Keli Rishon is forbidden according to some opinions and so is the final ruling.

[567] Admur 318:19 that Iruiy Keli Rishon cooks a Kelipa worth; Admur 318:12 that if food is baked it may not have a hot liquid Iruiy Keli Rishon poured on it. [see previous footnote]

[568] Tzemach Tzedek Mishnayos Shabbos 3, brought in Ketzos Hashulchan ibid footnote 31; Ketzos Hashulchan 124:12; Shevisas Hashabbos Hakdama Mivashel 19; Or Letziyon 2:30-10; Beis Meir brought in Biur Halacha "Vehu" that those who are lenient do not need to be protested; Igros Moshe 4:74 Bishul 18; Piskeiy Teshuvos 318:51
Background: See Admur 318:9 that the custom is to rule like the opinion that there is Bishul Achar Bishul by liquids; **See the following Poskim that one may nevertheless always pour liquid of a Keli Rishon onto water, even if not cooked:** Admur 318:20; Taz 318:18; Tosafos Pesachim 40b; Tur 318; Rashba, Ran and Rif on Shabbos 20a; Elya Raba Y.D. 68; Peri Megadim Yoreh Deah 68; Iglei Tal Ofeh 29; Tzemach Tzedek Mishnayos Shabbos 3:5, brought in Ketzos Hashulchan 124:12 footnote 31, and Tehilah Ledavid 318, in understanding of Michaber/Admur. **See Poskim who argue that one may not pour onto water from Keli Rishon:** M"A 318:35; Tosafos Shabbos 42a that pouring on a minute amount of cold water is forbidden; Tzemach Tzedek Mishnayos Shabbos 3:5, brought in Ketzos Hashulchan 124:12 footnote 31; P"M 318 A"A 35; Gr"a; Chayeh Adam; Tehilah Ledavid 318:28; M"B 318:78 and 85; Biur Halacha 318 "Vehu Shelo"; Kaf Hachaim 318:130; Ketzos Hashulchan 124:11-12; Igros Moshe 1:93; 4:74; Minchas Yitzchak 9:30-31; Beir Moshe 6:110; ; Az Nidbaru 2:20; Teshuvos Vehanhagos 1:207; Piskeiy Teshuvos 318:51. The Poskim ibid arbitrate that one may be lenient by an already cooked food, as this involves tow disputes 1) If there is cooking after cooking by liquids, and 2) If Iruiy Keli Rishon can cook liquids.

[569] Tzemach Tzedek ibid; Poskim ibid

leftovers from the previous course, as it will cause it to cook. Thus, one must make sure the plate is clean and dry prior to pouring, or is to make sure the food is being served from a Keli Sheiyni.

➤ May one pour a second serving of soup into his bowl which contains leftovers? Yes.[570]

42. May one use a peeler to peel fruits and vegetables on Shabbos?[571]

Inedible peels:[572] Those fruits and vegetable which majority of people do not eat together with the peel, and it is rather removed and discarded prior to eating, according to all opinions, it is [Biblically[573]] forbidden to use a peeler to remove the peel on Shabbos.[574] This applies even if one intends to do so in order to eat the food right away.

Edible peels: Those fruits and vegetables which majority of people eat together with the peel, some Poskim[575] rule it is forbidden to be peeled using a peeler, and rather may only be peeled with a knife for right away use.[576] Other Poskim[577] however rule it may be peeled using a peeler, and may even be peeled for later use on Shabbos.[578] Practically, those who are stringent are doing a proper act, although those who are lenient have upon whom to rely, and each person is to ask his Rav.[579] [Whenever one chooses to be lenient like the latter opinions, one must know that in truth the selected fruit/vegetable is eaten with its peel by majority of people. For example, cucumbers must be verified in each area if it is in truth eaten with its peel by majority of people, as explained next.]

Examples of fruits/vegetables and their peel status: According to the lenient opinion, it is permitted to peel, with the help of a peeler, all the following fruits and vegetables: apples, tomatoes, pears, apricots, plums, and peaches. According to all, it is forbidden to peel with a peeler a carrot, orange, grapefruit, Kiwi. The permissibility to peel cucumbers with a peeler is dependent on one's countries eating habits; if the majority of people are accustomed to eating the cucumber with the peel, then according to the lenient opinion, it may be peeled using a peeler, while if the majority of people remove the peel then according to all it is forbidden to use a peeler.[580]

One who is particular to never eat the peel: If a person is particular to always peel a certain

---

[570] As even if the ladle has remained a long time within the Keli Rishon, its pouring is defined as Iruiy Keli Rishon, which is permitted to be poured onto pre-cooked liquids, as explained above.

[571] See Rama 321:19, Admur 319:9, M"B 319:22 and 24 that peeling is subject to the Borer prohibition: Shabbos Kehalacha Vol. 2 p. 294 and 299-307; Piskeiy Teshuvos 321:34-35

[572] Iglei Tal Borer 6; Ketzos Hashulchan 125:16; Piskeiy Teshuvos 321:35

[573] As a peeler is the normal vessel used to remove the peel from a fruit/vegetable and hence is similar to a sieve and sifter, which is Biblically forbidden to be used. [See Admur 319:1; M"B 319:2; Rashi Shabbos 74a]

[574] The reason: As a peeler is a designated item for separating and negates the required condition of separating with one's hands. [ibid]

[575] M"A 321:19 regarding apples; Elya Raba 321:30; Tosefes Shabbos 321:41; M"B 321:84; Orchos Chaim 319:22 in name of Meorei Or; Igros Moshe 4:74 Borer 8; Az Nidbaru 9:10; Chut Shani 25:7

[576] The reason: As these Poskim hold that the separating prohibition applies to even edible peels and thus when peeling it one must abide by all Borer restrictions, which include not peeling it with a peeler, and even when using a knife, to only do it for right away use. The reason that even edible peels contain the Borer restriction is because when they are peeled off, they are generally thrown out, and hence have a status of Pesoles when one comes to peel it. [Piskeiy Teshuvos 321:34]

[577] Peri Megadim 321 A"A 30, brought in Shaar Hatziyon 321:97; Iglei Tal Borer 6:12; Shevisas Hashabbos Borer 24 and footnote 45; Kaf Hachaim 321:141; Ketzos Hashulchan 125:16 [see however Ketzos Hashulchan 126 footnote 19]; SSH"K 3:34

[578] The reason: As according to these Poskim, edible peels do not contain a Borer prohibition, and hence there is no need to abide by the Borer conditions which restricts one from using a Borer instrument and requires the peeling to be done for right away use. Regarding if the peeler contains an Issur of Muktzah or Uvdin Dechol-see Piskeiy Teshuvos 321:35 footnote 373-374

[579] Minchas Shabbos 80:69 that it is proper to be stringent when possible, and so concludes: Shabbos Kehalacha ibid; Piskeiy Teshuvos 321:34-35 that it is best to be stringent when possible, although one who is lenient has upon whom to rely; Michzei Eliyahu 1:51-52; Teshuvos Vehanhagos 1:208

Ruling of Rav Farkash in Shabbos Kehalacha ibid: Rav Farkash rules that one who wishes to be stringent like all opinions [which he rules one initially is to do], is to always apply the separating restrictions to anything being peeled. In a case that one is pressured to peel using a peeler, such as when one has a lot of fruits/vegetables to peel, or in a case that one is pressured to peel the fruits a while prior to the meal, such as in a case that one must leave one's house now and will only return when the meal will commence, then although one may be lenient like the latter opinions, nevertheless it is proper to also cut off part of the actual fruit together with the peel. [Shabbos Kehalacha 13:9; Piskeiy Teshuvos 321:34]

[580] See SSH"K 3:34; Shabbos Kehalacha ibid; Piskeiy Teshuvos ibid footnote 363

fruit/vegetable, despite it being eaten by majority of people, some Poskim[581] rule that even according to the lenient opinion, one must abide by the Borer restrictions and may not peel it using a peeler and may only peel it for right away use. Other Poskim[582] however rule that it is permitted for him to use a peeler even in such a case.

One who is never particular to remove the peel:[583] All fruits and vegetables that majority of people do not eat with the peel, retain all the Borer restrictions even if the person eating it is personally accustomed to eating the fruit/vegetable with the peel. Thus, it may not be peeled using a peeler or any other designated vessel, and may only be done in order to eat right away.

Pesach: Those who are particular to not eat peels on Pesach, and hence peel all their produce, seemingly may still abide by the leniency of using the peeler on Shabbos Pesach for peels that are generally eaten by majority of people, if they are accustomed to follow the lenient opinion during the other Shabbosim of the year.[584]

43. Salting salad on Shabbos:[585]

All foods which salt helps to change its natural state[586], [such as] to soften[587] it, or harden[588] it, or remove its bitterness, and other [changes] of the like, which includes all foods which are commonly pickled, may only be salted one piece at a time[589], and must be eaten immediately after the salting.[590] It is thus forbidden to salt another piece prior to eating the first piece, as doing so delays the eating of the first piece. Amongst foods included in the above category are: radish[591], onions, garlic[592], beans and lentils[593] that were cooked in their peels, cucumbers, and lettuce. Accordingly, it should be forbidden to salt a salad on Shabbos being that doing so transgresses both of the conditions, as it involves salting more than one piece of food at a time and one does not eat the salted food immediately. There is however one method available in which it is permitted to salt a salad on Shabbos, and that is through adding oil or vinegar to the food either before, or immediately after, the salting. If one adds oil or vinegar to the food immediately after salting, then it is permitted to salt even many pieces at the same time and they may even be eaten later on, on Shabbos, although one must do so in close proximity to the meal.[594] Practically, although one may place the salt first and then immediately add the oil[595], nonetheless, it is proper to first place the oil

---

[581] Shabbos Kahalacha Vol 2 13 Biurim 2 [p. 300] writes it is proper to be stringent and follow all the separating restrictions Orchos Shabbos 3:40

[582] SSH"K 3 footnote 88; See Piskeiy Teshuvos 321 footnote 363

[583] Piskeiy Teshuvos 321 footnote 363

[584] The reason: As the peel itself is still viewed as a food, and it is simply due to its Chametz contingency that people avoid it, and not because they suddenly view the actual peel as Chametz or inedible. Accordingly, at the very most they are removing the bad [Chametz] with the good [the peel] of which many Poskim rule is permitted, and hence the leniency would still apply according to the lenient opinion.

[585] Admur 321:4; Michaber 321:3-6; Shabbos 108b

[586] Admur ibid Taz ibid

[587] Admur ibid; Taz 321:6

[588] Admur ibid; Rashi ibid

[589] Stam opinion in Admur; Michaber 321:3; Rambam

The reason: The reason for this is because when one salts two pieces together, and certainly [when he salts] more [than two pieces], it appears like one is pickling pickled foods [which itself is forbidden due to cooking, or do due it being similar to tanning].

[590] 2nd opinion in Admur ibid; M"A 321:6; Raavan 352; Elya Raba 321:6; Bach; M"B 321:14; based on reason of Rashi behind the prohibition

The reason: According to the 2nd opinion, the reason [the Sages] prohibited to salt a few pieces at the same time is not because it appears like [one is] pickling pickled [foods], but rather is because that until one [finishes] eating the first [piece] the second piece remained in the salt and since the salt benefits it, this is similar to tanning.

[591] Admur ibid; Michaber 321:3; Shabbos ibid; See Shabbos Kehalacha 20 footnote 69 regarding radishes of today which are not very sharp, although he nevertheless concludes to be stringent.

[592] Admur ibid; Taz 321:2; M"B 321:13

[593] Admur ibid; Michaber ibid; Tur in name of Rabbeinu Peretz

[594] Admur ibid; Taz 321:1; M"A 321:6; M"B 321:14; Shiltei Giborim; Rashi ibid; Regarding why pouring vinegar is not considered like pickling- see Shabbos Kehalacha 20 Biurim 11

The reason: Even though salting many pieces together is forbidden [to be done] even to eat right away, nevertheless since [the pieces] do not remain at all alone with the salt, as one immediately pours on it vinegar and other species, it is [therefore] not similar to tanning. [ibid]

[595] So is wording in Shiltei Giborim; M"A 321:6; Admur ibid; M"B ibid; However see Shaareiy Teshuvah ibid in name of Shvus Yaakov which says to first place in the oil, although in truth in the Shvus Yaakov the word "first" is omitted.

and only then place the salt.[596]

44. May one eat biscuits, cakes, candies, chocolate, and the like, which have words/letters/pictures engraved on them?[597]

To break it and then eat it:[598] It is forbidden to break the letters that are on a food, even if the letters are engraved.[599] Accordingly, one may not break a piece off from the cake or biscuit if doing so entails breaking one of the letters.

To take a bite out from it: Some Poskim[600] rule that one may break engraved letters within the process of eating. Meaning, that one may break the letters in the process of taking a bite from the food, and the prohibition is only against breaking it with one's hands and then placing it into one's mouth.[601] However, other Poskim[602] rule they may not be broken even within the process of eating. According to this latter

---

[596] Ketzos Hashulchan 128 footnote 3 and 5; Menorah Hatehorah 321:6; Piskeiy Teshuvos 321:4; See Shaareiy Teshuvah 321:1 in name of Shvus Yaakov that "if one first places the oil, it is permitted"; See however Shabbos Kehalacha 20:31 and Biurim 12 and Tosefes Biur that there is no need to first place the oil, as is the simple implication of Admur ibid
The reason: As perhaps if one were to place the salt first he may come to forget to place in the oil immediately after. [Ketzos Hashulchan ibid 5] As well, this should be done being that according all opinions when the oil is placed first there is no question of a prohibition, and it is better to do an act that will go in accordance to all. [Ketzos Hashulchan ibid 3] As well, some Poskim explicitly write to place the oil first. [Shaareiy Teshuvah 321:1]

[597] See Ketzos Hashulchan 144 footnote 3

[598] Admur 458:8 "*The symbols which are made on the Matzos should not be made through forms of letters using a molded imprint [i.e. cookie cutter], or with one's hands (for the reason explained in chapter 470 and others) being that one is required to break them on Yom Tov, and there are opinions who prohibit to break a cake which has forms of letters on it even though he does not intend to erase the letters, but rather to eat them on Yom Tov, as was explained in chapter 340. Rather these symbols are to be made through holes or grooves, as long as one is careful to extremely speed their process, as was explained in chapter 460, see there.*"; Implication of Admur 519:6 regarding a Chosem; Teshuvas Rama 119; Chok Yaakov 475; Levush 473; M"B 475:57; Chazon Ish 61:1; Magen Avraham 340:6 leaves this matter with a Tzaruch Iyun; Kaf Hachaim 340:31 "One who is stringent is blessed" [although see Kaf Hachaim 473:118 regarding Matzah that it may be broken, as the majority are lenient]; Bris Olam Mocheik 4; Shevet Halevi 9:77 "Proper for each person to be stringent"
Other opinions: Some Poskim rule the erasing prohibition does not apply to the engraved letters that are on a food. [Ra"sh Halevy brought in Magen Avraham 340:6, although he himself concludes with Tzaruch Iyun; Maharil; Degul Merivava 340; M"B 340:15 [in contradiction of 475:57]; Kaf Hachaim 473:118 that so rule majority of Poskim; See Piskeiy Teshuvos 340 footnote 65; Har Tzevi 214; SSH"K 11:8 footnote 31 in name of Rav SZ"A]

[599] The reason: It is Rabbinically forbidden to erase letters on Shabbos even if one does not plan to write any letters in its place. [Admur 340:4]

[600] Ketzos Hashulchan 144 footnote 3 [His final ruling is written on page 151 at the end of the paragraph]; Shabbos Kehalacha Volume 3 20:74 [p. 369]; [To note that the Ketzos Hashulchan did not mention this ruling in chapter 144 and only later was it mentioned by him in the glosses to the end of the 7th volume, nevertheless, it is implied from there that his conclusion is to allow breaking the letters in the process of eating. See however the case of a bottle cap with engraved letters that the Ketzos Hashulchan allows one to break it on Shabbos, although contradicts himself in the glosses to the end of volume 7. Vetzaruch Iyun. The Rebbe was once addressed this question of whether one may break engraved letters according to Admur, and the Rebbe answered that no conclusive stance can be taken on this issue. Vetzaruch Iyun, being that this matter is explicitly ruled on in Admur 458:8]

[601] The reason: The basis of this ruling is that a) There are Poskim [Degul Merivava 340; M"B 340:15] who always allow breaking all letters within the process of eating [chewing it] and b) There are Poskim [See Poskim ibid in other opinions] who allow breaking engraved letters even with one's hands. Thus, although Admur rules stringently regarding on breaking within process of eating [with regards to letters written with icing], while the Magen Avraham leaves in question regarding breaking engraved letters, when both leniencies are combined, such as breaking engraved letters of a biscuit within the process of eating, then one may be lenient. [Ketzos Hashulchan ibid] This seemingly holds true as well in accordance to the ruling of Admur in Hilchos Pesach 458:8, as there he writes that a) **some** opinions rule and b) it is forbidden to **break** the Matzah with engraved letters. This implied that taking a bite from it is allowed, as in such a case there are two reasons to assume the Sages would not make a decree, and one may rely on those opinions who argue on the "some opinions rule". Likewise, we similarly see in Admur 460:9 in which he implies that it is permitted to break Matzos that contain engraved **pictures**. So is also the implied ruling of M"A 340:6 as he understood from the Mordechai [see Ketzos Hashulchan ibid] Now, in truth, pictures have the same status as letters regarding writing and erasing on Shabbos, as rules Admur 340:10, rather one must say that the Rabbinical decree against erasing was not made in all cases, and so too here, since there are two reasons to be lenient, it is permitted to be done.
The reason behind the leniency of engraved letters over external letters: The above allowance only applies to engraved letters, while external letters are prohibited to be broken even within the midst of eating. [Admur 343:10] Vetzaruch Iyun as why by engraved letters we are more lenient, as engraving is also prohibited due to writing. Some Poskim suggest that engraving letters is no longer common today, and thus, since one has no intent to write in the area that the letters are erased, in which case it is at the very most only a Rabbinical prohibition, therefore, the Sages did not make their decree, as they do not decree against uncommon cases, if it will prevent Oneg Shabbos. Now, although we see that Admur ibid and other Poskim ibid were stringent even regarding erasing engraved letters on foods, nonetheless, one can suggest that they did not extend the prohibition to a case of breaking them within the process of eating, in contrast to external letters, which Admur forbids breaking even within the process of eating. [Ketzos Hashulchan 144 footnote 3]
Ruling of Admur in 519:6: In Admur 519:6 he rules that one may not open a Chosem on Shabbos if it contains letters or pictures. This implies that it is forbidden to break engraved pictures, just as engraved letters. However, in truth, as the Ketzos Hashulchan ibid states, the above allowance was only given to food, for the sake of Oneg Shabbos, and not towards other cases.

[602] Rav Bistritzky in Shut Ara Degalil p. 35; Piskeiy Teshuvos 340:6 that from Admur ibid it is implied that this too is forbidden; Rav Eliyahu Landau that the custom is to be careful not to eat such foods on Shabbos; See article of Rav Shalom Dovber Hertzel in Koveitz Oholei Torah 1083 p. 108 [Rav Bistritzky does not make mention of the ruling of the Ketzos Hashulchan throughout his entire ruling. However, at the end in a

opinion, one may not give such foods to children that have reached the age of Chinuch. Practically, one is to speak to his Rav for a final ruling.

Engraved pictures:[603] Pictures and designs that are engraved onto a cake, biscuit and the like, may be eaten as normal on Shabbos.[604] One may even break a piece off and eat it, so long as there are no letters on the cake.

Summary:
One may not break the engraved letters found on a food, although some are lenient to do so in the process of eating, through taking a bite, as opposed to breaking a piece off with one's hands. One may break the engraved picture of a food even with one's hands.

Q&A
May one dip a biscuit with engraved letters into a tea?
One may dip a biscuit that contains engraved letters into tea if doing so will not inevitably cause the biscuit to break in the area of the letters. If, however, the biscuit will break in the area of the letters then doing so is forbidden. [One must beware to wash his hands without a blessing prior to eating biscuits dipped in coffee or tea and the like, prior to eating them.[605]]

May one make cheesecake using whole biscuits that contain engraved words?
It is not advised to do so due to the eating restriction to be explained. If one did so, then care must be taken not to break the biscuits in a way that the letters will break.[606] According to some Poskim[607], however, one may eat the biscuits whole, having them break in his mouth.

---

footnote he mentions that he found a ruling of the Ketzos Hashulchan which contradicts his ruling, and he writes that seemingly the Ketzos Hashulchan forgot the ruling of Admur in 458:8. However, in truth the Ketzos Hashulchan in his Hosafos does add the ruling of Admur there and nevertheless does not retract his final ruling said above.]

[603] Implication of Admur 460:9; Beis Yosef 460 in name of Rabbeinu Yerucham; M"A 340:6 in his understanding of Mordechai; Ketzos Hashulchan 144 footnote 3; Shabbos Kehalacha vol. 3 20:75; See Piskeiy Teshuvos 340 footnote 66; Mishnas Yosef 7:80; Orchos Shabbos 15 footnote 36 in name of Rav Gerelitz and Rav Chaim Kanievsy]

[604] The reason: It is unclear as to why Admur, and the Poskim ibid, are more lenient by engraved pictures than engraved letters, if they both are part of the same writing and erasing prohibition. However, perhaps the Sages did not apply their decree against erasing an engraved picture in such a situation, being it is not as common as erasing an engraved letter. [See Ketzos Hashulchan ibid] Alternatively, perhaps, since erasing a picture is only a Tolda of writing, therefore the sages were more lenient. [Shabbos Kehalacha ibid footnote 185; Rav SD"B Levin in Koveitz Oholei Torah 797 p. 43] Alternatively, some suggest that there is no writing or erasing prohibition involved in **engraved pictures** [See Tehilah Ledavid 340:3 in his initial understanding of Rambam-See Koveitz Oholei Torah 1083 p. 108] Now, although Admur 340:6 explicitly rules that one may not engrave into ash, perhaps that refers only to letters and not pictures. Now, although the Poskim do not differentiate between pictures and letters and rather rule that making a drawing is a Tolda of writing [See Admur 340:10; M"A 340:6; Rambam Shabbos 11:17; Degul Merivava 340; Tehilah Ledavid 340:3] perhaps Admur holds that when it comes to pictures, there is a difference between writing and engraving. See Admur 340:10 who writes "One who makes marks and designs on a document and the like, in the way that the artists design, is liable due to an offshoot of the writing prohibition. The same applies for one who erases it." Admur does not simply write that pictures have the same status as writing, and qualifies the case with "**on a document..in the way that artists design..**" This extra wording of Admur seems to imply that there are cases that the writing prohibition does not apply to making a picture, and perhaps an engraved drawing is one of those cases. See also Admur 302:5 who writes "For example one who designs a [picture of a] figure on a vessel which is waiting to be designed on, even if he only designed part of the figure, he has done part of the finishing touch of the vessel and is liable [for a sin offering]. **As although the figure on its own is not considered a [Biblically] forbidden form of work**, nevertheless now that the vessel is complete and fixed through his action it is considered [a Biblically forbidden form of] work." If the above is correct, then there would be no prohibition to engrave pictures into non-Muktzah sand, a cake and the like. Vetzaruch Iyun, as I have not found any Poskim who suggest such a ruling.

[605] 158:3

[606] Admur 458:8 regarding Matzah on Pesach; Vetzaruch Iyun if one may be lenient to permit cutting the case under the basis of Safek Pesik Reishei: See Admur 316:4; Kuntrus Achron 277:1; Taz 316:4; M"B 316:16; Biur Halacha 316:3 "Vilachen"
Other opinions: Some Poskim allow breaking engraved letters that is on food. [M"B 340:15; SSH"K 11:8. Ra"sh Halevy brought in Magen Avraham, although he himself concludes with Tzaruch Iyun]

[607] Ketzos Hashulchan 144 footnote 3; Shabbos Kehalacha Volume 3 p. 369; 20:73

45. May one make or undo a hair braid ["Tzama" in Hebrew] on Shabbos?[608]

It is [Rabbinically[609]] forbidden to braid one's hair [or another person's hair, or a child's hair] on Shabbos.[610] It is likewise forbidden to undo a braid on Shabbos [even if it was made before Shabbos].[611] [Those women who are lenient to do so, are to be protested.[612] This prohibition applies even if one will make a weak braid, and will use a soft brush that does not pull out hair.]

Summary:
It is forbidden to make a braid, or undo a braid, on Shabbos.

Q&A
May one make, or undo, the braid of a Sheitel on Shabbos?[613]
No.[614] Nevertheless, it is not required to protest those who do so, if they in any event will not listen.[615]

May one simply remove the elastic from the braid, without actually undoing it?
Some[616] write it is permitted to do so, even though the braid will eventually become undone on its own without the elastic.

-----------------*Rosh Chodesh*----------------
46. From which day of the new month may one begin saying Kiddush Levana?

There are various opinions regarding how many days into the month must pass for Kiddush Levana to be said. Some Poskim[617] rule one may say Kiddush Levana even on the first day of the moon's visibility. Other Poskim[618] rule one may only begin to say it after three days have passed from the Molad.[619] Other

---

[608] Michaber 303:26

[609] P"M 303 A"A 20; M"B 303:82; Rambam 20; Chachomim in Mishneh ibid; The following Poskim rule like Chachomim regarding makeup, and the same applies to a braid: Implication of Michaber 303:25 and Admur 320:27; M"A 303:19; Olas Shabbos 303:19; M"B 303:79; See Biur Halacha 303:25 "Mishum Tzoveia"; Kaf Hachaim 303:115-116

Other opinions: Some Poskim rule it is even Biblically forbidden to do so. [Rebbe Eliezer in Mishneh ibid, brought in Shaar Hatziyon 303:66; The following Poskim rule like Rebbe Eliezer regarding makeup, and the same applies to a braid: Elya Raba 303:40 in name of Rishonim who rule like Rebbe Eliezer in Mishneh ibid; Yireim, brought in Nishmas Adam; Semag; Ran; Ravan; See Biur Halacha ibid and Kaf Hachaim ibid]

The reason behind those who hold it is Biblically forbidden: Although it is farfetched to consider a hair braid similar to building a building, nevertheless, the Torah itself testifies that it is considered a category of building, as the verse states "Vayiven Hashem Elokim Es Hatzela" and the Sages teach that Hashem made a braid for Chava and presented her to Adam Harishon, and thus we see that a braid in the Torah is referred to as building. [Shabbos 95a; M"B 303:82]

Difference between doing it to a friend and to oneself: The Gemara Shabbos 95a differentiates between if a woman makes a braid on her own hair, in which case she is exempt [even according to the approach of Rebbe Eliezer], and only when she makes a braid on her friend's hair is she liable, as only then is the braid nice and beautiful.

[610] Michaber ibid; Mishneh Shabbos 94b "Hagodeles"

The reason: This is forbidden due to the building prohibition, as it is similar to building, and hence the Sages prohibited it. [M"A 303:20; M"B ibid; based on Shabbos 95a] This is supported in the Torah, as the verse states "Vayiven Hashem Elokim Es Hatzela" and the Sages teach that Hashem made a braid for Chava and presented her to Adam Harishon, and thus we see that a braid in the Torah is referred to as building. [Shabbos 95a; Machatzis Hashekel 303:20; M"B 303:82] It is not Biblically forbidden due to building, as the building prohibition only applies to structures. It is also not Biblically forbidden due to weaving, as this prohibition only applies a) To matters that are not attached to a person or the ground, and b) To a weaving that lasts and is permanent. [M"A 303:20; M"B 303:82; Tosafos Shabbos 94b] Regarding why it does not transgress the tying prohibition-see Or Sameach on Rambam 10:8 and Shevet Halevi 1:101

[611] Michaber ibid; Tosafos Shabbos 57a "Bema"

The reason: This is forbidden due to the destroying prohibition, as it is similar to destroying, and hence the Sages prohibited it. [P"M 303 A"A 20; M"B 303:83; Tosafos ibid]

[612] Darkei Moshe 303:7; Bedek Habayis; See Beis Yosef 303:26; Kol Bo 31

[613] M"B 303:82

[614] The reason: Although doing so does not transgress the building prohibition [as a braid is only considered building when attached to the body, just like Chava], nevertheless, it is forbidden due to the weaving prohibition. Now, although the braid is temporary, it is nevertheless Rabbinically forbidden. [M"B ibid] It is likewise forbidden to undo the braid due to the prohibition of Potzeia, which is undoing the weaving. [Shaar Hatziyon 303:71]

[615] M"B ibid; See Kol Bo 31, brought in Beis Yosef 303:26

[616] Chut Shani 36:15, brought in Piskeiy Teshuvos 303 footnote 87

[617] Rambam; Smag; Rashal; Sefer Hakaneh, brought in M"A 426:13; Gr"a and other Achronim brought in M"B 426:20

[618] Rabbeinu Yona; Levush 426; Bach 426; Taz 426:3; M"A 426:13; Peri Chadash; Beir Heiytiv 426:10; Siddur Yaavetz; main opinion in M"B 426:20

Poskim[620] rule one must wait until seven days pass from the Molad. [Furthermore, based on Kabala, one is not to begin to say Kiddush Levana until seven days from the Molad[621] have passed.[622] Practically, the Chabad custom, and the custom of many sects of Jewry, is to wait seven days from the Molad.[623] Other sects of Jewry are accustomed to say it after the passing of three days, and in a time of need, even prior to three days.[624] Even according to the Chabad custom, areas that do not experience much visibility of the moon due to cloudy skies[625], as is common in the winter months, then if Motzei Shabbos falls after three days but prior to seven days, Kiddush Levana is to be recited that Motzei Shabbos and is not to be delayed. In cases of question or doubt in this matter, one is to follow the ruling of the Rabbinical authority of his community.[626]]

Opinion of Taz 426:3: The Taz ibid brings the Bach who wonders at the above ruling that one must wait until seven days pass. The Bach rather rules, as rules Rabbeinu Yona, that after three days have passed one may say Kiddush Levana. The Bach concludes that practically the custom is to only wait three days, and hence if Motzei Shabbos falls on the fourth day or onwards Kiddush Levana is to be said and the Mitzvah is not to be delayed. The Taz ibid rules, as does the Levush, that if Motzei Shabbos falls after three days have passed then if the moon is already giving much light, Kiddush Levana is to be said, and one is not to delay until the seventh. [Hence the Levush and Taz conclude it is not enough for three days alone to pass, but the moon must also visibly be giving much light.]

Opinion of M"A 426:13: The M"A ibid brings all three opinions regarding when one may start saying Kiddush Levana. He concludes [so is implied] like the Bach, and if Motzei Shabbos falls within the first three days they are to delay until next Motzei Shabbos.

[619] The reason: As from three days after the Molad the moon is visible enough to benefit from it.

[620] Michaber 426:4 based on Kabalists brought in next footnote; Hagahos Maimanis brought in M"A 426:13

[621] Admur in Siddur and Peri Megadim brought in M"B 426:20; The Molad is the calculated time that the moon began its new cycle.

[622] Admur in Siddur based on Kabala; Michaber 426:4; Hagahos Maimanis, brought in M"A 426:13; This is based on the Kabalist Rav Yosef Gegetilya, the author of Shaareiy Orah; So is also written in: Mishnes Chassidim Miseches Motzei Shabbos; Maggid Meisharim Shir Hashirim; See Hagahos of Rebbe Rashab on Siddur Im Dach p. 321 for other Kabalistic sources, and sources in Chassidus. See Nimukei Orach Chaim 426:4; The Shaar Hakolel 33:2 suggests that there is no source for this in the Kabala of the Arizal or from the Gemara. The Rebbe Rashab however in the glosses ibid negates this remark and brings sources in Kabala, and Chassidus for this practice.

The reason: As one can only sanctify the moon after it has received from the seven Middos.

[623] The Chabad Custom: As stated above, Admur in the Siddur writes that based on Kabala one is to wait seven days past the Molad. So is also written in Torah Or [109b]. Practically, however, in the winter the Tzemach Tzedek would say Kiddush Levana even before seven days have passed from the Molad. The reason for this is because of the cloudy and rainy weather experienced in the Russian winter which prevents the moon from being seen. Hence, delaying Kiddush Levana when the opportunity arises prior to seven days could cause one to not say it at all due to the moon's inability to be seen past the seventh. [Glosses of Rebbe Rashab in Siddur Im Dach p. 321; Shaar Hakolel 33:2; See there [in Shaar Hakolel] that he suggests the reason the Tzemach Tzedek did not wait until seven days is because he found no source in the Kabala of the Arizal or from the Gemara. The Rebbe Rashab however in the glosses ibid negates this remark and brings sources in Kabala, and Chassidus for this practice.]

[624] The majority of Achronim [Bach; Taz ibid; M"A ibid; Peri Chadash; Beir Heiytiv 426:10; main opinion in M"B 426:20] dispute the ruling of the Michaber and Kabala, and rather rule that if Motzei Shabbos falls three days past the Molad or onwards one may say Kiddush Levana on Motzei Shabbos even though it is prior to the seventh of the month. Much of Lithuanian Jewry follows this ruling

Other Chassidim: In his glosses of the Siddur [p. 360], Rav Raskin records a tradition of the dynasty of Ruzhin that the Baal Shem Tov was not particular to wait until seven days pass to recite Kiddush Levana, while the Maggid of Mezritch was particular to wait. This is one of the instances that the custom of the Maggid differed from that of his teacher the Baal Shem Tov. See Nimukei Orach Chaim 426:4

Opinion of M"B: The M"B ibid brings that some Achronim, including the Gr"a, rule that one may say Kiddush Levana even before three days have passed, and even prior to Motzei Shabbos. He concludes that one who follows this opinion has upon whom to rely, and in an area of cloudy weather, he is praised for doing so.

[625] And hence delaying an opportunity of saying Kiddush Levana could cause one to not say it at all.

[626] Rebbe in Sichas Noach 5752, brought in Shaareiy Halacha Uminhag 2:179; See previous footnotes.

The Rebbe writes as follows: *If one is not **stringent**, one can say Kiddush Levana on Motzei Shabbos that falls after the 3rd day past the Molad, even though it is before the seventh. This especially applies in cloudy areas and particularly in the winter.* The Rebbe concludes that: *each community should follow in accordance to his level of cloudiness, and it is given to the discretion of the local Rav to decide whether to precede the Kiddush Levana to Motzei Shabbos that is before the seventh of the month.* It is implied from the above wording that [even according to the Chabad custom] one may choose to say Kiddush Levana on Motzei Shabbos that is prior to the seventh even if it is not cloudy or rainy. When it is cloudy or rainy one is specifically to do so. However, from footnote 14 there it is implied that in a non-cloudy area one is to wait.

Summary:
One should not say Kiddush Levana until seven days have passed from the Molad. However, if one suspects that the moon will not be visible after the seventh, then if Motzei Shabbos falls after three days but prior to seven days, Kiddush Levana is to be recited that Motzei Shabbos and is not to be delayed. In cases of question or doubt in this matter one is to follow the ruling of the Rabbinical authority of his community.

Q&A

Must one wait seven <u>complete</u> days [i.e. Zayin Shleimim] from the Molad to say Kiddush Levana?

Some Poskim[627] rule it is not necessary to wait until seven full days pass from the Molad, and rather as soon as six days have passed, and one has now entered the seventh day past the Molad, Kiddush Levana may be recited. Others[628] however rule that, based on Kabala, one is to wait for a full seven days to pass from the Molad before saying Kiddush Levana. Practically, one may be lenient in this matter.[629]

------------------Pesach----------------

47. Removing Chametz that is stuck in cracks and crevices of tiles and furniture:

Letter of law:[630] If one cannot remove Chametz <u>with his hands</u> due to it being stuck under cracks and crevices and the like, then it suffices for him to nullify the Chametz before the 6th hour of Erev Pesach [through saying the Bitul of Kol Chamira in Bedikas Chametz, or by Biur Chametz], and he is not required to destroy this Chametz before Pesach. One is not required to undo the floor [or undo furniture] to remove the Chametz even if he is capable of doing so, and rather the nullification suffices.[631] This

---

[627] Rameh Mepuno 78; Shiyurei Kneses Hagedola; Elya Raba 426:14 [brought in Shaareiy Teshuvah 426:10] that one may say Kiddush Levana on the night of the 7th; Ashel Avraham Buchach 426:2

[628] Birkeiy Yosef 426:4 brought in Shaareiy Teshuvah 426:10; Mateh Efraim 581:10 rules one is to initially say it only after seven complete days have passed, although if he suspects the moon will not be visible again, he is not to delay the blessing.

[629] So concludes Hiskashrus 454 p. 15 and so was the custom of Rav Yaakov Landau [as told to me by his son Rav Eliyahu Landau Shlita].
Seemingly the reason one may be lenient is because even regarding waiting seven days there is a dispute, and the Rebbe leaves room to be lenient. See also Sichas 1986 6th Adar Rishon that Kiddush Levana was said that Motzei Shabbos even though seven full days had not passed since the Molad.

[630] Admur 433:19; based on 433:21 regarding a hole in wall, 433:30 regarding a Mapoles and 438:11 regarding a pit; Rambam and Michaber 438:2 regarding a pit; Chok Yaakov 433:13; Ashel Avraham 433 according to Rambam; Olas Shabbos 433, although concludes with Tzaruch Iyun because of ruling of Bach; Peri Chadash 433; Makor Chaim 8; M"B 433:29; Implication of P"M 433 A"A 11; Kaf Hachaim 433:56; Piskeiy Teshuvos 433:4

Background from Admur:

Chametz found in the cracks of a wooden plank floor [433:19]: *If one has a [floor which has small deep crevices in between the tiles, such as by a] wooden board floor with small deep cracks in between the planks of wood, and one is thus unable to enter his hand into the hole to check for Chametz, he does not need to remove the tiles/wood in order to allow him to check under them. Even if one sees that Chametz has fallen into one of the small holes, and if one does not remove it from there, then it will be there throughout all the days of Pesach, nevertheless we do not trouble him to remove it from there, and rather he is to nullify it and that suffices.*

Chametz is inside hole of wall [433:20]: *The same law applies by a hole in one's wall or floor which is wide enough for one to fit his hand in, but is very deep, that one is not able to enter his hand to search the entire hole for Chametz, then one checks the hole to as deep that his hand reaches, and the remaining area suffices with one's nullification. This applies even if there is certainly Chametz there [and even if there is more than a Kezayis].*

The source of Admur's ruling: This case ruling of Admur ibid is not recorded in previous Poskim. Admur ibid learned this ruling from the ruling he brings next in 433:21 [as rules Michaber 433:7 and Pesachim 8a] regarding Chametz that is found in a hole in the wall that cannot be reached, in which case we rule that one is not required to check the hole past the area that one can reach with one's hand, and that this applies even if there is certainly Chametz there. This itself [that even by certain Chametz one is not required to remove it from a deep hole] is learned from 438:11 regarding Chametz found in a pit, in which case we rule that it may remain there over Pesach with Bittul. [Admur ibid; Michaber 438:2; Tur 438; Rambam Chametz 2] [Kuntrus Achron 433:4] It is likewise learned from the ruling in 433:30 regarding a Mapoles of three Tefachim, that even according to the second, stringent opinion, nullification suffices. Thus, in total, the basis of Admur's ruling is from the ruling brought in Michaber ibid regarding a pit, and the ruling regarding a Mapoles, which is the understood ruling regarding a hole in the wall, and hence the same applies to a crack.

Other opinions: Some Poskim rule that if one knows for certain that there is Chametz found in a hole, then he must destroy the Chametz even if it is not reachable by hand, and relying on Bittul does not suffice. [Bach 433; Raavad regarding the law by a pit, brought in Taz 438:4, Chok Yaakov ibid, Ashel Avraham ibid, P"M 433 A"A 11] The Chok Yaakov and Ashel Avraham ibid negate this ruling of Bach, as the Rambam, Tur and Michaber 438:2 all rule unlike the Raavad regarding a pit.

[631] The reason: The reason for this is because the main enactment of the sages for one to search for Chametz, despite having nullified it, is due to a decree that one may come to eat it on Pesach. Now, in the above case, being that this Chametz is in an area which one cannot place his hand in, certainly he will not come to eat it on Pesach. [433:19] Now, although by a Mapoles of less than three Tefachim, the Sages nevertheless required

applies even if one is able to see the Chametz. This applies even if there is a Kezayis of Chametz found there.[632] This applies even if the Chametz is visible.[633] Thus, the Chametz that is in between the deep crevices of one's floor, between the tiles [or in the cracks of one's table or other furniture], does not need to be removed or destroyed but is to merely be nullified. [If one did not nullify his Chametz before the 6th hour on Erev Pesach, and did not sell his Chametz to a gentile before Pesach, then he must destroy this Chametz on Pesach upon remembering, even if it entails taking apart the furniture and the like.[634] This applies even if the Chametz is less than a Kezayis.[635]]

Yisrael Kedoshim Heim-The Custom:[636] All the above is from the letter of the law, however practically, the Jewish people are holy and hence the custom is to destroy all Chametz that is in one's possession, even the Chametz found in unreachable areas. Thus, one is to pour bleach or other spoiling agent over Chametz that he is unable to reach with his hands. [There is however no basis to extend this stringency to require the taking apart the item in order to reach the Chametz.]

Summary:
Chametz that is stuck in a deep hole or crevice and cannot be reached with one's hands, is not required to be removed and it suffices for him to nullify the Chametz before Pesach. This applies even if there is a Kezayis of visible Chametz found in the crevice. Nonetheless, practically, the Jewish people are holy and destroy all Chametz that is in one's possession, even if the Chametz found in unreachable areas. Thus, when possible, one is to pour bleach or other spoiling agent over Chametz that he is unable to reach with his hands.

Q&A
Must one remove Chametz that is stuck in moveable items, and can fall out through shaking?
Chametz that is stuck inside a moveable item, but cannot be reached by hand, seemingly must be shaken out if one is able to do so.[637] If however, one is unable to shake out the Chametz, then it has the same status as any unreachable Chametz, of which we rule nullification suffices, and at the very most, one can spill a spoiling agent over it. Likewise, this only applies by a Kezayis of Chametz, or less than a Kezayis that is not dirty, if however, the Chametz stuck inside is less than a Kezayis and is dirty, then even shaking is not required, if one plans to nullify his Chametz before Pesach.[638]

---

one to destroy the Chametz [Admur 433:30], this is only because the Chametz may come to be revealed by a dog through the dog removing the mound. However, here, by Chametz stuck between cracks or in a deep pit, there is no possibility for a dog to undo the wall, or for it to happen on its own, as is common by a mound. There is also no need to suspect that an item of value may get lost in the crack over Pesach and he may come to undo the floor on Pesach in order to retrieve it, as this law is learned from Chametz found in a pit in which case we do not suspect for such a matter. There is also no need to suspect that a rat will remove the Chametz to a reachable area the same way we do not suspect regarding a pit. The reason we do not suspect for a rat dragging out Chametz is because there is no end to such a suspicion. If we were to suspect for such a thing then we should not allow Chametz of a gentile to be kept behind a Mechitza, and should continuously suspect perhaps Chametz in a gentile's house was brought to the house of a Jew. [Kuntrus Achron 433:4]

[632] Admur 433:30 regarding a Mapoles and 438:11 and Michaber 438:2 regarding Chametz found in a pit

[633] Pashut, see Admur ibid in all sources and Kuntrus Achron 433:4; Unlike Piskeiy Teshuvos 433 footnote 6 who says its implied from Admur in Kuntrus Achron ibid that if the Chametz is visible it should be destroyed. This is inaccurate. Upashut!

[634] Pashut! See 433:30 regarding a Mapoles

[635] See Admur 433/13; 442/28; 444/9; 446/3

[636] Admur 442:30 and Michaber 442:6 "If there is Chametz in a crack that one cannot remove, then one can place on it a little bit of cement over it". Now, although one can argue that the above refers to dough that is stuck in the crack of a wall, and bits and pieces can be removed, but it's difficult to remove in entirety, nonetheless, the spirit of the stringency should apply in this case as well. Vetzaruch Iyun why Admur made no mention here in 433:19 of this matter.

[637] This is derived from the ruling in Admur 3438:11 which requires one to remove Chametz from a high surface, lest it fall on Pesach and one come to eat. Thus, seemingly, the entire allowance brought above in 433:19 regarding unreachable areas is in a case that the Chametz cannot come to fall out on its own. If, however, it is possible for it to fall out on Pesach, then one should be required to do so. However, this only applies by a Kezayis of Chametz, or less than a Kezayis that is not dirty, if however, the Chametz stuck inside is less than a Kezayis and is dirty, then even shaking is not required, if one plans to nullify his Chametz.

[638] See Admur 442/28

Does one have to use toothpicks and the like to remove Chametz from areas that he cannot manage to remove with his hands, such as within the lining of a fridge?

No.[639] However, by a fridge and other items used for food, one is required to do so in order so Chametz does not Chas Veshalom fall into one's food.[640] In any event, *Yisrael Kedoshim Heim,* and it is thus proper to pour a damaging agent, such as bleach, onto the Chametz in all cases that one is able to do so.

Must one remove his car seats in order to remove the Chametz that is stuck under them?

All Chametz that is found under the car seat, and is reachable by hand, must be removed. All Chametz that cannot be reached by hand, is not required to be removed even if one is able to see it. There is no obligation to remove the car seats in order to reach Chametz that is stuck under it. One is likewise not required to vacuum out unreachable Chametz.[641] Nevertheless, practically, experience dictates that it is very difficult to remove even the reachable Chametz [due to abundance of crumbs] without either using a vacuum or removing the car seats. Likewise, in light of Yisrael Kedoshim Heim, Chametz that remains visible and unreachable under the car seat, is to have bleach or another spoiling agent over it, although is not required to remove the seat.[642]

Must one undo his chair if he sees Chametz in-between the crevices of the cushion and the chair?

This follows the same ruling as the previous Q&A. Thus, all the Chametz that is reachable by hand [or that can be shaken out] must be removed. All Chametz that cannot be reached by hand [and cannot be shaken out] is not required to be removed even if one is able to see it, and one is not required to undo the chair in order to remove it. Nevertheless, if there is Chametz that remains visible and unreachable under the cushion, it is proper, if doing so will not damage the cushion, to destroy it by pouring bleach, or other spoiling agent, over it. If, however, the Chametz stuck inside is less than a Kezayis and is dirty, then even shaking is not required, as explained in other Halachos.

Must one undo the keyboard of his computer to remove the Chametz stuck under the keys?

No.[643] This applies even if one knows for certain that there is Chametz found there. Nevertheless, in light of Yisrael Kedoshim Heim, those who desire to be stringent and undo the keyboard are not to be protested.[644] In any case that a thorough cleaning was not done, it is strongly advised not to use this keyboard over Pesach, as it is possible for Chametz to get onto one's finger and end up in one's food or mouth.

48. Pesach Barbecue-Does Charcoal require a Hashgacha for Pesach?

Charcoal briquettes: Charcoal briquettes [square shaped manufactured charcoal, typically used for barbecues] are compressed together using a starch binder, most notably corn or wheat starch.[645]

---

[639] This is derived from the fact that Admur ibid does not require one to use means other than his hands to remove the Chametz, and if his hands cannot remove it the nullification suffices. Accordingly, one does not need to use toothpick and the like to remove Chametz from cracks, if it is not reachable with one's hands.

[640] As since the moving of the fridge door can cause Chametz to fall out from the area that it is stuck in, it is similar to Chametz which is on a high surface which one must remove.

[641] As explained in the above Halacha from 433:19-20

[642] Although this is not required from the letter of the law as explained above, nevertheless "Yisrael Kedoshim Heim" and are thus accustomed to destroying all Chametz, even Chametz that is allowed to remain throughout Pesach. Hence, one should spoil the Chametz through pouring bleach on it.

[643] As a) The Chametz is unreachable by hand, and thus nullification alone suffices. b) The Chametz found there is less than a Kezayis and is certainly dirty. Due to the second reason, it is not required to even shake out the Chametz, if possible.

[644] See Michaber 442:6

[645] The charcoal making process: Charcoal is produced by drying wood, such as timber wood, and then heating the wood to a very high temperature until it blackens. The wood is then crushed into pieces of ash and combined together into small squares, known as briquettes, using a starch binder, either of corn or wheat.

Accordingly, it is proper for one to use charcoal briquettes that have a Hashgacha for Pesach to verify that they do not contain a Chametz starch which will then enter one's food.[646] [The Eida Hachareidis provides supervision over certain companies of charcoal, to enable its use for Pesach.] Certainly, one may not use unverified charcoal briquettes that were produced <u>during</u> Pesach.[647] Nonetheless, those who are lenient to use any charcoal that was produced before Pesach have upon whom to rely.[648] A company who was verified to use corn starch in their production, may have its charcoal used on Pesach even according to Ashkenazim who avoid Kitniyus.[649] [The company Kingsford[650], which is the leading charcoal manufacturer in the US, manufactures its briquettes using corn starch, and hence their products do not pose any Halachic issue.[651] One can contact any given company to verify its status.]

Lump Charcoal: Lump charcoal does not require a Hashgacha, as it is not known to contain any problematic additives. [The company Rockwood[652] does not manufacture briquettes, and hence all their products are lump charcoal which do not pose any Halachic issue.[653]]

---

[646] See Rabbi Blumenkrants Pesach digest p. 10-306

<u>The reason</u>: Although the charcoal is not edible, and is hence like all non-food products that are permitted to be owned and benefited from, nonetheless, they remain Rabbinically forbidden to be intentionally consumed due to Achshavei. [See Admur 442:22 and 32-33; 445:11] Now, since the coals release heat and smoke through which the food is cooked and flavored, the food certainly contains taste of the coal, which would include taste of the starch that is in it. One cannot argue that the Chametz starch is nullified to the other ingredients and hence permitted in use, as an intentional ingredient is not nullified even in 1000, even regarding the Rabbinical concept of Achshavei. [Admur 442:22] Now, although one can argue that perhaps the concept of Achshavei does not apply in such a case, as there is no actual starch that enters one food, and it is merely the burnt taste that penetrates, and hence we find ruled in 445:11 that one may cook using Chametz charcoal that was created prior to the 6th hour of the 14th, nevertheless perhaps that only applies in previous times when the intent was not to add flavor of the ash to the food, and it was simply the only cooking method available. However, by today's charcoal, since one certainly intends to enter the flavor of the coal/ash into the food [as this is one of the prime reasons people grill using charcoal-so it receive a smoked flavor] perhaps this would contain an Issur of eating due to Achshavei. In addition, regardless of the above, the custom is to abstain from using Chametz charcoal for cooking over Pesach, even if it became charcoal before Pesach. [Admur 445:11 and in Siddur; M"A 445:4; Tur 445; Maharshal; Maharil; P"M 445 A"A 4] The reason for this is because one may come to end up using Chametz charcoal that was created on Pesach. [Beis Yosef 445; P"M ibid; Rebbe in Hagada] Accordingly, one is to abstain from using charcoal briquettes that do not have a Hashgacha.

<u>Can one use a corn starch bound briquettes</u>? Yes, as a) The Kitniyus is not edible once mixed with the ash and we do not find the concept of Achshavei regarding Kitniyus, which is a mere Minhag. b) Kitniyus is nullified in majority. [See Admur 453]

[647] Admur 445:8 "Even the ash and charcoal of the Chametz are forbidden in benefit"; Many companies ship the briquettes the same day of production.

[648] The OU and CRC both write that charcoal does not require a Hashgacha for Pesach.

<u>The reason</u>: As the simple understanding of Admur 445:11 is that one may cook using Chametz charcoal, irrelevant of whether it adds flavor to one's food. The reason for this way of understanding is possibly due to that the Rabbinical prohibition of Achshavei does not apply to the smoked flavor of a product, and only when eating the actual Mamashus. This is in addition to the fact that some Poskim rule it is permitted to even eat Chametz that was destroyed before the 6th hour. [See Peri Chadash and Rashbatz, brought in Kaf Hachaim 442:99] Now, although earlier we stated the custom is not to use Chametz charcoal even if it was burnt before the 6th hour, nevertheless, perhaps this custom would not extend to this situation.

[649] See previous footnotes

[650] See https://www.kingsford.com; Currently, the Kingsford Products Company remains the leading manufacturer of charcoal in the US, enjoying 80 percent market share.

[651] Verified to me through a written correspondence with the company *"At this time, we do not claim to be gluten free. We can confirm that we use corn starch to bind the char in the briquettes. We do not use wheat starch."*

[652] See http://rockwoodcharcoal.com/; This is a S.L. Missouri based company.

[653] Verified to me through a written correspondence with the company *"You are correct that briquettes use binders such as potato or corn starch to bind them together.....some use a dextrin product (which ultimately comes from starch or gluten, I believe.) The good news is, we use NONE of that as we do not produce briquettes. Our charcoal is natural lump. It's just wood that has been carbonized to remove the moisture, tars, & liquors. It has ZERO fillers, binders, or additives such petroleum, starch, borax, limestone, etc. 100% natural untreated wood in ours. Our lump charcoal is probably the most natural and organic products you could ever buy, as it's mostly carbon.....the basis of all living organisms."*

49. May one begin the Seder prior to nightfall?[654]

It is forbidden to begin the Seder [i.e. Kadesh] prior to nightfall [i.e. Tzeis Hakochavim].[655] [If one is making a public Seder in an area that nightfall begins at a very late hour, and fears that people will not attend, he is to start the Seder early, after Plag Hamincha, through Davening Maariv, saying speeches, Pesach skits, and saying parts of Maggid, and then begin Kadesh after Tzeis Hakochavim. If this too is not viable, then some Rabbanim suggest making Kiddush after Pelag Hamincha and beginning the order of the Seder until Maggid. After Tzeis Hakochavim one is to begin Maggid and drink two cups of wine as part of the four cups. Practically, one is to contact a Rav for guidance in this matter.]

50. May one delay eating Matzas Mitzvah [of Motzi Matzah] until past midnight?

One is required to fulfill the Mitzvah of eating Matzah prior to midnight.[656] [If one eats the Matzah after midnight, some Poskim[657] rule he does not fulfill his obligation and has thus lost the Mitzvah. Other Poskim[658], however, rule he can nevertheless fulfill the Biblical Mitzvah up until Alos Hashachar. Other Poskim[659] rule that this matter is left in question, and hence one is to be stringent like both opinions, and eat Matzah without a blessing, if it is already after midnight. Practically, if one did not yet eat the Matzah and it is already after midnight, he is to eat the Matzah without the blessing of "Al Achilas Matzah."[660] If it is already close to midnight and one did not yet eat the Matzah, he is to skip from where he is holding and perform Motzi Matzah before midnight. The same applies to a person who awoke from sleep moments before midnight, that he should say Kadesh and immediately afterwards recite Motzi Matzah.[661] This applies for both the first and second Seder.[662]]

May one who is making a Seder for the public perform his own Seder afterwards?
Based on the above, those who desire to begin their Seder after the Mivtzaim Seder, must beware to at the very least eat the Matzah before midnight.

---

[654] Admur 472:2

[655] The reason: As a) One may not recite Kiddush, and fulfill the Mitzvah of four Kosos, until after nightfall. [Admur 472:2; 471:14] b) One does not fulfill his Biblical obligation of eating Matzah until nightfall [Admur 472:2] c) it is forbidden to eat Matzah on Erev Pesach prior to fulfilling the Mitzvah of eating Matzah at night. [Admur 471:4] d) It is forbidden to eat a meal past the 10th hour of the day, prior to the start of the Seder at night. [471:1]

[656] Admur 458:2; Reb Elazar Ben Azaria in Pesachim 120b
The reason: As just like the Karban Pesach may only be eaten until midnight, so too the Matzah may only be eaten until midnight, as the verse states Al Matzos Umerorim Yochluhu, thus teaching us that the eating of Matzah is connected, and follows similar laws, to the Pesach [Admur 458:2] This follows the opinion of Rebbe Elazar Ben Azaria, brought next.

[657] Reb Elazar Ben Azaria in Pesachim 120b; Zevachim 57b; Tosafos Zevachim ibid; Megillah 21a; Piskeiy Tosafos Pesachim 334; Zevachim 33; Rabbeinu Chananel in Arvei Pesachim; Semag in name of Riy; Mordechai end of Pesachim; Rabbeinu Yerucham 5:4; Conclusion of Or Zarua; Hapardes 9:16-26 "It is forbidden to eat Matzah after midnight"; See Biur Halacha 477:1 "Viyihei Zahir"

[658] Rebbe Akiva in Pesachim and Zevachim ibid; Rambam Karban Pesach 8:15; Chametz Umatzah 6; Rif [brought in Mishkanos Yaakov 139] Rav Hamaggid; Baal Haitur; Or Zarua in name of Rav Yaakov of Krubil; Kol Bo 90; See Biur Halacha 477:1 "Viyihei Zahir"

[659] Rosh; Rashba; Ran end of Megillah chapter 2; Rokeiach

[660] Degul Merivava 477; Shaareiy Teshuvah 477:1; P"M 477 M"Z 1; Derech Hachaim; Tov Ayin 38:87; Ikarei Hadat 19:14; Misgeres Hashulchan 119:11; Aruch Hashulchan 477:5; M"B 477:6; Biur Halacha ibid; Kaf Hachaim 473:16; 475:64; Beis Halevi 1:34; Nitei Gavriel 91:1
Other opinions: Some Poskim rule that the final ruling of the Talmud is like Rebbe Akiva that the Mitzvah of Matzah applies throughout the night, until Alos Hashachar. [Mishkanos Yaakov 139; Or Yisrael 475; Or Sameiach 6:1; Sdei Chemed Mareches Chametz Umatzah 14:11; See Nitei Gavriel ibid footnote 1]

[661] Degul Merivava 477; Shaareiy Teshuvah ibid; M"B 477:6; Ashel Avraham Buchach 477; Kaf Hachaim 477:10

[662] Admur 481:1 "There is no difference between the first and second night in any other matter"; Nitei Gavriel 91:5
Other opinions: Some Poskim defend the practice of those who recite a blessing over the Matzah even after midday. [Darkei Chaim Veshalom 605; See Nitei Gavriel ibid footnote 6]

-----------------*Yom Tov*----------------

51. Taking a shower on Yom Tov?[663]

A. Showering with **hot** water:

Water heated on Yom Tov:[664] It is forbidden to bathe [or shower[665]] one's entire body with water that was heated on Yom Tov.[666] This applies even out of a bathhouse. This applies even if the water was heated [in a permitted method, such as] for the sake of drinking.[667] This applies even if one does not bathe his entire body simultaneously, but rather bathes one limb at a time.[668] It is however permitted for one to wash one's face, hands and feet[669] [and according to some Poskim[670], even minority of one's body] with the water, even if it was heated on Yom Tov.[671] [It is debated as to whether the water in a boiler which is automatically heated by the sun, or a timer, receives the Halachic status of water heated before Yom Tov or the Halachic status of water heated during Yom Tov.[672] Practically, one is to be stringent not to bathe majority of one's body in such water, even if he does so one limb at a time.[673]]

Water heated before Yom Tov: Some Poskim[674] rule it is permitted to bathe [or shower] one's entire body simultaneously, using water that was heated before Yom Tov.[675] Other Poskim[676] however rule it is forbidden to bathe (or shower[677]) the entire body on Yom Tov, even if the water was heated before Yom Tov, and even outside of the bathhouse.[678] However, even according to this opinion, the prohibition only applies against bathing one's entire body simultaneously. However, one may wash his entire body through washing one limb at a time, if the water was heated before Yom Tov.[679] Practically, although the main opinion follows the former approach in all these matters[680], nevertheless, it is already accustomed in these provinces [Ashkenaz] to be stringent like the latter opinion, and one may not swerve from this custom.[681] [Furthermore, there are even some Sephardic communities who are stringent in this matter, and each community is to follow their custom.[682]]

Bathing in a bathhouse:[683] The above allowances only apply outside of a bathhouse, however in a bathhouse, it is forbidden for one to bathe [i.e. enter the limb into the water, such as in a bathtub] even his

---

[663] See Admur 511:1; Michaber 511:2; Piskeiy Teshuvos 511:4-6; Nitei Gavriel 31:7

[664] Admur 511:1; Michaber 511:2; Rambam 1:16; Mishneh Shabbos 38b

[665] Admur ibid parentheses in original; Tosafos ibid; Rashba Shabbos 40a

[666] The reason: This is due to the Rabbinical bathing prohibition, explained in 326:1.

[667] Admur ibid; M"A 326:6

[668] Admur ibid; Michaber 511:2; Braisa Shabbos 40a; Avodas Hakodesh 3:5; Magid Mishneh 1:16; Kneses Hagedola 511; Shulchan Gavoa 511:4; Mamar Mordechai 511:1; M"B 511:11; Kaf Hachaim 511:16

[669] Tzaruch Iyun as to the exact measurement of area that may be washed on one's hand and feet. [SSH"K 14 footnote 23 in name of Rav SZ"A]

[670] Biur Halacha 511 "Aval"; Kaf Hachaim 511:14 based on implication of Rosh, brought in Beis Yosef 326 and Y.D. 299:6; Beir Moshe 8:169 in a time of need

Other opinions: Some Poskim however rule one may not heat water to bathe the other limbs of the body, and the allowance is limited to the face, arms, and feet. [Shach Y.D. 199:12 in name of Masas Binyamin 5; Aruch Hashulchan 511:6] The Kaf Hachaim ibid concludes to only be lenient in a time of need

[671] Admur ibid; Michaber ibid; Mishneh Beitza 21b

[672] See Q&A

[673] Piskeiy Teshuvos 511:5

[674] 1st opinion in Admur ibid "Therefore, even Rabbinically, it is permitted to bathe the entire body in water that was heated before Yom Tov."; Michaber 511:2; Rambam 1:16; Rif Beitza 11a

[675] The reason: As according to this opinion, Biblically, since extending a fire and cooking was permitted for the sake of eating and drinking, therefore, it was also permitted for bathing on Yom Tov. Accordingly, we do not suspect that if we permit one to bathe in hot water on Yom Tov that perhaps one will come to heat up water on Yom Tov, being that heating water on Yom Tov is only Rabbinically forbidden, and we do not make a Gezeira Legezeira. [Admur ibid; Taz 511:3; Kaf Hachaim 511:24]

[676] 2nd opinion in Admur ibid; Rama 511:2; Tur 511; Ran in opinion of Tosafos Shabbos 39b; Rosh 3:8 in name of Riva

[677] Admur ibid parentheses in original; Tosafos ibid; Rashba Shabbos 40a

[678] The reason: As according to this opinion, extending a fire and cooking water for the sake of bathing on Yom Tov is Biblically forbidden. Accordingly, we suspect that if we permit one to bathe in hot water on Yom Tov that perhaps one will come to heat up water on Yom Tov for the sake of bathing his entire body, and transgress a Biblical prohibition. [Admur ibid; Taz 511:4; Ran ibid]

[679] Admur ibid; Elya Raba 511:1; Rashba and Ritva ibid; Braisa Shabbos 40a; M"B 511:18; Kaf Hachaim 511:28

The reason: As every limb that he washes is being washed in a permitted method. There is no reason to decree that this may lead one to heating the water on Yom Tov itself, as even if he does, it is permitted to heat up water for the sake of bathing a single limb. The prohibition of heating water only applies if one heats water for the sake of bathing his entire body, being that it is only needed for the pampered. [Admur ibid]

[680] Admur ibid; Ran Beitza ibid

[681] Admur ibid; Rama ibid; Levush 511; M"B 511:18

[682] Kaf Hachaim 511:30

[683] Admur ibid; Michaber 511:1; Ran Beitza 11a; Ateres Zekeinim; Shulchan Gavoa 511:6; M"B 511:9; Kaf Hachaim 511:25

face, hands and feet in hot water, even if the water was heated before Yom Tov.[684] It is likewise forbidden for him to shower his entire body simultaneously, even if the water was heated before Yom Tov.[685] [However, to shower one's entire body one limb at a time, seemingly remains permitted if the water was heated before Yom Tov. Our bathtubs today have the status of a bathhouse.[686]]

Heating water on Yom Tov for bathing purposes: It is permitted for one to heat water on Yom Tov for the sake of washing one's face, hands and feet[687] [or in a time of need, other limbs, so long as it is minority of one's body[688]].[689] [This applies even if the water in not drinkable.[690]] It is however forbidden to heat water on Yom Tov for the sake of bathing one's entire body.[691] According to some Poskim[692], this latter prohibition is only Rabbinical.[693] According to other Poskim[694], this latter prohibition is Biblical.[695] [This applies even today.[696] Nonetheless, even according to this opinion, there are cases in which heating the water for bathing the entire body is only Rabbinically forbidden.[697] Some of the ramifications between these opinions is regarding a) Benefiting from the water if one transgressed and heated the water; b) If one may asking a gentile to heat the water in a time of need; c) Heating the water for the sake of an ill person.[698]]

Turning on the hot water faucet:[699] It is permitted to open the hot water faucet on Yom Tov, so long as it does not cause an automatic ignition of gas or electricity to heat up the water in the boiler [i.e. automatic boiler].

B. Showering with <u>cold</u> water:[700]

The Sages did not decree against bathing in cold water on Shabbos [or Yom Tov[701]] and it is thus permitted to do so from the letter of the law.[702] Nevertheless, the custom in the Ashkenazi provinces is to

---

[684] The reason: This is due to a decree that one may come to heat up the water on Yom Tov [i.e. Gzeiras Habalanim]. Even minority of the body is forbidden due to a decree that one may come to bathe his entire body. [M"B 511:9; Kaf Hachaim 511:25 and 27]

[685] Admur ibid; Beis Yosef in name of Ran ibid; Shulchan Gavoa 511:6; Mamar Mordechai 511:3; M"B 511:16; Kaf Hachaim 511:26

Other opinions: It is permitted for one to shower in the outer room of the bathhouse [Beis Hachitzon] with water that was heated before Yom Tov. [Poskim ibid]

[686] See Piskeiy Teshuvos 511:4

[687] Tzaruch Iyun as to the exact measurement of area one's hand and feet that may be bathed. [SSH"K 14 footnote 23 in name of Rav SZ"A]

[688] Conclusion of Kaf Hachaim 511:14

Background: Some Poskim rule it is permitted to heat water on Yom Tov to bathe any limb, so long as it is minority of one's body. [Michaber Y.D. 199:6; Implication of Rosh, brought in Beis Yosef 326; Rashba Shabbos; Noda Beyehuda Tinyana 25; Machazik Bracha 511:3; Shaareiy Teshuvah 511] Other Poskim however rule one may not heat water to bathe the other limbs of the body, and the allowance is limited to the face, arms and feet. [Shach Y.D. 199:12 in name of Masas Binyamin 5; Aruch Hashulchan 511:6] The Kaf Hachaim ibid concludes to only be lenient in a time of need

[689] Admur 511:1; Michaber 511:2 [hands]; Beis Hillel Mishneh Beitza 21b [feet]; Rambam 1:16 and in Pirush Hamishneh; Kol Bo 58; Rokeiach 299; Levush 511; Beis David 290; Shulchan Gavoa 511:2; Biur Hagr"a; Bigdei Yesha; Kaf Hachaim 511:12

The reason: As since extending a fire was permitted for the sake of eating, therefore, it was also permitted for even other non-food needs, so long as it is a Yom Tov need. Therefore, it is permitted to heat up a little bit of water on Yom Tov for the sake of bathing with one's face, arms and feet. [Admur ibid and 495:3; Beis Yosef 511] Alternatively, the washing of the face, arms and feet is considered a matter of equal necessity to all people, and therefore is permitted under the pretense of Lechol Nefesh Yeiaseh Lachem. [Rashba Avodas Hakodesh 3:4; Kaf Hachaim 511:10]

[690] Rashba Avodas Hakodesh 3:4; Rabbeinu Yerucham; Elya Raba 511:3; M"B 511:8; Kaf Hachaim 511:10

[691] Admur 511:1; Michaber 511:1; Rambam 1:16

The reason: See next that it is disputed as to whether the prohibition is Biblical or Rabbinical.

[692] 1st opinion in Admur ibid; Ran in opinion of Rif; Rambam ibid; Shita Mekubetzes Beitza ibid in name of Ritva

[693] The reason: As Biblically, since extending a fire and cooking was permitted for the sake of eating and drinking, therefore, it was also permitted for bathing on Yom Tov. [Admur ibid]

[694] 2nd opinion in Admur ibid; Rama 511:2; Tur 511; Tosafos Shabbos 39b; Rosh 3:8 in name of Riva

[695] The reason: As the bathing of the entire body is not a need of every person, but rather only for the pampered and spoiled, and the Torah only permitted doing work even for the sake of food, if the work is the need of every person. If, however, it is only needed by the pampered, then it is forbidden to do on Yom Tov. [Admur ibid; Beis Yosef 511 in name of Tosafos ibid; Taz 511:2; M"A 511:4]

[696] SSH"K 14 footnote 21; Beir Moshe 8:159; Piskeiy Teshuvos 511:5

[697] Such as if one places all the water on the fire in one shot, and intends to use the water to also wash his hands feet and legs. [Admur ibid in parentheses]

[698] See Kaf Hachaim 511:13

[699] Piskeiy Teshuvos 511:7

[700] Admur 326:1 and 6; Michaber 326:1; Shabbos 40a

[701] Piskeiy Teshuvos 511:7

[702] Water in a vessel: It is permitted to do so even if the cold water is within a vessel. [Setimas Haposkim that only prohibit the hot springs that are within a vessel and not cold water; Implication of M"A 326:8]

Other opinion: Some Poskim rule it is forbidden to bathe in cold water that is in a vessel. [Mordechai, brought in M"A ibid]

avoid doing so being that there are many bathing restrictions involved which people are not aware of.[703] [However, if one is bothered by the heat or the perspiration, then he is allowed to shower in cold water.[704]]

C. Warm water:[705]
Whenever it is permitted to shower one's entire body in cold water, it is permitted to use even warm water for this purpose.[706] Warm water is defined as water which is below body temperature, and its heat is not felt in it, as explained in Q&A
Turning on the hot water faucet: It is permitted to turn on the hot water tap in order to achieve warm water in a shower, so long as it does not cause an automatic ignition of gas or electricity to heat up the water in the boiler [i.e. automatic boiler].

D. The restrictions one must beware of when showering on Yom Tov:
Whenever it is permitted for one to bathe or shower on Yom Tov, one must beware of the following matters:
1. Not to squeeze one's hair.[707]
2. Not to swim in the water, if entering a Mikveh or river.
3. Not to splash away debris in the water.

Summary:

Hot shower: It is forbidden to take a hot bath/shower on Yom Tov. This applies even if one is using water that was heated before Yom Tov. However, if the water was heated before Yom Tov, one may shower one limb at a time, even if he ends up showering his entire body in this method. One, however, may not bathe even minority of his body in the bathtub, and only showering is permitted. If the water was heated on Yom Tov, it may only be used to wash one's face, hands and feet, and in a time of need, other limbs of the body, so long as it is minority of the body in total, and one does not immerse the limb in a bathtub.

Cold/warm shower: One may shower the entire body in cold, or lukewarm, water if one feels extreme

---

[703] Admur 326:6; M"A 326:8; Bach; Maharil 139; Terumos Hadeshen 255; Beis Yosef Y.D. 199; M"B 326:21

Other opinions and Sephardic custom: Some Poskim rule that today the custom has spread to allow bathing in cold water. [Olas Shabbos 326:16] Accordingly, some Sephardic Poskim rule it is permitted to bathe in cold water. [Or Letziyon 2:35-2; Implication of Rav Poalim 4:12 and Y.D. 15 regarding a shower, however see Yaskil Avdi 6:1 who is stringent] Practically, each community is to follow his custom. [Kaf Hachaim 326:25 and 31] This custom is omitted by the Michaber and Rama, although is mentioned by the Beis Yosef ibid

When does the custom apply? Admur ibid writes "Due to that not everyone knows to beware in all the below mentioned matters, therefore the custom spread in these provinces to not bathe at all on Shabbos." From this wording it is implied that only when all these suspicions are applicable are we accustomed to avoid bathing, however from the concluding wording of Admur "therefore the custom spread in these provinces to not bathe at all on Shabbos, not even with cold water" it is implied that the custom spread to all cases. Perhaps this is because the main worry which brought about this custom is that one may come to squeeze the hair, and so writes Beis Yosef and M"B ibid; However see Ketzos Hashulchan 133 footnote 8 that the decree only applies when all the suspicions are applicable.

[704] Ketzos Hashulchan 133 footnote 8 [towards end]; Igros Moshe 4:74; Beir Moshe 6:73; Dvar Yehoshua 2:54; Az Nidbaru 1:61; SSH"K 14:1; Piskeiy Teshuvos 326:8; Shabbos Kehalacha 18:40; Minchas Yitzchak 6:32 implies that one may not bathe in cold water even to cool off, and may only do so for the sake of a Mitzvah, such as to use a Mikveh, however he then concludes by bringing the Ketzos Hashulchan ibid who is lenient.

The reason: Being that in any event from the letter of the law it is allowed, and it is only a custom to be stringent, and in a case of pain this stringency need not be kept. [Poskim ibid]

[705] Piskeiy Teshuvos 511:5

[706] Supplement from Mahadurah Basra chapter 259 Page 884 in the new Shulchan Aruch regarding water heated before Shabbos, and the same would apply here to water heated on Yom Tov, which has the same status as before Shabbos; Chacham Tzevi 11 who forbids for women to immerse in water on Shabbos that is called hot, rather it must be cold or slightly warm; Nodah Beyehudah Tenyana Orach Chayim 24 that women may bathe in warm Mikvaos but not hot Mikvaos; Aruch Hashulchan 326:3; P"M 511 M"Z 5; Ashel Avraham Buchach 326; Tehilah Ledavid 326:3; Minchas Shabbos, brought in Ketzos Hashulchan 133 footnote 1; Shevisas Hashabbos Mevasheil 125; M"B 326:7; Igros Moshe 1:126; SS"K chapter 14 footnote 3; Piskeiy Teshuvos ibid; Shabbbos Kehalacha ibid;

Other Poskim: Some Poskim rule that it is forbidden to bathe in warm water just like hot water [Beis Meir Y.D. 197:3; Rambam brought in Biur Halacha; However the M"B himself 326:7 writes that bathing in warm water is allowed [for Mikveh]. Some however write that in truth the M"B holds that only water in which some coldness is felt is allowed, and it is by this warmth that he allows to bathe, however water which its heat is felt is forbidden as writes the Rambam, as he brings in Biur Halacha. [Az Nidbaru, brought in Piskeiy Teshuvos 326:2].

[707] 326:6

discomfort by the heat. If one is not in a state of discomfort, he may not shower in even cold water, just as is the law on Shabbos.

Q&A

What is defined as warm water as opposed to hot water?[708]

There is room to learn from Admur, and the Poskim[709], that so long as the water is less than Yad Soledes, then it is not considered hot and is thus allowed. Practically, however, the Poskim[710] rule that even less than Yad Soledes is considered hot[711], and so long as the water is warmer than body temperate [37 Celsius; 98.6 F], or its heat is felt in it, then it is forbidden to bathe in it, just like hot water. Others[712] however write that since the measurement of hot water is not recorded, it most likely refers to all waters that people call hot, [and not necessarily to water that is above or below body temperature].

Is water that was heated on its own on Yom Tov [i.e. solar boiler, or electric boiler on timer] defined as water heated before Yom Tov?[713]

Some Poskim[714] rule that water which became heated on its own on Yom Tov has the same status as water that was heated before Yom Tov, and it is hence permitted for one to bathe one's entire body in such water one limb at a time. Other Poskim[715] rule the water is defined as heated on Yom Tov, and it is hence only permitted to bathe minority of one's limbs in such water. Practically, one may not bathe majority of one's body in such water, even if he does so one limb at a time.[716]

---

[708] See Shabbos Kehalacha 18:29; Piskeiy Teshuvos 326:1 and footnote 14

[709] Regarding water heated on Shabbos Admur 326:4 mentions "even if it will not be heated to Yad Soledes", implying that before Shabbos only water that is heated to Yad Soledes is forbidden. [Ketzos Hashulchan ibid]; See Shabbos Kehalacha ibid 18 Tosefes Biur 1

[710] Tehilah Ledavid 326:3; Ketzos Hashulchan 133 footnote 1 in name of Minchas Shabbos; Minchas Yitzchak 4:44; Or Letziyon 2:35-3; See SS"K chapter 14 footnote 3; Piskeiy Teshuvos 511:4-6; Nitei Gavriel 31:7 based on Tehilah Ledavid 326:3

[711] As the Rashba explicitly writes that people do not generally bathe in hot water that is above Yad Soledes.

[712] Aruch Hashulchan 326:3; This ruling is also found in the Chacham Tzevi 11 who forbids for women to immerse in water on Shabbos that is called hot, rather it must be cold or slightly warm; Zera Emes 71

[713] See Piskeiy Teshuvos 326:2 and 511:5

[714] Tehilah Ledavid 326:3 regarding water heated by the sun; See also regarding water placed on a fire before Shabbos: Rav Akiva Eiger on M"A 326:4; Setimas Harishonim; SSH"K 14:3 in name of Rav SZ"A; Final position of Shevet Halevi 3:33; 4:31; 7:32; Shabbos Kehalacha 18:34; Piskeiy Teshuvos 326:2; See Shabbos Kehalacha 18 Biurim 5

[715] See Admur 326:4 that even if the water was heated Biheter on Shabbos it has the status of heated on Shabbos; Implication of Admur in Supplement from Mahadurah Basra chapter 259 Page 884 in the new Shulchan Aruch regarding solar heated water; Implications of M"B 511:12; SSH"K 14 footnote 17 and so concludes Piskeiy Teshuvos 326:2 and 511:5

[716] So is the ruling of Admur ibid; Piskeiy Teshuvos 511:5

Yoreh Deah

------------------*Kashrus-Hashgacha's*----------------

1. Does baby formula require a Hashgacha?[1]

It is forbidden to feed non-Kosher food to a child, even one day old.[2] Baby formula, which serves as an alternative to breast milk, contains various Kashrus concerns including, non-Kosher milk and non-Kosher animal products which is used to create the vital nutrients necessary for the infant.[3] Accordingly, one is to beware to only purchase baby formulas under a reliable Hashgacha. This applies towards all baby formula's, whether dairy or soy. In the past, there were no dairy baby formula's available with a Hashgacha, due to the inability to produce the Chalav Yisrael milk powder. Today, there are various companies which carry a Mehadrin Chalav Yisrael Hashgacha for dairy formula, such as Materna [Eida Hachareidis]; Similac [Iggud Harabanim-Westheim]; Kendamil [Kadasia UK]. Other dairy formulas are available under an OUD Hashgacha and are not Chalav Yisrael.

What to do in a case that there is no alternative? In a case that there is no Mehadrin formula available[4] and there is no alternative food that the baby can be fed, then the infant may consume non-Chalav Yisrael baby formula that is under Rabbinical supervision [such as OUD]. If there is no formula available under Rabbinical supervision which the infant can consume, then the infant may be given even non-Kosher formula, in the situation that no other proper food alternative is available.[5] In such a case, it is also best to mix the formula with an edible but bitter substance, if the infant is willing to consume it.[6] In all cases, when using non-Kosher formula, one is to designate separate utensils for its use, and is not to use these utensils with other Kosher foods. Likewise, one is to monitor as to when using the formula no longer becomes necessary, or an alternative option becomes available.[7]

---

[1] See Hakashrus 8:23-24; Hakashrut Kehalacha [Edry] 45:26 [p. 421]

[2]

[3] Non-Kosher milk: One of the major ingredients in baby formula is powdered milk, as well as powdered Casein which is a protein product found in milk. In the past, Casein was only produced in Chalav Akum plants. Both the powdered milk and Casein face the issue of Chalav Akum. According to some Poskim, powdered milk does not contain a prohibition of Chalav Akum [Har Tzevi Y.D. 113; Rav Yosef Mashash in Otzer Hamichtavim 3:1392; Shearim Hametzuyanim Behalacha 38 in name of Zekan Aaron; Tzitz Eliezer 16:25; Yalkut Yosef 81:14] while according to other Poskim it does contain a prohibition of Chalav Akum. [Chazon Ish Y.D. 41:4; Teshuvos Vehanhagos 1:141; 2:373; Rav Mordechai Eliyahu in Mamar Mordechai 1:155; See Avnei Nezer 103; Divrei Yisrael] In addition, the powdered casein is extracted through the use of an enzyme or rennet which in many instances is a non-Kosher animal derivative, hence entering the prohibition of Gevinas Akum. [See Hakashrus ibid footnote 24 that Casein is not available in Chalav Yisrael plants and that it is derived from the whey of the milk which is subject to dispute into whether it carries the prohibition of Chalav Akum.]

Non-Kosher animal products: Since infant formula is designed to emulate mother's milk, it must contain a source of fat, protein, amino acids, vitamins, minerals, sugar, and other micronutrients. Fatty acids that are ideal for infant nutrition may be of animal origin. Vitamins may come from non-Kosher fish or from animal organs. Micronutrients can be derived from an array of non-Kosher sources. All may be found in infant formula. Reading the label" is a very inadequate means of ascertaining the Kosher status of an infant formula, since potentially non-Kosher ingredients may be listed in a seemingly inconspicuous manner, or, as a trace ingredient. For example, beef fat is commonly referred to as "oleo," and "natural vitamins" may be obtained from non-Kosher fish oil.

[4] Such as one who is stuck in an area without Kosher baby formula, and there are no alternative options of feeding available. Or, one whose doctor instructed the child to have a specific type of formula which does not contain a Kashrus supervision.

[5] Hakashrut Kehalacha [Edry] 45:26 [p. 421]

The reason: As a) This may lead to Sakana. and b) There are various Halachic disputes associated with the Kashrus status of the ingredients, and possibly, at the very most it would only be a Rabbinical prohibition [such as Chalav Akum, Gevinas Akum, animal products are nullified in 60x], of which some Poskim rule may even initially be fed to a child if he is in need of it, even if he is not in danger. However, in such a case, it is best to have it done through a gentile. [See Admur 343:6]

[6] Making a food bitter and inedible removes its non-Kashrus status from a Biblical level, and is only forbidden Rabbinically due to Achshavei, which would not apply to a sick person or infant without eating alternative. [See Rambam Yesodei Hatorah 5:8 "Or he is fed something that has a bitter substance mixed with the non-Kosher food"; Rama Y.D. 155:3; Yad Avraham Y.D. ibid; Admur 442:22 and 30; Kaf Hachaim 554:34; Hakashrus 21:12]

[7] Hakashrut Kehalacha [Edry] 45:26 [p. 421]

----------------*Basar Bechalav*----------------

2. What makes a food Fleishig-Must one wait six hours after eating a Pareve food that was cooked in a meat pot or that came into contact with meat:[8]

If Pareve food was cooked in a meat pot it is permitted to eat dairy products after eating that food without waiting at all. There is no custom to be stringent. [This applies even if the pot is Ben Yomo.[9] One is not even required to wash his hands or clean his mouth prior to eating dairy.[10] One may even eat the food in the same meal as actual dairy, without needing to recite Birchas Hamazon beforehand.[11] However, if the pot was Ben Yomo one may not eat the food with actual dairy.]

If the pot was dirty with meaty leftovers:[12] Even if the pot was not washed well and contained some leftover meat when the Pareve food was cooked inside it, one does not need to wait six hours prior to eating milk products [and one is also not required to wash his hands or mouth or to recite an after blessing beforehand[13]], although one may not eat this food with dairy products.[14] [Some Poskim[15], however, rule that this only applies if the food contains 60x versus the meat, and there is no meat taste felt in the food. Other Poskim[16] rule that this applies even if the food did not have 60x the meat.[17] Even in their opinion, however, this only applies if there is very small amount of meat fat or gravy in the food, while if there is a large amount, then one must wait six hours.[18] Likewise, it only applies if one does not eat any actual meat.[19] Likewise, this only applies if one did not intentionally leave the meat in the pot to be mixed with the Pareve food, however if one purposely did so then he needs to wait six hours.[20] However, some Poskim[21] are lenient even in the case that one intentionally added a small amount of meat. In all cases, one is to clean and wash his mouth prior to eating dairy.[22]]

Summary:
Pareve food that was cooked in a meat pot one does not need to wait six hours prior to eating dairy. This applies even if the pot contained a small amount of leftover meat gravy/fat, in which case although it may not be eaten together with dairy, one does not have to wait six hours prior to eating dairy. However, in such a case, one should clean and rinse his mouth prior to eating dairy. If the pot

----

[8] Rama 89:3; Darkei Moshe 89:6; Beis Yosef O.C. 173

[9] Pashut as otherwise there is no novelty in the Rama, and so is evident from Shach 89:19.

[10] Elya Raba 173:4; Birkeiy Yosef 89 Shiyurei Bracha 34; Zivcheiy Tzedek 89:38; Kaf Hachaim 89:61

[11] See Birkeiy Yosef 89 Shiyurei Bracha 24; Zechor Leavraham 3 Y.D. 54:2; Zivcheiy Tzedek 89:39; Kaf Hachaim 89:62

[12] Shach 89:19; Bach 89; Minchas Yaakov on Toras Chatas 77:13; Peri Chadash 89:19; Beir Heiytiv 89:11; Lechem Hapanim 89:24; Beis Lechem Yehuda 89:15; Orach Mishar on Darkei Moshe ibid, brought in Darkei Teshuvah 89:42; Zivcheiy Tzedek 89:36; P"M 89 S.D. 19; Pischeiy Teshuva 89:7; Chochmas Adam 40:13; Aruch Hashulchan 89:13; Kitzur Shulchan Aruch 46:10; Kaf Hachaim 89:59; Igros Moshe Y.D. 2:26; Kitzur Yalkut Yosef 89:37 [Yalkut Yosef p. 426]

Other Opinions: Some Poskim rule that if the pot had leftover meat, one is required to wait [a full 6 hours] prior to eating dairy. [Elya Raba O.C. 173:4; Elya Zuta 173:3]

[13] See Poskim in Kaf Hachaim 89:61-62

[14] The reason: As since there is a very minute amount of meaty leftover inside, and one has no intent to eat and simply does not want to bother to clean it, therefore the Sages did not decree that one must wait six hours. [Yad Yehuda Pirush Haruch 89:5, brought in Darkei Teshuvah ibid]

The proof: The Rama states that one does not have to wait 6 hours after eating Pareve foods cooked in a meat pot. The source of this statement is in the Beis Yosef ibid. Now, if the Rama and Beis Yosef were referring to a case that the pot is clean, there is no novelty at all in this ruling, as according to the Beis Yosef it is even permitted to eat it with actual dairy. Hence, one must conclude that the case refers to a dirty pot, in which case the food may not be eaten with dairy, but nevertheless one does not need to wait six hours. [See Shach ibid; P"M 89 S.D. 19; Yad Avraham 89]

[15] Beis Lechem Yehuda 89:15; brought in Pischeiy Teshuvah and Darkei Teshuvah ibid; Megadim Chadashim 89:5; Yad Yehuda Pirush Haruch 89:5; Zivcheiy Tzedek 89:36; Ben Ish Chaiy Shelach 2:12 [rules to wait one hour if there isn't 60x and one who waits 6 hours is blessed]; Kaf Hachaim 89:59

[16] Yad Avraham 89 and 95; Pischeiy Teshuva 89:7; Aruch Hashulchan 89:13

[17] The reason: As otherwise what would be the novelty of the ruling of the Rama. [ibid] As the entire issue of waiting six hours according to Ashkenazi ruling is a Minhag, and there is no custom to wait six hours after such a case. [Aruch Hashulchan ibid; See Darkei Moshe ibid]

[18] Orach Mishur ibid, and Yad Yehuda ibid, brought in Darkei Teshuvah; See there that it is implied that only when there remains a little bit of fat in the pot did the Shach/Bach rule that waiting is not required, while if there is a large amount of fat/gravy, or actual meat, then one must wait.

[19] So seems Pashut; See Darkei Teshuvah ibid

[20] Yad Yehuda ibid, brought in Darkei Teshuvah ibid

[21] Pischeiy Teshuvah ibid

[22] Ben Ish Chaiy ibid

contained a large amount of meat gravy, or one ate actual pieces of meat, he must wait six hours.

Q&A

If a dirty meat spoon was used to mix a Pareve food, must one wait six hours?

➢ Example: One used a spoon that was used to mix chicken soup to mix or serve the rice/spaghetti that was cooked as Pareve in a meat pot. Must one wait six hours?

No. [If, however, one sees pieces of meat in his food and eats them, he is to wait six hours.]

If one placed Pareve spaghetti in a pot that contains a small amount of meatball sauce, must he wait six hours?

If one did so intentionally, so the spaghetti gain taste of the sauce, then he must wait six hours irrelevant of the amount of sauce added. If he did so simply due to lack of desire to clean the pot, then if the amount of sauce was minute, he is not required to wait six hours.

If one deep fried falafel or French fries in oil that was used to deep fry chicken, must one wait six hours prior to eating dairy?
Yes.[23]

-------------------*Machalei Akum*----------------

3. The Prohibition of Pas Akum and its reason:[24]

The Sages forbade eating bread [and other grain bakery products] of the gentile nations, as a precaution against intermarriage.[25] [This prohibition is referred to as Pas Akum. The Sages did not completely prohibit the consumption of gentile bakery products and rather restricted its allowance, only permitting it with the fulfillment of certain criteria, such as Jewish involvement in the baking process, as will be explained in future Halachos. The reason behind this prohibition is because partaking in the meal of a gentile induces closeness and friendship, which can lead to intermarriage. The reason the Sages forbade specifically their bread is because the bread is the main staple of the meal.]

The law if the suspicion of intermarriage is inapplicable: The above prohibition, against eating the baked grain products of a gentile, applies even if there is no suspicion that one may come to intermarry with the gentile's family.[26] Thus, even if the gentile is not married and does not have any children, and even if he is a priest who opposes marriage and will never have children, his baked products remains forbidden.[27] Even if the gentile is still a child, and even if he is physically incapable of having children, the prohibition remains.[28] Even the baked grain products of a gentile king and aristocrat are forbidden, even though the King will certainly not allow his family to marry with a Jew.[29] Even if the gentile is not an idol worshiper the bread is forbidden.[30]

Pas Paltar-Bakery bread of a gentile: This will feature IY"H in a future Halacha.

---

[23] Such a food is considered a Tavshil Shel Basar and hence requires one to wait if chewed or swallowed.

[24] 112:1; Mishneh Avodah Zara 35b

[25] Michaber ibid; Gemara ibid 36b "The Sages decreed against their bread and oil due to that this leads to drinking their wine, and they decreed on their wine due to it leading to intermarriage, and idol worship"

[26] Rama ibid; Rashba 248; Shach 112:4; Taz 112:1; Peri Chadash 112:4; Erech Hashulchan 112:2; Chochmas Adam 65:1; See Kaf Hachaim 112:9

[27] Shach 112:4

The reason: As even if he does not have any daughters, certainly he has friends with daughters, and the intermingling with the childless gentile can lead to intermarriage with one of his friend's daughters. [Shach ibid in name of Rashba] Alternatively, the reason for this prohibition is due to a Lo Pelug. [Taz 112:1]

[28] Kaf Hachaim 112:9 in name of Rashba ibid

[29] P"M 112 M"Z 1; Kaf Hachaim 112:10

[30] P"M 112 S.D. 2; Peri Tohar 112:3; See Mateh Yehonason 112

When was the decree against Pas Akum and Bishul Akum first initiated?[31]
The decree against Pas Akum was instituted in the times of the Tannaim.

The Kabalistic reasons:
The Ben Ish Chaiy[32] comments that although the bread of a gentile is prohibited due to a Rabbinical decree, in truth, this prohibition contains deep and mystical meaning. The Arizal[33] was very careful to avoid eating Pas Akum even if there was a mere doubt if it was Pas Akum.

---

3. What types of bakery products are prohibited due to Pas Akum?

A. Which grains of bread need to be Pas Yisrael? Must gluten free bread be Pas Yisrael?[34]

Only breads [or baked Mezonos products] that are made of the five grains [oat, spelt, wheat, barley, and rye] are forbidden due to Pas Akum.[35] However, bread made of legumes or rice [or potatoes] is not included in the prohibition of Pas Akum.[36] Nevertheless, legume bread falls under the prohibition of Bishul Akum and thus is only permitted to be eaten if the legume bread is not fit for a kings table.[37] Some Poskim[38], however, argue that legume bread is never fit for a kings table, and is hence never forbidden neither due to Pas Akum or Bishul Akum.[39] [Practically, all bread, irrelevant of the type of grain that it is made from, must contain a Hashgacha to verify that it contains only Kosher ingredients.[40] Thus, there is no extra leniency associated with gluten free bread, and a Hashgacha is required. However, regarding whether it must be baked by a Jew, while non-Mehadrin Hashgacha's would not be particular in this matter[41], a Mehadrin Hashgacha is to make sure that it is baked by a Jew even if it is made of grains that do not derive from the five grains listed above. Those who keep a Mehadrin Kashrus standard are certainly to be stringent in this matter.[42]]

Is low quality grain bread which is not served on a kings table forbidden due to Pas Akum?
Some Poskim[43] rule that low-quality breads made from the five grains which are not served on a kings table, are nevertheless forbidden due to Pas Akum. Other Poskim[44] however rule that such breads are permitted, just as is the law regarding Bishul Akum.

---

[31] Taz 112:4

[32] Chukas 2 Hakdama

[33] Shaar Hakavanos Hakashrus 19 footnote 9

[34] Michaber Y.D. 112:1; Rosh 19:21, brought in Tur 112:1; Rabbeinu Yerucham 17:7

[35] Michaber ibid

The reason: As these foods are considered of significance and bring towards closeness amongst people. [Taz 112:2]

[36] Michaber ibid

[37] Rama ibid

[38] Bach 112; Rabbeinu Yerucham Nesiv 17:7; Tur; Levush, brought in Shach 112:5 and Taz 112:3; Ben Ish Chaiy 2 Chukas 1

[39] The reason: Although actual cooked legumes is considered Bishul Akum, as it is served on a kings table, nevertheless its bread is not considered Bishul Akum being that the bread is not served on a kings table. [Ben Ish Chaiy ibid]

[40] There are various ingredients that bakeries enter into their bread which can be of Kashrus concern, and at times be explicitly not Kosher, such as: 1) Non-Kosher oils that derive from animals which are entered into the dough or placed to grease the pan 2) Hafrashas Challah if owned by a Jew; [See https://www.kashrut.com/articles/bread/; https://oukosher.org/blog/behind-the-scenes-theoretical-kashruth/the-local-bakery/]

[41] As a) Non-Mehadrin Hashgacha's are not particular to require that bread baked by a gentile bakery [I.e. Pas Paltar] be Pas Yisrael, and b) Non-Mehadrin Hashgacha's are generally lenient with their definition and inclusion of "Eino Rauiy Al Shulchan Melachim," and hence in this case may rely on the dissenting opinion who argues on the Rama

[42] As a) The Rama rules that it is fit for a kings table and b) Perhaps today even the dissenting opinion would agree that it is fit for a kings table, as times have changed, and gluten free bread is served today by many fancy caterings.

[43] Peri Megadim 112 M"Z 3

[44] Avnei Nezer Y.D. 1:92-7 based on Shach

B. Dough of a gentile:[45]

The dough of a gentile is not considered Pas Akum, as the prohibition of Pas Akum only applies towards <u>baked</u> products of a gentile. [Thus, all dough products that are sold, may be made by gentiles and do not require any Jewish intervention within the processing of making the dough.]

Q&A

If the dough was made by a Jew but was baked by a gentile, is it forbidden due to Pas Akum?[46]
Yes. The bread is forbidden due to Pas Akum, unless there was some Jewish intervention in the baking process, such as turning on or raising the flame or entering the bread into the oven.

Is yeast of a gentile forbidden due to Pas Akum?
No. The yeast of a gentile is not forbidden due to Pas Akum, even if it was made from gentile baked products.[47] Nevertheless, it requires a reliable Hashgacha, as yeast can be derived from various sources, some of which are not Kosher.

C. Mezonos products:

Pas Akum or Bishul Akum: The prohibition of Pas Akum extends towards Mezonos products.[48] Nevertheless, the Poskim[49] explain that this only applies towards Mezonos products that can become Hamotzi upon setting a meal over them [as will be explained], however other Mezonos products, do not retain the Pas Akum prohibition, but rather the Bishul Akum prohibition. Those Mezonos products which are forbidden due to Pas Akum, are not also forbidden due to Bishul Akum and hence they retain all the leniencies and stringencies attributed to Pas Akum. The other Mezonos products however receive all the leniencies and stringencies of Bishul Akum.

Mezonos foods which can become Hamotzi:[50] All baked Mezonos products that are made from one of the five grains, and require a Hamotzi and Birchas Hamazon if one were to set a meal over them, fall under the prohibition of Pas Akum and not Bishul Akum. These products receive all the leniencies [and stringencies[51]] attributed to Pas Akum, and hence in those places that are accustomed to be lenient to eat Pas Akum [of a gentile bakery] may do so by these products as well [so long as their ingredients are certified as Kosher, and so long as they are not filled with foods that contain a prohibition of Bishul Akum[52]]. A Mezonos food can only become Hamotzi upon setting a meal over it if it is made of dough that is baked, such as Pas Haba Bekisnin, as explained in Orach Chaim chapter 168 regarding the laws of blessings.[53]

Mezonos foods which cannot become Hamotzi:[54] All Mezonos products that remain Mezonos even if one were to set a meal over them, do not fall under the category of Pas Akum but rather of Bishul Akum. The laws of Bishul Akum will be explained in the next chapter. A Mezonos food always remains Mezonos

---

[45] Shach 112:1 that so is the implication of Michaber and Rama throughout the chapter; Rambam and Rashba brought in Beis Yosef; Toras Chatas 75:2 in name of many Achronim; Chachmas Adam 65:5; Hakashrus 19 footnote 9
<u>Other opinions</u>: Some Rishonim rule that the dough of a gentile also contains the prohibition of Pas Akum, and it hence must be made with Jewish involvement. [Ran, brought in Beis Yosef and Shach ibid]
[46] P"M 112 S.D. 1
[47] Beis Yosef 112; Taz 112:10; Beir Heiytiv 112:14
[48] Rama 112:6 regarding pastries such as honey cake and Kichlich; Michaber 112:6 regarding the Infanda/Pashtida, however to note that the Infanda is Hamotzi if made from real dough.
[49] Taz 112:6; Shach 112:18; Toras Chatas 75:12; Beis Yosef 12 in name of Rav Yechiel; Peri Chadash 112:17; Beis Lechem Yehuda 112:11; Kaf Hachaim 112:35; See Hakashrus 19:2
[50] Taz 112:6 based on Rama 112:6 which mentions that Lekach and other sweet pastries have a prohibition of Pas Akum; Shach 112:18; Toras Chatas 75:12; Beis Yosef 12 in name of Rav Yechiel; Peri Chadash 112:17; Beis Lechem Yehuda 112:11; Kaf Hachaim 112:35; See Hakashrus 19:2
[51] Such as that even if they are unfit for a kings table, it is forbidden.
[52] See Q&A
[53] See also Seder Birchas Hanehnin chapter 2
[54] Based on Poskim ibid; Rivash 28; Peri Chadash 112:17; Beis Lechem Yehuda 112:14; Kaf Hachaim 112:36

even upon setting a meal over it if it is a cooked product, such as cooked dough, or a Mezonos food that was made from a very thin batter[55], as explained in Orach Chaim chapter 168 regarding the laws of blessings.[56]

Summary:

All baked Mezonos products that can become Hamotzi upon setting a meal over them fall under the prohibition of Pas Akum, both for leniency and stringency. All Mezonos products that can never become Hamotzi even if one were to set a meal over them, fall under the prohibition of Bishul Akum, both for leniency and stringency

List of foods which fall under the prohibition of Pas Akum:[57]
1. Pretzels
2. Bread crumbs
3. Croutons
4. Crackers
5. Biscuits
6. Cookies
7. Mezonos cereals
8. Malawah baked by a gentile
9. Jachnun baked by a gentile

Pastries:

Baked pastries that do not contain stuffing's of other foods fall under the prohibition of Pas Akum and not Bishul Akum. Thus, those who are accustomed to eating Pas Akum bakery products, may eat these products made by a gentile baker, so long as their ingredients are certified as Kosher.

Sufganiyot:[58]

Sufganiyot are deep fried and hence fall under the prohibition of Bishul Akum and not Pas Akum. Thus, Kashrus agencies must ensure that their Sufganiyot follow the standards required for Bishul Yisrael, such as having a Jew light the flame or [according to the Sephardim[59]] enter the Sufganiyot into the oil.

Are pastries and casseroles that are stuffed with food forbidden due to Bishul Akum?

Although all Mezonos products that can become Hamotzi are under the laws of Pas Akum, nevertheless, if the Mezonos contains stuffing of food, those foods are subject to the laws of Bishul Akum].

Are baked Mezonos foods that are first cooked and then baked, such as soft pretzels and bagels, considered Pas Akum or Bishul Akum?[60]

Such foods are subject to the laws of Pas Akum.

---

[55] Shach 112:17; Beir Heiytiv 112:9; Rivash 28; Peri Chadash 112:17; Beis Lechem Yehuda 112:14; Kaf Hachaim 112:36; See however in Sefer Hakashrus 19 footnote 14 that R. Moshe Shternbuch in Teshuvos Vehanhagos 3:248 rules Mezonos foods that are baked very thin can be considered Pas Akum and not Bishul Akum.

[56] See also Seder Birchas Hanehnin chapter 2

[57] Birkeiy Yosef 112 Shiyurei Bracha 9; Kaf Hachaim 112:38

[58] Rivash 28; Peri Chadash 112:17; Beis Lechem Yehuda 112:14; Birkeiy Yosef 112:11; Kaf Hachaim 112:36 and 43; Sefer Hakashrus 19 footnote 14

[59] Michaber 113:7; Birkeiy Yosef ibid; Kaf Hachiam 112:43; See Yechaveh Daas 5:53

[60] Igros Moshe Y.D. 2:33

Mezonos morning cereals:
All Mezonos cereals are subject to the laws of Pas Akum rather than Bishul Akum. Non-Mehadrin Hashgachas [OU; OK and others] provide their Hashgacha despite that the product is not Pas Yisrael, under the leniency associated with Pas Paltar [industrial bread of gentile]. Those who are particular to eat Pas Yisrael even by industrial products [Pas Paltar] are to only purchase morning cereals that contain a Mehadrin Hashgacha.

-----------------*Kashrus-Kashering*-----------------
4. Must new pots or pans be Kashered or contain a Hechsher?

In the manufacturing process of cookware, it is common for an oil based primer and/or polish to used. Occasionally, this polish/primer is made from non-Kosher animal fats, and hence enters the cookware into the question of whether it is permitted to be used without Kashering.

The ruling: Many Poskim[61] rule that based on the current way that the non-Kosher oil is applied, there is no need to Kasher new pots, pans, or aluminum cookware, even if one knows for certain that a non-kosher based oil was used as a primer or polish during the manufacturing process.[62] However, other Poskim[63] rule stringently that the pot requires Kashering. Some[64] say the pot requires Hagalah, while others[65] suffice with Iruiy Keli Rishon. [The above reflects the current known method of pot manufacturing. In the event that cookware manufactures change how the oil based polish is used, then this will also affect the law, whether for leniency or stringency.[66]]

The custom:[67] The widespread custom is not to require new cookware to be Kashered. However, in certain areas, such as Eretz Yisrael, many are accustomed to be stringent.[68] It is for this reason that there exists cookware, and aluminum pans, with Rabbinical certification. The Hashgacha of Rav Landau in Bnei Brak is accustomed to Kasher all new cookware and cutlery.

Cast iron cookware: Cast iron cookware which is preseasoned, may only be used without Kashering if one verifies that a Kosher [non-animal based] oil was used for the seasoning. If one is unsure, and certainly if he knows for certain that it was seasoned using a non-Kosher oil, then the pot must be koshered prior to use.[69]

---

[61] Minchas Yitzchak 4:112; Tzitz Eliezer 12:55; Mishneh Halachos 7:112; Yabia Omer 1:7; Rivivos Efraim 6:212; The laws of Pesach [Blumenkrantz] p. 3-73; Rav Shmuel Furst in name of Rav Moshe Feinstein; See Koveitz Mibeis Levi 1:32; Avnei Yashpei 2:58 in name of Rav Elyashiv; Halichos Shlomo Moadim 2

[62] As the heat of the manufacturing process is so great that it would burn any possible non-Kosher fat. [The pot is commonly entered into an oven that is 500 degrees Celsius.] Furthermore, the fat is not edible even in its original state, as it is mixed with other items, and is hence deemed Nosein Taam Lepegam. [Poskim ibid]

[63] Mishmeres Shalom Yoreh Deah 121:12; Chazon Ish Moed 44; Har Tzevi Y.D. 110; Teshuvos Vehanhagos 1:422; Moadim Uzmanim 4:282; Kinyan Torah 4:92; See Seridei Eish 2:35; Rav Eli Landau Shlita informed me, based on directives of his brother, the Chief Rabbi of Bnei Brak and head of the Landau Hashgacha, that all new cookware must be Kashered, including spoons, forks, cups, and especially pots and pans. The reason for this is because they use hot non-Kosher animal oils to compress and polish the items, and some specifically use lard for this process.

[64] Har Tzevi ibid; Chazon Ish ibid; Rav Wozner, Rav Elyashiv hold even for those who are stringent, it suffices to do Hagala on the inside; Rav Landau ibid; Regarding if Libun or Hagala is required when an item absorbs non-Kosher liquid directly, see Shach 121:8 in name of Rameh Mipuno 96; Rav Akiva Eiger 121; Aruch Hashulchan 121:11

Teflon: Rav Landau related to me that Teflon coated pans that have suspicion of having a non-Kosher oil primer placed under the Teflon coating, it requires Libun Kal, and hence is not Kasherable.

[65] Tzitz Eliezer ibid regarding those who desire to be stringent

[66] Minchas Yitzchak ibid

[67] Mishneh Halachos 7:112; The laws of Pesach [Blumenkrantz] p. 3-73

[68] Piskeiy Teshuvos 451:4; Kashrus Manual of the Eida Hachareidis;

[69] The reason: The seasoning that is added to a cast iron pot is very different than the polishing/premier added to regular pots, as a) The seasoning is not entered into a libun level oven which cures the pot and burns any of the Issur, and b) The seasoning is edible for a human and is not Pagum. [See Kinyan Torah ibid]

How to Kasher a preseasoned cast iron pot: There are several points that require clarification when Kashering such a pot, such as a) Must one first remove all the oil seasoning that is absorbed inside the metal of the pot, through scrubbing it with soap and detergent? b) Does Hagala suffice, or is Libun required. See Shach 121:8 and Rav Akiva Eiger there [concludes with Libun]; P"M 451 M"Z 16 [concludes with Hagalah]. In order to Kasher according to all opinions, the pot is to be Kashered with Libun, and placed through a self clean oven cycle.

5. Leaving a gentile, or non-religious Jew, alone in one's home and how it effects the Kashrus of one's kitchen:[70]

Important note 1-The food in the home: The law below only discusses the issues posed to the kitchen utensils by leaving a gentile alone in one's home. A second severe issue that is relevant, is the status of the open foods left in the home, as all foods which are not properly sealed become Rabbinically forbidden if left in the hands of a gentile. This especially applies to an open meat packet in the freezer, or an open bottle of wine.

**Important note 2-Rentals*: The law below only discusses the case that the gentile, or non-religious Jew, that was left alone in the home is a mere visitor, guest, or maid. However, if the gentile or non-religious Jew rented the home, such as a Tzimmer rental, then all the vessles must be Koshered in all cases, as explained in Q&A.

A. Lechatchila:

It is initially forbidden to allow a gentile [or non-religious Jew[71]] to remain alone with one's eating utensils/vessels due to worry that he may use the vessels to cook non-Kosher foods [either non-Kosher ingredients or meat with milk[72]].[73] This applies even if one plans to not use the vessels again until after 24 hours.[74] This applies whether one desires to leave a vessel in the house of a gentile, or desires to leave a gentile alone in his home.[75] [This applies even if one instructs the gentile not to use the utensils.]

Yotzei Venichnas:[76] If one is coming in and out of the house constantly, then it is permitted to leave the gentile alone in one's home even initially.

Leaving a gentile at home while food is cooking: One is to be stringent not to leave pots [of cooking food] with one's gentile maid, if no Jews will remain at home.[77] If, however, one is constantly coming in and out of the house, than one may do so, as stated above.[78] If, however, the maid knows that one will be gone for quite some time, such as he will be leaving to go to Shul and the like, one should be stringent.[79]

B. Bedieved:[80]

Important note: This law of Bedieved only applies in a case that the gentile or non-religious that was left alone in the home is a mere guest or maid. However, if the gentile or non-religious Jew rented the home, such as a Tzimmer rental, then all the vessles must be Koshered, as explained in Q&A.

---

[70] Michaber/Rama Y.D. 122:9; Mordechai Perek Ein Mamidim, quoted in Taz 122:8; Igros Moshe Y.D. 3:61

[71] See Q&A!

[72] Igros Moshe Y.D. 3:61

[73] Michaber ibid; Mordechai ibid

[74] Rama ibid; Shach 122:8; Taz 122:8

[75] Michaber Y.D. 122:9 regarding bringing to house of gentile; Rama ibid that the same applies to leaving a gentile in one's home *"And initially one is to be careful in all cases even regarding maids and slaves in ones home, that our vessels should not remain with them as they amy come to use them with not Kosher food"*; Mordechai ibid likewise mentions both cases; See Igros Moshe Y.D. 3:61 who even regarding bedieved treats the latter case the same as the former

[76] Shach 122:9 that so is custom today being that one may even initially rely on Yotzei Venichnas; Rama 118:12 brought next

[77] Michaber 118:12; Tur in name of Rosh Kelal 19:18; Vetzaruch Iyun why the Poskim here make no mention of the discussion of Bedieved in 122:9; Perhaps one can say there is a difference between one's maid working in one's house [the case here], in which we are always lenient Bedieved, and a case where one sends his item to the gentile's house [the case in 122]. Vetzaruch Iyun. See coming footnotes in Bedieved.
The reason: As she may cook non-Kosher food in it. [Shach 118:37]

[78] Rama ibid

[79] Shach 118:37 in conclusion of opinion of Rama in Tur and Rosh ibid

[80] Rama Y.D. 122:9

Other opinions: Some Poskim rule that the entire issue of not leaving one's vessel entrusted with a gentile is only initially, while Bedieved, it may be used at all times. [Implication of Michaber 118:12 and 122:9 who simply writes "Yeish Lehachmir and Yeish Lizaher" and so learns Aruch Hashulchan 122:18 in Michaber] The reason for this is because "Lo Machzakinan Issura" for a mere Chashash. [See Aruch Hashulchan 122:20]
Is there a difference between if one left the vessel by the gentile's home or left the gentile in one's home alone regarding Bedieved? The Michaber and Rama ibid entirely deal with a case that one brought his vessel to the house of a gentile, and only in the end does the Rama conclude that one is to be stringent Lechatchila even when leaving a maid in one's home. This seems to imply that they have different laws Bedieved. If correct, this would explain why in 118:12 no mention is made in Poskim regarding Bedieved, as is done here. See also Taz ibid and Mordechai ibid who seem to differentiate and say that in the Jews home, we do allow the Sfeik Sfeika to permit using the vessel after 24 hours. However, see Mordechai ibid who concludes even by knives in Jews home "Venachon Lehachmir." See also Igros Moshe ibid who makes no differentiation between the cases and applies the Bedieved ruling of here to a case where a gentile was left in one's home for some time. Vetzaruch Iyun!

Within 24 hours: If one transgressed, and left a gentile alone with his vessels, then he may not use his vessels [with hot foods] until the passing of slightly more[81] than 24 hours from when the vessel was first left by the gentile.[82] If one transgressed and cooked food in the vessel within 24 hours, the food is forbidden.[83] Some Poskim[84], however, are lenient in a time of need, while others[85] forbid the food in all cases.

After 24 hours: After slightly more than 24 hours have passed [since it was first left alone with the gentile], the vessels may be used as usual [even with a Davar Charif[86]].[87] [Thus, if the gentile was left alone in the home starting from 10:00 am that morning and remained there until 7:00 pm, then it may be used again starting from 10:00 am the next morning and one is not required to wait until 7:00 pm the next day.] Certainly, it may be used after 24 hours have passed since he retrieved the vessel from the gentile [i.e. 7:00 pm].[88] Some Poskim[89] however rule that if one left the vessels with the gentile Bemeizid, then the vessels are forbidden even after 24 hours and either must be Kashered [i.e. metal] or broken [i.e. earthenware]. If, however, the vessels were left with the gentile by mistake, then one may be lenient after 24 hours if the vessel is not Kasherable, while if it is Kasherable it is to be Kashered.[90] [Practically, if one left the vessels with the gentile Beshogeig and 24 hours passed since one retrieved the vessels, one may be lenient to use them without Kashering.[91]]

---

[81] As it takes time for the gentile to cook his food, and hence, enough time must pass for one to be able to question whether 24 hours has passed since his first use. [See Rama ibid who directly implies this] However, see Shach ibid whose wording is "If it stayed by the gentile for 24 hours.."; See Mahariy Bruno 27, brought in Darkei Teshuvah 122:40 "Stayed by gentile for two days"

[82] Rama ibid; Shach 122:8; Taz 122:8; Mordechai ibid
The reason: So long as 24 hours have not passed since the gentile could have possibly used the vessel, then there is only one doubt, which is that perhaps he used it and perhaps he did not. [Rama ibid] Alternatively, we assume the gentile used it, and it is not considered a doubt at all. Nevertheless, what is a doubt is whether he used it for a food that is Pogem or not. [Taz 122:8 in negation of Ram's doubt; Mordechai ibid]

[83] Rama ibid; Taz ibid
The reason: As there is only one Safek, perhaps he cooked food in it or perhaps he didn't, and by a Biblical doubt one must be stringent. [Rama ibid] Alternatively, we assume for certain that he cooked in it, and the doubt is whether he cooked a Davar Pogem or not. [Taz ibid; Mordechai ibid]

[84] Rama ibid based on Svaras Atzmo; Poskim brought in Darkei Teshuvah 122:40; Aruch Hashulchan 122:20 and that so is implied from Shach ibid
The reason: As one can argue that even here there is a Sfek Sfeika: a) Perhaps he did not cook in it at all, and b) Even if he did, perhaps he cooked a Davar Pogeim. [Poskim brought in Darkei Teshuvah 122:40; See Taz ibid] Alternatively, as the entire matter is a mere Chashash, and thus Bedieved, Lo Machzikinan Issura. [Aruch Hashulchan 122:20]

[85] Taz ibid; Mordechai ibid; Aruch; Beis Lechem Yehuda 122:9, brought in Darkei Teshuvah 122:40

[86] Chamudei Daniel Taaruvos 7, brought in Darkei Teshuvah 122:42, that so is implied from Setimas Haposkim
The reason: As perhaps the non-Kosher food that was cooked is Pegam in the new food. [ibid]

[87] Rama 122:9 as explained in Shach 122:8 and so is final ruling of Shach ibid; Reah; Toras Chatas 59:4; Taz 122:8 regarding if left by gentile Beshogeg and not Kasherable
The reason: As within the 24 hours there is only a single Safek; whether he used the vessel for non-Kosher or not. [Rama ibid] This doubt is a Biblical doubt. However, after 24 hours from the time it began staying with the gentile, it is a Sfek Sfeika, as a) Perhaps he did not use it at all and b) Even if he did, perhaps he used it 24 hours ago and it is no longer Ben Yomo. Now, throughout the entire Torah we permit Sfek Sfeika even by a Biblical prohibition. [Implication of Rama ibid; See Taz ibid] Alternatively, we assume that he definitely used the vessels for non-Kosher food and the Sfeik Sfeika is as follows: a) Perhaps 24 hours have passed since he used it and b) Even if used within 24 hours, perhaps it was used with a Davar Pogeim. [Taz ibid based on Mordechai ibid]
Other opinions: Some Poskim rule one may not use the vessel even after 24 hours, and hence if made of metal it must be Kashered, while if made of earthenware it must be destroyed. [Implication of Mordechai, brought in Taz ibid; Implication of Issur Viheter, brought in Shach ibid; Bach 122 and 137] Some Poskim rule it is never permitted until 24 hours pass from the time it was retrieved from the gentile. [Chesed Leavaraham Kama Y.D. 40, brought in Darkei Teshuvah 122:40]

[88] See Chesed Leavaraham Kama Y.D. 40, brought in Darkei Teshuvah 122:40, who establishes the case of allowance to be only when 24 hours pass since retrieving from the gentile, as perhaps he used it towards the end of the day. See also Igros Moshe ibid
The reason: As now we know for certain that 24 hours have passed since a last use and the entire doubt is only Rabbinical, as after 24 hours the taste is Pagum and is only Rabbinically forbidden. Now, by a Rabbinical doubt we rule leniently. [See Shach 122:8 in name of Maharash Mebonburg]
Other opinions: The above stringent Poskim are stringent even in this case, as no differentiation is made. Seemingly, the reason is as suggests the Taz ibid, that we never allow one to initially rely on a Safeik.

[89] Taz 122:8; Other Poskim who are stringent after 24 hours [but make no distinction of Shogeg/Meizid: Implication of Mordechai, brought in Taz ibid; Implication of Issur Viheter, brought in Shach ibid; Bach 122 and 137
Is there a difference between if one left the vessel by the gentile's home or left the gentile in one's home alone? See Taz ibid and Mordechai ibid who seem to differentiate and say that in the Jews home we do allow the Sfeik Sfeika to permit using the vessel after 24 hours. However, see Mordechai ibid who concludes even by knives in Jews home "Venachon Lehachmir"

[90] The reason: As we never allow one to initially rely on a Sfek Sfeika [or Safeik Derabanan]. [Taz ibid]

[91] Igros Moshe Y.D. 3:61

Vessels not commonly used for hot foods and law of cups:[92] The above requirement to wait 24 hours only applies to vessels that are commonly eaten with hot foods [of a Keli Rishon[93] or vessels that are used to drink wine[94]]. However, those vessels that are not commonly used with hot foods [of a Keli Rishon, and are not used to drink wine] may be used even within the 24 hours, so long as they are properly washed. [Accordingly, only pots, pans and serving spoons that are commonly used with a Keli Rishon or Iruiy Keli Rishon must be delayed 24 hours prior to use. However, forks, spoons, and knives, and the like that are only commonly used for a Keli Sheiyni, or for cold, may be used even right away.[95] Cups that are designated for use of drinking wine, such as wine glasses[96], must be Kashered even after the passing of 24 hours.[97]]

Leaving the vessel by the gentile for short amount of time:[98] The above law only applies if the vessels remained in the home with the gentile for a considerable amount of time, such as half a day, however if it remained there for a mere hour, the vessels may be used as usual.

Summary:
It is forbidden to leave one's eating utensils, cookware, or food that is in the midst of cooking, in the care of a gentile [or a non-religious Jew], unless one is entering and exiting the area constantly. If one accidently did so [and the gentile was a mere visitor or guest, and not a renter], then all vessels that are commonly used with hot Keli Rishon foods are not to be used until after 24 hours. Vessels that are only commonly used with cold or Keli Sheiyni foods are permitted to be used right away. Vessels that are designated to be used to drink or store wine, may not be used even after 24 hours, until they are Koshered. All open foods that require seals when left with a gentile become non-Kosher.

Practical application with maids:
Based on the above, all those who have gentile maids who work at home must beware to never leave the maid alone in the house for a long period of time, in a way that is not defined as "entering and exiting constantly." Thus, by a family outing, the maid is to come with them. Likewise, during the day hours when the parents are out at work and the children are out at school, the maid is not to be employed or be allowed to remain in the home. Accordingly, employing a gentile live-in-maid poses a serious Kashrus challenge, and may not be done if the parents both work and the children are in school, as there is no one who remains with her at home.

Q&A
May one leave eating utensils alone with a non-religious Jew?
A Jew who is known to desecrate Shabbos in public is considered like a gentile for all matters and is hence to be treated like a gentile regarding the above law.[99] It is thus forbidden to leave him/her alone in one's home with one's Kosher kitchen unless a Jew is constantly coming in and out of the house.

---

[92] Shach 122:8 [towards end]

[93] Aruch Hashulchan 122:20

[94] See Rama 136:1; Tur 136; Shach 122:8; Taz 122:8

[95] Aruch Hashulchan 122:20

[96] See Y.D. 135:1 that by Yayin Nesech even glass vessels can absorb and require Koshering; Vetzaruch Iyun regarding Kiddush cups as gentiles don't usually know that they are designated for wine.

[97] Rama Y.D. 136:1 that it must be Kashered if no Chosem; Tur 136; Shach 122:8 and 136:3
The reason: Although it is not possible for the vessel to absorb wine in such a short amount of time, nevertheless, it may not be used until it is Kashered being the Sages considered a temporary stay of the vessel by the gentile, as if it had stayed there permanently. [Shach ibid; Tur ibid; Beis Yosef 136] Accordingly, we are only stringent in this case that the vessel was in possession of the gentile, although if he simply drank wine from it in front of us, the vessel does not need to be Kashered. Furthermore, perhaps this stringency of wine cups only applies if one sends it to a gentile, and not if one left a gentile in one's home. Vetzaruch Iyun
Other opinions: Some Poskim rule one may use the cup after 24 hours. [Bach 122 and 136, brought in Shach ibid] Other Poskim rule it does not need to be Kashered at all, and may be used even within 24 hours. [Beis Yosef 136 in name of Ran Avoda Zara 39a in name of Reah, in name of Ramban]

[98] Rama ibid; Mordechai in name of Rabbeinu Tam; See Shach 122:8; Taz 122:7

[99] See Michaber 119:7 that such a Jew is like a gentile for all matters and is hence Chashud for everything; See also Michaber Y.D. 2:5 and Admur Shechita 2:10; Regarding a Jew who keeps Shabbos but eats non-Kosher: See Michaber 119:3 that one who is Chashud to eat Treif is not Chashud to steal Treif; See Rama 1181 and Shach 118:16

Bedieved, if one transgressed and left him in the home alone, it follows the same law as a gentile being left alone in the home in which case all the vessels are permitted after 24 hours, and vessels commonly used with cold are permitted even within 24 hours. Regarding cups, seemingly one may be lenient even within 24 hours.[100]

If one rented his home or Tzimmer to a gentile, or non-religious Jew, what is the status of the vessels?[101]
In such a case, all the vessels must be Koshered, and the leniency of waiting 24 hours does not apply.[102]

May one do a home swap with a gentile or non-religious Jew?[103]
One may not do so, due to the Kashrus issues stated above. If one did so, then the kitchen and its utensils must be Koshered, as it contains the same status of a home rental, as stated above.

May one do a home swap with a religious Jew who follows different Hashgacha's or Kashrus standards?[104]
Yes. However, if they plan to make use of the kitchen, then one should instruct them as to the Hechsheirim that they can use. For example, if a Sephardi is home swapping with an Ashkenazi, then the Ashkenazi should be forwarned not to cook any Chadash grain products, or any meat that is no Glatt Kosher. Likewise, one who does not eat Heter Mechira during the Shemita year is to instruct the family accordingly.

If one has a home video surveilince system [i.e. CCTV] may a gentile or non-religious Jew be left there alone?[105]
It is only valid if all the following conditions are fulfilled:
a) The gentile or non-religioius Jew is aware of the video surveilince.
b) The gentile or non-religioius Jew is made aware that they do not have permission to use the kitchen utensils.
c) The Jew will look at the surveilince video.

------------------*Tevilas Keilim*----------------
6. Must one immerse electrical appliances?[106]
Electrical appliances which are used to cook food, and come in direct contact with food, are obligated in immersion in a Mikveh with a blessing. This includes toasters[107], sandwich makers, water urns and the like.

---

[100] The reason: As many Poskim hold a Michalel Shabbos of today does not make wine Yayin Nesech.

[101] Heard from Harav Yaakov Yosef z"l

[102] The reason: This is not similar to the case mentioned above where the gentile did not have permission to use the vessels as he wishes, in contrast to here where the gentile has become a temporary owner of the vessels and was able to use it for whatever he wishes. It is thus no different than purchasing a vessel from a gentile, in which the law is that it must be Koshered.

[103] Heard from Harav Yaakov Yosef z"l

[104] Heard from Harav Yaakov Yosef z"l

[105] See Koveitz Or Yisrael 65 pp. 61-70; and Netiv Hachalv and Sefer Ohel Yaakov Yichud p. 146

[106] Igros Moshe Y.D. 1:57; 3:24; Chelkas Yaakov 1:126; 2:62-3; Minchas Yitzchak 2:72; Shevet Halevi 2:57-3; Beir Moshe 4:100; 7:57; Kinyan Torah 4:90; Sharaga Hameir 4:105; Mishneh Halachos 9:162; Teshuvos Vehanhagos 1:450; Rav SZ"A in Sefer Tevilas Keilim p. 185; Hakashrus 4 footnote 88; Kashrus Halacha Lemaaseh p. 275-277

Other opinions: Some say that since electrical appliances are plugged into the ground, they therefore do not require immersion. [So rules Rav Asher Lemel Hakohen and other Rabbanim; Rav Yaakov Yosef] The Poskim ibid negate this opinion.

[107] Beir Moshe 4:100; Mishneh Halachos 9:162; Teshuvos Vehanhagos 1:450; Rav SZ"A in Sefer Tevilas Keilim p. 185; Hakashrus 4 footnote 88; Kashrus Halacha Lemaaseh p. 275-277

Other opinions: Some Poskim rule a toaster does not need to be immersed, as it is not a table vessel [Klei Seuda] and is not a true cooking vessel being the bread is already edible prior to the toasting. [Igros Moshe 3:24; Rivivos Efraim 4:405]

How to immerse and avoid damage: One is to fully immerse the item, and not use it for at least 24 hours in order to give it time to dry.[108] One may also choose to disassemble the item, and immerse only the parts that come in contact with the food and require Tevila [such as the grates of a toaster, and knives of a blender].[109]

Other alternatives: If immersing the vessel will damage it, then there remains only one other alternative, and that is to give it to a Jewish professional take it apart and reassemble it.[110] It does not suffice for one to give it to a gentile as a present and borrow it back from him for permanent use.[111]

7. Circumventing the need to Toivel-Giving a vessel to a gentile and then borrowing it back:

Vessels that are borrowed or rented from a gentile do not require immersion.[112] Accordingly, in a case that one is unable to immerse a vessel in a Mikveh, such as on Shabbos or in an area without a Mikveh, he can give the vessel to a gentile and then borrow it back and use it without immersion.[113] However, this only helps to allow one to use the vessels without immersion on temporary basis. It is however forbidden to use the vessels permanently without immersion, even though they are considered borrowed from the gentile. He is to thus immerse the vessel without a blessing [or immerse it together with a vessel that requires a blessing[114], or acquire it back from the gentile and immerse it with a blessing[115]] in a Mikveh at his first opportunity.[116] [See Q&A for how long one has]

How to give the gentile the vessels as a gift-Which Kinyan must be done?[117] When a gentile is given a present from a Jew, according to all it suffices for him to carry the object in order for a valid acquisition to take place. [Accordingly, every person who has a gentile adjacent to him and the vessel, can perform the above acquisition with the gentile by simply giving him the vessel and placing it into his hands and then borrowing it back.] If, however, one sells him the item, then additional Kinyanim are needed and it is only to be done through a Rav who is expert in this field. [Thus, if one does not have a gentile adjacent to him and must thus do the acquisition over the phone, and the like, then a Rav is to be contacted. *See our Sefer "The Laws & Customs of Pesach" Chapter 5 Halacha 6 for the full details of this subject!*]

Tevilas Keilim under Quarantine:
Due to the coronavirus breakout many individuals in many different countries are unable to immerse their new vessels either due to quarantine laws or due to the closing of the Mikvaos. This poses a dilemma especially prior to Passover when it is commonly accustomed to purchase new vessels in honor of the festival. In Halacha, there exists a precise solution for this situation, to temporarily circumvent the need to Tovel the vessel in a Mikveh. This is done through giving the vessels to a gentile as a gift and then borrowing them back, as stated above.

---

[108] Kinyan Torah 4:90; Beir Moshe ibid
[109] See Hakashrus Kehalacha chapter 35 in name of Rav Mordechai Eliyahu
[110] Beir Moshe 4:100; Tevilas Keilim 4:16 in name of Rav SZ"A
[111] See Admur 323:5; Taz Y.D. 120:18
[112] Michaber Y.D. 120:8
[113] Michaber Y.D. 120:16 and Admur 323:8 regarding Shabbos; Rama 120:16 that so applies even during the week in an area without a Mikveh; Mordechai Beitza Remez 677
Other opinions: Some Poskim question this allowance to give a vessel as a present to a gentile and then to take it back, as this is not a true acquisition to the gentile and is rather Harama. Additionally, it is forbidden to give a present to a gentile. [Rashbash 468; Pischeiy Teshuvah 120:15] See M"A 13:8 and Yeshuos Yaakov 13:4 who invalidate this option regarding Tzitzis Vetzaruch Iyun as to why they allow it regarding Tevilas Keilim
[114] Taz Y.D. 120:18; M"B 323:35; Ketzos Hashulchan 146 footnote 6 that this applies even according to Admur, and the reason Admur did not state this explicitly is because he is dealing with a case that one only has this vessel to immerse.
[115] Ketzos Hashulchan 146 footnote 6
[116] Admur ibid; Taz O.C. 323:6; Y.D. 120:18; Chelkas Binyamon 120/133
The reason: One cannot use the vessel forever on the basis that it belongs to a gentile as when an item remains forever in the hands of the Jew it is similar to him having acquired it. Furthermore, it is similar to a borrowed Tallis which requires Tzitzis after 30 days being that after 30 days it appears as if it belongs to him. Based on this it should be immersed even with a blessing. Nevertheless, since I have not found the matter explicitly ruled in Poskim I am hesitant to rule this way, and rather one should immerse another vessel that requires a blessing together with it. [Yoreh Deah Taz 120/18]
Other opinions: Some Poskim rule it is not necessary to immerse the vessel. [Kneses Hagedola 120]
[117] Admur 448:9

Q&A

For how long may one retain the "borrowed" vessel of the gentile without it requiring immersion?

As stated above, the vessel is to be immersed at its first opportunity. This applies even if the vessel is still within 30 days of the borrowing.[118] From some Poskim[119] it can be understood that the maximum limit for this is 30 days, and hence after 30 days, even if the opportunity has still not risen, it becomes forbidden to use the vessel. Practically, however, one may continue to use it even after 30 days so long as a Mikveh has not yet become available.[120]

Does it help to be Mafkir the vessels and then take it back from Hefker without intent to acquire?[121]

No.[122] Nonetheless, some Poskim[123] suggest that in a time of need one can be Mafkir the vessel by throwing it into a public area and declaring it Hefker and then take it back with intent to not acquire it. [Practically, one should not rely on this opinion.]

Where to find a gentile to perform the sale:

Not everyone has a gentile available to perform the above-mentioned acquisition. One should try calling his local rabbi or Kashrus organizations to see if he has set up with a gentile the above procedure of acquisition. Otherwise, one could do so online for a small fee, using the Israeli Tzomet organization's sale. The following is the link for their website https://tickchak.co.il/10922/form/tickets. Another possibility is to do so through the Montreal Beis Din using the following link https://mk.ca/mechiras-keilim-form/

---

[118] Taz ibid "This Takana is only temporary, meaning for that Shabbos, or on a weekday so long as a Mikveh is not available."; Implication of Admur ibid who instructs to immerse the vessel after Shabbos.

[119] See Taz ibid who brings a proof regarding Tzitzis that it can only be used without Tzitzis for up to 30 days, from which some Rabbanim understand that past 30 days the allowance become void. Regarding the 30 day period of Tzitzis see: Admur 14:4; Michaber 14:3; Menachos 44a

[120] Setimas Haposkim; See Taz ibid who explicitly writes that one can use it until a Mikveh becomes available, and does not give a time limit of 30 days. His later statement regarding the 30 day period for Tzitzis was simply used as a proof for the idea that one cannot use it forever. As for the difference between Tevilas Keilim versus Tzitzis, one can possibly explain that only by Tzitzis did the sages give a 30-day limitation, while by Tevilas Keilim they did not, as tying Tzitzis to the garment is more feasible then finding a Kosher body of water to immerse the vessels in. See the wording in Admur 14:4 *"As after thirty days it appears that the garment belongs to the person, and hence the Sages decreed that it is to have Tzitzis tied to its corners.";* So is also evident from the fact that the M"A 13:8 invalidates the ability to lend the Tzitzis to a friend even though he agrees to the ability to do so by Tevilas Keilim, as he explicitly writes, hence proving a difference between the two and therefore one cannot recruit rulings from Hilchos Tzitzis to that of Tevilas Keilim. Vetzaruch Iyun.

[121] See Minchas Shlomo 2:66-16; Regarding the ability to not acquire something even though it is in your property by having explicit intent to not acquire it, see: Admur 448:5 [that it helps remove liability]; M"B 448:6; Chok Yaakov 448:8; Mahariy Mintz 82; Mahariy Asad 83; Hamakneh; Beis Meir Sireideiy Eish 2:26; Kaf Hachaim 306:47

[122] Setimas Kol Haposkim; Maharil Diskin Kuntrus Achron 5-136 p. 79; P"M 13 A"A 8 "To make it Hefker was not given as an option as he requires it when he takes it"

The reason: The Shulchan Aruch does not offer this as an option and simply offers the option of giving the vessel to a gentile as a present, as stated above. Seemingly, this is because such an option would be invalid being that he requires it when he takes it, and at the very least it appears as if he has acquired it, and indeed he has total intent to keep the item. [See P"M ibid; Minchas Shlomo ibid]

[123] Rav SZ"A in Minchas Shlomo ibid; See also M"B 13:15; Artzos Hachaim 13; based on advice of brother of M"A

------------------ *Sakana*----------------

8. Closing off the window or door of a room/home:[124]

One may not completely [and permanently[125]] close off a window or door, being that demons use openings to enter and exit and hence closing it off can lead to danger. Rather one must leave a small hole in the area. [The custom is to place a hollow tube, such as a tin can, that is open from both ends within an area of the window or door, and the remaining area may then be sealed.[126] So was the ruling of the Tzemach Tzedek.[127]]

Q&A

How large of a circumference must the remaining hole contain?
From the letter of the law, a hole of any size suffices.[128] However, the Rebbe Rayatz records that the custom is for the hole to have a circumference of 1.5 Tefach, which is 12 centimeters.[129]

May one cement, paint over the remaining hole [i.e. the open ends of the tube]?[130]
Yes. The hole may be covered over by a plug, thin layer of cement, paint, and the like, so long as the hole remains hollow inside, and one is able to easily remove the covering, if he so wishes.

May one completely seal off a door or window if there is another exit adjacent to it?[131]
No.[132]

May one close [not seal] a window or door if he plans to leave it closed for a very long time?[133]
Yes.

May one seal a window or door if he leaves the window/door frames intact?
Some[134] write this is allowed.

May one demolish a building and then rebuild a new project with different areas of windows and doors?
Sefer Chassidim[135] writes that his warning applies even in such a case, and hence one must be careful not to change the areas of the doors and windows, and to rebuild all the doors and windows that

---

[124] Tzavah Yehuda Hachassid 20; Sefer Chassidim 461; 1146; Teshuvos Upesakim Chachmaei Ashkenaz Tzarfat 83; Brought in: Kneses Hagedola Y.D. 179:10; Beis David C.M. 2:95; Yosef Ometz 37; Ikarei Dinim 8:40; Zivcheiy Tzedek 116:78; Ben Ish Chaiy Pinchas 2:17; Kaf Hachaim 116:122; Shivim Temarim 23 p. 60; Mila Dechasidusa 461; Makor Chesed 461; Igros Kodesh Rebbe Rashab 1:159 and 174 [printed in Shut Toras Shalom Halacha 36-37]; Igros Kodesh 13:296; 15:346 [printed in Shulchan Menachem 4:27-29]; Shemiras Hanefesh p. 15; Shemiras Haguf Vihanefesh p. 219; Shevet Halevi 6:111

[125] However, one may completely close off an opening for temporary basis, such as to close a window or door of a room, even if he plans to leave it closed for a very long time.

[126] Igros Kodesh Rebbe Rashab 1:159 [printed in Shut Toras Shalom Halacha 36]; Shivim Temarim 23 p. 60; Shemiras Hanefesh p. 15; Igros Kodesh 13:296; 15:346 [printed in Shulchan Menachem 4:27-29]; Shevet Halevi 6:111

[127] Igros Kodesh Rebbe Rashab 1:159 [printed in Shut Toras Shalom Halacha 36]; Shivim Temarim 23 p. 60; Igros Kodesh 13:296; 15:346 [printed in Shulchan Menachem 4:27-29]

[128] Tzava ibid "a small hole"; Yosef Ometz ibid "Any size hole"; Shivim Temarim 23 p. 60 in name of Yosef Ometz; Ben Ish Chaiy ibid "any size hole"; Mila Dechassidusa "By leaving some hollow area.."; Toras Yekusiel Kama 15; Shemiras Hanefesh p. 15; See Sefer Beis Chayeinu 770 p. 277 that the Rebbe directed to leave a hole the size of a needle

[129] Igros Kodesh Rayatz 9:385, brought in Igros Kodesh 13:296 [printed in Shulchan Menachem 4:27-29]

[130] Igros Kodesh Rebbe Rashab 1:159 [printed in Shut Toras Shalom Halacha 36] "May cover with cement"; Shivim Temarim 23 p. 60 "May cover with a plug"; Igros Kodesh Rayatz 9:385 "After it is plugged, it is painted over"; Igros Kodesh 13:296; 15:346 [printed in Shulchan Menachem 4:27-29]; Shevet Halevi 6:111

[131] Sefer Chassidim 461; 1146

[132] The reason: As angels and demons only have permission to use a specific exit. [See Shivim Temarim ibid]

[133] Shivim Temarim 23 p. 60

[134] Shivim Temarim ibid; Shemiras Hanefesh p. 15; Koveitz Mibeis Levi 7:44; However see Beis Chayeinu ibid

[135] Sefer Chassidim 461

existed in the first building. Nevertheless, the custom is not to be stringent in such a case and rather the doors and windows are rebuilt in whatever manner one desires.[136]

May one install an air-conditioning unit into his window?
Yes, as there remains some empty space that is not covered over.

------------------*Machalei Sakana*----------------
9. Mayim Shenisgalu-Liquids that were left uncovered:[137]

The letter of the law: Liquids that were left uncovered [without supervision[138], for even a very short amount of time[139]] were forbidden by the Sages to be consumed [or used[140]] due to worry that perhaps a snake entered venom into the liquid [and one will come to drink it and die].[141] [This prohibition applies to all liquids, including wine.[142] The prohibition applies whether the liquid was left uncovered during the day, or during the night.[143]]

The custom today: Today, being that snakes are no longer commonly found in inhabited area, it is permitted to drink liquids that remained uncovered.[144] It is thus no longer accustomed to be careful in this matter.[145] [However, some Poskim[146] rule that even today one is to avoid drinking liquids that were left uncovered.[147] Certainly in those areas in which poisonous snakes are commonly found, it is forbidden from the letter of the law even today to drink liquids that were left uncovered.[148] Due to this, some Poskim[149] rule one is to be stringent in this matter in Jerusalem, and Eretz Yisrael, and any area that they are slightly found. Each person is to verify how common it is to find poisonous snakes in the homes of one's area, and act accordingly. In any event, in all cases, it is proper to beware from leaving foods and liquids uncovered due to the insects that can enter them and cause one to stumble in eating them.[150]]

[136] Mila Dechasidusa 461; Makor Chesed 461
[137] Michaber Y.D. 116:1; O.C. 272:1; Admur O.C. 272:1; Tosefta Terumos 7:13-19; Avoda Zara 30a-b; Chulin 9b
[138] Tur 116 that a live person who is guarding the liquid will prevent a snake from coming out to drink from it.
[139] Tur 116; Aruch Hashulchan 116:3
Regarding the amount of time that it must be left revealed to be prohibited: Seemingly this includes even a short amount of time, so long as the snake has enough time to reach it and place venom into it.
[140] Tur and Beis Yosef 116 rule the water is not to be spilled in a public area and is not to be given to animals or birds and is not to be used to wash one's floor.
[141] Michaber Y.D. ibid
[142] Admur ibid; Michaber O.C. ibid; Some Poskim rule that this includes honey and even ground garlic. [Perisha 116:2]
[143] Beis Lechem Yehuda 116:1; Poskim in Kaf Hachaim 116:7; See Hakashrus p. 431 footnote 67; So is proven from fact that the Poskim make no differentiation in this matter.
[144] Michaber Y.D. ibid
The reason for this allowance: As the entire prohibition of the Sages was due to the snakes. [Taz 116:1] Now, although, in general, when the Sages make a decree the decree remains in place, even if the reason behind the decree is no longer applicable, until a larger and more scholarly Beis Din nullifies it. Nevertheless, this only applies in decrees that were made due to a reason but not made contingent to the reason, such as the decree not to do Melacha on Erev Pesach due to the Pesach sacrifice. However, in this scenario, the Sages explicitly made the decree contingent to its applicable reason, and hence in a scenario that the reason is not applicable, the Sages initially never decreed against drinking it. [See Tosafos Avoda Zara 35a that at times the decree is not applicable] Water that was left revealed in an area without snakes, is similar to revealed water that was supervised to make sure no snakes entered, in which case it is certainly permitted. [Mateh Yehonason 116:1, brought in Otzer Mefarshim]
[145] Admur ibid; Michaber O.C. ibid; Tur 116; Taz ibid; Levush 116; Peri Toar 116:2; Peri Chadash 116:1; M"B 160:23; Rebbe in Likkutei Sichos 23:35; All Poskim in later footnotes who only require in area that snakes are commonly found
[146] Shlah p. 79 "One who guards his soul is to distance himself from this" [brought in Elya Raba 170:24; P"M 170 M"Z 10; Piskeiy Teshuvah 116:1; Aruch Hashulchan 116:2; Likkutei Sichos 23:35 footnote 32] Custom of the Gr"a who was very careful in this [Maaseh Rav 95, brought in Pischeiy Teshuvah 116:1]; Peas Sadcha 86; The M"B 160:23 holds that there is no need today to be stringent in drinking revealed waters, although there are those who are stringent; Kitzur SH"A 33:5 [To note that in the Kitzur SH"A with the rulings of Admur brought by Rav Bistritzky no mention is made in that Halacha that Admur argues on the Kitzur in that regard.] Tosafos Yerushalayim 116 [brought in Hakashrus ibid] writes based on the Mishneh in Derech Eretz 11 that the nighttime is more severe than the day in this regard and hence all waters that were left revealed, even at night are not to be drunk.
[147] The reason: Seemingly this is due to Ruach Raah. [Peias Hasadeh ibid]
[148] Peri Toar 116:2; Peri Chadash 116:1; Yeshuos Yaakov 116:2; Birkeiy Yosef in Shiyurei Bracha 116:3; Mor Uketzia 170; Aruch Hashulchan 116:2; Kaf Hachaim 116:6
[149] Peri Chadash 116:1 "In all areas that they are even slightly found, such as Yerushalayim, it is proper for every G-d fearing Jew to avoid drinking it"; Birkeiy Yosef ibid that so is the custom today in all Eretz Yisrael
[150] Zivcheiy Tzedek 116:2; Kaf Hachaim 116:9

Wine that was left uncovered: Wine that was left uncovered for some time is invalid to be used for Kiddush, as explained in 272/1.

Summary:

It is permitted to drink liquids that were left uncovered unless one lives in an area that poisonous snakes are commonly found. Some are accustomed to be stringent against drinking uncovered liquids in all cases. In any event, it is proper to beware to cover the liquids in order to prevent insects and the like from entering the food.

Q&A

May one perform Netilas Yadayim with revealed water [in those places that snakes are commonly found, or according to those who are always stringent]? Is one to cover the Negel Vasser water at night prior to going to sleep?[151]

Many Poskim[152] rule there is no need to be stringent against washing hands with water that was left revealed overnight. This applies even in an area where snakes are commonly found.[153] However, there are opinions[154] who are stringent and rule one is to avoid washing with revealed waters. Practically, the custom is to be lenient completely even regarding drinking revealed waters, and certainly regarding using it for washing[155], and so is the apparent Chabad custom.[156] There is likewise no problem to wash hands for bread using revealed waters even in areas that snakes are common.[157]

May pots on the fire be left uncovered [in areas that snakes are commonly found or according to those who are stringent]?[158]

Once the pot has been brought to a boil, or has begun to release steam, it can be left uncovered.

May liquids in the fridge or in a closet be left uncovered [in areas that snakes are commonly found or according to those who are stringent]?[159]

Yes.

What is the law if water that was left uncovered became mixed with other foods/liquids [in areas that snakes are common]?[160]

The liquids are not nullified in 60x.

---

[151] See Hakashrus p. 432; Piskeiy Teshuvos 4:12

[152] Shalmei Tzibur brought in Shaareiy Teshuvah 4:7; Pischeiy Teshuvah Yoreh Deah 116:1; Peri Toar Yoreh Deah 116:2; Birkeiy Yosef 116:4; So is also implied from M"B 160:23; Admur 272:1 rules we are no longer careful regarding revealed waters as snakes are no longer commonly found.

[153] Shalmei Tzibur ibid, as the stringency of not drinking from revealed waters in areas with snakes only applies to drinking and not washing. [Shaareiy Teshuvah ibid; M"B 160:23]; See however Poskim in next footnote that one is to be stringent in those areas that snakes are common, even regarding washing.

[154] Rav Sheptal brought in Shaareiy Teshuva ibid; Seder Hayom: "Every G-d fearing Jew needs to prepare for himself prior to going to sleep two vessels, one that contains water and one that is empty, into which he will pour the water upon awakening. One is to place the water filled vessel into the empty vessel, **covered** and clean."; Chesed Lealafim 4:10; Kaf Hachaim Falagi 8:11; Kaf Hachaim 116:8 and Artzos Hachaim 4:1 that one is to be stringent in those areas that snakes are common [brought in Hakashrus 18:19]

[155] Conclusion of Shaareiy Teshuvah ibid

[156] See Migdal Oz story 114 from which it is proven that it was not an acceptable Chabad custom to cover the waters. This is seen from the fact the servant of the Tzemach Tzedek could not understand why he covered the water, as well as from the fact one Chassid complained to the Rebbe Rashab about the stringencies of another Chassid who followed this ruling of covering the water. Nevertheless, as is evident from the story, this was the custom of the Tzemach Tzedek. However, from his response it is understood that this custom is not meant as a directive for the public.

[157] Levush 160:5; Aruch Hashulchan 160:1; M"B 160:23 [It is implied from there that he rules even regarding washing hands upon awakening there is no need to be stringent]; See however Kaf Hachaim 116:8 that one is to be stringent in those areas that snakes are common.

[158] Tur and Beis Yosef 116; Hakashrus 18:15

[159] Kaf Hachaim 272:9; Hakashrus 18:17

[160] Peri Chadash 116:3; Birkeiy Yosef Shiyurei Bracha 116:5

------------------ *Ribis* ----------------

10. Using check cashing services:

A. Introduction-What is check cashing and what Halachic issue does it face?

Using a Jewish owned check cashing service is, for Halachic purposes, similar to selling a loan to a third party who is Jewish, and follows all the restrictions to be explained [in B]. The difference between cashing a check by a bank versus a check cashing service, is that by a bank, the money is not accredited to one's account until the check is cleared, which often entails collecting the funds from the bank account of the check writer. This is similar to a lender [i.e. the person who owns the check] asking an individual [i.e. the bank] to collect the money from the person who owes him [i.e. the check writers account]. However, by a check cashing service, the client receives cash at the time of the transaction, and in exchange for this cash payment, he signs over the collection of the check to the check cashing Service Company. Thus, in essence, he has sold his check, or his loan document, to the check cashing company. Another difference between a bank and a check cashing service, is that a bank does not take a percentage on the check, and provides the service in exchange for one holding an account with the bank. Now, how does a check cashing service provide income for their business? The check cashing service charges a fixed percentage rate towards the check, and hence on every check they make a certain amount of money. For example, on a $1000 check, a service fee of 3% will give the client $970, while the company will eventually collect $1000. This enters one into the Halachic question regarding Ribis associated with selling a loan for a lower price to a Jew, and clarifying the final Halachic ruling requires a number of introductions. At first, we will explain the general issues of Ribis involved of selling a loan [B], then we will define the status of a check [C] and then finally we will discuss the applicable law of using a check cashing service [D]. These laws must be followed both by the client and by the service owner, if they are Jewish. If either the client or the check cashing company is owned by gentiles, then no restrictions exist.

B. The general rule of selling a loan:[161]

This subject was explained in detail in Volume 1 of our Sefer, under Choshen Mishpat Halacha 4. The following is a summary of what is explained there.

It is forbidden for a Jewish lender to sell a loan to a Jewish third party for a lesser amount, unless the seller relinquishes liability on the payment of the loan.[162] He may however retain liability of the authenticity of the loan and its current unpaid status. A loan given to a gentile may not be sold and the only option is to forgive the loan and have the buyer acquire his rights.[163]

---

[161] Admur Ribis 57; Michaber 173:4; Sefer Haterumos 4:13 in name of Ramban; Rashba 3:261; Yerushalmi 5:1; See Bris Pinchas 17:9-11

[162] Thus, if Reuvein lent Shimon $1000 and the money is due in six months and Reuvein is currently in need of the cash, it is permitted for him to sell the debt contract to Levi for $700, and Levi will collect the $1000 in six months from Shimon, so long as Reuvein is removed from all liability of payment. Hence, if at the conclusion of the six months Shimon has still not paid back the loan to Levi, Reuvein has no accountability towards providing Levi with his money. If, however, Reuvein retains liability for the payment of the debt, such as that in the event that Levi became poor and cannot pay the loan after six months then Reuvein will give Levi the money he is owed, then it is forbidden to sell it for a lesser price than the amount of the loan. Furthermore, it is forbidden to do so even if he will not have to give Levi the money that he is owed on the contract, but will simply have to return to Levi the money which he received from him when he purchased the contract. [Admur ibid; Shach 173:9; Darkei Moshe 173:5]

The reason: As this is a case of "Karov Leschar and Rachok Lihefsed", as the buyer of the contract will for sure gain the original investment back, either from Reuvein or Shimon, and also stands a chance to make more money through having the full amount paid by Shimon. Thus, according to Halacha this is not considered a sale at all but rather a loan, and consequently when the buyer collects the owed funds from Shimon, which is more than the amount which he gave Reuvein the seller, this is considered a profit on his loan [and is complete interest]. [Admur ibid; Taz 176:3; Rashba ibid]

[163] Admur 69; Shach 169:61; Perisha 169:41; Michaber 169:18; Semak 260

Other opinions: Some Poskim rule that if the debt is documented then it may be sold to another even if the debt is owed by a gentile. [Rama C.M. 66:32]

Q&A

May the lender sell his debt for a lesser amount, and retain liability, if the lesser amount is in exchange for the expenses the buyer will entail in collecting the debt [i.e. Sechar Tircha]?[164]

- For example: Reuvein lent $1000 to Shimon, and now desires to sell the debt to Levi with liability. For Levi to collect the debt he will have to travel to Shimon and request the money. May Levi charge Reuvein a $50 fee for collecting the debt, and thus buy the debt from Reuvein for only $950?

Yes.[165]

Shiur of Sechar Tircha:[166] The amount of money that the buyer may diminish from his payment in exchange for the loan must be a set fee irrelevant of when the loan is due. Thus, the buyer may decide to charge the seller 5% for his Sechar Tircha. This charge however must be the same whether the loan is due to be paid immediately, or only in a number of months. If he charges more money for a loan that is not yet due, then it reveals he is not charging Sechar Tircha but rather Ribis for the delay of payment.

C. Definition of a check in Halacha:[167]

Prior to discussing the law of cashing a check by a check cashing service we must first determine the status of a check according to Halacha; is a check considered a loan document, a promissory note, an equivalent to cash payment? The practical ramification regarding Ribis is if the check may be sold for a lesser amount with or without liability. There is a dispute amongst today's Poskim as to the status of a check according to Halacha. Some Poskim[168] rule it is viewed as a mere promise document which has no Halachic validity. It is similar to promising to pay someone money, and is not a document of a debt. According to this opinion, a check cannot be sold to another and hence one may never exchange a check for less than its value, even if the seller does not have liability on the check, unless he is only taking Sechar Tircha. Other Poskim[169] rule a check is identical to a loan document for all Halachic purposes, and hence may be sold just like a loan may be sold.[170] Accordingly, it may be sold for a lesser amount if the seller does not retain liability. Other Poskim[171] rule a check is similar to an oral loan that can be purchased through Mamad Shelashton, otherwise, it cannot be sold for a lesser amount. Other Poskim[172] rule that a non-postdated check is considered like actual cash payment, as under law the person must honor the check he signed. Practically, majority of today's Poskim conclude that a check has the status of a loan document which can be sold following the same rules as a loan document. Based on this, the following is the summary of cashing a check by a check cashing service:

---

[164] Bris Pinchas p. 219-221; So rules regarding charging a consumer more money for a later payment that involves Tircha: Beis Efraim Y.D. 41; Mayim Rabim 38; Mishpat Ribis 20:8; Bris Yehuda 22 footnote 6

[165] One may diminish money from the loan contract in order compensate for the work and fees that the buyer of the loan must go through in order to collect the payment.

[166] Bris Pinchas 17:14; Bris Yehuda 9:9; Toras Ribis 19:22 footnote 44; Mishpitei Ribis p. 3423 in name of Rav SZ"A

[167] See Mishpitei Ribis p. 342

[168] Ateres Shlomo 1:65 of Rav Shlomo Garelitz; Chut Shani Ribis 16:115 of Rav Gerelitz; Vayaan David 2:219; Rav Z.N. Goldberg in Techumin 12:295; leaves this issue in doubt; Kinyan Torah 3:93

[169] Minchas Yitzchak 5:120; Igros Moshe C.M. 2:15; Lehoros Nasan 8:106; Ohala Shel Torah 1:84

[170] The reason: Various Halachic considerations can render a check as a valid loan document:
   1. Mamrani: The Poskim rule that a Shetar Mamrani [I owe you document] is a valid document as has the same status as a loan. [See Shut Bach 15; Tzemach Tzedek 10
   2. Dina Demalchusa Dina: Since according to law the check writer must honor his check, therefore it is considered like a loan document, as Halacha accepts the laws of the country regarding monetary matters. [Rama C.M. 369:11; Chasam Sofer 5 C.M. 44; Rashba 22]
   3. Situmta: Since using a check is an accepted way of business, it receives the Halachic status of a "Situmta", which is considered a Halachically binding Kinyan. [See Choshen Mishpat 129:5 and Keses Kodshim on 201:1]
   4. Umdana: When one can assess the intents of a transaction to be of a certain form, it has Halachic status of Umdana, which is Halachically binding. [See Rav Z.N. Goldberg in Techumin 35:346]

[171] Rav Abba Shaul, brought in Mishpitei Ribis ibid

[172] See Mishpitei Ribis ibid; Pischeiy Choshen Halvaa 10 footnote 21; See Shevet Halevi 7:222

The Final Law:
D. Using a check cashing service-Gentile service or client:
Gentile check cashing service: A Jew may use any gentile owned check cashing service, irrelevant of fees, liability and the like.[173]
Jewish check cashing service-gentile client: A Jewish owned check cashing service may charge a gentile client whatever rate he desires for exchange of cashing his check, irrelevant of liability and the like.[174] Furthermore, it is even a positive command to take a surcharge for the exchange.[175]

E. Jewish check cashing service-Jewish client:
Non-postdated check:[176] Some of today's Poskim rule that Ribis does not apply to a non-postdated check, as it is viewed as cash payment. Majority of today's Poskim however rule that it is considered like a loan document and hence follows the same laws as a post-dated check, as explained next.
Postdated check [and non-postdated check according to most Poskim]:[177] A Jewish client may not cash a check by a Jewish owned check cashing service unless the Jew does not accept liability for the check's payment, or the Jew is charged a fixed fee that covers only the expenses of the service [i.e. Sechar Tircha]. This applies even [and even more so] if the check writer [i.e. payer] is a gentile, as explained in B. Being that all check cashing services make the check holder retain liability to repay the money in the event that the check is not respected, irrelevant of reason, therefore, the only option that remains is the second option, which is for the check cash service to charge a fixed fee for their service. Accordingly, it is forbidden for the client to be charged a greater rate for a postdated check, as this reveals that the extra fee is in exchange for the delay of payment. Thus, in summary, a check cashing service may charge only a fixed rate for all checks that they cash, irrelevant of the due date of the check.
Heter Iska:[178] In addition to all the above, it is proper for the check cashing service to have a Heter Iska for all of his transactions in order to prevent any issues of Ribis that may come up. [Some check cashing services charge more money for post-dated checks based on a Shtar Heter Iska. One should contact a Rav regarding if such a Shtar should be relied upon.]
Exchange fees:[179] So long as the company has a fixed exchange fee for all checks, whether postdated or non-postdated, and it covers only the expenses of the service [Sechar Tircha], it is valid, and is not considered Ribis.

Summary:
When a Jewish client desires to cash a check by a Jewish owned check cashing service, he may only do so if they charge a set fee for all checks, whether postdated or not. If they charge a greater percentage for a post-dated check, it is forbidden to use their services, unless they contain a Shtar Heter Iska, in which case a Rav is to be contacted.

---

[173] The reason: As the laws of interest do not apply to transactions between gentiles and a Jew. [See Admur Ribis 70 and 75]
[174] The reason: As the laws of interest do not apply to transactions between gentiles and a Jew. [Admur Ribis 75]
[175] Admur ibid
The reason: This is similar to the collection of an actual debt from the gentile in which the surcharge collection is interest, and hence fulfills the positive Biblical command to take interest from a gentile.
[176] See Mishpitei Ribis p. 342
[177] Bris Pinchas 17:11-16
[178] Bris Pinchas 17:16
[179] Bris Pinchas 17:16

> **May one write a postdated check for himself and exchange it by a Jewish owned check-cashing service for less money?**[180]
>
> One may only do so if there is a fixed fee or percentage rate being taken for the check [as Sechar Tircha] and this rate would be the same even if the check was not postdated. If, however, the check cashing services charges a greater fee or percentage for the postdated check, it is forbidden to exchange it by them due to Ribis.

------------------ *Avoda Zara* ----------------

11. May one celebrate thanksgiving?

Thanksgiving is celebrated annually in the United States on the fourth/last Thursday of November, and is considered a Federal holiday, in which people have off from work and spend time with family. Customarily, a special Thanksgiving dinner is served, which includes Turkey and other foods. The question is raised regarding if a Jew may celebrate this Holiday by either attending or making a party, or eating Turkey in its honor. The Halachic questions involved is regarding whether the Holiday derives from a foreign religion, and whether celebrating it transgresses the prohibitions of "Darkei Emori" and "Bechukoseiheim Lo Seileichu." To understand this subject properly, we will preface it with a general introduction as to its history and initiation.

A. The history:

Historically, the celebration of Thanksgiving can be traced back to the early 1600's and possibly earlier. Famously, Thanksgiving was celebrated by the early pilgrims who came on the mayflower ship in 1620 and settled in Plymouth, Massachusetts. These pilgrims were a fringe group of Puritans, a group of reformed Protestants originally from England, who broke off from the Church of England and came to search for a homeland where they can follow their religion without persecution of the English church. The Puritans desired to abolish the common Catholic Holidays celebrated by the Roman and Catholic church and in its place to have celebratory days of thanksgiving, in which they give gratitude to G-d for saving them and helping them in the course of their lives. One year later, in 1621, they celebrated a three-day Thanksgiving celebrating the successful Harvest of crop, and using the days to give thanks to G-d. While this Thanksgiving celebration is the oldest record attained of the event [found in writing], nonetheless, there are records of Thanksgiving days of celebration by non-Puritan pilgrims, as well as Indian Natives of America.[181] Residents of New England for example, were accustomed to rejoice after a successful harvest, based on ancient English harvest festivals, not relating to their religion. The celebration was colony based and not considered a national widespread Holiday until 1789. In 1789, Congressman Elias Boudinot of New Jersey proposed in Congress a resolution urging President Washington to: "*Recommend to the people of the United States a day of public Thanksgiving and prayer to be observed by acknowledging with grateful hearts the many and signal favors of the Almighty God, especially by affording them an opportunity to establish a Constitution of government for their safety and happiness.*" The official proclamation was then passed by George Washington as a day of giving thanks to the Almighty for all of His greatness and goodness that He has done.[182] This day did not become an official

---

[180] Bris Pinchas 17:11

[181] Florida, Texas, Maine and Virginia each declare themselves the site of the First Thanksgiving, and historical documents support the various claims. Spanish explorers and other English Colonists celebrated religious services of thanksgiving years before *Mayflower* arrived.

[182] The following is the original letter of proclamation: *By the President of the United States of America, a Proclamation. Whereas it is the duty of all Nations to acknowledge the providence of Almighty God, to obey his will, to be grateful for his benefits, and humbly to implore his protection and favor-- and whereas both Houses of Congress have by their joint Committee requested me to recommend to the People of the United States a day of public thanksgiving and prayer to be observed by acknowledging with grateful hearts the many signal favors of Almighty God especially by affording them an opportunity peaceably to establish a form of government for their safety and happiness. Now therefore I do recommend and assign Thursday the 26th day of November next to be devoted by the People of these States to the service of that great and glorious Being, who is the beneficent Author of all the good that was, that is, or that will be-- That we may then all unite in rendering unto him our sincere and humble thanks--for his kind care and protection of the People of this Country previous to their becoming a Nation--for the signal and manifold mercies, and the favorable interpositions of his Providence which we experienced in the course and*

national Holiday with leave from work, until 1863 when Abraham Lincoln signed a proclamation, turning Thanksgiving into an official national Holiday.

History of Eating Turkey: While wild fowl was a commonly available poultry eaten by the Pilgrims and Native Americans, there is no known Historical record connecting specifically the eating of Turkey with Thanksgiving, although this has been the tradition for quite some time.

B. The Halacha:

It is forbidden to take any part in a celebration associated with idolatry.[183] It is likewise forbidden for one to follow the path of gentiles or try to be like them.[184] It is likewise forbidden to perform actions that have no meaning and are considered Darkei Emori.[185] Accordingly, some Rabbanim[186] rule that one is not to celebrate Thanksgiving with a party, or through having a customary Thanksgiving menu, due to it infringing on some, or all, of the above issues.[187] Other Poskim[188] however rule it is permitted to celebrate the day with family and friends and have a special Thanksgiving menu, including Turkey, and doing so is not related to any of the above prohibitions.[189] Nevertheless, some of these Poskim[190] maintain that it is forbidden to make it into a set Holiday that must be celebrated annually, and rather it is to be voluntary each year and only done on occasion.[191] [Seemingly, after researching the history behind Thanksgiving, as stated above in A, it appears there is no issue at all involved in celebrating Thanksgiving, as stated in the lenient opinion. Practically, many Frum Jews are accustomed to celebrating the day with Turkey, however others are particular not to do so, and one is to contact his Rav for a final ruling. The Rebbe in a talk[192] made mention of the day of Thanksgiving and praised the United States for being a G-d oriented

---

conclusion of the late war--for the great degree of tranquility, union, and plenty, which we have since enjoyed--for the peaceable and rational manner, in which we have been enabled to establish constitutions of government for our safety and happiness, and particularly the national One now lately instituted--for the civil and religious liberty with which we are blessed; and the means we have of acquiring and diffusing useful knowledge; and in general for all the great and various favors which he hath been pleased to confer upon us. and also that we may then unite in most humbly offering our prayers and supplications to the great Lord and Ruler of Nations and beseech him to pardon our national and other transgressions-- to enable us all, whether in public or private stations, to perform our several and relative duties properly and punctually--to render our national government a blessing to all the people, by constantly being a Government of wise, just, and constitutional laws, discreetly and faithfully executed and obeyed--to protect and guide all Sovereigns and Nations (especially such as have shown kindness unto us) and to bless them with good government, peace, and concord--To promote the knowledge and practice of true religion and virtue, and the increase of science among them and us--and generally to grant unto all Mankind such a degree of temporal prosperity as he alone knows to be best. Given under my hand at the City of New York the third day of October in the year of our Lord 1789.

Go: Washington

[183] See Shulchan Aruch Y.D. 148

[184] Michaber and Rama Y.D. 178:1

[185] Admur 301:33

[186] So held some American Rabbanim of the past generation; See Igros Moshe O.C. 5:20-6; 5:30-6

[187] The reason: As a) Some Poskim rule that due to the prohibition of "Ubechukoseihem Lo Seileichu" one may not imitate a practice of the gentiles unless it originated from Jewish sources. [See Gr"a Y.D. 178:7; Darkei Teshuvah Y.D. 178:14] b) Eating Turkey on Thanksgiving has no understandable source or reason and is hence considered Darkei Emori. [See Igros Moshe O.C. 5:30-6]

[188] See Igros Moshe E.H. 2:13; Y.D. 4:11-4; O.C. 5:11-4; So held some American Rabbanim of the past generation

[189] The reason: As a) It is not a religious Holiday. b) It is not sourced in idolatry; c) It has a valid reason; to give thanks to G-d. d) The eating of Turkey is done as a celebratory food because it tastes good and serves many at a meal, and is not related to unknown practices. Therefore, it does not transgress any of the above issues, as only the ways of the gentiles that are done for idolatry purposes or have no source for their meaning are forbidden under the clause of Darkei Emori and Bechukoseihem Lo Seileichu. [See Rama 178:1; Maharik 88; Igros Moshe ibid] Furthermore, one can learn that only is it permitted to celebrate the day but that this day should be celebrated by Jews, as it gives thanks to Hashem for giving us the United States of America, which has served as a place of refuge for millions of Jews from religious and physical persecution.

[190] Igros Moshe Y.D. ibid; 5:20-6; O.C. 5:30-6

[191] The reason: As doing so transgresses the prohibition of Darkei Emori and "Ubechukoseiheim Lo Seileichu" as there is not enough logical explanation to set the day for all generations as a day of celebration. It also transgresses Baal Tosif. [Igros Moshe ibid]

[192] Sichas 19th Kisleiv 5747; Free Translation from SIE: *"It is appropriate to reiterate that the character of this nation is based on faith in G-d. And we speak not of an abstract Super Being; but of G-d, Creator and Master of the world. One can profess belief in a Creator while failing to recognize G-d's interest in the details of the world and in man's mortal actions. Our nation however, is built on the principles established by the founding fathers. When they landed on these shores one of their first acts was to set and proclaim a holiday of Thanksgiving to the Creator and Master of the world who had saved them from danger and brought them to these safe shores. Here they could live without fear, religious persecution or oppressive decrees. Here they could conduct their lives according to their sacred beliefs. Their thanksgiving expressed this faith: G-d not only created the world but also directs the events of the world. They recognized the providence of G-d in their salvation. This holiday has become tradition and every year we offer sincere thanksgiving to the Al-mighty for showing those early settlers His abundant kindness. Even the estranged souls, who in their heart believe in G-d but outwardly boast of atheism or relegate G-d to the seventh Heaven, certainly participate in the customs of the holiday of Thanksgiving established by those original Americans."*

country, setting aside a day to give thanks to G-d. While the Rebbe praised the idea of the National Holiday and its meaning, no mention was made regarding whether a Jew may or may not celebrate it.]

Summary:
Some are accustomed to celebrating Thanksgiving and have a Turkey dinner menu, and those who do so have upon whom to rely. Others are stringent to avoid doing so. One is to contact his Rav for a final directive.

12. Yoga/Meditations/Therapies:[193]

Rabbinical supervision: Yoga[194] and many eastern meditations, contain aspects of idolatry that are forbidden for a Jew, of which one is required to give up his life rather than perform. Nonetheless, the aspect of seclusion and meditation in it of itself does not contain idolatry and is not Halachically forbidden, and on the contrary, can be found rooted in Torah. Likewise, much of the physical exercise of Yoga is not idolatry related. One who desires to perform any of the above types of therapies is to beware to do so in a Kosher manner, making sure that it is removed from any idolatry tainted practices. The same way a food requires Rabbinical supervision so it does not contain any non-Kosher ingredients, so too eastern meditations and Yoga style practices require Rabbinical approbation to verify that they have been ridden of their prohibited aspects of idolatry. The Rebbe encouraged Rabbanim to seek G-d fearing psychologists and mental health experts to study the field of meditation and make Kosher forms of meditations available for the public in need of these therapies. In addition, the Rebbe proposed that the meditations include a Jewish spiritual content, such as the concept of Shema Yisrael, G-d's oneness.

Who should use this therapy? The Rebbe's position, even regarding Kosher meditations, was that it is not meant for the healthy minded and should only be used, as proscribed by a medical or mental health professional. The same way a healthy person does not take medicines for ailments he does not have, and if he does so it will damage his body, so too, taking part in these therapies if it is not medically needed, can prove detrimental to one's mental health. Furthermore, even one who needs these therapies, it should be used like a medicine, only on occasion and according to need. Just as one can overdose on medicine, and become addicted, similarly one can become indoctrinated and infatuated with the therapy given to the point that what was once a healer of mental health becomes its destroyer. Kosher meditations must be regulated. Once one becomes stable and healthy, he is to leave this therapy all together and continue to lead a normal and healthy life without external dependencies.

13. Giving presents to a gentile:

A. May one give a present to a gentile?[195]

It is forbidden to give a free present to a gentile who one is not acquainted with.[196] This applies even if the gentile is not an idolater, such as a Muslim.[197] If, however, one is acquainted with the gentile, he may give him a free present, as certainly the gentile will repay him for the favor.[198] Regarding if one may give a gentile acquaintance a present in honor of his Holiday-See Halacha C!

---

[193] See Sichos Kodesh 5739 3:314; Likkutei Sichos 36:335-336; Heichal Menachem 1:48, two letters of Rebbe to Rav Yaakov Landau, Chief Rabbi of Bnei Brak; Healthy in Body Mind and Spirit chapter 9

[194] Yoga is a group of physical, mental, and spiritual practices or disciplines which originated in ancient India. There is a broad variety of Yoga schools, practices, and goals in Hinduism, Buddhism, and Jainism. Many of the positions and mantras in Yoga contain pure idolatry, summoning deities and spiritual forces and showing one's subservience towards them.

[195] 151:11; Avoda Zara 20

[196] Michaber ibid

The reason: As this brings closeness amongst the Jews and gentiles, and can cause him to learn from his ways. [Chinuch Mitzvah 426]

[197] Shach 151:18

Ger Toshev: It however does not apply to a Ger Toshev [Shach ibid], who are those gentiles that have accepted the seven Nohadite laws. [Chinuch 426]

[198] Taz 151:8

The reason: Being that the Gentile will repay him, it is thus not considered like a present at all, but rather like a sale. [ibid]

B. Giving Charity to a gentile:[199]

It is permitted and encouraged to distribute charity to a gentile.[200] This applies even if the charity is being given to an individual gentile or a group of gentiles without it also being distributed to Jewish paupers on that occasion.[201]

C. May one give a present to a gentile in honor of his Holiday, such as chr--tmas and New Years?

It is forbidden to give presents to an idol worshiper [even if he is an acquaintance] on the day of his Holiday. If, however, the gentile does not believe in the idol, and does not worship it, then it is permitted to do so.[202] Christians, who believe in the deity of a human [Yoshka] and worship him, are considered to be practicing idolatry[203], and it is therefore forbidden to give them presents on the day of their Holiday, which includes chr--tmas and New Years.[204] Nevertheless, some Poskim[205] rule that the above prohibition only applied in previous times, when people were much more religiously observant of idolatry, however today that the worshippers are no longer expert in idolatry, it is therefore permitted to do business with them on the day of their holiday [and give them presents, if they are an acquaintance].[206] This especially applies if segregating ourselves from the gentiles on the day of their Holiday will bring enmity and hatred towards us, being we live amongst them and have business relationships with them throughout the year. Nevertheless, a Baal Nefesh is to distance himself from rejoicing with them if he is able to do so inconspicuously, in a way that will not arouse enmity. Thus, practically, if one needs to send gifts to a gentile [acquaintance, such as an employee] on the day of their Holiday, such as New Years[207] [or chr--tmas], it is permitted to do so. However, if possible, the present should be sent before the Holiday begins, such as the afternoon prior to the Holiday. If this is not possible, then the gift may be sent on the Holiday itself.[208]

14. *May one pray to G-d on behalf of a gentile or Mumar?*[209]

May one Daven for a gentile or Mumar, such as for him to recover from an illness, or for him to have blessing in his Parnasa, or to find a spouse and have children?

It is permitted to pray to G-d for blessing on behalf of a gentile, or Mumar, who does good acts for the Jewish people.[210] This applies even if the gentile is an idolater.[211] Thus, for example, one may pray for a gentile acquaintance or business partner who is ill, or is undergoing legal troubles.[212] One is not to pray

---

[199] Michaber Y.D. 151:12; Rama 251:1 *"One distributes charity to gentile paupers together with Jewish paupers due to Darkei Shalom"*; Tur 151 and 251; Gittin 61a; Regarding Matanos Laevyonim see: Michaber 694:3; M"A 694:6; Taz 694:2; M"B 694:10

[200] The reason: This is permitted and encouraged to be done in order to keep the state of peace with our gentile neighbors [Michaber ibid; Rama ibid; Tur ibid] It thus does not contain a prohibition of Lo Sichaneim. [See Taz 151:8]

[201] Shach Y.D. 151:18; 251:2; Taz 151:9; Darkei Moshe 251; Bach 151 and 251 "and so is the custom"; Ran Gittin ibid

Other opinions: Some Poskim rule one may not distribute charity to a gentile pauper if one is not also distributing charity to Jewish paupers at the same time. [Perisha 251; Gr"a in his opinion of Rama ibid; Mordechai Gittin ibid] Seemingly, the reason for this is because when one is not distributing charity to others Jews, there will be no enmity caused if one withholds from giving to a gentile, as he is not expecting the money and does not notice any racism towards him. It is thus forbidden to give him the money, being it is forbidden to give a present to a gentile. [Michaber 151:11] If, however, one is giving out to other Jews and one specifically does not give a gentile pauper, this causes enmity.

[202] Michaber 148:5; Avoda Zara 65a

[203] Rambam Machalos Assuros 11:7; Avoda Zara 9:4; Pirush Hamishnayos Avoda Zara 1:3; Teshuvas Harambam 448; Rama 148:12 [in uncensored editions] lists Xmas and New Years as Holidays of idolatry; Likkutei Sichos 37 p. 198; Rebbe in handwritten editing remarks to a letter "Christianity is Avoda Zara, is in contrast to the seven Nohadite laws, as opposed to Islam. However, the Christians of today are simply "Maaseh Avoseihem Beyadeihem".

The reason: As they believe that Yoshka is one of the three parts of Hashem and they worship him. [In truth however, there are different sects of Christianity with different belief systems. See Haemuna Vehadeios of Rasag 2:7 that there are four groups of Christians and not all are idol worshipers; See here https://www.thoughtco.com/faith-groups-that-reject-trinity-doctrine-700367]

[204] Rama 149:12 [in uncensored editions]; Terumos Hadeshen 195

[205] Opinion in Michaber 148:12; Tur in name of Rashbam; Tosafos

[206] Michaber ibid

[207] Rama 149:12 [in uncensored editions]; Darkei Moshe Haaruch 148:5; Terumos Hadeshen 195

[208] Rama 149:12; Terumos Hadeshen 195

[209] Sefer Chassidim 790; Chaim Bayad [Falagi] 33; Darkei Teshuvah 151:29; Yechaveh Daas 6:60; Ateres Paz 1:3

[210] Sefer Chassidim ibid based on the fact Rebbe Yochanon in the Talmud praises and blesses Charvona; Bava Metzia 114b that Eliyahu Hanavi went to save a certain gentile from Gihenom being that he did good for the Jewish people; Chaim Bayad ibid that it is completely permitted. He brings many cases in history that Rabbanim have Davened for gentiles to recover from illness, or find favor in the eyes of the king etc.

[211] So is implied from Sefer Chassidim who includes a Jewish Mumar

[212] Chaim Bayad ibid

on behalf of a gentile, or Mumar, who performs evil acts towards the Jewish people.[213] [If the gentile does not perform either good or evil for the Jewish people, it is permitted to Daven on his behalf for the purpose of Darkei Shalom or other potential benefit.[214] The Rebbe was publicly witnessed by Dollars to bless many gentiles of all walks of life. It however requires further analysis if one may even privately pray on behalf of a gentile, when there is no benefit involved, and one is doing so simply out of his good will.]

Ger:[215] A convert's prayer on behalf of his parents does not help [to the same extent as a regular son who Davens for his father[216]]. [However, he may Daven for him if he so chooses, and such a prayer does have some affect.[217]]

------------------ *Kishuf and Darkei Emori*-----------------

15. Starting a new activity on Mondays and Wednesdays:[218]

It is customary not to begin a new activity on Mondays and Wednesdays.[219] [Some[220] rule that this only applies for mundane matters and not for matters that involve a Mitzvah. Practically, so is the custom.[221] One may thus get married on Mondays and Wednesdays without worry. One is to however avoid moving on Mondays and Wednesdays.[222] If this is unavoidable, then one is to at least move some items into the home, the day before.[223] Alternatively, one is to bring Torah books, and/or have a Chassidic gathering, at the home on the day before.[224] Some[225] rule that one may be completely lenient regarding starting activities on Monday's, and one is only to be careful on Wednesdays. The custom of the world today is to be completely lenient in this regard[226] although some segments of Jewry are stringent even today.[227]]

16. Making a Tattoo:[228]

The verse[229] states "And the writing of a tattoo you shall not place on yourselves." From here it is learned that it is Biblically forbidden to make a Tattoo on one's skin.[230] One who does so transgresses the above negative command, and according to some Poskim[231], also transgresses the negative command of "Lo Seilechu Bechukos Hagoyim."

Definition-How is it done? The tattoo [that is forbidden by the Torah] is made by making a cut in one's skin and then filling it with sand, or ink, or other pigments that leave a mark.[232] Alternatively, one first marks an image on the skin using a pigment and then cuts open the skin for the ink to enter into its pours.[233] [Today, tattoos are made through first sketching an image onto the skin and then using a fine

---

[213] Sefer Chassidim ibid

[214] So is implied from Sefer Chassidim ibid who only states not to Daven for one who does evil to the Jewish people. Vetzaruch Iyun as to why Davening for a gentile from whom one receives no benefit does not transgress "Lo Sechanem" [Y.D. 151:11] See Chaim Bayad ibid

[215] Sefer Chassidim 790

[216] Yechaveh Daas 6:60

[217] Yechaveh Daas ibid

[218] Michaber Y.D. 179:2 based on Teshuvas Ramban 282 [104] who states "Those that do not begin on ב"ד [Mondays or Wednesdays]...", Based on Zohar p. 273

[219] The reason: As on Mondays the Mazal of the moon shines, and the Mazal of the moon is not good omen. [Ramban ibid; Shabbos 156a "One who is born by Mazal Levana" will have difficulties-Banaiy Vesoser"] On Wednesday the Mazal of Shabsai Kochav shines, which is also not a good omen. [Ramban ibid] The Mazal that shines on that day or night rules over everything of that entire day. [Pirkei Direbbe Eliezer 6]

[220] Ruach Chaim brought in Darkei Teshuvah 179:11

[221] Ruach Chaim ibid

[222] Igros Kodesh 15:390 [brought in Shulchan Menachem 6:237]

[223] Dvar Eliyahu 37 brought in Darkei Teshuvah 179:13

[224] Ruach Chaim ibid

The reason: As then it is considered done for the sake of a Mitzvah, and is hence allowed.

[225] Birkeiy Yosef 179 in Shiyurei Bracha 3 in name of Derech Chaim brought in Darkei Teshuvah 179:12

[226] Heard from Rav Asher Lemel Hacohen

[227] The custom in Belz is to be very particular regarding this matter. They hence do not marry, get engaged or even start the learning semester on Mondays or Wednesdays.

[228] Shulchan Aruch Y.D. 180; Mishneh Makos 21a

[229] Vayikra 19:21

[230] Chinuch Mitzvah 253

[231] Bach 180 in implication of Tur 180 who writes that a tattoo is "Mechukei Hagoyim Hu"

[232] Michaber 180:1; Mishneh Makos 21a that one must both <u>cut</u> and <u>fill</u> it with ink

[233] Shach 180:1; Bach

needle that is filled with ink to puncture the skin and enter the ink. Thus, the cutting and filling is done simultaneously.]

Where on the skin?[234] The Biblical prohibition against making a tattoo applies anywhere on the skin.

What writing is forbidden?[235] The Biblical prohibition against making a tattoo applies to any type of writing. [Some Poskim[236], however, rule that it only applies to letters of a language, and does not apply to making a mere mark, or line, and the like, although doing so is Rabbinically forbidden.[237] Seemingly, however, tattooing a picture or design falls under the Biblical prohibition of making a tattoo.[238]]

Having someone else make the tattoo on one's body: If someone else makes a tattoo on one's skin, then if he assisted him in the tattooing, he is liable. If he did not assist him in making the tattoo, then he is exempt from Biblical liability.[239] Nevertheless, it remains Rabbinically forbidden.[240]

Placing a pigmented ointment on a wound if will leave a mark:[241] It is permitted to place ash [or any other ointment[242]] onto a wound [even though it will leave a permanent mark].[243]

Branding a slave: One who brands his slave is exempt from Biblical liability[244], although it nevertheless remains initially forbidden [if the slave was circumcised and immersed in a Mikveh[245]].[246]

Q&A

Why did the Torah prohibit tattoos?

The act of tattooing is rooted in the act of idol worship[247], in which the worshipers would tattoo their god onto their skin, thus showing their subordination to him.[248]

May one write a tattoo onto the skin of a gentile?[249]

Yes.

May one write on one's skin?[250]

➤ Example: One does not have paper and needs to write down a phone number, may he do so on his skin? Likewise, may one doodle a picture on his skin?

One who writes on his skin, without making a cut into his skin which allows the ink to penetrate, is exempt from Biblical liability.[251] Nevertheless, some Poskim[252] rule it is Rabbinically forbidden to do

---

[234] Shach 180:2
[235] Shach 180:2; Beis Yosef 180; Tur 180; Rabbeinu Yerucham 5 Nesiv 17; Chachamim Makos 21a
Other opinions: Rebbe Shimon rules one is only liable for lashes if he tattoos the name of an idol. [Makos ibid] We do not rule like this opinion. [Beis Yosef ibid]
[236] Meil Tzedaka 31, brought in Pischeiy Teshuvah 180:1; Implication of Semak Mitzvah 72 "Write similar to letters"; Karban Ahron on Sifri
Other opinions: From some sources it is implied that the Biblical tattoo prohibition applies irrelevant of whether one writes letters or makes marks and the like, as the mere act of engraving ink into the skin is the Biblical prohibition. [Initial understanding of Meil Tzedaka ibid as is implied from wording in Michaber 180:1 and Rambam "Kesoves Kaka, which is that he **marks** on the skin" as opposed to "writes on the skin, as writes Tur 180; So is also implied from Michaber 180:3-4] The Meil Tzedaka however rejects this interpretation in his conclusion.
[237] The reason: As the Torah calls it "Kesoves Kaka" which implies writing, and writing is defined as letters of an agreed upon language, and so is implied from all Poskim who use the term "One who **writes** a tattoo"
[238] Implication of Michaber 180:1 who does not differentiate between letters and pictures; Implication of Michaber 180:3-4 regarding branding a slave; See Meil Tzedaka ibid that so long as its defined as "Kesav" it is forbidden and so rule regarding Shabbos, that drawings have the same status as writing: Admur 340:10; M"A 340:6; Rambam Shabbos 11:17; Degul Merivava 340. Vetzaruch Iyun from the wording of Admur ibid, as well as 302:5.
[239] Michaber 180:2 and 11
[240] Shach 180:4
[241] Michaber 180:3
[242] Taz 180:1; Shach 180:5
[243] The reason: As the wound shows that it was not done for the sake of tattooing as do the idol worshipers, but rather for healing purposes. [Shach 180:6; Taz 180:1] Even after the wound heals there is still some mark left of the wound which shows the intent of the remaining ink mark. [Taz ibid]
[244] Michaber 180:4
[245] Noda Beyehuda Tinyana E.H., brought in Pischeiy teshuvah 180:2
[246] Rama ibid "however it appears that initially.."
[247] Shach 180:6; Chinuch Mitzvah 253
[248] Rambam Avoda Zara 12:11
[249] Noda Beyehuda Tinyana, brought in Pischeiy Teshuvah 180:2
[250] See Minchas Chinuch Mitzvah 253:1; Nishmas Avraham Y.D. 180

so. It is however unclear if this applies even with ink that is erasable.[253] Other Poskim[254], however, rule it is permitted to do so even Rabbinically. Practically, the widespread custom is to be lenient even initially.[255] However, if the ink is permanent and cannot be removed at all from the skin even with the passing of time, one is to be stringent.[256]

May one place a Tattoo sticker on his skin [i.e. temporary tattoo]?

A temporary tattoo, or a tattoo sticker, involves stamping a picture or design onto the external layer of the skin, which lasts for anywhere between a few days to several weeks. Its Halachic status follows the same debate mentioned above regarding writing on the skin, in which the conclusion was that it is not Halachically considered a tattoo. Nevertheless, making a tattoo like design on the skin seemingly falls into a separate prohibition of "Thou shall not go in the ways of the gentiles." Just as the Torah prohibits one to wear clothing of gentiles, and have a haircut like a gentile[257], so too, and even more so, should he not make a tattoo like gentile.[258] [In any event, regardless of the technical Halachic discussion, it is certainly not a proper thing for a G-d fearing Jew to do, aside for the possible Biblical prohibition involved, as mentioned above. This applies even for children, and hence one is to prevent one's children from placing a color tattoo on their skin. Nonetheless, those children who place mild images, such as a flower and the like, and do so out of mere playfulness for temporary purpose seemingly have upon what to rely.[259]]

May one have a temporary mark or number stamped on his hand when entering a park and the like?

Yes.[260]

---

[251] Michaber 180:1; Mishneh Makos 21a

[252] Minchas Chinuch ibid based on Beis Shmuel E.H. 124:16 "Even if the witnesses just wrote their signatures and did not fill it with ink, nevertheless they become Rabbinical Reshaim" [However see next footnote for alternative explanation of Beis Shmuel]; Implication of Rambam in Avodas Kochavim 7 who writes exempt; Implication of Tosafos Gittin 20b

[253] The law if the ink is erasable with time: The Minchas Chinuch ibid writes that even according to the stringent opinion, the Rabbinical prohibition is only regarding ink that is not erasable, however if the ink is erasable then the prohibition does not apply. So records also Shevet Halevi 3:111-1 in name of Minchas Chinuch. See however Pashegen Hakesav of Rav Chaim Kanievski p. 74-75 that such ink does not exist, as all writing on skin is erasable and hence one must conclude that according to the stringent opinion, any writing on the skin is Rabbinically forbidden. So is also implied from the Mishnas Chachamim brought in next footnote that according to the stringent opinion any writing is Rabbinically forbidden.

[254] Mishnas Chachamim 57; Kesef Mishneh on Rambam ibid; Shevet Halevi 3:111-1 that all the above Poskim in previous footnote, recorded by the Minchas Chinuch ibid only referred to one who made a cut into the skin and did not fill it with ink, in which case it is Rabbinically forbidden, however to simply write on the skin without making any cut was never discussed by them and there is thus no such source to Rabbinically prohibit it [Rav Chaim Kanievsky, brought in Nishmas Avraham ibid makes the same claim]; Implication of the Poskim who all omit the above Rabbinical prohibition against writing on the skin even without cutting it, including the Michaber 180, Chochmas Adam 89:11; Kitzur SHU"A 169:1; Ben Ish Chaiy Maaseiy 2:15

[255] Rav SZ"A, brought in Nishmas Avraham ibid, rules one may be lenient even initially; Rav Chaim Kanievsky, brought in Nishmas Avraham ibid that the Achronim write the custom is to be lenient; See Minchas Chinuch ibid that even according to the stringent opinion, if the ink is erasable it is permitted. [see previous footnotes]

[256] As rules the Minchas Chinuch ibid; To note however that to date there does not exist any ink that permanently remains on the skin with simply writing on it, without cutting into the skin with a needle and the like. If such a thing existed, the entire tattoo industry would change to this method which is painless and woundless.

[257] See Michaber 178:1

[258] See Bach 180 based on Tur 180 that in addition to the tattoo prohibition, a tattoo also transgresses the prohibition of Bechukoseihem Lo Seileichu. Seemingly, there is no reason to limit this latter prohibition to only a case that an incision was made in the skin, and hence even a temporary tattoo, would transgress this prohibition. However, perhaps one can suggest that only by an incision, which is done for the sake of mimicking idolatry and showing one's subservience, does one transgress, however a sticker tattoo which is not done in such a way, and one does for decorative purposes, would not transgress the above, as it is done for a reason, and is not considered an immodest or idolatry tainted practice. So is also implied from the fact that all Poskim ibid who discussed the question of writing on one's skin, made no mention of the separate prohibition of Bechukoseihem Lo Seileichu, hence implying that it does not exist. Vetzaruch Iyun.

[259] As explained in the previous footnote, that there is room to learn that it does not transgress the Issur of Bechukoseihem Lo Seileichu, especially if it is done for reasons of playfulness and beauty, and hence has no similarity to the actions of gentiles. However, stickers that contain horrible looking images, as is done by the gentiles, would certainly be more severe.

[260] As a) We rule that if it is temporary and does not penetrate the skin it is not considered a Halachic tattoo, and b) It is done for identification purposes, and hence does not transgress the prohibition of Chukos Hagoyim.

May a Jew who has a tattoo be buried in a Jewish cemetery?
A Jew that has a tattoo must be buried in a Jewish cemetery just like any other Jew.[261] Despite the common misconception, there is no Halachic source that bares a Jew with a tattoo, or a Jew who has committed any sin, from being buried in a Jewish cemetery and this is also not the common practice.

------------------ *Beged Isha*----------------

17. Cross-dressing-Lo Silbash:[262]

A. The prohibition:

A woman may not wear the clothing of a man, such as to place on herself a male turban, or male hat, or wear a shield and the like. She may likewise not get a male haircut. Likewise, a man may not wear the clothing of a woman, such as to wear colored female clothing, or a gold necklace, in those areas that these clothing and ornaments are only worn by women.[263] The general rule is, any clothing that is customarily worn in one's area by only one gender, is forbidden to be worn in that area by the opposite gender.[264] [Thus, in most areas of the world, it would be forbidden for men to wear a skirt. However, in Scotland, it would be permitted to wear kilts.] One who transgresses the above, transgresses a Biblical negative command and is liable for lashes.[265]

Wearing a single garment of the opposite gender:[266] It is forbidden to wear even a single garment of the opposite gender, even though one's gender remains recognizable due to other clothing that he is wearing. [One who transgresses the above, transgresses a Biblical negative command and is liable for lashes.[267]]

Tumtum/Androgynous:[268] It is forbidden for a Tumtum or Androgynous to dress like a woman. [It is, however, also forbidden for them to shave their hair like a man.[269]]

The reason behind the prohibition:[270]
Two reasons are recorded in Rishonim:
- Some[271] write the reason behind this prohibition is because cross-dressing leads to promiscuity.
- Others[272] write the reason is because idolaters practiced cross-dressing.

B. Cases of exception:

Wearing clothing of the opposite gender due to the cold, or for purposes of shade, or Tznius: Many Poskim[273] rule the prohibition of Lo Silbash only applies when one wears clothing of the opposite gender

---

[261] See Yoreh Deah 362:5; Sanhedrin 47a that one is not to bury a Rasha next to a Tzaddik, which is the source we find for the custom of having a Jewish cemetery that is free of gentiles. Based on this, it would likewise be prohibited to bury a Rasha who is a Jew near a gentile, and hence one with a Tattoo may not be buried with gentiles even though he has committed a sin. See Igros Moshe 147 that even a Jew who is married to a gentile must be buried in a Jewish cemetery.
[262] Yoreh Deah 182:5; Rambam Avodas Kochavim 12:10; Nazir 59a; Parshas Ki Seitzei "Lo Yihyeh Keli Gever.." "Lo Yilbash Gever Simlas Isha"
[263] Michaber ibid
[264] Rama 182:5
[265] Taz 182:6; Chinuch Mitzvas 542 [women cross-dressing] 543 [Men cross-dressing]; Rambam Sefer Hamitzvos Mitzvah 40; In Hilchos Avodas Kochavim it is listed as two Mitzvos;
[266] Rama ibid; Chochmas Adam 90:1
[267] Taz 182:6
[268] Rama ibid
[269] Shach 182:8; Kol Bo; Rambam
[270] See Arugas Habosem 138:4
[271] Chinuch Mitzvas 542-543; Rashi Dvarim 22:5; See Nazir 59a that it is a Toeiva
[272] Rambam Moreh Nevushim 3:37, brought in Chinuch ibid
[273] Shach 182:7 in name of Bach; Taz 182:4; Avnei Tzedek 72; Shraga Hameir 7:124 that the Shach agrees with the Bach on this matter; See Darkei Teshuvah 182:9; See also Admur 301:6 based on M"A 301:16 and Gemara Shabbos that a female ring is not considered a Shinuiy for a

for the purpose of resembling the opposite gender.[274] It is however permitted for one to wear the clothing of the opposite gender for other purposes, such as to protect one from the cold, or from the sun [or for other purposes]. Other Poskim[275] however rule that doing so is forbidden. [Practically, one may be lenient in this matter in a time of need.[276]] This, however, only applies if one's gender is still recognizable. It is however forbidden in all cases to wear clothing of the opposite gender in a way that his gender is no longer recognizable.[277] However, some Poskim[278] are lenient even in such a case.

Garments and items that are not ornaments of beauty: Some Poskim[279] rule that the prohibition of Lo Silbash only applies towards garments and items that are ornaments for a woman and make her look beautiful. However, other items are permitted to be worn by a man, even if he does so for the purpose of appearing like a woman. Other Poskim[280] however question this ruling.

Wearing out of jest and fun/Purim/Chasana:[281] It is accustomed on Purim [and by Chasunas[282]] to allow males to wear the clothing of females, and vice versa.[283] [However, many Poskim[284] challenge this custom[285] and thus, practically, one is not to do so. Some write it is to be avoided even by children.[286] If it is recognizable that the person is a man or woman, and he or she merely wears a single clothing of the opposite gender, there is room to be lenient.[287] The Rebbe in one letter expressed contempt for those who cross-dress for playful purposes, however it is unclear if this refers to completely dressing like the opposite gender, or even wearing a single garment.[288]]

Q&A

Does the prohibition against cross-dressing apply even if someone else places the clothing on oneself?[289]

Yes. This prohibition applies even if a gentile places the clothing on him.

Does the prohibition against cross-dressing apply even if one plans to remove the clothing right after trying them on?[290]

Yes. The prohibition applies even against wearing the clothing of the opposite gender for a mere

---

man to carry through wearing on his finger on Shabbos, being that at times, during the week, they wear it on their finger to bring it to be fixed. Thus, we see that if one wears the item for non-cross-dressing purposes, it is permitted

[274] The reason: As the verse states "Eideiy Isha" which refers to ornaments that beautify a woman and make her appear like a woman. [see Taz ibid]

[275] Yad Haketana 2:6 [p. 279], brought in Darkei Teshuvah 182:9; Binas Adam 90:94; The Shach ibid questions the ruling of the Bach, although some write that his question is not relating to this matter, of which he also agrees; See Divrei Chaim 2:62 [prohibits even to prevent pain]; Maharsham 2:243; Yabia Omer 6:14-4

[276] Shraga Hameir 7:124; Maharsham 2:243 rules one may only be lenient if it is recognizable to the viewer that one is doing so due to the cold and the like; Bach writes one may be lenient because one has no other choice; See Minchas Yitzchak 2:108-4

[277] Shach ibid; Bach brought in Taz Yoreh Deah 182:4 [Taz concludes "One who is stringent is blessed"]; Yireim 96; Teshuvas Harambam; Shalah; Kneses Hagedola; M"B 696:30; Kisei Eliyahu 696:3; Birkeiy Yosef 696:13 and Yoreh Deah 182:3; Beis Oved 696:10; Kaf Hachaim 696:57; Aruch Hashulchan 696:12

[278] Rama 696:8 regarding Purim; Mahriy Mintz 16; Hisorerus Teshuvah 500

[279] Bach, brought in Shach 182:7

[280] Shach ibid

[281] Rama 696:8; Mahriy Mintz 16; Hisorerus Teshuvah 500

[282] Yireim 96, brought in Taz Yoreh Deah 182:4; Shach 182:7

[283] The reason and other opinions: This is not forbidden due to the cross-dressing prohibition as the intent is for mere joy [as opposed to promiscuity]. Nevertheless, according to some opinions, there remains a prohibition for a man to wear women's clothing, or vice versa, even in such a case. Practically the custom is like the lenient opinion. [Rama ibid]

[284] Bach brought in Taz Yoreh Deah 182:4 [Taz concludes "One who is stringent is blessed"]; Shach 182:7; Yireim 96; Teshuvas Harambam; Shalah; Kneses Hagedola; M"B 696:30; Kisei Eliyahu 696:3; Birkeiy Yosef 696:13 and Yoreh Deah 182:3; Beis Oved 696:10; Kaf Hachaim 696:57; Aruch Hashulchan 696:12

[285] The reason: As the allowance to wear clothing of the opposite gender for mere playfulness is only in a case that one does not appear like the opposite gender, being that he/she remains wearing clothing of also his/her gender. [See Shach ibid and Atzei Levona 182]

[286] Piskeiy Teshuvos 696:14; Nitei Gavriel 75:7

[287] P"M 696 M"Z 4; M"B 696:30 in name of P"M; Implication of Shach 182:7 as explained in Atzei Levona

[288] Igros Kodesh 10:238, printed in Shulchan Menachem 5:56

[289] Maharsham 2:243

[290] See Minchas Chinuch 543:1 that one who cross-dresses and was warned many times while wearing it, is liable for lashes each time he was warned, just like the law by Kilayim, and by Kilayim it is forbidden to wear it for even a mere moment. [Rambam Kilayim 10:30]

moment.

May one cross-dress in the privacy of his room, not in the view of others?[291]
No.

May one wear under clothing of the opposite gender that is not apparent to outside view?[292]
No. A Rabbinical prohibition applies even if people cannot see that one is wearing the clothing of the opposite gender.

May one wear clothing of the opposite gender in an irregular way, such as to wear a woman's blouse around his neck as a scarf?[293]
This matter requires further analysis. Practically, one is not to do so unless he is cold and the like.

May one wear his wife's socks or undershirts if he desires?
One may do so for clothing purposes if he does not have any socks, or undershirts available. It is forbidden to do so for purposes of appearing like a woman.

If one realized that he wore his wife's sock or undershirt, must he remove it?
If one is unable to change into other clothing, it is permitted to remain wearing it.[294] If, however, one is able to change into men's socks or undershirt, then he is to do so.

May women wear pants?[295]
It is forbidden for women to wear pants. This applies even towards women pants that are made specifically for women and are not worn by men.[296] In the latter case, it is disputed as to whether this prohibition is due to Lo Silbash or only due to reasons of modesty.[297]

Under a skirt: Women are not initially to wear pants outside even for protection from the cold, and even if they wear a skirt on top.[298] However, in a time of need, one may be lenient.[299] [See below regarding skiing]

Children: It is forbidden for girls who have reached the age of three years old to wear pants.[300] Some Poskim[301] rule it is even forbidden prior to this age.[302] Practically, girls below three years old may

---

[291] Minchas Yitzchak 2:108-3; Betzeil Hachochma 5:126
[292] See Beis Yosef 182 that if the clothing are "concealed from the eye, then even though they are different between a man and a woman, since they are not apparent to the outside, they are not included in the Biblical prohibition" as they cannot lead towards an abomination"; See however Ohel Yaakov 182:20 that many Achronim are stringent in this matter that it is nevertheless Rabbinically forbidden.
[293] See Betzeil Hachochma 5:126 for an analysis on this subject
[294] As he has no intent to look like a woman by wearing it in order.
[295] Minchas Yitzchak 2:108; Shevet Halevi 2:63; See Ohel Yaakov 188:44-45
[296] The reason: As pants is mainly a men's clothing and hence it is considered Beged Ish for a woman to wear it even if it is a woman's style. [Minchas Yitzchak ibid; Shevet Halevi ibid] In addition, these clothing are Bigdei Zima, clothing of promiscuity, which shape a woman's legs, thighs and private area. [Minchas Yitzchak ibid; Shevet Halevi ibid] Some Poskim however rule that women pants which are different than men pants, do not contain Beged Ish as it is not similar to men's clothing, although it would nevertheless be forbidden due to being immodest. [See Avnei Tzedek Y.D. 72; Mishneh Halachos 12:353]
[297] See previous footnote
[298] The reason: Although doing so is not forbidden due to Beged Ish, being she is wearing it for protection from the cold, nevertheless it is not a modest and elegant form of dress.
[299] Avnei Tzedek Y.D. 73; Shevet Halevi 2:63; See Minchas Yitzchak ibid
The reason: As according to most Poskim, it does not transgress Lo Silbash being she is not intending to wear it in order to resemble a man, and even according to the dissenting Poskim, if she is wearing women pants, perhaps they do not at all contain a prohibition of Lo Silbash. Regarding modesty, since the pants is covered by a skirt it does not present any prohibition.
[300] The reason: As starting from three years of age we educate a girl to dress modestly. Furthermore, once she reaches the age of Chinuch, it is forbidden for her to wear men's clothing.
[301] Minchas Yitzchak 2:108
[302] The reason: As it is forbidden to feed children a prohibition even from one day old. [See Admur 343:2] Furthermore, by Lo Silbash, perhaps the person who places the clothing onto another also transgresses. [Minchas Yitzchak ibid]

wear girl pants[303], however they are not to wear pants of boys unless there is no other clothing available and they need to wear it to protect them from the cold or the sun.[304]

May a woman wear pants while skiing?

Some Poskim[305] rule it is forbidden to do so.[306] Practically, however, if she is wearing it in order to protect her from the cold, or for Tznius purposes, then she may wear pants under a skirt for extra modesty and protection.[307] It is forbidden to go skiing without a skirt due to reasons of modesty.]

May women wear pajama pants?

Some Poskim[308] rule it is forbidden for women or girls to wear pajama pants even at night in an only girl's room, and even if it is worn under a nightgown, unless she is wearing it to protect from the cold.[309] Other Poskim[310] however rule that pajama pants are permitted to be worn in private, while not in the presence of other men. Practically, it is permitted for women and girls to wear women pajama pants in private, under a nightgown or long T-shirt, for Tznius purposes or in order to protect from the cold, and so is the widespread custom even amongst Chassidic and G-d fearing women.[311] They are however not to wear the pants in front of other men that are in the house.

May one dress children in clothing of the opposite gender?[312]

Children or all ages [even below Chinuch and even a baby] may not wear clothing of the opposite gender unless there is no other clothing available and they need to wear it to protect from the cold or the sun.[313]

May children cross dress for a skit, play and the other purposes of the like?

This matter is subject to the same dispute mentioned regarding cross-dressing on Purim, or for a wedding. Practically, if it is recognizable that the person is a man or woman, and he or she merely wears a single clothing of the opposite gender, there is room to be lenient.[314] Nonetheless, the Rebbe expressed contempt for children who cross-dress for school plays and the like.[315]

---

[303] As a) They are different than boys pants and do not contain Lo Silbash [Avnei Tzedek Y.D. 72 and perhaps even according to Minchas Yitzchak 2:108 and Shevet Halevi 2:63 they would agree that by a toddler it is not considered at all a boys clothing any more than a girl being that so is the common practice] B) There is no immodesty involved, as they are below the age of three.

[304] See Minchas Yitzchak ibid

The reason: As it is forbidden for an adult to dress even a child with men's clothing as it is forbidden to feed a prohibition to a child of any age.

[305] Minchas Yitzchak 2:108

[306] The reason: As although many Poskim rule a woman may wear men's clothing to protect her from the cold and the like, nevertheless, here she is placing herself into the situation, and in this case, according to all Poskim we tell her simply not to go skiing and thus not have a need to wear the pants, [Minchas Yitzchak ibid]

[307] See Avnei Tzedek Y.D. 73; Shevet Halevi 2:63

The reason: As according to most Poskim it does not transgress Lo Silbash being she is not intending to wear it in order to resemble a man. It is difficult to accept the argument of the Minchas Yitzchak ibid as if so "Nasnu Devarecha Leshiurim."

[308] Minchas Yitzchak 2:108

[309] The reason: As the prohibition of Lo Silbash applies even when wearing the clothing in private, not in front of men. [ibid]

[310] See Avnei Tzedek Y.D. 73 and Rivivos Efraim 5:534 and Ohel Yaakov p. 308 in name of Rav Elyashiv and Rav Wozner and many Poskim of today that pajama pants do not contain the prohibition of Lo Silbash as they are not men's clothing at all and are not made to appear in public

[311] Avnei Tzedek Y.D 73

The reason: As according to most Poskim it does not transgress Lo Silbash being she is not intending to wear it in order to resemble a man.

[312] Igros Moshe 4:62-3

[313] See Minchas Yitzchak ibid

The reason: As it is forbidden for an adult to dress even a child with men's clothing, as it is forbidden to feed a prohibition to a child of any age. [Minchas Yitzchak ibid, based on Admur 343:2]

[314] P"M 696 M"Z 4; M"B 696:30 in name of P"M; Implication of Shach 182:7 as explained in Atzei Levona

[315] Igros Kodesh 10:238, printed in Shulchan Menachem 5:56

----------------- *Nidda*----------------

18. Kallah going to Mikveh:

Every Kallah prior to her wedding must purify herself from Nida blood through counting Shiva Nekiyim and immersing in a Mikveh. This applies even if the Kallah is not a Nida [i.e. is after menopause] as the Sages suspected for fresh sighting of blood as a result of her excitement for the wedding [i.e. Dam Chimud].[316] This law applies even for one who is remarrying his divorcee.[317] The following are the detailed laws of this immersion:

A. How many days before the wedding may a Kallah go to Mikveh?[318]

[Lechatchila], a Kallah is to immerse in the Mikveh as close as possible to the night of the wedding.[319] Nevertheless, the custom is that a Kallah may immerse in a Mikveh up until four nights prior to her wedding.[320] [Thus, if her wedding is on Thursday night, she may immerse starting from Sunday night.] She may not immerse prior to this time [i.e. prior to 4 nights before the night of her wedding[321]]. [However, in a time of great need, a Kallah may immerse even prior to four nights before the wedding.[322]]

B. Doing Bedikos until the wedding night:[323]

A Kallah who immerses prior to her wedding must continue doing two daily Bedikos after her Shiva Nekiyim until she has marital relations with her Chasan after the wedding.[324] These two daily Bedikos are required during all the days in-between her seven clean days and the marital relations which occurs after the wedding, and hence must be performed daily in the days between her Shiva Nekiyim and immersion [if the event that there are days in-between], and in the days between her immersion and the wedding. Thus, if she completed her Shiva Nekiyim on Sunday, went to Mikveh on Tuesday night, and is getting married Thursday night, she must continue doing two daily Bedikos until Thursday night. Furthermore, even after the wedding, if for whatever reason she did not have marital relations that first night, she must continue to do 2 Bedikos each day until she has successful intercourse.[325] Nevertheless, some Poskim[326] are lenient in this matter once the Chuppah has taken place, and hence those who are lenient to forgo these Bedikas once she has become married, have upon whom to rely.[327] In the event that the Kallah did not do any of these Bedikos past her seventh day, she nevertheless remains pure.[328] If, however, seven

---

[316] Michaber Y.D. 192:1; Rava Nida 66a

[317] Michaber Y.D. 192:5; Teshuvas Rashbatz

If one's divorcee is nursing or pregnant from his child: See Toras Hashlamim that it applies even if she is Meulekes Bedamim [i.e. nursing; pregnant]. See Taharah Kehalacha 9:14 for all the Poskim on this matter

If groom was intimate with his Kallah before the wedding: The above requirement applies even if one lived with his Kallah before the wedding and had marital relations with her, nevertheless, she must immerse prior to the wedding even if she is not a Nida [i.e. after menopause], as stated above. [Radbaz 3:423; Birkeiy Yosef 192 in Shiyurei Bracha; Taharah Kehalacha ibid, unlike Shiureiy Shevet Halevi 192:5]

[318] Rama 192:2

[319] Rama ibid; Beis Yosef 192; Hagahos Maimanis Issurei Biyah 11:5 in name of Rashbam; Mordechai in name of Rashbam; Rokeiach 317 in name of his father and teachers

[320] Rama ibid based on Mordechai ibid regarding one who immerses on Tuesday night for a Motzei Shabbos wedding, and the same applies any other time of the week, as explained in Sidrei Taharah 192:7; Darkei Teshuvah 192:20

[321] As there is to be no more than five nights between the immersion and intercourse. [Sidrei Taharah 192:7; Darkei Teshuvah 192:20]

[322] Pesach Habayis 192 brought in Darkei Teshuvah 192:19; Taharas Yisrael 192; Taharah Kehalacha 9:7

[323] Rama 192:2; Taz 192:5' Beis Yosef 192; Hagahos Maimanis Issurei Biyah 11:5; Tosafos Yuma 18; Kitzur SHU"A 157:1 [regarding until she immerses]; Maharam Merothenberg 320; Bach; Chochmas Adam [These Poskim apply this even after she immersed in the Mikveh, until the marital relations]; Taharah Kehalacha 9:8

Background: The Rama ibid rules that if a Kallah will have five nights between her immersion and marital relations, then she must check herself daily until the Beilas Mitzvah is performed. The Poskim ibid conclude that in truth this law applies to all the days between the 7th clean day and the Beilas Mitzvah.

Other opinions: Some Poskim rule a Kallah is not required at all to check herself before her wedding [unless she saw her period, in which case she is required to check herself for Shiva Nekiyim, and no longer]. [Opinions brought in Rosh, recorded in Tur 192]

[324] The reason: As we suspect perhaps she will see "Dam Chimud", blood of affection, until she has the first marital relations. [Taz 192:5 in name of Beis Yosef; Hagahos Maimanis Issurei Biyah 11:5]

[325] Implication of Rama ibid; Lechem Vesimla 192:9; So conclude Kitzur Dinei Taharah 12:5; Darkei Taharah p. 98; Taharah Kehalacha 9:9; 12:5

[326] Chovos Daas 192 [brought in Piskei Dinim 192:20]

[327] Taharah Kehalacha 9:9 footnote 14

[328] Rama ibid; Beis Yosef 192

days have passed without Bedikos prior to her Chuppah [irrelevant of when she went to Mikveh], she must recount the seven days.[329]

Machzir Gerushaso-Remarrying one's ex-husband: A woman who is remarrying her ex-husband is required to perform Shiva Nekiyim, immerse in a Mikveh, and perform Bedikos until the marital relations after the wedding, just as is the law by any other Kallah, as stated above.

C. May a Kallah prior to her wedding go to Mikveh during the daytime?[330]

If a Kallah prior to her wedding desires to immerse during the day time [for whatever reason she prefers] then she may do so even initially, so long as she has completed her Shiva Nekiyim and is immersing on her eighth day and onwards.[331] Practically, while many Kallahs immerse at night, it is also common for Kallahs to immerse during the day, in order to have greater privacy and calmness in their first immersion.[332]

Day of wedding-past Shiva Nekiyim: A Kallah may immerse on her eighth day and onwards, even on the day of her wedding [if the Chuppah will take place at night[333]].[334] Nevertheless, a Kallah is not to initially schedule her immersion for the day of her wedding, even if she is past the Shiva Nekiyim and the Chuppah will take place at night.[335] She is rather to schedule the immersion for the previous night or another time prior. If, for whatever reason, she did not immerse prior to the day of her wedding, then she is to immerse on the day of the wedding, although making sure that the Chuppah will take place at night.[336] In a time of need, she may immerse on the day of her wedding even if the Chuppah will take place during the day.[337] Regarding if she may immerse on the day of her wedding even if it falls on her 7th day, see the next Halacha!

D. May a Kallah go to Mikveh on the seventh day, if that is the day of her Chuppah?[338]

If the seventh day of Nekiyim of the Kallah falls on the day of her wedding, some Poskim[339] rule she may immerse during the day, being that she will not be with her Chasan until nighttime. Other Poskim[340],

---

The reason: As the suspicion of "Dam Chimud/blood of affection" in approximation to the wedding, is not as strong as the suspicion at the time of proposal to get married. [Taz 192:5]

[329] Sidrei Taharah; Chochmas Adam; Piskei Dinim; Taharah Kehalacha 9:10; See Rokeiach 317 that the Rabbinical institution was to count Shiva Nekiyim within seven days before the wedding.

[330] Rama 197:3; Shach 197:9; Maharil; Pardes Rimonim 197; Shulchan Hamareches Kiddushin p. 79; Nitei Gavriel Niddah 1 4:2 and 3 34:6

[331] Shach ibid; unlike Rama ibid who implies to permit even on the 7th day. Now, although majority of the Poskim are lenient like the Rama, and so is the final ruling, nevertheless this only applies in a time of need, such as the 7th day is the day of her wedding. However, when there is no time of need, certainly one is to be stringent like the Shach.
Other opinions: Some Poskim rule she may immerse even on the 7th day. [Implication of Rama ibid as bring all Achronim]

[332] Nitei Gavriel ibid footnote 3 that so is the custom in many places

[333] Degul Merivava 197:3; Pischeiy Teshuvah 197:10; Nitei Gavriel in next footnote; See regarding immersing on the 7th day: Rav Akiva Eiger ibid; Rav Poalim 4:21; Poskim brought in Nitei Gavriel 34 footnote 4
Other opinions: Some Poskim rule she may immerse during the day even if the Chuppah will take place by daytime. [Implication of Sidrei Taharah 197:11; Teshuvah Meahava 197 that so is custom; Mishnas Yaakov 3:128; Meiy Niddah 197:1; Poskim brought in Darkei Teshuvah 197:22; Poskim brought in Taharah Kehalacha 9 footnote 26 and Nitei Gavriel 34:2 footnote 6 Nitei Gavriel 3 34:2]

[334] Rama 197:3 even regarding 7th day; Maharil; implication of Shach 197:9 regarding 8th day and onwards and so learns Minchas Yaakov, brought in Yad Efraim 197:3; So rules Nitei Gavriel 3 34:6 that she may even initially immerse on her eighth day even if it is the day of her wedding so long as the Chuppah will take place at night, and that so is the custom

[335] Yad Efraim 197:3
The reason: As the Shach 197:9 argues on the Rama 197:3 regarding the seventh day, and the same should apply regarding the 8th day unless it is a time of need. [Yad Efraim ibid]

[336] Yad Efraim ibid

[337] Nitei Gavriel 3 34:2

[338] 197:3; See Yad Efraim 197:3; Taharah Kehalacha 9:16; Nitei Gavriel 1 5:3 and 3 34

[339] Implication of Rama 197:3, and so learns and rules: Beir Heiytiv 197:8; Sidrei Taharah 197:11; Degul Merivava 197:3; Gilyon Maharsha 197; Panim Meiros 2:4; Pischeiy Teshuvah 197:10; Chochmas Adam 115:14; Rav Akiva Eiger 71; Pardes Rimonim 197:3; Meiy Niddah 197:1; Pischeiy Niddah p. 67 in name of Rav Yonason Eibashitz; Teshuvah Meahava 2:366; Poskim brought in Yad Efraim ibid; Ben Ish Chaiy Shemini 2:17; Kovetz Zalman Shimon p. 11 suspects for Shach ibid initially although permits in time of need.

[340] Shach 197:9 in his understanding of Rama; Toras Hashelamim 197:8; Chasam Sofer 189 agrees with Shach; Avnei Nezer 250; Misgeres Hashulchan 197; Tzemach Tzedek 153 seems to suspect for ruling of Shach ibid although is lenient in a time of need; Minchas Yaakov [brought in Degul Merivva, Yad Efraim ibid] questions the ruling of the Shach although does not argue on him; Yad Efraim ibid concludes that she is to immerse twice, one time before the Chuppah in order to avoid Chuppas Niddah, and then a second time after the Chuppah. She is not to have Yichud with the Chasan until after her second immersion. See however Beis Shlomo 2:42 who argues against having her immersing twice; See Minchas Yitzchak 4:72

however, rule she may never immerse during the seventh day, even if the Chuppah will take place at night.[341] According to this opinion, she is to immerse at night prior to the Chuppah, or if not possible, then after the Chuppah.

The law if the Chuppah takes place during the day: Many Poskim[342] rule that even according to the first opinion above, it is only permitted for her to immerse during the day if the Chuppah will take place at nighttime, after Tzeis Hakochavim. It does not suffice to make the Chuppah close to nighttime, even if the Yichud will occur at night.[343] Other Poskim[344] however rule that she may immerse during the day even if the Chuppah will take place during the day.

Final ruling and custom:[345] Practically, when the seventh day of her count falls on the day of the wedding, if possible, she is to immerse at night prior to the Chuppah and delay the Chuppah until after the immersion.[346] If it is not possible for her to immerse at night, and to delay the Chuppah for this long, then she is to immerse during the day but delay the Chuppah until nighttime. If the Chuppah cannot be delayed until night, then she is to contact a Rav.[347]

When on the 7th day may she immerse:[348] She may immerse beginning from sunrise. If she immerses prior to sunrise but after Alos, it is valid Bedieved. If she immersed before Alos, then she must re-immerse after sunrise. [Some[349] write that she is to initially immerse after Pelag Hamincha, after completing her last Bedika.]

------------------ *Respecting Sages/teachers/elders* -----------------

19. Standing for your teacher, elders and Torah scholars:[350]
A. Standing for a Teacher and Torah scholar:[351]
It is a positive command in the Torah to stand in front of any Torah scholar.[352]

The age of the Sage: The command to stand before a Torah scholar applies even if the Torah scholar is not old but is young and wise. [This applies even if he is a child below the age of Bar Mitzvah.[353]]

The amount of wisdom that defines a Sage: The command to stand before a Torah scholars applies even if the Torah scholar is not one's teacher.[354] It applies to any Torah scholar who is greater than oneself [in Torah knowledge] and it is fit to learn from him.[355] This, however, only applies to a Torah scholar whose knowledge is excelled far beyond the normal common folk, in which case if the person has more knowledge than oneself, then he is to stand for him. If, however, the person's knowledge is not excelled far beyond the normal folk, then there is no obligation to stand for him, even though he is more

---

[341] The reason: As the reason for the prohibition of immersing on the seventh day is not only due to Serach Bita but also due to Shema Tistor Reiyasa, and it is thus more severe. [Shach ibid] The Poskim ibid, however, question the ruling and reason of the Shach based on the fact that if the Chuppah will not take place until night, there is also no chance of Tistor Reiyasa, so why is it any more severe than Serach Bita. See however Toras Hashelamim who defends the ruling of the Shach ibid.
[342] Degul Merivava ibid; Pischeiy Teshuvah ibid; Rav Akiva Eiger ibid; Rav Poalim 4:21; Poskim brought in Nitei Gavriel 34 footnote 4
[343] Degul Merivava ibid
[344] Implication of Sidrei Taharah 197:11; Teshuvah Meahava 197 that so is custom; Mishnas Yaakov 3:128; Meiy Niddah 197:1; Poskim brought in Darkei Teshuvah 197:22; Poskim brought in Taharah Kehalacha 9 footnote 26 and Nitei Gavriel 34:2 footnote 6
[345] Taharah Kehalacha ibid
[346] As rules the Shach ibid and so rules Kovetz Zalman Shimon p. 11
[347] Taharah Kehalacha ibid writes, that in such a case, she is to follow the ruling of the Yad Efraim ibid that she is to immerse twice, one time before the Chuppah in order to avoid Chuppas Niddah, and then a second time after the Chuppah. She is not to have Yichud with the Chasan until after her second immersion. [See Taharah Kehalacha ibid footnote 25] If even this is difficult for her to perform, Taharah Kehalacha concludes that she is to contact a Rav regarding if she may nevertheless immerse by day. [ibid] Nitei Gavriel 34:2 concludes that in a time of need, such as during the long summer days, she may immerse during the day and have her Chuppah take place by day, although avoid having a Halachically valid Yichud until night. He concludes that so is the ruling that he received from Rabbanim and that is done in practice.
[348] Chidushei Rav Akiva Eiger 197:3; Pischeiy Teshuvah ibid
[349] Nitei Gavriel 5:3
[350] Shulchan Aruch chapter 244; Kiddushin 32b
[351] 244:1
[352] Michaber ibid; Rambam Talmud Torah 6:1; Sefer Hamitzvos Mitzvas Asei 209; Chinuch Mitzvah 257; Semag 13
The reason: As the verse [Vayikra 19:32] states "Mipnei Seiva Takum", which means that one is to stand for those who have acquired wisdom.
[353] Shach 244:1; Perisha; Darkei Moshe; Beis Yosef, all in name of Shivlei Haleket
[354] Michaber ibid
[355] Rama ibid; Tur in name of Rambam [or Rameh [see Shach 244:2; See however Beis Yosef and Beir Hagoleh] and Ran

knowledgeable than oneself.[356] Practically, however, today the custom has become to only stand on behalf of the Rosh Yeshiva or Ravad [i.e. head of the Beis Din], although the validity of this custom requires further clarification.[357]

Teacher: One is obligated to stand for his Rebbe.[358] This applies even if he is not his main teacher from whom one has learned majority of his Torah.[359] A teacher, however, is not obligated to stand for his student, even if his student is a very great Torah scholar.[360]

A scholar standing for other scholars:[361] A scholar is not required to stand for another scholar and it rather suffices to simply show him some form of respect.

A scholar who is not G-d fearing:[362] A scholar who belittles the Mitzvos, and does not have fear of heaven, is considered like the lowest of the common folk [and one is certainly not to stand in respect of him].

Standing for one who is a Baal Mitzvos or is in process of doing a mitzvah:[363] It is permitted even for an exceptional Sage [even if he is the Gadol Hador[364]] to stand in honor of a person who is a man of good deeds [such as charity, philanthropy, Hiddur in Mitzvos].[365] Some Poskim[366] rule that he is even obligated to stand on his behalf [and certainly the common folk are obligated to stand for a Baal Mitzvos]. [Due to this, it is proper to stand in front of anyone who is performing a Mitzvah in one's presence, such as a Gabaiy Tzedaka when he is collecting money, and so too anyone else who is doing a Mitzvah.[367] Some Poskim[368] hold it is an actual obligation to stand. This, however, only applies if the person is doing a Mitzvah without payment. If, however, he is being paid, then one is not to stand on his behalf.[369]]

An Avel:[370] An Avel during Shiva is not obligated to stand in the presence of even the Gadol Hador, [and certainly HE is not obligated to stand for a Torah scholar or elder].[371]

Q&A

Must one stand for the wife of a Torah Sage?[372]

Some Poskim[373] rule one is obligated to stand for the wife of a Torah Sage, just as one is required to stand for the Torah Sage himself.[374] Some Poskim[375] rule this applies even after the death of the Sage.

---

[356] Shach 244:2; Tosafos; Semak 32; Rosh; Rameh

Other opinions: Some Poskim rule one is only required to stand for a Sage who is excelled far beyond even the Sages of his generation, even if he is more knowledgeable than oneself. [Rif, brought in Shach ibid]

[357] Shach 244:11

The reason: Seemingly, the reason for this is in order not to differentiate between Sages [and hence avoid offending those people who one thinks is not a Sage], however the Rosh yeshiva or Raavad is a recognizable and undisputable Sage to whom all are to stand for. [Shach ibid]

[358] Michaber 242:16

[359] Michaber 242:30

[360] Shach 242:39 in name of Bach and Derisha

[361] Michaber 244:8

[362] Michaber 243:3; Rosh in Teshuvah

[363] Michaber 244:12; Shabbos 31b

[364] See Rama 244:10

[365] The novelty of this ruling is that although in general we prohibit a Sage from doing matters that are beneath his dignity, in this case, it is permitted. [Shach 244:10 in name of Tur; Taz 244:6]

[366] Shach 244:10 in name of Tur and Ran and Bach; Taz 244:6; The Beis Yosef 244 brings two opinions regarding this matter

Other opinions: Some Poskim rule it is not obligatory to stand for a man of good deeds. [Opinion of Michaber as understood by Bach 244; Birkeiy Yosef 244; Ran; Ramban]

[367] Ben Ish Chaiy Ki Seitzei 2:19

[368] Taz 361:2 based on Michaber 361:4 and Tur 361 in name of Maharitz Geios and Yerushalmi who rules that one must stand by funeral because of the Gomlei Chassadim; and based on Kiddushin 33; Tanya chapter 46 "Therefore, the Sages obligated one to stand in front of one who is doing a Mitzvah even if he is a complete ignoramus"

The reason: As Hashem resides and becomes invested in the soul of the Mitzvah performer at the time of performance. [Tanya ibid]

[369] Ben Ish Chaiy Ki Seitzei 2:19;

[370] Rama 376:1

[371] The reason: As standing up in such a state of mourning is not considered a Hiddur. [Shvus Yaakov 3:26] Alternatively, because the Aveilim are busy. [Levush, brought in Gilyon Mahrsha 376] The practical ramification is regarding Tisha Beav. [Gilyon Mahrsha ibid]

[372] The Talmud [Shavuos 3b] states that the wife of Rav Huna came to a court case before Rav Nachman and debated whether he should stand for her, despite the fact that doing so may discourage the other party. It is discussed in Poskim as to whether this standing up is from the letter of the law or a Midas Chassidus.

Other Poskim[376], however, rule that doing so is not obligatory even when her husband is alive, and it is rather an act of piety. Some Poskim[377] write, that according to the Arizal, there is no need to stand for the wife of a Torah sage even as an act of piety. Other Poskim[378], however, negate this claim.

Must one stand for a scholarly woman?
Some Poskim[379] rule one is required to stand for a female Torah scholar. Other Poskim[380], however, rule one is not required to do so.

Must one stand for a blind Torah Scholar?[381]
Yes.

If one is holding a Chumash in his hands, must he stand up for a Torah scholar?
Some[382] rule that if one is holding a Chumash, he is not required to stand in honor of a Sefer Torah or Torah Scholar.[383]

If one is in the midst of learning Torah, must he stand for a Torah scholar/elder?[384]
Yes.

Must one stand for a Torah scholar on Tisha Beav?
Some Poskim[385] rule one is not required to stand for his teacher, or Torah Scholar, on Tisha Beav. Other Poskim[386], however, rule one is obligated to stand on Tisha Beav, and so is the custom.

Must one who is now an adult stand for the person who was his Melammed in Cheder?[387]
If one has vastly exceeded his Melammed in Torah knowledge, then he is not obligated to stand for him. If, however, most of one's knowledge is from this Melammed, then he is obligated to stand for him just the law by a main teacher.[388] [The Rebbe was witnessed to show much respect to his Melammed in Cheder, Rav Schneur Zalman Vilenkin, even many years later.]

---

[373] Taz 242:14 that the positive command to honor a Torah Sage applies also for his wife; Bach 242; Shiyurei Kneses Hagedola 244; Sheilas Yaavetz 2:135; brought in Pischeiy Teshuvah 244:1; See Birkeiy Yosef 244 in name of Bach and Taz 242, and Birkeiy Yosef C.M. 17:5 and Ben Ish Chaiy Ki Seitzei 2:16

[374] The reason: As Eishes Chaveir Kechaveir, as is proven from the above Gemara. [ibid]

[375] Taz ibid based on Maharam Mintz; Yaavetz ibid

Other opinions: Some Poskim rule one is not required to honor a Sages wife after his passing. [Taz ibid in name of Tosafos Shavuos Haeidus 36]

[376] Opinion who argues on Kneses Hagedola, brought in Sheilas Yaavetz ibid; Implication of all Poskim who omitted this ruling from the Shulchan Aruch; See there for a thorough discussion on the matter

[377] Brought in Birkeiy Yosef 244:1

[378] Ben Ish Chaiy Ki Seitzei 2:16

[379] Zera Yitzchak 1 p. 88 that he found a manuscript of the Peri Chadash who left this matter in question, although he rules that one is obligated; Yechaveh Daas 3:72 based on Sefer Chassidim 578 and all Poskim who require standing for an elderly woman, and he concludes that this matter is a Biblical doubt

[380] Ben Ish Chaiy Ki Seitzei 2:16; Rav Poalim 2 Kuntrus Sod Yesharim 9 based on Arizal in Shaar Hamitzvos Kedoshim; See Halachos Ketanos 1:154 that one is not required to stand for an elderly woman; See Minchas Chinuch 257:3 that according to the Rambam [whom is how we rule] there is no wisdom by a woman, as honoring one's wisdom only applies if he is commanded to learn it

[381] Shaar Efraim 78; Ginas Veradim Y.D. 4:1; See Birkeiy Yosef 244; Ben Ish Chaiy Ki Seitzei 2:15

[382] Sefer Chassidim 930; See Chaim Sheol 71:2; Shiyurei Bracha 244

[383] The reason: As it is improper for the Torah to stand for those who are learning it. [Chaim Sheol ibid] Alternatively, because one who is involved in a Mitzvah is exempt from another Mitzvah. [Sefer Chassidim ibid]

[384] Michaber 244:11; Chaim Sheol 71:2

[385] Shvus Yaakov 1, brought in Pischeiy Teshuvah 242:12

[386] Machazik Bracha, brought in Pischeiy Teshuvah 242:12

[387] See Ben Ish Chaiy Ki Seitzei 2:11 in name of Birkeiy Yosef in Shiyurei Bracha

[388] The reason: As this is a belittling of Torah to stand for an ignoramus. Likewise, if the teacher was paid, it is less respectable to stand for him. [ibid]

> **Must one stand in front of the body of a deceased Torah scholar?**
> Some Poskim[389] rule one is obligated to stand in the presence of a deceased Torah scholar. Other Poskim[390] rule one is not required to stand in the presence of a deceased scholar. According to all opinions, one must stand when a funeral procession is taking place, irrelevant of the scholarly status of the deceased.[391]

B. Standing for an old person:[392]

It is a Mitzvah [a possible Biblical obligation[393]] to stand in front of the elderly.[394]

The age defined as elderly:[395] An elderly person is defined, in this regard, as a person who has reached 70 years of age. [According to the Arizal and Kabala, one is to stand for a person who has reached 60 years of age.[396]]

Standing for an elderly ignoramus/Rasha:[397] The above obligation to stand before the elderly applies even if the old man is an ignoramus, so long as he is not a Rasha. [One who does not wear Tefillin, or Daven, is considered a Rasha, and one is not obligated to stand in his honor.[398] It is unclear if this applies even in a case that the person is a Tinok Shenishbah.]

Standing for a gentile elder:[399] [One is not required to stand in honor of an elderly gentile, however] one is to honor and respect him with words, and give him a hand of support.

A Sage standing for an elder:[400] Even a young Sage must stand for an elderly man who is very old. [If, however, he is a greater Sage than the elderly man[401]] he is not required to fully stand, and it suffices to slightly [get up to] show him honor.

An elderly man standing for another elder:[402] An elderly man is not required to stand for another elderly man, and it rather suffices to simply show some form of respect.

> **Q&A**
> **Must one stand for an elderly woman?**
> Some Poskim[403] rule one is obligated to stand for an elderly woman. However, other Poskim[404] rule one is not obligated to do so.

---

[389] Implication of Taz Y.D. 361:2 based on story in Moed Katan; Pischeiy Teshuvah Y.D. 361:3 based on Taz ibid

[390] Yad Eliyahu 54, brought in Pischeiy Teshuvah ibid

[391] Michaber 361:4; Tur 361 based on Yerushalmi and Maharitz Geios

[392] 244:1

[393] Implication of Rav Issi Bar Yehuda in Kiddushin 32a who includes a Zakein Ashmaiy in the verse and Rashi ibid states "The word Seiva in the verse implies every old man"; Implication of Minyan Hamitzvos of Rasag; Implication of Beis Yosef 244 who brings Rashi ibid; Implication of Minchas Chinuch Mitzvah 257; See Chinuch Mitzvah 257 who only adds "standing for elders" later on in the Mitzvah and Minchas Chinuch ibid questions if the Chinuch learns it is part of the Biblical Mitzvah or not, nonetheless, he concludes that we rule like Rav Isi Bar Yehuda; See however Rambam Mitzvah 209 who makes no mention at all that it is included in the Biblical command, and likewise in Hilchos Talmud Torah 6:9 he does not write it as a command at all, and simply states that "One is to stand for him." This strongly implies that he does not learn this to be a Biblical command. Likewise, the Michaber ibid and Tur ibid writes standing for elders only in the end of the Halacha, and states "Likewise it is a Mitzvah." It is unclear if the intent of the Michaber/Tur is to state that it is likewise a positive command, or if his intent is to say that it is a Mitzvah, but not a positive command. See Sefer Hamitzvos Rasag of Rav Perlow Mitzvah 11-12. Vetzaruch Iyun.

[394] Michaber ibid; Tur 244; Rambam Talmud Torah 6:9; Chinuch Mitzvah 257; Semag 13; Rebbe Isi Ben Yehuda in Kiddushin 32b; Rebbe Yochanon in Kiddushin 33a that the Halacha is like Isi

The reason: As the verse in Parshas Kedoshim [Vayikra 19:32] states "Mipnei Seiva Takum", which means that one is to get up for his elders.

Other opinions: Some rule there is no obligation to stand for an elder who is not a Torah scholar. [Tana Kama and Rebbe Yossi Hagelili in Kiddushin ibid; Pesikta on Parshas Kedoshim omits opinion of Issi ben Yehuda; Implication of Sheilasos on Kedoshim ibid; Implication of Rashi Kedoshim ibid; Implication of Or Zarua, Yireim, Ravaan p. 137 who omit the words "Elder"; See Sefer Hamitzvos Rasag of Rav Perlow ibid]

[395] Michaber ibid

[396] Brought in Birkeiy Yosef 244; Ben Ish Chaiy Ki Seitzei 2:12; Minchas Chinuch 257

[397] Rama ibid; Beis Yosef in name of Tosafos Kiddushin 32; Hagahos Maimanis 6; Mordechai; Rabbeinu Yerucham; Ran; Rabbeinu Tam

[398] Ben Ish Chaiy Ki Seitzei 2:12

[399] Michaber 244:7; Kiddushin 33a

[400] Michaber 244:7

[401] Shach 244:5

[402] Michaber 244:8

[403] Sefer Chassidim 578; Beis Yehuda Y.D. 1:28; Minchas Chinuch 257:3 based on final ruling like Rebbe Issi Bar Yehuda; Kiryat Chana David 1:15; Yechaveh Daas 3:72; Implication of Chinuch ibid, and all other Rishonim who record "This Mitzvah applies to both men and women"

C. In what circumstances must one stand for the Sage/elderly?

Within four Amos:[405] One is obligated to stand for a scholar/elder upon them reaching within one's four Amos [196 cm].[406] One is not [i.e. forbidden[407]] to stand in his honor, prior to him reaching within one's four Amos.[408] The same applies for one's teacher, if he is not his main teacher from which he learned majority of his wisdom, then he must stand upon him reaching within one's four Amos.[409]

Rabbo Hamuvhak/Gadol Hador/Ravad/Nassi: One must stand in honor of his main[410] Rebbe [i.e. Rabbo Hamuvhak] upon his Rebbe entering within his sight [even though he is not within four Amos of him].[411] [This is approximately the distance of 128 meters.[412]] The same law applies towards an exceptional Torah Scholar, even if he is not one's teacher, one must stand upon him entering within one's sight.[413] The definition of an exceptional Torah scholar, in this regard, is one who is considered the Gadol Hador and is famous amongst his generation for his wisdom.[414] This refers to a Sage who is exceptionally greater than the other Sages of his generation.[415] The same applies for a Nassi; that one must stand in his honor upon him entering within one's sight.[416] The same applies for a Rosh Av Beis Din [Ravad], that one must stand on his behalf upon him entering within one's sight.[417] Some Poskim[418] however rule, that in today's times we no longer have a concept of a Rosh Av Beis Din.

Riding:[419] If the scholar/elder is riding on a horse, or wagon [or car], and reaches within one's four Amos, it is considered as if he is walking in one's four Amos, and one must stand on his behalf.

In the Beis Midrash/Shul/room:[420] When the Nassi enters the Beis Midrash, everyone is to stand for him, and they do not sit down until he tells them to sit down. When the Ravad [i.e. head of Beis Din] enters the Beis Midrash, they make for him two rows through which he walks in-between, and they remain standing until he sits in his place. When a regular Sage enters the Beis Midrash, whoever is within his four Amos upon him walking by, is to stand for him, thus having some people sitting and some people standing, until the Sage reaches his place to sit. [Some Poskim[421] however rule that in today's times, whenever a Sage or elder enters into a room that is surrounded by walls, everyone in the room must stand for him, even if he is not within one's four Amos.[422]]

---

[404] Halachos Ketanos 1:154; Ben Ish Chaiy Ki Seitzei 2:16; Rav Poalim 2 Kuntrus Sod Yesharim 9 based on Arizal in Shaar Hamitzvos Kedoshim; Shevet Halevi 1:114; See Avnei Yashpei 1:188

[405] Michaber 244:2 and 9 and 13-14

[406] Michaber 244:2; Kiddushin 33a

The reason: One is required to stand in a way that is recognizable to the elder that it is being done out of honor and respect, and it is only recognizable once the person reaches his four Amos. [Taz 244:3; Kiddushin ibid]

[407] Shach 244:6 and Birkeiy Yosef 244 based on implication of Michaber, as the Michaber 244:2 already taught us that one is not obligated to stand until the Sage reaches the four Amos, so what need is there to repeat this ruling if not for the fact the Michaber is now teaching us that it is even forbidden to stand prior to this point; Ben Ish Chaiy Ki Seitzei 2:13

[408] Michaber 244:9

The reason: It is forbidden to stand prior to the Sage reaching within one's four Amos being that it is not recognizable that it is being done in his honor, being that there is no obligation to stand for him yet. [Shach ibid; Birkeiy Yosef ibid]

[409] Michaber 242:30

Other Poskim: Some rule that one must stand Kimalei Einav for any teacher from which one learned Torah from, even if he did not learn majority of his Torah from him. [Maharik 12]

[410] This refers to one from who one has learned majority of his Torah from. [Rama 242:4; Michaber 242:30; See Bava Metzia 33; Sheilasos 131]

[411] Michaber 242:16; 244:9; Kiddushin 33a

[412] Shach 244:8 in name of Semak 52

[413] Michaber 244:10

[414] Rama ibid; Terumas Hadeshen 138; Tosafos

[415] Shach 244:2

[416] Michaber 244:14

[417] Michaber 244:13

[418] Shach 244:11 based on Semak 32

[419] Michaber 244:2; 242:16; Kiddushin 33b; Rashi ibid

[420] Michaber 244:15; Horiyos 12b

[421] Kneses Hagedola 244 and Birkeiy Yosef 244:5 leaves this matter in question; Ben Ish Chaiy Ki Seitzei 2:13 and in his Sefer Mekabtziel concludes that one must be stringent by a Biblical command.

[422] The reason: As perhaps in a closed area, the entire area is considered to be within one's four Amos. Now, although the above law states that only for a Nassi must all the people in the Beis Midrash stand up, perhaps this only applied in previous times, and only in a Beis Midrash was the above order of standing given out, being that only students sat in the Beis Midrash and each day the Nassi/Avaad/Rebbe would enter, and they thus wanted to delegate different levels of respect. However, today, this is no longer applicable. [Birkeiy Yosef ibid]

Closing one's eyes:[423] It is forbidden for one to close his eyes prior to the scholar/elder entering one's four Amos, simply in order to refrain from needing to stand for him upon him reaching his four Amos.

Bathroom/bathhouse:[424] One is not required to stand for the scholar/elder in a bathroom or bathhouse.[425] This however only applied in the inner room of the bathhouse, however in the outer room [including the middle room in which people change[426]] one is required to stand.[427]

During work:[428] Workers are not obligated to [stop and] stand for a scholar [or elder] while they are working.[429] [If, however, one is self-employed, he may choose to stop his work and stand, if he wishes to be stringent.] If, however, one is working for another [i.e. an employee], it is forbidden for the worker to be stringent upon himself and stand during his work. [This applies even in the presence of one's main Rebbe.[430]]

Learning Torah:[431] Even while one is learning Torah, he is obligated to stand for [a sage/elder]. [One must stand for a Sage/teacher/elder even in a Shul, and even during Davening.[432]]

Rebbe in presence of his Rebbe:[433] One may not delegate honor to a student in the presence of his Rebbe, unless the Rebbe also delegates respect to the student.[434] This applies even to the student's student; that the student may not stand in the presence of his Rebbe, when his Rebbe is in the presence of his own Rebbe, unless his Rebbe's Rebbe also delegates respect to his Rebbe [which is his student].[435]

Q&A

If one hears the voice of the Sage/elderly, but does not see him, must he stand in his honor?
Some Poskim[436] rule that if one hears the sound of the Sage, or elderly, coming within his vicinity he must stand in his honor.

Who is defined as a Rabbo Hamuvhak, one's main teacher?[437]
A Rabbo Hamuvhak is defined as any person from whom the student has received majority of his Torah wisdom, whether in Chumash, Mishneh, or Talmud.[438] In today's times, however, this mainly relates to the Rebbe from whom one learned majority of his knowledge in Halacha, and directed him in the proper path, and not one who taught him the ways of Pilpul and Chakira.[439]

One's Melammed in Cheder:[440] If most of one's Torah knowledge is from his Melammed in Cheder, then he is obligated to stand for him, just like a main teacher.

A Maggid Shiur/Shul Rabbi:[441] If most of one's Torah knowledge comes from the classes given by a certain Rabbi, then this Rabbi is considered his Rabbo Hamuvhak. This applies irrelevant of Torah

[423] Michaber 244:3; Kiddushin 32b
[424] Michaber 244:4; Kiddushin 32b
[425] The reason: As the verse states "Stand and honor" from which we learn that only when the standing respects and honors the person, must one stand. [Michaber ibid]
Rabbo Hamuvhak/One's Rebbe: Some Poskim rule that the above allowance [not to stand] applies even towards one's main Rebbe, Rabbo Hamuvhak. [Lechem Mishneh Talmud Torah 6, brought in Pischeiy Teshuvah 244:3] Others however rule that it does not apply by one's main Rebbe, and one is required to stand even in a bathhouse, in respect of his main Rebbe [Turei Even on Rambam ibid, brought in Pischeiy Teshuvah ibid]
[426] Shach 244:3; see Admur 84:1
[427] Rama ibid in name of many Rishonim
[428] Michaber 244:5
[429] The reason: As the Torah did not obligate one to honor the elderly if doing so will cause one a loss of money. [Kneses Hagedola 244 in name of Mahariy Beiy Rav 52; Birkey Yosef 244 in name of Toras Kohanim; Bavli; Yerushalmi]
[430] Kneses Hagedola 244 in name of Reb Avraham Halevi; Ben Ish Chaiy Ki Seitzei 2:17
[431] Michaber 244:11; Abayey in Kiddushin 33b; See Chaim Sheol 71:2
[432] Ben Ish Chaiy Ki Seitzei 2:15
[433] 242:21
[434] Michaber ibid
[435] Rama ibid; Shivlei Haleket
[436] Gilyon Maharsha 240:7 regarding a father, and 244:1 regarding a Sage or elderly, based on Rama 282:2 that in such a case one must stand for the Sefer Torah even if he does not see it
[437] 242:30
[438] Michaber ibid; Baba Metzia 33a
[439] Rama ibid; Maharik 170
[440] Ben Ish Chaiy Ki Seitzei 2:11 in name of Birkeiy Yosef in Shiyurei Bracha

subject, whether it be Tanach, Gemara, or Halacha.

<u>One who learned majority of his knowledge from Sefarim:</u>[442] One whose majority of knowledge was personally acquired through the study of Sefarim, is not considered to have a Rabbo Hamuvhak, and hence, even one's primary teacher is only considered a teacher.

If one is sitting on the Bima and a Sage/teacher/elder walks by, must one stand up if he passes within his four Amos, below the Bima?[443]
Yes.

If one is sitting in a room, and a Sage/teacher/elder walks by in a different room, must one stand up if he passes within his four Amos?[444]
No.

One must stand for a Sage/teacher/elder even if he is in the middle of Davening?[445]
Yes.

D. For how long must one remain standing?[446]

Regular Sage/elderly: One must remain standing until the scholar/elder passes from in front of his face.[447] As soon as the scholar [or elder] passes in front of him, he is [i.e. must[448]] to sit down.[449] [Thus, he is to sit down prior to the Sage passing a four Amos distance from him.[450]] Some Poskim[451] however, rule he is to remain standing until the Sage passes a distance of four Amos from him.

Ravad:[452] One must remain standing in honor of the Rosh Av Beis Din until he passes a distance of four Amos from him. Some Poskim[453], however, rule that in today's times we no longer have a concept of a Rosh Av Beis Din.

Teacher/Gadol Hador/Nassi:[454] One must remain standing in honor of his main Rebbe [i.e. Rabbo Hamuvhak], and Gadol Hador, and Nassi, until his Rebbe/Gadol/Nassi sits down or until he passes from within his sight. Once his Rebbe [sits[455]], or passes from his sight, he is to sit down.[456]

In a Beis Midrash: See Halacha C!

Q&A
If the elder/Sage remains standing within one's four Amos, for how long must one remain standing?
This matter requires further analysis. Seemingly, one should remain standing until the amount of time it takes him to pass from before oneself.

---

[441] Ben Ish Chaiy ibid
[442] Ben Ish Chaiy Ki Seitzei 2:20 in name of Binyan Tziyon 83; See also Admur 429:3
[443] Ben Ish Chaiy Ki Seitzei 2:13
[444] Ben Ish Chaiy Ki Seitzei 2:13
[445] Ben Ish Chaiy Ki Seitzei 2:15 in name of Birkei Yosef
[446] Michaber 244:9 and 14-15
[447] Michaber 244:2 and 9; Kiddushin 33b
[448] See Shach 244:6 regarding him learning in the Michaber that it is prohibited to stand prior to entering the four Amos, as otherwise the ruling of the Michaber would be repetitive. The same then should apply here regarding this law, as the Michaber already stated this law in 244:2. As for the reason that it is an obligation for one to sit, it is to show that the only reason he stood is in honor of the Sage/elder. [ibid]
[449] Michaber 244:9
[450] See Shach 244:7 and Michaber 244:13
[451] Shach 244:7 in name of Bach; Rashi; Rosh
[452] Michaber 244:13
[453] Shach 244:11 based on Semak 32
[454] Michaber 242:16; 244:9-10 and 14; Based on Yuma 53b; Kiddushin 33a
[455] Shach 242:35
[456] Michaber 242:16

E. How to stand:[457]
One must fully stand up in front of the scholar/elder with exception to those cases mentioned above in which only slight standing is required.

F. How often is one required to stand for a Torah Sage or elderly person?[458]
Some Poskim[459] rule that one is only obligated to stand for his Rebbe twice a day, one time in the morning and a second time in the evening.[460] This, however, only applies in the house of the Rav [i.e. in private], however, in public, when one is in front of others who do not know that he already stood, he is obligated to stand [each time]. [Even in the privacy of the Rebbe's home, it is permitted for one to stand for his Rebbe more than two times a day if he so wishes, and it is only that he is not obligated to do so.[461] Other Poskim[462], however, rule one is obligated to stand for his Rebbe even 100 times. Some Poskim[463] rule that this stringency only applies to a Torah scholar and not to an elder. It is questionable if this dispute applies likewise towards standing for one's parent.[464]]

G. Avoiding making people stand for you:[465]
It is improper for a Sage to trouble the public, and deliberately pass in front of them, in order so they stand up for him. Rather, he is to take a short path while walking from one area to another in order to diminish the amount of people that need to stand for him. If the Sage is able to walk a different route, and bypass the congregation, it is considered meritorious for him. Alternatively, the Sage is to enter the Shul prior to the congregation.[466] [This mainly applied in previous times when the congregation would sit on the ground, and it was troublesome to make them stand for him. However, today that people sit on benches and there is no trouble involved, one need not be particular in this matter. Although even today, one is not to deliberately walk in front of the congregation in order so they stand for him.[467] However, some Poskim[468] rule that even today one is to specifically take a different route in order not to trouble the congregation to stand, and that so is the custom of the elderly Sages.]

H. A scholar/elder who forgives his honor:[469]
All [people for whom one is required to stand, such as a Sage; Avad; Gadol Hador; Nassi; elder] if they forgive their honor, then their honor is forgiven [and it is no longer obligatory to stand for them]. Nevertheless, it remains a Mitzvah to honor them and slightly stand up for them. [Some Poskim[470] rule that only a Rav may forgive his respect, however, one who is not a Rav but learns Halacha or Talmud cannot forgive his respect.[471]]

Summary:
For whom must one stand? One is required to stand in the presence of one's teacher of Torah, Torah scholar, and elderly person. One is also to stand for the wife of a Torah Sage, a Baal Mitzvos, and one

---

[457] Taz 244:4
[458] Rama 242:16; See Kiddushin 33b
[459] Tur in name of Rambam
[460] The reason: As the honor of his teacher should not be any greater than the honor of Hashem in Kerias Shema. [Taz 242:12]
[461] Shach 242:36 based on wording of Rama ibid; Bach 242 and Semag 13 who write "not obligated"; however, the Rambam, Tur and other Poskim write "not permitted." The Rama ibid hence interprets this to mean "not obligated." [Shach ibid]
[462] Shach 242:37 in name of Rosh Tur; Levush; Sefer Chassidim 23
[463] Shevet Halevi 5:130; However, see Sefer Chassidim 23 who writes one must stand for a Zaken even 100 times
[464] Aruch Hashulchan 240:24 leaves this matter in question; Chayeh Adam 66:7 rules one does not need to stand for a parent more than twice a day, once in the morning and once in the evening.
[465] Michaber 244:6; Kiddushin 33a
[466] See Michaber 244:16 "It is not praiseworthy for a Torah Sage to enter last"; See Taz 244:8
[467] Shach 244:4
[468] Birkeiy Yosef 244
[469] Michaber 244:14; Kiddushin 32a
[470] Chida in Shiyurei Bracha 243
[471] The reason: As the Torah is not considered his that he can forgive his respect, while by a Rav the Torah is considered already his. [ibid]

who is performing a Mitzvah. However, the custom of many today is to only stand on behalf of the Rosh Yeshiva or Ravad, although the validity of this custom requires further clarification. If any of the above people forgive their honor, it is no longer obligatory to stand for them, although it still remains a Mitzvah to honor them and slightly stand up for them. One may not delegate honor to a student in the presence of his Rebbe, unless the Rebbe also delegates respect to that student.

Who is defined as a Sage/teacher/elder? A Sage is defined as any G-d fearing person whose Torah knowledge far exceeds that of the common folk. An elder is defined as any Jew who is above 70 years of age, and according to Kabala, above 60 years of age, and is not Rasha. A teacher is defined as anyone who has taught one Torah, even if he did not learn from him majority of his Torah.

When must one stand? One is required to stand upon the above people entering one's four Amos, whether on foot or in a vehicle, and must remain standing until the person passes from in front on him, in which case he is then to be seated. This is with exception to a main teacher/Gadol Hador/Ravad/Nassi, in which case one must stand upon them entering within his sight, and by a Ravad, must remain standing until he passes a distance of four Amos from him, while by a main teacher/Gadol Hador/Nassi he must remain standing until his Rebbe/Gadol/Nassi sits down, or until he passes from within his sight. Some Poskim however rule that in today's times we no longer have a concept of a Rosh Av Beis Din. Likewise, one whose majority of knowledge was personally acquired through the study of Sefarim is not considered to have a main teacher. Some Poskim rule that in today's times, whenever a Torah scholar or elder enters into a room that is surrounded by walls, everyone in the room must stand for him. It is forbidden for one to close his eyes prior to the scholar/elder entering his four Amos, simply in order to refrain from needing to stand for him upon him reaching his four Amos. One is not required to stand for the scholar/elder in a bathroom, or the inner room of a bathhouse. Workers are not obligated to [stop and] stand for a scholar [or elder] while they are working. Even while one is learning Torah he is obligated to stand for [a sage/elder].

How to stand: One must fully stand up in front of the scholar/elder with exception to those cases mentioned above in which only slight standing is required.

How often to stand: In public, one must stand in face of his Rebbe/scholar/elder even 100 times that day. However, in private, it is disputed as to whether one needs to stand more than twice a day, one time in the morning and one time in the evening.

Q&A

May a Torah scholar belittle himself for the sake of a Mitzvah, such as to play music by a wedding?[472]

It is permitted for a Sage to belittle himself for the sake of Heaven out of service of Hashem and fulfillment of his Mitzvos, such as to rejoice the Chasan and Kallah. According to some Poskim[473], however, he may not belittle himself for the sake of a Mitzvah Bein Adam Lechaveiro, such as to return a lost object.

---

[472] Chavos Yair 202; brought in Shaareiy Teshuvah 244:4
[473] Rosh brought in Michaber C.M. 263:3

---------------- *Talmud Torah*----------------

20. Siyum Misechta:[474]

The making of a Siyum:[475] When one completes a Misechta, it is a Mitzvah to rejoice and hold a [public[476]] festive meal for the occasion. [One may make several meals, throughout several days, in honor of the Siyum.[477]]

The status of the meal:[478] The festive meal held for the occasion of a Siyum Misechta is considered a Seudas Mitzvah.

When to finish the Misechta and make the Siyum:[479] Upon reaching the end of a Misechta, one is to leave a small section at the end of the Misechta to be learnt on the day that he plans to make the Siyum and festive meal, thereby completing the Misechta on that occasion.

Attendance:[480] It is a great Mitzvah and obligation for others to join the Siyum celebration, and take part in his Simcha, even though they did not complete the Misechta.

The order of the Siyum-Kaddish and Asara Bnei Rav Papa:[481] After completing the final lines of the Misechta, during the Siyum celebration, Kaddish Derabanan is to be recited if a Minyan is present. One is to strive to have a Minyan by the Siyum in order to say this Kaddish. The prayer of [Hadran Alach and] Asara Bnei Rav Papa is recited [before the Kaddish].[482] [Other prayers are customarily added, including a prayer within the Kaddish Hagadol. The Chabad custom is to recite the regular Hadran Alach, Aseres Bnei Rav Papa, and then go straight to a regular Kaddish Derabanan.[483]]

Q&A

On which Misechtos can a Siyum be performed?

One may make a Siyum celebration, with a Seudas Mitzvah, after completing any of the following:

- Finishing Chamisha Chumshei Torah with a commentary.[484]
- Completion of one of the Sefarim of Navi together with a commentary of the Rishonim.[485] However, it is disputed in Poskim if one may learn a single Sefer simply for the sake of making a Siyum and exempting oneself from a fast.[486]
- A Misechta in Shas.[487] This includes even one of the short Misechtos, such as Miseches Kallah, Sofrim, and Avos Derebbe Nasan.[488] Some Poskim[489] rule one may make a Siyum even on one Perek of a Misechta. It is best to make a Siyum that follows all opinions.[490]

---

[474] See Sefer Askinu Seudasa for a full digest on this topic

[475] Rama Y.D. 246:26; O.C. 551:10; Nimukei Yosef Bava Basra Perek Yeish Nochalin; Shabbos 118b "Abayey said "When we would see a Torah scholar complete a Misechta we would have a celebratory day."; Midrash Raba Koheles; Midrash Raba Shir Hashirim; Lekach Tov Tzav in name of Pesikta;

[476] Igros Kodesh 14:374

[477] Chavos Yair 70 that a meal may be held also the next day, and perhaps even the day later, brought in Pischeiy Teshuvah 246:78; Aruch Hashulchan 246:27

[478] Rama Y.D. 246:26; O.C. 551:10; Nimukei Yosef Bava Basra Perek Yeish Nochalin; Or Zarua 2:407

[479] Shach 246:27 in name of Mahram Mintz 2:119; Aruch Hashulchan 246:44 based on Moed Katan 9a; Kaf Hachaim 551:161

[480] Shach 246:27 in name of Mahram Mintz 2:119; Taz 246:9 in name of Rashal

[481] Shach 246:27 in name of Mahram Mintz 2:119

[482] Shach ibid; Maharam Mintz 2:119; Teshuvas Harama in end; Rashal in Yam Shel Shlomo Bava Kama 37; Rav Haiy Gaon, brought in Sefer Haeshkol

The reason: Some suggests that Rav Papa was wealthy, and was accustomed to make a large Siyum for his sons when they would complete a Misechta. The ten sons also correspond to the ten utterances with which the world was created. [Rama ibid] Alternatively, the sons of Rav Papa are mentioned because they all passed away Al Kiddush Hashem during the lifetime of their father, and hence we mention their name Leilui Nishmas. [Zecher Yehoseif on Miseches Brachos]

[483] Reshimos Devarim of Rav Chitrik 4:219; Directive of Rebbe to Rav Binyamin Althouse; Toras Menachem 4:239 that the Rebbe remarked to Rav Meir Ashkenazi who said the long Kaddish "This is a novelty to me, and I have never seen this done beforehand."; See also Hisvadyus 5745 3:1700

[484] Igros Moshe O.C. 1:157; See Rama 669; Askinu Seudasa Miluim 1

[485] Minchas Pitim Y.D. 246:26; Pnei Yehoshua Brachos 17a; Halef Lecha Shlomo 386; Igros Moshe O.C. 1:157; Teshuvos Vehanhagos 1:300

[486] See Piskeiy Teshuvos 470:9

[487] Rama ibid

[488] Pischa Zuta in name of Hadras Kodesh; Rebbe in meeting with Pnei Menachem of Ger, printed in Hisvadyus 5744 13th Adar Rishon

[489] Mentioned in Hisvadyos 5749 4:86; 5750 1:97; Rebbe in meeting with Pnei Menachem of Ger, printed in Hisvadyus 5744 13th Adar Rishon

[490] Rebbe ibid

- A Misechta of Talmud Yerushalmi.[491]
- A complete Seder of Shisha Sidrei Mishneh.[492]
- Some Poskim[493] rule one may make a Siyum on a single Misechta of Mishnayos in Shisha Sidrei Mishneh, if one learned it in depth with the commentaries. However, it is disputed in Poskim if one may learn a single Misechta simply for the sake of making a Siyum and exempting oneself from a fast.[494] Practically, it is best to make a Siyum that follows all opinions.[495]
- A Sefer of Zohar, even if one does not understand.[496]
- Completion of one of the four sections of Shulchan Aruch.[497]
- Completion of the Rambam's Mishneh Torah.[498]
- Completion of the writing of a Sefer in Chidushei Torah.[499]

Can one make a Siyum if he did not comprehend what he learned?[500]
No. the Siyum can only be made if one understands, to some level, the words that he read [with exception to the Sefer HaZohar[501]]. However, a Siyum may be made if one understands majority of the material, even though some of the material was not understood.[502]

Can one make a Siyum on a later date if he already completed the Misechta?
The Siyum celebration must be made in close proximity to the completion of the Misechta, as otherwise the Simcha dissipates.[503] [In the event that the Misechta was completed many days earlier, seemingly, the Siyum celebration does not have the status of a Seudas Mitzvah. Perhaps, however, if he concluded the last lines only superficially, with intent to study it in greater depth on the day of the Siyum, then this is also valid. Vetzaruch Iyun!]

May one make a Siyum if he learned the Misechta out of order?[504]
Yes.

May one make a Siyum Misechta if it was studied in parts by several individuals?[505]
Yes.

---

[491] Rebbe in meeting with Pnei Menachem of Ger, printed in Hisvadyus 5744 13th Adar Rishon
[492] Pnei Meivin 103; Betzeil Hachochma 4:99
[493] Peri Hasadeh 3:91; Binyan Shlomo 59; Betzeil Hachochma 4:99; Afrakasa Deanya 1:154-3; Mentioned in Hisvadyos 5749 4:86; 5750 1:97; See Yabia Omer 1:26
[494] See Piskeiy Teshuvos 470:9
[495] Rebbe ibid
[496] Yabia Omer 1:26
[497] Beis Avi 2:52; Mishneh Halachos 6:166
[498] Likkutei Sichos 32:271
[499] Shearim Hametzuyanim Behalacha 113:10 in name of Tiferes Shmuel 55
[500] Piskeiy Teshuvos 470:9
[501] Yabia Omer 1:26
[502] Afrakasa Deanya 1:154
[503] See Shach ibid in name of Maharam of Mintz that one who desires to delay the Siyum celebration is to leave some lines unlearned.
[504] Minchas Yitzchak 2:93; Betzeil Hachochma 2:28
[505] Kinyan Torah 5:52

--------------- *Tzedaka*---------------
21. Using Maaser money to pay tuition for school/Yeshiva/seminary or other Torah education:[506]

The letter of the law:[507] If one cannot afford[508] to pay the tuition for Torah education from non-Maaser, or non-Chomesh funds, it is permitted for him to use his Maaser or Chomesh money [which he separated], for the sake of paying for the tuition of his older sons [Torah education].[509] [If, however, one can afford to pay tuition from his regular income, then he is not use Maaser or Chomesh money to pay tuition.[510] Furthermore, some Poskim[511] learn that in locations where sending one's children to a school of education is compulsory according to law, one may not use any Maaser money towards paying tuition, whether of a son or daughter.[512] However, once the child graduates from compulsory education, one may use Maaser money to pay for their education, even according to this opinion. Other Poskim[513], however, dispute the above opinion, and state that one may deduct tuition from Maaser even in areas that the education is compulsory.]

The ideal practice:[514] Despite the above allowance, one who does not deduct tuition payments from his Maaser or Chomesh funds [and instead minimizes his expenses so he can afford to pay tuition from his regular income] is considered clever[515] and is rewarded. This is in light of the teaching of the Sages[516] who state that all the [annual] income of an individual is decided from Rosh Hashanah until Yom Kippur. Whatever income he will make that year, from which he can sustain himself with, is already pre-decided in an exact amount. For this reason, one is to be careful not to overspend, as he will not have more money added to his predetermined annual budget. This however is with exception to the expenses endured in celebrating Shabbos and Yom Tov **and educating his sons in Torah learning**, of which we rule that whoever adds [in expenses] Hashem adds to his annual budget, and allocates to him extra funds at that time, or later on.

How much of the tuition may be deducted from Maaser/Chomesh:[517] All the expenses necessary for facilitating the Torah education of one's older son may be deducted from Maaser or Chomesh, if one

---

[506] Admur Hilchos Talmud Torah 1:7; See Glosses of Rav Ashkenazi volume 2 p. 482-506; Tzedaka Umishpat 6:14; Hilchos Maaser Kesafim chapter 16

[507] Admur Hilchos Talmud Torah 1:7; 3:4; Michaber 251:3 "One who gives money to his older sons and daughters who he is not obligated to support, in order to teach them Torah and direct the daughters in a straight path is considered Tzedaka"; Rambam Hilchos Matanos Aniyim 10:16; Peas Sadcha 118; Tzedaka Umishpat 6:14

[508] So writes Admur in 1:7 based on Shach 249:3 in name of Maharam regarding using Maaser money for a Mitzvah that it may only be used if one cannot afford it otherwise, however, no mention of this condition is made in Admur 3:4 or Michaber 251:3 or Rambam ibid, and on the contrary, from Shach 251:5 it is clearly evident that one may pay for their education even if he can afford it. See Chasam Sofer Y.D. 231; Glosses of Rav Ashkenazi ibid 46a and 49a

[509] The reason: As any matter which is a Mitzvah, but is not an obligation, one may use Maaser money to pay with, and one cannot afford it otherwise. [Shach 249:3; Taz 249:1; Maharshal; Derisha 249:1; Maharam Menachem 459; Toras Menachem 34:272 [brought in Shulchan Menachem 5:110]

[510] Implication of Admur ibid who makes the entire allowance contingent on "If he cannot afford"; See Poskim in previous footnotes

[511] Igros Moshe Y.D. 2:113; See Teshuvos Vehanhagos 1:560; Hilchos Maaser Kesafim 11:16-17

[512] The reason: As one may not use Maaser money to pay for things that are considered an obligation, and since sending him to an educational institution is an obligation, one may not deduct tuition from those funds. [ibid]

[513] So is evident from all of today's Poskim recorded in the footnotes below who allow deducting tuition from Maaser: Shevet Halevi 5:133; Tzedaka Umishpat ibid; Orchos Rabbeinu 1:301; Rav Mordechai Ashkenazi

[514] Admur ibid 1:7; See also Likkutei Sichos 9:346; Toras Menachem 34:272 [brought in Shulchan Menachem 5:110] that it is proper for each person to push himself to not need to use Maaser money for Mitzvah purposes, and rather he is to use his own money for purchasing Mitzvos, while saving the Maaser money to support paupers.

[515] Literally "Zariz"

[516] Beitza 16a

[517] Admur ibid "All the expenses of the education of his older son, in contrast to the tuition paid for the actual learning" [To note however that in the new printing of the Shulchan Aruch there is a "Lamed" in parentheses added to the word "Atzmo" which word completely change the understanding of this statement of Admur, and it would be interpreted to mean that he cannot deduct from Maaser/Chomesh tuition for his personal Torah education, however for his older son, he may deduct the entire tuition, including the money's given to the teachers. This extra Lamed can be found in the printing of Hilchos Talmud Torah in the year 1799 in Levov, which was one of the earliest editions. Rav Mordechai Ashkenazi learns like the former approach and does not include the extra Lamed in his Nussach of Admur. See Hilchos Talmud Torah of Rav Ashkenazi ibid p. 497] Beir Sheva 41; Elya Raba 156:2; Tuv Taam Vadaas Telisa 2:96; Ahavas Chesed 2:19; See Orchos Rabbeinu 1:301; Tzedaka Umishpat 6:14 footnote 36

The reason: As one is obligated to teach his son the entire Torah, both the written and oral [Admur Hilchos Talmud Torah 1:4 and Kuntrus Achron 1:1], and any matter which is an obligation may not be deducted from Maaser. [Poskim ibid] Furthermore, some Poskim rule it is forbidden, being one may not use Maaser money towards Mitzvos. [Rama Y.D. 249:1]

Other opinions: Some Poskim rule that one may deduct even the salary of the Rebbe from Maaser. [Leket Yosheer Y.D. p. 76; Rishon Letziyon 249; Meishiv Devarim Y.D. 137 in name of Sefer Hagan; Peri Yitzchak 2:27; Tzedaka Umishpat 6:14; Yabia Omer Y.D. 58:1; See Orchos

cannot afford it otherwise. However, the actual payment for the Rebbe teaching him Torah may not be deducted from the Maaser or Chomesh. [Thus, one may deduct the part of tuition that covers room and board, and any other expense associated with facilitating the son's presence in the Torah education. However, the amount of the tuition that is given to the son's Rebbe, may not be deducted. Furthermore, some[518] learn that one must deduct the amount of money he would have in any event spent on supporting his son at home. This, however, is not the implication of Admur. The above limitation is only regarding an older **son**, however, for the Torah education of an older **daughter**, one may deduct the entire tuition from Maaser.[519]]

Son versus daughter and child versus adult: One may only deduct the tuition of Yeshiva for his <u>older</u> children from Maaser [if he cannot afford it otherwise].[520] However, he may not deduct the tuition for his <u>younger</u> children from Maaser.[521] A young child is defined as any child below six years of age, while an older child is defined as above the age of six.[522] [However, some Poskim[523] learn that even children above age six are defined as a young child, and hence one may not deduct their tuition from Maaser until they become older.[524] Practically, one may follow the former opinion.[525] One may deduct the tuition for his older daughter's [i.e. six years and up] Torah education, from Maaser, just as is permitted to be done for a son.[526] [Furthermore, by a daughter, one may deduct even the salary of the Rebbe/teacher from Maaser, as stated above.[527] This amount [i.e. the salary given to the teacher] may be deducted from Maaser even prior to the daughter reaching six years of age.[528]]

If one is poor and cannot pay tuition even of his younger children, or of the Rebbe:[529] If one is a true pauper, and cannot afford to pay tuition even if he cuts back on all expenses to the utmost, then he may use his Maaser money to pay for all the tuition, just as any poor person may receive Tzedaka to help pay tuition.

Rabbeinu 1:298; Shevet Halevi 5:133 permits in a time of need; See Divrei Malkiel 5:115] The reason for this is because one is only obligated to teach his child the written Torah and not the oral Torah. [Michaber Y.D. 245:6; Poskim ibid]
[518] Tzedaka Umishpat 6 footnote 35
[519] Minchas Yitzchak 10:85
The reason: As one is not obligated to teach his daughter Torah. [ibid]
[520] Admur Hilchos Talmud Torah 1:7; 3:4; Michaber 251:3; Rambam Hilchos Matanos Aniyim 10:16; Peas Sadcha 118; Tzedaka Umishpat 6:14
[521] Shach 251:5; See Taz 249:1; Birkeiy Yosef 249; Chavos Yair 224; Beis Din Shel Shlomo Y.D. 1; Hilchos Maaser Kesafim 11:12;
[522] Shach 251:5; Shevet Halevi 5:133; Hilchos Maaser Kesafim 11:12; Heard from Harav Yaakov Yosef Za"l that so we rule Halacha Lemaaseh;
The reason: As a father is obligated to provide all his children below age six with all their needs [Michaber E.H. 71:1] and one cannot deduct an obligatory payment from Maaser. [Shach ibid; See Taz ibid and Poskim ibid] Now, although the Sages [E.H. ibid] instituted to support one's children until they become older [Bar/Bas Mitzvah] this is not an absolute obligation but a mere Rabbinical moral practice which cannot be enforced. Thus, one may use Maaser money to pay for the logistics of their Torah education. This is further proven from the fact we see that if the father has enough money to give to charity, then we do enforce him to support his children from the charity. It is hence clear that charity may be used to support one's children who are above age six. [Shevet Halevi 5:133] To note, however, that in Eretz Yisrael, in 5704, the Chief Rabbanut instituted that its courts can even enforce a father to pay child support until age 15, and it is thus a complete obligation [See Yaskil Avdi E.H. 4:15; Hilchos Maaser Kesafim 11 footnote 371], nonetheless, they never established in their Takana that one cannot use Maaser/Tzedaka money's to support the children past age six, as their main intent is that support is given, irrelevant of how it is paid. [Heard from Harav Yaakov Yosef; Orchos Rabbeinu 2:140]
[523] Rav Ashkenazi in Hilchos Talmud Torah p. 488; So rule regarding that one may not support one's children above age six from Maaser money: Possible way of learning Taz 249:1 that although its considered Tzedaka to give past age six, one cannot deduct it from Masser and so learns Shevet Halevi 5:133 in the Taz ibid; Igros Moshe Y.D. 1:143; Piskei Rav SZ"A, brought in Hilchos Maaser Kesafim 11:16; Derech Emuna Matanos Aniyim 7:57 that so ruled Chazon Ish; Orchos Rabbeinu 1:291; Pear Hador 4:69; See Meishiv Devarim Y.D. 137; Hilchos Maaser Kesafim 11:16
[524] The reason and the definition of "older" according to this approach: Some rule that it is defined as any child below the age of Bar or Bas Mitzvah, and older child must be above this age to have his tuition deducted from Maaser. [See Hilchos Talmud Torah of Rav Ashkenazi p. 488 who states that older children is defined as above Bar and Bas Mitzvah, as the Sages obligated the father to support his children until that age. See Michaber E.H. 71:1; Rambam Ishus 12:14] Other Poskim rule it is defined as the age that it is common for a child to become employed and begin supporting himself. [Igros Moshe ibid] Accordingly, some rule it applies until one's child gets married, as it is accustomed to support him until this time. [Rav SZ"A] Others rule that in any area that the law of the land obligates one to support his children, he may not deduct it from Maaser. [Pesakim of Rav SZ"A, brought in Hilchos Maaser Kesafim 11:16; Igros Moshe Y.D. 2:113]
[525] Shevet Halevi ibid; Rav Yaakov Yosef
[526] Michaber Y.D. 251:3; Minchas Yitzchak 10:85; See Tzedaka Umishpat 6:14 footnote 35
[527] Minchas Yitzchak 10:85; Article of Rav Ashkenazi
[528] See article of Rav Ashkenazi who says that even by a boy, if he is below age 6, the tuition for the actual teacher may be deducted from Maaser, as one is not obligated to hire a teacher before age 6, even for a boy.
[529] Rama 251:3 "Supporting himself comes prior to supporting others"; Hilchos Maaser Kesafim 16:16

Summary:

One may only use Maaser/Chomesh money to pay for a child's Torah education if the following is fulfilled:

1. One cannot afford to pay otherwise, [unless he cuts back on expenses].
2. The child is above age six.
3. <u>By a son</u>: One does not deduct the sum of the tuition that goes to pay for the salary of the teachers, from Maaser.
   <u>By a daughter</u>: One may deduct even the sum of tuition that goes to pay the salary of the teachers, from Maaser. If she is below six years old, one may only deduct the sum of the teacher's salary of the tuition [and not meals etc] from Maaser. If, she is above six years old, one may deduct the entire tuition from Maaser.
4. <u>One who is poor</u>: One who is poor and cannot afford to pay tuition even if he cuts back on all possible expenses, may use Maaser money to pay the entire tuition.
   *Important note: Some Poskim learn that in locations where sending one's children to a school of education is compulsory according to law, one may not use any Maaser money towards paying tuition, whether of a son or daughter. Other Poskim however dispute this ruling.

Q&A

Can travel expenses to the Torah institution be deducted from the Maaser or Chomesh?

Seemingly, the travel expenses to and from the Torah institution may be deducted from Maaser, just as all other learning expenses. However, some[530] learn that the travel expenses of a son to learn Torah is an actual obligation upon the father and hence cannot be paid using Maaser/Chomesh money [unless the person is poor and will be unable to pay otherwise]. However, even in their opinion, the traveling expenses for the Torah education of daughters may be deducted from Maaser/Chomesh.

Who is defined as "one who cannot afford" which allows him to use Maaser/Chomesh funds for tuition?

This means that if one does not make enough income to live the lifestyle he desires <u>and also pay tuition</u>, then he may deduct [only] the above-mentioned tuition expenses from Maaser/Chomesh. He is not required to cut back on expenses from matters that he desires, and live a poor lifestyle, in order to not use his Maaser funds for tuition. If, however, the person is in truth a real pauper, and cannot afford to pay tuition even if he cuts back on all expenses to his utmost, then he may use his Maaser money to pay for **all** the tuition, of any age child, just as is the law by any poor person.

May one deduct from Maaser the sum of tuition used to pay the secular education department?

This matter requires further analysis.

May a single mother use Maaser or Chomesh money to pay tuition of her children who are above age six?[531]

Yes. She may even use Maaser money to pay for the part of the tuition that goes to pay the teacher's salary.[532]

If one received a discount from tuition, may he use Maaser money to pay the amount of the discount?[533]

Yes.

---

[530] Rav Mordechai Ashkenazi OBM in a written reply
[531] See Orchos Rabbeinu 1:302
[532] <u>The reason</u>: As she is not obligated to teach her children Torah.
[533] Orchos Rabbeinu 1:301; Hilchos Maaser Kesafim 16:4

> **If there are two Torah institutions available for educating one's children and one sends his child to the better and more expensive institution, may he deduct the difference from Maaser?[534]**
> Yes.

---------------- *Sefarim/Geniza*----------------
22. Bayis Malei Sefarim-The Mitzvah of purchasing Torah books:[535]

Today [being that writing the oral Torah has become permitted[536]] it is a Mitzvah [and Biblical obligation[537]] to write [publish, and purchase[538]] Chumashim, Mishnah, Gemara and their commentaries. [Some Poskim[539] rule that today this positive Biblical command is actually in place of the Mitzvah of writing a Sefer Torah and not just an additional obligation.[540] Practically, the custom today is like this opinion, to fulfill the Mitzvah of writing a Sefer Torah through purchasing Sefarim.[541] The purpose of this Mitzvah is in order to have Sefarim available for learning[542] and it is hence an affiliate of the Mitzvah of learning Torah.[543] Thus, the completion of this Mitzvah is fulfilled through learning the purchased Sefarim.[544]]

What Sefarim is one to buy to fulfill the above Mitzvah?[545] One is to write [publish or buy] Chumashim, Mishnah, Gemara and their commentaries [Nonetheless, in truth, this Mitzvah is fulfilled through writing or purchasing any Torah Sefarim, and not just those listed above. The Mitzvah is fulfilled even upon purchasing Sefarim in other languages, such as in English.[546] One is not required to purchase all available Sefarim in order to fulfill this Mitzvah, and any time one purchases a Sefer, the Mitzvah is fulfilled.[547]]

---

[534] Orchos Rabbeinu 1:302; Hilchos Maaser Kesafim 16:6

[535] Michaber 270:2; Tur 270:2 in name of Rosh [quoted in next footnote]; Rabbeinu Yerucham in name of the Geonim; See Likkutei Sichos 23:17 Shavuos 1; 24:209 Parshas Vayelech [printed in Shulchan Menachem Yoreh Deah 6:178]

[536] See Admur 334:12

[537] Rosh ibid, brought in Tur ibid, "*Today it is **a positive command** of every Jew who can afford to do so, to purchase Sefarim of Cumashim and Gemara's*"; It appears that even in accordance to the Michaber ibid [and Beis Yosef and Bach ion next footnotes] who simply write that it is a Mitzvah to do so, and the Mitzvah of writing a Sefer Torah remains in place, nevertheless they do not argue on the Rosh that writing Sefarim is included in the Biblical Mitzvah of writing a Sefer Torah and is hence considered part of the Biblical command according to all. [See Likkutei Sichos ibid]

[538] See Aruch Hashulchan 270:9 and Likkutei Sichos 23:17 in length for explanation of why all Poskim agree that by Sefarim, the Mitzvah is fulfilled by purchasing them, even though by a Sefer Torah, some Poskim require it to be written; Hisvadyos 1988 Hei Teves
The reason: Although the Rama 270 rules one does not fulfill his obligation if he purchases a Sefer Torah nevertheless, regarding Sefarim the obligation is fulfilled even with purchasing them, as the entire purpose of this Mitzvah is to learn from the Sefer. The only reason there is a Mitzvah to write a Sefer Torah and one does not fulfill his obligation with purchase is because a Sefer Torah has laws of writing, as opposed to other Sefarim. [See Likkutei Sichos ibid]

[539] Implication of Rosh ibid; Shach 270:5 "The main opinion is like the Rosh and unlike the Beis Yosef"; Derisha and Perisha 270 in his understanding of the Rosh; Taz 270:4 that so is the implication of the Rosh; Aruch Hashulchan 270:8-9; Rebbe in Likkutei Sichos 23:17 Shavuos 1
Other Poskim: Many Poskim rule that the Mitzvah of purchasing Sefarim is not in place of the Mitzvah of writing a Sefer Torah, and rather is simply in addition to it. The Mitzvah of writing a Sefer Torah remains intact even today. [Implication of Michaber 270:1; Beis Yosef and Bach 270 in explanation of Rosh, brought in Taz 270:4 and Shach ibid; Conclusion of Taz ibid "*The words of the Beis Yosef are correct, as how can we nullify a positive command of "Vikisvu Lachem" with the passing of the generations*"; Levush and Magid Mishneh brought in Shach ibid in their opinion of the Rosh; Shagas Aryeh 36 negates Perisha] Nevertheless it appears that even in accordance to their opinion writing Sefarim is included in the Mitzvah of writing a Sefer Torah and is hence considered part of the Biblical command according to all. [So is implied from Rosh ibid; See Likkutei Sichos ibid]

[540] The reason: As today we no longer learn from a Sefer Torah, and it is even forbidden to do so, as it is belittling to the Sefer. Thus, the Mitzvah of writing a Sefer Torah can no longer be fulfilled through writing one and rather can only be fulfilled today through writing/buying Sefarim that one can learn from, as the entire purpose of the Mitzvah is to learn from the Sefarim. [Derisha ibid, brought in Taz ibid and Shach ibid; Likkutei Sichos 23 ibid]

[541] Rebbe in Likkutei Sichos 23:17 "The custom of Israel today to not write one's own Sefer Torah is like the opinion of the Rosh"; See there in length and in Aruch Hashulchan 270:9

[542] Rosh ibid as explained in Derisha ibid and Shach and Taz ibid;

[543] Likkutei Sichos 23:17; See Aruch Hashulchan 270:9

[544] Likkutei Sichos ibid; See Aruch Hashulchan 270:9

[545] Michaber 270:2; Tur 270 in name of Rosh; Rabbeinu Yerucham in name of the Geonim

[546] Likkutei Sichos 23 Shavuos 1

[547] Likkutei Sichos 23 Shavuos 1

Q&A
Are women obligated in the Biblical Mitzvah to purchase a Sefer Torah/Sefarim?
Some Poskim[548] rule that women are not Biblically obligated to purchase a Sefer Torah, or Sefarim. Others[549] however leave this matter in question.[550]

Q&A on what to buy
Purchasing practical Halacha Sefarim:[551]
In fulfillment of the above Mitzvah, one is to especially purchase Sefarim dealing with practical Halacha which will be studied frequently in order to know what one is to practically follow.

Having a Keser Shem Tov, Or Torah and Tanya in every home:[552]
Every home is to contain the following three Sefarim: Keser Shem Tov of the Baal Shem Tov, Or Torah of the Maggid, and Tanya. The books should be published in separate volumes as opposed to being bound together in a single volume. One should study these books daily, as much as one wishes, or at least on Shabbos and holidays and other days of special occasion.

Purchasing a Chitas [Siddur and Chumash, Tehillim and Tanya] for one's child:[553]
Every child is to have a Siddur, Chumash and Tehillim of his own [Chitas]. These Sefarim are to be placed in the room of each child.

Donating books to libraries:[554]
In fulfillment of the above Mitzvah, one is to donate Sefarim to public libraries and help them expand.

---------------- *Mezuzah*----------------
23. Covering the Mezuzah-Mezuzah Cases:
This Halacha tackles three different subjects associated with covering a Mezuzah. 1) The need to cover a Mezuzah in areas of filth and immodesty. [Halacha A] 2) The custom to leave the name Shakaiy of the Mezuzah visible to the outside, in areas that a cover is not required [Halacha B] 3) The material that should be used as a Mezuzah cover. [Halacha C]

A. The obligation to cover the Mezuzah parchment, and when it applies?
The parchment of the Mezuzah that is placed on the doorpost is to be covered.[555] One is to place the parchment of the Mezuzah in a tube [Mezuzah case] and then attach it to the doorpost, as explained in the C. The remainder of this Halacha will discuss the cases in which the covering is required from the letter of the law, the cases in which the Mezuzah must be covered in a non-transparent case, and the cases in which a double covering is required.
Is the Mezuzah to remain visible through the cover/Should the cover be transparent? It is best for the

---

[548] Rambam Sefer Hamitzvos Mitzvah 18, Listed in end of 248 positive commands as one of the Mitzvos that women are exempt from.
[549] Shaagas Aryeh 35
[550] The reason: As even women are obligated to learn Torah, in those topics relevant to them, and hence they recite Birchas Hatorah. [Shagas Aryeh ibid]
[551] Sichas Hei Teves 1988 printed in Hisvadyus 2:170-173
[552] Sichas 1950 p. 265; Sefer Haminhagim [English] p.
[553] Sichas Hei Teves 1988 printed in Hisvadyus 2:170-173
[554] Sichas Hei Teves 1988 printed in Hisvadyus 2:170-173
[555] Michaber 289:1; Taz 286:5; Vetzaruch Iyun Gadol on Michaber 286:5 who rules the Mezuzah is to remain revealed and uncovered in an area of purity, perhaps however in 286:5 he only refers to the name of Hashem, and not the entire Mezuzah. [See Mikdash Me'at 289:21]
The reason: From the letter of the law, the parchment of the Mezuzah does not need to be covered, with exception to areas of impurity. Nevertheless, it should have a covering over it in all areas, as otherwise, the touching of the parchment upon leaving/entering the room can cause the name of Hashem, which faces the outside, to become erased. [Taz ibid] Another reason for covering the Mezuzah, is to suspect for those Poskim who prohibit touching Holy writings with their bare hands. [R. Akivah Eigar brought in Pischeiy Teshuvah 285:4; Seemingly the Taz is not bothered by this issue]

Mezuzah [parchment] placed on the doorposts to be visible.[556] This especially applies to the name Shakaiy written on the external part of the Mezuzah, which is meant to remain visible, as explained in B.[557] Thus, one should use a transparent casing of clear plastic, or glass, for his Mezuzah parchment. This, however, is with exception to a room in which marital relations take place, and according to many Poskim, it is also with exception to a room in which women are not modestly dressed, in which case the Mezuzah is not to be visible even through glass or plastic, as will be explained below.

Hiding the Mezuzah within the doorpost:[558] If, for whatever reason, one cannot allow the Mezuzah to be visible, it may be placed in a non-transparent cover, and even hidden within a hole in the doorpost, as the main Mitzvah of Mezuzah does not require it to be noticeable.

Covering the Mezuzah in a room with feces and a diaper changing room:[559] By a room which contains filth [i.e. urine or excrement], such as rooms in which children are found [and have their diapers changed in that room[560] or use the potty in the room], it is best[561] for the Mezuzah of its doorpost to be covered. However, one may [and should[562]] use a **transparent** covering in such areas, so the Mezuzah remains visible.[563]

Covering the Mezuzah in rooms in which people are not fully clothed:[564] When placing a Mezuzah on the door of rooms in which women [or men[565] or even children[566]] are at times undressed, the Mezuzah is to be covered.[567] Many Poskim[568] rule, that in such areas, the Mezuzah is to be covered by a **non-transparent** covering. However, from other Poskim[569], it is implied that one may [and should] use a

---

[556] Michaber 286:5; Taz 286:5

[557] Rama 288:15; See next Halacha!

[558] Taz 286:4

[559] Michaber 286:5; Shach 289:9; Taz 286:5; Regarding the general obligation of not having feces revealed in front of Sefarim-See Siddur Admur; Our Sefer "Awaking like a Jew" 7:16
Other opinions: Some Poskim rule one should not place Mezuzahs in such a room. [Bach, brought in Shach 286:9] The Shach ibid concludes that one should place a Mezuzah in the room and cover it.

[560] Pashut, as certainly the Michaber does not require a Mezuzah to be covered in a room that has children that have simply made in their diapers, and rather the intent is that the children either do their needs inside that room, or in a potty in the room, as was common back then when bathrooms were not commonly found in the home.

[561] So is the wording of the Michaber ibid; Taz ibid "It does not even require a glass covering, however this is the best option"
Letter of law: From the letter of the law, a Mezuzah that is attached to the doorpost does not need to be covered even in the face of filth and excrement, and women who bathe, as since the Mezuzah is above 10 Tefach from the ground, it is considered as if it is in a different area. [Taz ibid based on Semag; See 79:4 and Siddur Admur that Sefarim may be left on a table ten Tefach high in front of feces] Alternatively, since the Torah obligated one to place a Mezuzah in such rooms, it does not require it to be covered in face of belittling acts. [Mamar Mordechai 40:2; Aruch Hashulchan 286:15, see there!]

[562] In order so the name Shakaiy remain visible, as brought in Rama 288:15 and Taz ibid

[563] Taz 286:5; Aruch Hashulchan 286:10; Ben Ish Chaiy 2 Ki Savo 15; Shulchan Melachim 162; Yad Hekatana Mezuzah 3:13
The reason the Mezuzah may remain visible in face of the feces: Although the Mezuzah still remains visible through its case, in full view of the excrement, nevertheless, this is permitted, as regarding the laws of Shema, the Torah only forbade having the feces revealed outside of a cover, while if it is covered even by glass, it is permitted to read the Shema, as the Torah only requires a covering and covered it is. This same law applies here in the opposite case where the name of Hashem is covered by glass, as that since the name is covered, there is no prohibition involved, as the Torah was not particular in it remaining visible. [Taz ibid; See also Admur 76:1]
Other opinions: Some Poskim rule that the Mezuzah may not be visible through its covering, in face of excrement. [Rishon Letziyon 286:5; Pischeiy Teshuvah 286:8 in name of Chomos Yerushalayim 277; Birkeiy Yosef]

[564] Shach 286:9; Taz 286:5; M"B 84:7; Regarding the general obligation of not being naked in front of Kisveiy Kodesh/Sefarim-See Admur 45:3; M"A 45:2; Shabbos 120b that one may not be naked if Hashem's name is written on his skin as "it is forbidden to stand before Hashem naked"; Michaber Y.D. 281

[565] Daas Kedoshim 286; Shevet Halevi 2:156; Shulchan Melachim 161; Pischeiy Shearim 286:25

[566] Admur 45:3 in parentheses based on 275:13 that prohibits children being naked in front of candles

[567] Letter of law: Some Poskim rule that this is not required from the letter of the law. [So proves Mamar Mordechai 40:2; Aruch Hashulchan 286:15, see there!; Taz ibid: From the letter of the law, it does not need to be covered, as since the Mezuzah is above 10 Tefach from the ground it is considered as if it is in a different area. [See also Siddur Admur that Sefarim may be left on a table ten Tefach high in front of feces] These words of the Taz seemingly also apply to being naked in front of the Mezuzah. To note, however, that in 40:5 regarding marital relations, Admur a) Mentions it is forbidden to be naked in front of the Mezuzah and b) does not mention ten Tefach and c) In 45:3 rules it is forbidden to be naked in front of Kisveiy Kodesh.

[568] Aruch Hashulchan 286:10; Ben Ish Chaiy 2 Ki Savo 15; Shulchan Melachim 162; Yad Hekatana Mezuzah 3:13
Opinion of Admur: It is implied from Admur 40:5 that it is definitely forbidden to be naked in front of a Mezuzah, even if it is covered by glass, as Admur forbids marital relations being it is similar to Erva, and hence certainly he would forbid Ervah itself! Vetzaruch Iyun.

[569] Taz 286:5 "By placing a **glass** covering over the Mezuzah one nullifies the claim of some who refrain from placing Mezuzahs on rooms that women bathe in occasionally, as through this [glass] the Mezuzah is covered even though it is visible"; Beir Heiytiv 286:8 in his summary of Taz "**only** in a room of marital relations is glass invalid"; However, some of the above Poskim [in previous footnote] seem to understand the Taz ibid is not referring to women who are at times naked in the room, and that in such a case in truth a non-transparent cover is required. So is implied from Aruch Hashulchan ibid and Shulchan Melachim ibid. Furthermore, the Mikdash Me'at 286:12 explains the statement in the Taz of "women

transparent covering even in such areas, in order so the name of Hashem remains visible.[570] [According to all opinions, one may/should have a transparent covering if people will not be naked in front of it, even if they are not fully clothed in front of it[571], although some[572] write to be stringent even in such a case.]

Rooms that are not of dwelling in which people are unclothed:[573] All rooms which are not actual rooms of dwelling, such as a storage room, in which a woman or man are accustomed to be naked in, such as a shower, are not to have a Mezuzah placed by their entrance.[574] This applies even if one desires to cover the Mezuzah.[575]

Covering the Mezuzah in the Parents' bedroom-Room of marital relations: In a room where a couple has marital relations, and the Mezuzah is inside the room[576], the Mezuzah must be covered in a way that it cannot be seen, and hence a transparent covering [such as plastic or glass] is invalid.[577] If the Mezuzah is only covered by a transparent covering, such as glass [or plastic], it is forbidden to have relations in such a room while the Mezuzah remains visible.[578] Regarding if the Mezuzah must contain a double covering, this matter is disputed amongst Poskim: Some Poskim[579] rule the Mezuzah needs to be within two vessels, and must thus contain a double covering. Other Poskim[580], however, rule the Mezuzah is not required to be within two vessels, and hence a single covering [that is not transparent] suffices.[581] Practically, one

---

bathe in occasionally" to refer to women who are not naked while they bathe. It is however clearly implied from the Taz ibid, as he writes in his conclusion, that only marital relations in a room requires a non-transparent cover, and not a mere undressed woman.

[570] The reason: Although the Mezuzah will remain visible through its case, nevertheless, the Torah was only stringent that the Mezuzah be covered, and covered it is. This is similar to the law regarding covering excrement before praying. [Taz ibid] Now, although by Davening in front of the Ervah, we rule that being covered does not suffice and it must also not be visible [see Admur 75:8-9] nevertheless, perhaps the Taz holds that this only applies regarding Davening, while regarding simply being naked in front of Kisveiy Kodesh, it is allowed. See also P"M 75 in Hakdama, and 74 A"A 1, Kaf Hachaim 75:38, Chazon Ish 16:7 [brought in Piskeiy Teshuvos 75:15] that Min Hatorah, a glass covering is valid for Erva, and it is only due to Hirhur that we prohibit it by a man. Thus, there is a clear reason to say that regarding Kisveiy Kodesh, if the Mezuzah is covered even with glass, it is valid, as Hirhur is not applicable.

Opinion of Admur: It is implied from Admur 40:5 that it is forbidden to be naked in front of a Mezuzah, even if it is covered by glass, as Admur forbids marital relations being it is similar to Erva, and hence certainly he would forbid Ervah itself! Vetzaruch Iyun, as marital relations is stricter than revealed Erva, as everyone agrees that sefarim require two coverings by marital relations, which is unprecedented in all the laws of Tzoa and Erva, and hence we see marital relations is a different category of Erva and is more strict.

[571] So is implied from even the stringent opinions, as they only mention being naked in front of the Mezuzah; See also Mikdash Me'at ibid who learns this way in the Taz ibid

The reason: As we have no source anywhere in Poskim for forbidding immodest dress [that is not nudity] in front of Sefarim, and on the contrary, we find Poskim who explicit write it is permitted [Taz ibid]. The only prohibition we find is to Daven and learn in front of immodestly dressed women, and who says this applies regarding a Mezuzah? Furthermore, even by Davening and Shema, the Biblical prohibition is only if the actual Erva is revealed, while immodest dress is only Rabbinically forbidden due to erotic thoughts; something that is not applicable to a Mezuzah. [See Admur 75:1; Panim Meiros 1:74; Maharam Brisk 2:70; Chayeh Adam 4:1]

[572] See Ateres Paz 2:15 that for this reason one should not sell transparent covers to the unscrupulous; He however does not address any of the points mentioned above for why it should be permitted according to all when mere immodesty is in question and not actual nakedness.

[573] Michaber 286:2

[574] The reason: It is not honorable towards G-d to place a Mezuzah in such areas. [Michaber ibid]

[575] See Michaber and Rama ibid; Shach 286:8 and 12

[576] This means that the doorpost in which the Mezuzah is placed is inside the room. This often happens when the room has a door leading to another room, in which case its Mezuzah is placed inside the actual room. Alternatively, it can happen if the door of the room opens to the outside, in which according to Chabad custom of Heker Tzir, the Mezuzah is placed inside the room. Even if the Mezuzah is outside the room, as is the case with most bedrooms, nevertheless, if the door is opened and the Mezuzah is visible, seemingly the same law applies, as explained in Admur 75:98.

[577] Admur 40:5; Taz 286:5

The reason: A glass covering is not valid, and thus forbids marital relations, as the Mezuzah is visible through it. By Erva [a naked private part] the Torah forbids saying Shema even if the Erva is in a transparent covering, due to the verse "Lo Yiraeh Becha Ervas Davar". Now, marital relations is also a belittling matter [to be done in front of Kedusha items] and is similar to the Ervah prohibition and thus requires that the Mezuzah be covered in a way that it cannot be seen at all through the covering. [Admur ibid; Taz ibid; See also Admur 75:8-9]

Other Poskim: Some Poskim rule that from the letter of the law, one is not required to cover the Mezuzah even in a room where marital relations occurs. [So proves Mamar Mordechai 40:2; Aruch Hashulchan 286:15, see there!]

[578] Admur ibid

[579] M"A 40:2; 1st opinion brought in Admur; Chesed Leavraham; Kaf Hachaim 40:13 concludes it is best to be stringent

[580] Taz 186:5; 2nd opinion brought in Admur; Mamar Mordechai 40:2

[581] The reason: As the wall is considered its own domain, and hence everything that is inside the wall is considered to be in a separate domain than the inside of the room. Furthermore, even if the Mezuzah is not inside the wall, but placed in a tube that is attached to the doorpost of the wall, it is nevertheless considered a separate domain, as since it is attached to the wall, it is considered like the wall. [Admur ibid; See Pischeiy Teshuvah 286:8 in name of Chomos Yerushalayim 277] The Taz ibid however makes no mention of this reason of Admur [that the wall is a separate domain] and rather states that the fact the Mezuzah is above ten Tefach makes it a separate domain. This idea [of ten Tefach separating domains] is also brought in Admur 79:4 and in Siddur Admur regarding Sefarim being in sight of feces. It however was omitted in Admur 40:5.

If the Mezuzah is inside the wall but the name of Hashem is visible through a hole: Admur ibid requires that one place a **permanent** piece of wax or other material over the hole, in order to consider it within a separate domain. A temporary covering over the hole would not suffice.

may be lenient like the latter opinion and the Mezuzah does not require a double covering.[582] [This however only refers to a Mezuzah that is on the doorpost, however, a loose Mezuzah that is lying in the bedroom, according to all must be placed within two coverings, just as is the law by Sefarim.] The above requirement of covering the Mezuzah during marital relations is only in a case that the Mezuzah is visible within the room. If, however, upon closing the door of the room, the Mezuzah is left outside the room, it does not need any covering while the door is closed.

Summary:
It is best for the Mezuzah [parchment] placed on the doorposts to be covered, although within a transparent covering. If one at times is naked in the room, or feces is revealed in it, then according to many Poskim this covering is treated as mandatory, although in the latter case of feces, it suffices to have a transparent covering. If a couple has marital relations in the room, and the Mezuzah is placed inside the room, then according to all, the Mezuzah must to be covered with a non-transparent cover. If, upon closing the door, the Mezuzah is outside the room, it does not need any covering, and marital relations may take place while the door is closed. In all cases that a covering is required, it suffices to have a single covering, even if it is designated for the Mezuzah.

Doing belittling acts in front of a Mezuzah:[583]
It is forbidden to perform belittling acts in front of a Mezuzah on a constant basis. This applies even if a non-transparent covering covers the Mezuzah. It is thus forbidden to constantly change diapers in front of a Mezuzah or wash soiled clothing in front of it. However, on mere occasion, this may be done if the Mezuzah is covered, as explained above. The Mekubalim[584] write that one is to be careful that the four-cubit area surrounding the Mezuzah always remains clean.

May a visible Mezuzah parchment be inside a room in which women change clothes, if it is not visible from the area that they change?
Yes.[585]

B. Leaving the name Shakaiy visible:

The [Divine name of Shakaiy which is written on the outside of the Mezuzah[586]] is to be revealed and not covered [unless the Mezuzah is found in an unclean area, in which case it is to be covered, as explained in A].[587] [Thus, when the Mezuzah is placed in a non-transparent tube] the custom is to make a hole in the tube opposite the name Shakaiy [the Shin-Daled-Yud] which is written on the outside of the parchment, in order for it to be visible to the outside.[588] The name of Hashem, however, is to be covered by glass or plastic in order to prevent it from being erased upon being touched often.[589] [Thus, based on the above, one should use a transparent casing of clear plastic or glass for his Mezuzah parchment. This, however, is with exception to a room in which marital relations takes place, and according to many Poskim, is also with exception to a room in which women undress, in which case the Mezuzah and name of Hashem is

---

[582] Admur ibid; Mamar Mordechai 40:2; Zivcheiy Tzedek 2:38

The reason: As this matter is only Rabbinical, and one may be lenient in a Rabbinical dispute. Furthermore, one can say that even according to the stringent opinion [of the M"A ibid] who requires a double covering, this was only in a case that the Mezuzah is placed in a temporary vessel, as such a vessel is not permanently nullified to the wall [being that one will remove it], and it is only for this reason that it does not help to cover the hole of the wall of the Mezuzah to refrain the Mezuzah from being considered part of the room. [Admur ibid; See Hearos Ubiurim 369:26]

[583] Yad Ketana 3:13; Pischeiy Teshuvah 286:7; Ben Ish Chaiy 2 Ki Savo 15; See also Taz 289:5 "An area that **at times** has filth, and on **occasion** women bathe"

[584] Shela Hakadosh Miseches Chulin; Yosef Ometz 600 in name of Rav Chaim Vital

[585] This follows the same law as Davening with an Erva in the room, in which case it is permitted to pray so long as the Erva is not within one's sight. [Admur 75:9]

[586] However, the rest of the Mezuzah is to be covered by the tube, as ruled in Michaber 289:1; See Mikdash Me'at 286:21

[587] Michaber 286:5; Kol Bo

[588] Rama 288:15; Mordechai and Hagahos Maimanis; Zohar Vaeschanan brought in Biur Hagr"a 2

[589] Taz 286:5

not to be visible even through glass or plastic, as explained above.]

Q&A
Should the <u>entire</u> name of Hashem [Shakaiy] be left visible?[590]
Yes. The entire name is to be left visible and not just the letter Shin.

C. The Mezuzah case:

The parchment of the Mezuzah that is placed on the doorpost is to be covered, as explained in A.[591] The Mezuzah is to have its parchment [rolled and] placed in a tube made of reed, or of any other material.[592] *What material is to be used as a Mezuzah case?* Any material may be used as a case for the Mezuzah.[593] [Nevertheless, based on the above requirement to leave the name Shakaiy revealed, it is best to use a transparent Mezuzah case, such as a plastic or glass case, for one's Mezuzahs. Alternatively, one can use a case of other materials that leave a glass opening opposite the name of Hashem. There is a tradition from the Baal Shem Tov that one is not to use tubes made of metal or iron.[594] Some[595] learn that this only applies to iron and not to other metals. There is an unsubstantiated tradition that the Rebbe instructed in the 1940's, that according to Kabala one is not to place the Mezuzah in any casing, but rather in a paper or plastic wrapping.[596] Practically, the Mezuzahs in 770 and the Rebbe's home are covered in a soft plastic cover, and many Chabad Chassidim are accustomed to use a soft plastic or paper cover.[597] There is a written testimony, that in the house of the Tzemach Tzedek the Mezuzahs were wrapped in paper.[598]]

Final Summary:
The parchment of the Mezuzah is to be rolled and placed in a tube or covering. The name Shin-Daled-Yud is to remain visible through the tube/covering, although is nevertheless to be covered by plastic or glass. This can be accomplished by having a Mezuzah case with a hole by Hashem's name that is covered with plastic or glass, or through simply using a transparent Mezuzah cover [i.e. glass or plastic] for one's Mezuzahs. This, however, is with exception to a room in which marital relations take place, and according to many Poskim, is also with exception to a room in which people undress, in which case the Mezuzah and name of Hashem is not to be visible even through glass or plastic.

---

[590] Meorer Yisheinim 172

[591] Michaber 289:1; Taz 286:5; Vetzaruch Iyun Gadol on Michaber 286:5 who rules the Mezuzah is to remain revealed and uncovered in an area of purity, perhaps however in 286:5 he only refers to the name of Hashem, and not the entire Mezuzah. [See Mikdash Me'at 289:21]
The reason: From the letter of the law, the parchment of the Mezuzah does not need to be covered, with exception to areas of impurity. Nevertheless, it should have a covering over it in all areas, as otherwise, the touching of the parchment upon leaving/entering the room can cause the name of Hashem, which faces the outside, to become erased. [Taz ibid] Another reason for covering the Mezuzah, is to suspect for those Poskim who prohibit touching Holy writings with their bare hands. [R. Akivah Eigar brought in Pischeiy Teshuvah 285:4; Seemingly the Taz is not bothered by this issue]

[592] Michaber 289:1; Tur 289
The reason: This is to prevent the Mezuzah from falling and from getting ruined due to moisture on the wall. [Sefer Hayashar; Bach 289; See Pischeiy Shearim p.190] Alternatively, it is done so the parchment remains in a rolled state and not unroll and get ruined. [Levush 289:1]
Other opinions: Some Poskim rule that one is not to place the Mezuzah in paper or parchment, as one should not have any matter blocking between the doorpost and the parchment, as the parchment needs to lie directly on the doorpost. [Gra in Maaseh Rav, brought in Pischeiy Teshuvah 289:22] Seemingly, in his opinion, the Mezuzah case should not completely surround the parchment, but rather only cover its external side. [However, see Mikdash Me'at 289:1] Some Poskim rule one is to suspect for this opinion. [Mikdash Me'at ibid] Practically, the Poskim negate this opinion and so is the custom. [Aruch Hashulchan 289:19 "certainly the Gr"a did not say this"; Tuv Taam Vedaas 245; Maharahm Shick Y.D. 288; Divrei Malkiel 5:65; Maharsham 4:139; Halichos Shlomo Pischeiy Shearim 289]

[593] Michaber 289:1

[594] Daas Kedoshim 289:1; Pischiey Shearim 190
The reason: There is a known tradition in the name of the Besht, not to use tubes made of iron since iron is used to make weapons which kill, while the Mezuzah is grants long life. This follows that which is stated regarding the Mizbeiach, that it is unfit for that which shortens to be placed on that which lengthens. [ibid]

[595] Daas Kedoshim ibid, although he received in the tradition he heard that also metal is included.

[596] Mikdash Melech 2:439

[597] So was told to me by Harav Groner

[598] Kerem Chabad 2 p. 85

In one sentence: The Mezuzah parchment is to be placed in a transparent glass or plastic casing on the doorpost, unless marital relations take place within the room, or people are naked within the room, in which a case a non-transparent cover is to be used.

Nylon wrap:[599]
The custom is to wrap the parchment of the Mezuzah in plastic [saran-wrap] to prevent the parchment from drying out. It is then placed into the tube.

Why today are many people not particular to use a transparent glass or plastic Mezuzah case that allows the Shin to be seen?
Several reasons can be attributed to this matter: 1) By Mezuzah's placed on doors that lead to the outside, transparent cases are not used as the sun can penetrate the transparent case and ruin the Mezuzah; 2) People are not careful to not undress in face of the Mezuzah. Practically, when no sun damage is foreseen, one is to be particular to use a transparent Mezuzah case, and be particular that family members do not undress in front of it.

------------------ *Kohen* ----------------
24. May a Kohen travel from Eretz Yisrael to the diaspora?
It is forbidden for a Kohen [in Eretz Yisrael], to enter into the lands of the gentiles [in the Diaspora].[600] It is, however, permitted for him to do so [for the sake of a great Mitzvah[601], such as for the sake of] finding a wife, or to learn Torah [if he plans to eventually return to Eretz Yisrael[602]].[603] Furthermore, some Poskim[604] rule the above prohibition only applied in previous times, when Eretz Yisrael was pure, however today, it is permitted for a Kohen to enter the Diaspora. Other Poskim[605], however, argue that this law applies even today. [Practically, the custom today, is to allow Kohanim to travel from Eretz Yisrael to the Diaspora.[606] This custom is practiced even amongst Gedolei Yisrael who are Kohanim.[607]]

------------------ *Aveilus* ----------------
25. Eating regulations during Shiva:[608]
There are no eating regulations during Shiva and the mourner may eat whatever foods he desires, including meat and wine, as will be explained.
Meat:[609] It is permitted for a mourner to eat meat during Shiva.[610] [This applies towards all Kosher meat and poultry, without restriction.]
Wine:[611] It is permitted to drink wine during Shiva.[612] [Furthermore, some Poskim[613] rule it is even a Mitzvah and obligation for the mourner to drink wine during the meal.[614] Practically, one is not required

---

[599] Pischeiy Shearim 190
[600] Michaber Y.D. 369:1; 372:1; Tur 369 and 372; Rif Hilchos Tuma; Rambam Avel 3; Rosh Tuma; Sheilasos Emor; Avodas Kochavim 13a; Eiruvin 47a; Mishneh Ohalos 18
The reason: As the Sages decreed impurity upon the land of the gentiles [Shabbos 15], as they bury their dead in all areas. [Shach 369:2]
[601] Beis Yosef 372 based on Tosafos Avoda Zara ibid; Perisha 372
[602] Beis Yosef 372 based on Tosafos ibid; Perisha 372
[603] Michaber 372; Avoda Zara ibid
[604] Shach 369:2; Taz 369:4; Bach 369; Perisha 369:3; Rashal on Tur 369, brought in Perisha ibid; Aruch Hashulchan 369:11
[605] Shvus Yaakov 2:98, brought in Pischeiy Teshuvah 369:5, that "The law is so clear that it is forbidden even today, that if only all the other laws would be this clear."
[606] Maharikash; Rav Akiva Eiger 369; Chochmas Adam 159:1; Igros Kodesh 11:281
The reason: Seemingly today people are lenient because it is considered for the sake of Parnasa, or because today we are in any event considered Tamei Miesim. [Rebbe Akiva Eiger ibid]
[607] Igros Kodesh 11:281
[608] Michaber 378:8; Rambam 4:6
[609] Michaber 378:8; Rambam 4:6
[610] The reason: The prohibition of eating meat only applies prior to the burial, when the mourner is an Onen, however during Shiva, it is permitted to drink wine and eat meat. [Shach 378:7]
[611] Michaber 378:8; Rambam 4:6

to drink wine if he does not want to.[615]] Nevertheless, he is to limit his intake of wine, and is only to drink it during the meal, to help digest the food, and not during other times to get drunk.[616]

Q&A

May people who come to comfort the mourner [i. e. Menachem Avel] eat food in the Shiva home?[617]

Some[618] are accustomed not to eat any food, or take any item, from the Shiva home, throughout the seven days of Shiva.[619] Others[620], however, rule there is no need to be particular in this matter, and that the custom of many is to eat food in the Shiva home after Shacharis. Some[621] write that [even according to the first opinion] the custom to be stringent in this matter only applies to the house in which the person passed away. However, if the person did not pass away in the Shiva house, then there is no need to refrain from eating food in the home. [Practically, the widespread Ashkenazi custom is not to eat any foods in any Shiva house, throughout Shiva. However, the Sephardic custom is on the contrary, for the Avel to honor the visitors with food, of which they partake in eating. Many Chabad Rabbanim have testified to this custom of avoiding eating in a Shiva home and that one is to abide by it.[622] However, there are Chassidishe homes that offer the comforters food and drink.[623] Seemingly, on Shabbos there is room to be lenient according to all.[624]]

Lechaim:[625] It is not our custom to offer a Lechaim in the Shiva home during the Shiva, with exception to on the seventh day, after Shacharis.

May one eat or drink his own food in the house of the mourner?[626]

The Ashkenazi custom stated above, is not to eat any food in the house of the Avel, even if it is one's own food that he brought with him. [Due to this, it is proper [for those who follow this practice] not to bring any food to the house of the Avel even if he desires to eat it later on when he leaves the house.]

May one drink from the cup of an Avel?[627]

The custom is not to drink from the cup of an Avel, unless one washes the cup in-between.[628] This,

---

[612] The reason: The prohibition of drinking wine only applies prior to the burial, when the mourner is an Onen, however, during Shiva, it is permitted to drink wine and eat meat. [Shach 378:7]

[613] Kesubos 8b, brought in Tur 378, "The Sages instituted 10 cups of wine to be drunk in the Shiva home"; The Tur ibid learns this Gemara literally that one is meant to drink wine and concludes "and so is the custom"; Beis Hillel 378 that for this reason even a Nazir who is in Aveilus may drink wine, as it is a Biblical Mitzvah and obligation; See however Yad Avraham 378 who argues on his conclusion

Other opinions: Some Poskim rule that the above statement of the Gemara is not to be taken literally as an obligation, but rather simply as a giving of permission. [Beis Yosef 378 in explanation of Rambam]

[614] The reason: As the whole purpose of creation of wine was to comfort mourners. [Eiruvin 65a, brought in Beis Hillel ibid]

[615] Setimas Michaber and Nosei Keilim in Shulchan Aruch; Beis Yosef 378 "The custom is not like this approach"

[616] Michaber ibid; Tur ibid in name of Ramban; Kesubos ibid "Since they saw people were drinking and getting drunk they amended their decree."

[617] See Nitei Gavriel 92:1

[618] Elya Raba O.C. 224:7; Rav Akiva Eiger 376; Beis Lechem Yehuda 376 that so is the custom in these provinces; Aruch Hashulchan 376:11; Mishmeres Shalom Mem 60; Keser Shem Tov p. 684; Kaf Hachaim 224:46

[619] The reason: As there is a spirit of impurity that resides in the house of the Avel throughout the seven days. [ibid]

[620] Yosef Ometz p. 330; Noheg Katzon Yosef p. 50; Ikarei Hadaat 34:30; Chaim Bayad 125; Yabia Omer 4:35; Nitei Gavriel ibid footnote 5; Nishmas Yisrael p. 130

[621] Nitei Gavriel ibid in name of Misgeres Hashulchan 376 and Even Yaakov 42

[622] Rav Eli Landau stated to me that his father was very careful in this matter, and so he saw accustomed amongst Chassidim to be careful; Rav Yeruslavsky stated the custom is to be stringent; Rav Gluchovsky stated the Chabad custom is to be stringent; Rav A.L. Hakohen told me the custom in all Ashkenazi circles is to be stringent in this.

[623] Nitei Gavriel ibid footnote 5; Rabbi Leibel Groner in a correspondence related that he witnessed in many Chassidishe homes that they offer Lechaim and Mezonos after Shacharis.

[624] See Shivlei Haleket 23 that the adherence of not drinking from the cup of an Avel does not apply on Shabbos; See Nitei Gavriel ibid footnote 21

[625] See Toras Menachem-Reshimos Hayoman p. 414 that the Rebbe Rayatz instructed the Rebbe to have Lechaim distributed only on the 7th day. See Shulchan Menachem 5:282 footnote 5

[626] See Keser Shem Tov ibid

[627] See Nitei Gavriel 92:8; Pnei Baruch 10:12

however, does not apply on Shabbos.[629] Likewise, women are not accustomed to be careful in this matter.[630] Even men can choose not to be particular in this matter.[631]

May the mourners sit on regular chairs during the meal?
One is to sit on a low stool even during the meals, however some are accustomed to be lenient to sit in regular chairs, as explained in the next Halacha.

---

[628] Bach 403 in name of Rokeiach; Shivlei Haleket 23; Maavor Yabok 35
[629] Shivlei Haleket ibid
[630] Shivlei Haleket ibid
[631] Shivlei Haleket ibid "In all these matters there is no need to be careful" a different Nussach reads "In all these matters it is proper not to be particular, as the verse states Tamim Tihyeh Im Havaya Elokecha."

Even Haezer

-----------------Marriage----------------

1. At what age is a man to get married?[1]

A. The minimum age of Marriage:

Child marriages-Marrying prior to 13 years old:[2] Prior to 13 years of age, a boy may not get married, as it is considered like promiscuity.[3] It is thus forbidden to wed a boy to a woman prior to reaching this age.[4] If a child transgressed and consecrated [Kiddushin], or married, a woman prior to this age, it is meaningless, [and the woman does not need a Get[5]].[6] [This Halacha implies that a child may not get married until he has reached his 13th birthday.[7] However, some Poskim[8] rule that Rabbinically, a child may get married starting from 12 years old and onwards, and if he does so, his wife Rabbinically requires a Get.]

B. The suggested age for marriage:

It is a Mitzvah upon every man to marry a woman at 18 years of age.[9] [The Rebbe strongly encouraged this approach.[10] Some Poskim[11] rule this means that one should get married as soon as he begins his 18th year, which is after turning 17 years of age.] One who precedes and marries at 13 years of age [has fulfilled] the Mitzvah Min Hamuvchar.[12] [However, in today's times, one is not to get married this young.[13]]

C. By what age must one be married:

In any event, one may not pass 20 years of age without being married [and is thus to place effort to be married prior to reaching 20 years of age].[14] One who does not get married by 20 years old transgresses

---

[1] Michaber E.H. 1:3

[2] Michaber E.H. 1:3; 43:1; Tur 1; Rambam Issurei Biya 21

[3] Michaber ibid; Tur 1; Bach 1; Rav Akiva Eiger that so is implied from Rashba 803 and 1181; Aruch Hashulchan 1:11; See Taz 1:3 that this means that it appears the relationship is for the sake of promiscuity, even though in truth it is not promiscuity, as they are doing so in a way of marriage.

Other opinions: Some Poskim rule it is not considered like promiscuity. [Beis Shmuel 1:4; Tosafos Sanhedrin 77b; Rosh; See Beir Heiytiv 1:5 in name of Kneses Yechezkal 55; Pischeiy Teshuvah 1:3]

[4] Michaber 43:1

[5] Chelkas Mechokeik 43:1

[6] Michaber 43:1; Mishneh Yevamos 96b; Rami Bar Chama 112b

[7] Chelkas Mechokeik 1:3; 43:1 negates the ruling of Bach; Beis Shmuel 1:3; Beis Yosef 1; Implication of Rambam and Tur ibid

[8] Bach 1 if father marries him off, brought in Chelkas Mechokeik 43:1; Rashi and Tosafos on Sanhedrin 77b "A year or half a year before his Bar Mitzvah"; Some Achronim in interpretation of Rambam and Tur, brought in Chelkas Mechokeik ibid; Bach 1, brought in Chelkas Mechokeik and Beis Shmuel ibid, rules that only the father may marry him off from age 12, and the Sages instituted a Rabbinical Kiddushin for him at this age, and his wife needs a Get!

[9] Michaber ibid; Kiddushin 29b; Pesachim 113a; Mishneh Pirkei Avos end of chapter 5:22; Rambam Ishus 15:2 writes from 17 years of age

The reason: Although in general, a person must fulfill all the Mitzvos as soon as he turns 13 years of age, nevertheless, the Sages received that regarding the Mitzvah of Peri Urevu, it only begins at age 18. The reason for this is because one is required to learn Torah, and one only has time to properly do so prior to marriage. [See Michaber Y.D. 246:2] Now, the Torah learning of the Talmud begins from age 15, as stated in the Mishneh in Avos, [and therefore the Sages gave 2-3 years of learning the Talmud prior to marriage]. [Chelkas Mechokeik 1:2; Beis Shmuel 1:3; See Admur Hilchos Talmud Torah 3:1] The reason why the Sages stated one should get married at 18, even though it takes five years to complete Talmudic studies, is because it is possible to learn after marriage without too many distractions for about 2-3 years, prior to having many children. [Admur ibid]

[10] Igros Kodesh 13:23; 18:436; 20:175 "If only that the Ashkenazim would also get married at a very young age"; 23:221-222; 29:272; Letter 5,974 "You should be Makpid on the teaching in the Mishneh of 18 years old for marriage, as certainly the Mishneh is reliable and it applies to all types of Jews"; On the other hand, see Igros Kodesh 10:202; 28:341 [printed in Shulchan Menachem 6:95] where the Rebbe seems to resolve with the custom of getting married in the early 20's and not 18 or even 20 years old.

[11] Beis Shmuel 1:3; Taz 1:3 in name of Maagid Mishneh; Biur Hagoleh 1:3 in name of Rambam; Maggid Mishneh on Rambam 15:1; Rambam Ishus 15:2 writes from 17 years of age; Aruch Hashulchan 1:11

Other opinions: Some Poskim rule one is to get married after completing his 18th year, which is after his 18th birthday. [Bach 1, brought in Taz 1:3]

[12] Michaber ibid; Yevamos 62b; Sanhedrin 77b; Rav Chisda in Kiddushin 29b "If I would have married at 14"

The reason: As he quashes his lusts and passions from the Yetzer Hara, and is like sticking an arrow into his eyes. [Kiddushin 30a; Rambam Issurei Biyah 21:25]

[13] Birkeiy Yosef 1 in name of Rabbeinu Yona in his Tzava, brought in Pischeiy Teshuvah 1:2; Aruch Hashulchan 1:11; See Igros Kodesh 29:272

The reason: As the people are weaker [i.e. less mature] and the generations have changed [and are thus unable to handle marriage at such a young age]. [ibid]

[14] Michaber ibid; Rambam ibid; Kiddushin 29b "Until twenty years Hashem waits for a man to marry. When he reaches age 20 and is still not married, Hashem says let his bones swell."

and nullifies a Biblical Positive command.[15] [If, however, he is not married by twenty years old due to matters beyond his control, then he does not transgress any prohibition.[16] Likewise, some Poskim[17] rule it is permitted to delay marriage until 24 years of age in order to find a proper Zivug, or due to other reasons.] One who passes 20 years of age of and does not wish to get married, then [in previous times[18]] the Beis Din would coerce him to marry in order to fulfill the Mitzvah of having children.[19] However, in today's times, one is no longer coerced by Beis Din to get married.[20]

D. Delaying marriage past 20 due to learning Torah:

If one is involved in Torah learning, and toils in it, and fears marrying a woman lest he be required to toil after sustenance and thus nullify his Torah learning, then it is permitted for him to delay getting married [even past the age of 20].[21] [Some Poskim[22] rule he may delay marriage for as long as he wants, so long as getting married will prevent him from learning Torah due to the need for him to get a job to support his family. He may likewise choose to marry a woman who is infertile in order so he can dedicate his entire life for Torah learning.[23] Other Poskim[24] however rule there is a limit to this matter, and one cannot delay marriage forever.[25] Some Poskim[26] rule that one may delay until 24 years of age. However, according to Admur, he may delay marriage until he learns and remembers the entire oral Torah in a summarized fashion[27], if he is capable of doing so.[28] Practically, in many Litvishe Yeshivos, the custom was to delay marriage until the early 30's. However, the practice in Yeshivas Tomchei Temimim was, and is, to get married in the early 20's, and so is the proper approach.[29] Chabad Rabbanim and Mashpi'im around the

---

The reason: As it takes up to five years to learn the [entire Talmud], and in previous times they would learn with the children five years of Mishneh from age 10 and 5 years of Talmud, which are the Mitzvos with their reasons in a summarized fashion, [and hence by age 20 they completed their Mitzvah of Yedias Hatorah]. Hence, since there is no longer a need to delay marriage past 20 years old due to Torah learning, therefore, one who went past age 20 without getting married transgressed the Biblical positive command of Peru Urevu. [Admur Hilchos Talmud Torah 3:1] Alternatively, as once one turns 20 years old he is liable for Heavenly punishment. [Aruch Hashulchan 1:11]

Other opinions: Some Poskim rule one may delay marriage until 22 years of age. [See Shaiy Lamoreh 1 that the Peri Chadash got married at 22, and this is based on opinion of Rava in Kiddushin ibid]

[15] Admur Hilchos Talmud Torah 3:1; Rambam Ishus 15:2
[16] Aruch Hashulchan 1:11
[17] Maharikash, brought in Pischeiy Teshuvah 1:5
[18] Rama ibid
[19] Michaber ibid; Tur in name of Rosh
[20] Rama ibid

The custom of Jerusalem Jewry: In Jerusalem, an institution was made that any man who reaches 20 years of age and is still single, must leave the city. This institution was enforced in previous times, and has been around for at least 300 years. [See Sefer Asos Mishpat p. 263; Hatakanos Al Yerushalayim p. 41 that the father of the Chida signed on this Takana, which was a reinstitution of a previous Takana. It is also signed by the following Rabbanei Yerushalayim: Author of Admas Kodesh; Peri Hadama; Get Mekushar; Rav Yaakov Algazi] In the mid 1900's, the Sephardic Yeshiva "Porat Yosef" experienced a series of tragedies, which the Roshei Yeshiva attributed to lack of enforcement of this Takana. They desired to remove the Cherem, although not all the Rabbanim agreed to do so, and it hence has remained in place. There is discussion amongst Rabbanim as to whether this Takana applies to all of Jerusalem, or only to the old city. [Heard from Harav Yaakov Yosef za"l] Practically, Harav Yaakov Yosef za"l would rule for Bochurim who have reached 20 years of age to leave the city of Jerusalem and go study elsewhere.

[21] Michaber Y.D. 246:2; E.H. 1:3; Admur Hilchos Talmud Torah 3:1; Kiddushin ibid "Learn Torah and then get married"

The reason: If one gets married prior to learning Torah, he will be under financial burden to support his wife and children, and will thus be unable to study Torah as much. Now, although the one must stop learning in order to fulfill a positive command, this only refers to a positive command that can be fulfilled momentarily, as one can shortly afterwards resume his Torah learning. However, if one were to get married, then he would be unable to continue learning at all, as he must now sustain his family. [Admur Hilchos Talmud Torah 3:1]

[22] Beis Shmuel 1:5 in implication of Rambam; Rav Akiva Eiger 1 in name of Maharam Mintz 42
[23] Chochmas Shlomo based on Beis Shmuel ibid
[24] Rosh Kiddushin 1:42, brought in Tur E.H. 1 and Beis Shmuel ibid; Levush 1; Rashal Kiddushin; Aruch Hashulchan 1:13; Shevet Halevi 3:173; See Admur Hilchos Talmud Torah Kuntrus Achron 3:1 who learns in Rashi and the Rambam that the limitation is five years for Mishneh and five years for Talmud.
[25] The reason: As this allowance was only given to Ben Azaiy. [Rosh ibid] However, the Beis Shmuel ibid explains, that the novelty of Ben Azaiy is that even if getting married would not disturb him from his learning, such as if he is wealthy, he is still not required to get married.
[26] Rashal Kiddushin; Aruch Hashulchan 1:13; Sefer Hamitzvos of Chofetz Chaim "Until 25 years of age"; Shevet Halevi 3:173
[27] This includes all of the Jewish laws, all the 613 commands together with all their details, Biblical and Rabbinical, and their summarized reasons. [Admur Hilchos Talmud Achron 3:1] This includes even knowledge of those sections of laws that are not applicable, and are not practical, for all people, such as Kodshim, Zeraim, Nashim and Nezikin. However, one may not delay marriage simply for achieving greater depth of understanding and Pilpul in Torah. [Admur Hilchos Talmud Torah Kuntrus Achron 3:1]
[28] Hilchos Talmud Torah 3:1; See Hilchos Talmud Torah Kuntrus Achron 3:1 that one cannot delay marriage forever simply to further his in depth understanding of the Torah, as this is a study that has no end, and in any event one will never reach the final depth of his research.
[29] Igros Kodesh 10:202; 14:30 [printed in Shulchan Menachem 6:95]

world have proclaimed the necessity for Bochurim to begin Shidduchim as soon as they complete their study in Yeshiva Gedola. At age 20, they are to begin their search for a wife, and only those who are truly dedicated to assiduous Torah study may delay for another one to two years.[30] A similar ruling has been given by other Gedolei Yisrael of today's generation.[31]]

Delaying marriage forever for the sake of learning:[32] Furthermore, one whose soul yearns to learn Torah constantly like Ben Azaiy, and he attached himself to it his entire life, and thus did not get married, he carries no sin for doing so.[33] [Some Poskim[34] rule this applies even if getting married would not trouble him from his learning, such as he is wealthy. However, Admur negates this opinion, and implies if one is able to do both, to constantly fulfill his Mitzvah of Yedias Hatorah and get married, then he must do so.[35] Some Poskim[36] rule that initially, even one who desires to learn like Ben Azaiy, must get married, and it is only after the fact, if he did not marry, that he carries no sin. Furthermore, some Poskim[37] rule that a person of the such stature and nature of Ben Azaiy is not found at all today. However, from Admur[38], it is implied even initially one may choose to follow Ben Azaiy and not get married in order so he can constantly review his Torah learning and not come to forget parts of the Oral Torah and his Mitzvah of Yedias Hatorah.[39] Nonetheless, even in his opinion, the Sages advised one to get married once he has completed his Mitzvah of Yedias Hatorah, even if there is worry that he may come to forget.[40] If, however, there is no worry of forgetting the Mitzvah of Yedias Hatorah, and he simply wants to delay marriage in order to continuing learning the depth and Pilpul, then it is forbidden to do so, even according to Ben Azaiy.[41]]

Who may delay marriage past 20 for the sake of Torah learning? One may only delay marriage past the age of 20 due to Torah learning, on condition that his inclination does not overcome him with erotic thoughts to the point that his mind is unable to focus [and he is able to thus learn without thoughts of sin]. If, however, he is troubled by erotic thoughts[42] to the point that his mind is unable to focus, then he is to first get married, in order to learn Torah with purity of mind, without erotic thoughts.[43] [The Rebbe encouraged this approach.[44]] Furthermore, this allowance of delaying marriage due to Torah study is only for a person who has the intellectual capacity to learn and remember the entire Oral Torah, in which case he is to first learn the entire oral Torah and only then get married.[45] This includes all of the laws; all the

---

[30] See the letter which was signed by Rabbinical leaders, Mashpim and Roshei Yeshiva's from various Chabad communities.

[31] Shevet Halevi 3:173 [as soon as possible; age 24]; Chazon Ish E.H. 148 and in Peas Sadcha 1:149 [until age 20]; Rav SZ"A [until age 20], brought in Sod Hanissuin p. 73 [he married all his children prior to age 20]

[32] Michaber 1:4; Rambam Ishus 15:3; Ben Azaiy in Yevamos 63b; See Hilchos Talmud Torah Kuntrus Achron 3:1 that even the Chachamim agree with Ben Azaiy, and hence the Rambam and Michaber rule that one has the option of doing like him; See Aruch Hashulchan 1:14 that the Rif omitted this ruling and according to some Ben Azaiy did get married, and possibly it was literally Sakanas Nefashos for Ben Azaiy to stop learning Torah, and therefore he could not get married.

[33] The reason: As one has a constant Mitzvah of Yedias Hatorah, and if he gets married, and has no time to review, he will come to forget his Torah learning. Thus, one can choose to not get married in order so he review his Torah learning his entire life and not come to forget any aspect of it. This is why Ben Azaiy did not marry, as he feared he would forget his Torah learning. Now, although we rule that one must stop his Torah learning in order to fulfill a passing Mitzvah, this is only in a case that one can then return to his Torah learning, however if the Torah learning of Yedias Hatorah will be pushed off forever, then one is not required to stop to perform the Mitzvah. [Hilchos Talmud Torah Kuntrus Achron 3:1]

[34] Beis Shmuel 1:5

[35] Admur Hilchos Talmud Torah Kuntrus Achron 3:1

[36] Taz 1:6

[37] Aruch Hashulchan 1:14

[38] Hilchos Talmud Torah Kuntrus Achron 3:1

[39] The reason: See previous footnotes for reason in Admur.

[40] See lengthy explanation in Admur Hilchos Talmud Torah Kuntrus Achron 3:1 and how Admur learns this in the Rosh

[41] Implication of Admur Hilchos Talmud Torah 3:1 and Kuntrus Achron 3:1

The reason: One cannot delay marriage forever simply to further his in depth understanding of the Torah, as this is a study that has no end, and in any event one will never reach the final depth of his research. [Admur Hilchos Talmud Torah Kuntrus Achron 3:1]

[42] See Shevet Halevi 3:173 that erotic thoughts is defined as literally thoughts, even if it does not lead to sinful activity [i.e. Zera Levatala], as thinking such thoughts is itself Biblically forbidden.

[43] Admur Hilchos Talmud Torah 3:1-2; Michaber Y.D. 246:2; E.H. 1:4; Beis Shmuel E.H. 1:5; Taz E.H. 1:4; Rambam Talmud Torah 1:5; Kiddushin ibid "and if he is unable to be without a wife, he should first marry"; Based on Yuma 29a; Vetzaruch Iyun why it was not mentioned in Michaber 1:3! See Divrei Yatziv E.H. 3

[44] Igros Kodesh 13:23

[45] Admur Hilchos Talmud Torah 3:1

The reason: As only if one learns and remembers the entire Torah does he fulfill the Mitzvah of Yedias Hatorah, which is even greater than the Mitzvah of Peru Urevu. [Admur Hilchos Talmud Torah Kuntrus Achron 3:1]

613 commands together with all their details, Biblical and Rabbinical, and their summarized reasons.[46] If, however, he does not have the intellectual capability to learn and remember all of the Torah, then he must get married prior to the age of 20.[47]

Summary:
One is to get married at 17/18 years of age, and no later than 20 years of age. It is permitted to delay marriage due to Torah learning, if certain criteria is fulfilled, as explained next. Some Poskim rule it is permitted to delay marriage until 24 years old in order to find a proper Zivug, learn Torah, or due to other important reasons. The Rebbe strongly advocated for bringing down the marriage age, and encouraged people to get married starting from age 18. Nonetheless, the Chabad custom in Yeshivos is for Bochurim to get married in the early 20's. Chabad Rabbanim world over have ruled that at age 20, Bochurim are to begin their search for a wife, and only those who are truly dedicated to assiduous Torah study may delay for another one to two years.

The criteria for delaying marriage due to Talmud Torah:
According to the ruling of the Alter Rebbe, the allowance of delaying marriage past age 20 for the sake of Torah study only applies if the following four conditions are fulfilled:
1. One is learning Torah and is capable of fulfilling the Mitzvah of Yedias Hatorah, through learning and memorizing all the details and reasons of the 613 commands, in a summarized fashion.
2. One will be unable to fulfill this Mitzvah of Yedias Hatorah if he gets married, due to his preoccupation in making a living to support his family.
3. One has not yet already fulfilled the Mitzvah of Yedias Hatorah. If he has already fulfilled this Mitzvah, he may no longer delay marriage, unless he is worried it may lead him to forget his Torah learning.
4. One is <u>not</u> troubled by erotic thoughts that prevent him from learning Torah in purity.

Practically, by what age must Yeshiva Bochurim today get married by?
As stated above, in the summary, the Rebbe strongly encouraged people to marry early, from age 18, although the current custom mentioned by the Rebbe, is to marry in the early 20's. The Chabad Rabbanim in recent years ruled that at age 20, Bochurim are to begin their search for a wife, and only

---

The reason: If one gets married prior to learning Torah, he will be under financial burden to support his wife and children, and will thus be unable to study Torah as much, and will be unable to learn and remember all the Halachos with their reasons, which is the explanation of the 613 Mitzvos, and the main part of the Oral Torah. Therefore, the great Mitzvah of Peru Urevu is delayed due to this learning, even though it is the greatest of all the Mitzvos, as Talmud Torah is greater than all the Mitzvos and hence makes him exempt from the Mitzvah of Peru Urevu. Now, although one must stop learning Torah in order to fulfill a positive command that cannot be fulfilled by others, this only refers to a positive command that takes up a limited amount of one's time, as one is only nullifying the command to constantly learn Torah. However, it does not refer to nullifying forever the Mitzvah of Yedias Hatorah, which is knowledge of all the Halachos and their reasons in a summarized fashion. [Admur Hilchos Talmud Torah 3:1; Kuntrus Achron 3:1]

[46] Admur Hilchos Talmud Torah 3:1 and Kuntrus Achron 3:1

[47] Implication of Admur Hilchos Talmud Torah 3:1 and Kuntrus Achron 3:1; Implication of Tzemach Tzedek in "Maaseh Chassidim Harishonim", printed in Hilchos Talmud Torah [Ashkenazi] Volume 5 p. 645, regarding that one who cannot learn all Torah may lengthen his Davening as he is not applicable to the Mitzvah of Yedias Hatorah.

Tzaruch Iyun from other sources: Tzaruch Iyun from Admur Hilchos Talmud Torah 2:8 and 4:6 in parentheses which seems to imply that even one who cannot learn and remember all 613 commands in detail, can still fulfill the Mitzvah of Yedias Hatorah through learning and remembering the maximum of their ability. Accordingly, they too would be allowed to delay marriage until they fulfill their limited version of the Mitzvah of Yedias Hatorah. This contradicts the implication above that such people cannot fulfill the Mitzvah of Yedias Hatorah and hence do not have the above allowance relevant to them. See, however, the statement of the Tzemach Tzedek ibid, who seemingly learns in Admur 4:6 that they do not have an ability to fulfill the Mitzvah of Yedias Hatorah. Vetzaruch Iyun on how to fit all this into Admur. See Hilchos Talmud Torah of Rav Ashkenazi ibid who leaves this in a Tzaruch Iyun. See also Hearos Ubiurim 770 5764 for an article on this subject; See Shevet Halevi 3:173 who brings the ruling of Admur ibid and concludes that from the spirit of his ruling we can conclude that the allowance applies to anyone who desires to acquire knowledge in Shas and Poskim even if he will not complete it all.

The reason: As the Mitzvah of learning Torah is only greater than Peru Urevu if one can fulfill the Mitzvah of Yedias Hatorah, which is to learn and remember the entire Torah. If however one cannot do so, then although he can still fulfill the Mitzvah of Vehigisa Bo Yomam Valayla, nevertheless this does not push off the Mitzvah of Peru Urevu, as the Mitzvah of learning Torah is pushed off by any Mitzvah that cannot be fulfilled by others. [Admur ibid]

those who are truly dedicated to assiduous Torah study may delay for another one to two years. We will now explore whether this custom of delaying marriage past age 20 has Halachic basis.

Is there a Halachic allowance for Yeshiva Bochurim to delay marriage past age 20 for Bochurim today? Based on the criteria mentioned above, from the letter of the law, in today's times, most Yeshiva students do not have a Torah learning allowance to differ marriage, and must get married before the age of 20, as most students are not born with the intellectual ability to learn and remember the entire Torah. Furthermore, even of those who are able to reach this state of learning, many are troubled by erotic thoughts.[48] On what then does the custom rely upon to delay marriage past age 20 despite their ineligibility for the allowance of the Torah learning deferral? This will be addressed next.

On what do people rely upon today to delay marriage past age 20, even if they do not fall under the criteria which allows delaying marriage due to Torah learning?

Seemingly, Bochurim today are not mature enough for marriage until their early 20's, and hence, irrelevant of the Heter of learning Torah, they are unable to marry beforehand. We find basis for this approach in the Poskim[49] who state that the dictum of the Sages which encouraged marriage from age 13 is no longer applicable today due to the change of times, and lack of maturity. Hence, seemingly, the same would apply regarding even past age 20, that if times change, and people are no longer mature enough to marry this early, then the marriage age automatically becomes delayed. In other words, the Torah did not obligate one to get married by any specific age, and rather obligated one to get married as soon as is able to, once he becomes Bar Mitzvah. Now, in previous times, since Talmudic Torah learning extended from age 15-20, therefore the marriage age was up until age 20, to suffice one to learn five years of Talmud.[50] We see from here that delaying marriage for a necessary purpose is permitted. The same should certainly apply to delaying marriage due to lack of maturity, as if one is not mature enough to marry, the marriage will not last, and certainly the Mitzvah is not yet applicable to him. Alternatively, one can say that the age by which one must marry is dependent on the community system, and if the system in one's community is to only marry after age 20, after concluding the educational system, then for that community, the marriage age is differed until later. This is similar to the establishment of the original age 20 which was based on the system to learn Talmud from age 15-20. Vetzaruch Iyun on all the above, as no matter what one says, it contradicts the simple ruling in Shulchan Aruch that one must marry by age 20 without giving any exception to the rule, unless one is learning Torah. The above is thus only a Limud Zechus on the current custom, in order to defend how it does not transgress the clear ruling in Shulchan Aruch that one must marry by age 20. Nevertheless, in truth, it is possible even today for Bochurim to be mature enough for marriage by age 18-20, and hence fulfill the Mitzvah of Peru Urevu according to Biblical requirement, through educating them at an early age that they should expect to get married by that time, and so is done in many Chassidic communities until this very day. As stated earlier, the Rebbe strongly encouraged and advocated for early marriages, from age 18.

Yuchsin

2. Who is a Jew-Determining Jewish identity in cases of question and doubt:

According to Jewish law, a person is only determined to be a Jew [i.e. to contain a G-dly soul, be obligated in the Torah and Mitzvos, and be part of the Jewish nation in the eyes of G-d and his people] if his mother is Jewish [i.e. direct maternal lineage[51]], or he converted to Judaism in a Halachically valid conversion, as will be explain in A. This Halacha will mainly focus on the verification of these two claims. What if someone is unsure if his/her mother was Jewish, or if he had a Kosher conversion?

---

[48] See Shevet Halevi 3:173 "Who today can say they are clean from erotic thoughts, when the streets are filled with immodesty and promiscuity, and certainly it is obvious that one must get married as soon as possible."
[49] Birkeiy Yosef 1 in name of Rabbeinu Yona in his Tzava, brought in Pischeiy Teshuvah 1:2; Aruch Hashulchan 1:11; See Igros Kodesh 29:272
[50] See Admur Hilchos Talmud Torah 1:3
[51] This means that either all her maternal lineage goes back to Har Sinai, or that someone in her maternal lineage converted a Kosher conversion.

Furthermore, even if one claims to be sure that his mother was Jewish, or that he converted in a Kosher method, how do we determine that his claim is true? Do we simply believe the claim of Jewish identity of any person, and if he says his mother is Jewish, or that he converted, he is believed, or do we require investigation and verification of proofs?

Note: To follow is a mere synopsis of the subject. In all cases of question or doubt one is to bring the issue to a Beis Din that is familiar in these matters.

A. Definition of a Jew:[52]

Jewish mother:[53] According to Jewish law, a person [who did not convert in a Kosher method] is only considered Jewish if his/her mother is Jewish [i.e. direct maternal lineage]. [This means that all his/her direct maternal ancestors are descendants of a woman who was present at the giving of the Torah on Har Sinai, or that someone in her direct maternal lineage converted a Kosher conversion.] One who was born from a Jewish mother is a full-fledged Jew even if one's father, or someone in the paternal lineage, is/was not Jewish.[54] One whose mother is not Jewish, is not considered Jewish even if their father is Jewish.[55] One who is Jewish, remains Jewish even if he or his direct maternal ancestors converted r"l to a different religion.[56] [Accordingly, there is no such thing in Halacha as a half Jew or quarter Jew, either someone is

---

[52] See "Who is a Jew" by Rabbi Emanuel Shochat for a full overview on this subject.

[53] Michaber E.H. 4:5 *"A Jew who has relations with one of these woman, the offspring follows the mother's identity."* 4:19 *"A gentile who had a child with a Jewess, the child is a Jew"*; 7:17; 44:9 [regarding Kiddushin]; Rama O.C. 282:3 [regarding getting Aliyah]; Y.D. 159:3 [regarding Ribis]; E.H. 16:2; 44:9; Shach Y.D. 159:7; Admur 282:8 *"A slave who has not been emancipated has the same status as a woman. However, if his mother is Jewish, then he is considered a complete Jew for all matters."*; Admur Hilchos Ribis 79; Rambam Hilchos Issurei Biyah 12:7; 15:3-4, 6; Rebbe Yochanon in Yevamos 17a and 23a and 45b based on Devarim 7:3-4; Mishnah Kiddushin 66b, 68b; Ramban on Vayikra 24:10

Did we ever follow paternal lineage and not maternal lineage? According to some sources, prior to the giving of the Torah, paternal lineage was followed to determine the identity of a Jew, and not maternal lineage. [See Sifra Toras Kohanim Emor 14 and Chochmei Tzarfat brought in Ramban on Vayikra 24:10] The Ramban ibid negates this suggestion, and claims we always followed maternal lineage, even prior to Matan Torah.

[54] Michaber and Rama ibid; Rambam ibid; Gemara ibid

Conversion: Some Poskim rule that the daughter of a gentile father and Jewess requires conversion. [Yearos Dvash Derush 17, brought in Pischeiy Teshuvah E.H. 4/1; Avnei Nezer 16 on Tosafos Yevamos 16b] Practically we do not rule this way. [Avnei Nezer 16; Yeshuos Yaakov 4/8; Beis Yitzchak 26; Achiezer 21; Chazon Ish 6/7]

[55] Michaber and Rama ibid; Rambam ibid; Gemara ibid

Other opinions: The Midrash records the opinion of Rebbe Yaakov Kfar Nevorai who held we follow paternal lineage, and not maternal lineage. His teacher, Rebbe Chagaiy negated this opinion as inaccurate and told his student, Rebbe Yaakov, that he deserves lashes for making such a statement. [Bereishis Raba 7b] This Rebbe Yaakov Kfar Nevorai is considered a controversial figure in the Talmud, and some considered him a sinner and heretic.

[56] Michaber and Rama E.H. 44:9 regarding Kiddushin *"A Yisrael Mumar who did Kiddushin, it is valid. And even if the Mumar had a child later from a Jewish woman, his Kiddushin is valid"* [They do not differentiate between if converted out of duress or willingly]; Rama Y.D. 159:3 [regarding Ribis]; Beis Yosef E.H. 157:6 *"The children and all descendants of a Jewish mother who became a Mumar [remains Jewish and their Kiddushin is valid] even after many generations. This matter is an obvious Jewish law and those students who wrote differently, should have been persecuted by the Sages and excommunicated , as certainly these matters have no root and branch to rely on, and woe top one who is lenient in this"* Maharik Shoresh 85; Maggid Mishneh Ishus 4, brought in Beis Yosef 44; Teshuvas Reim 47 and 49 [Rav Eliyahu Mizrachi] that this applies for all the future descendants, see there in length; Noda Beyehuda Tinyana 162, brought in Pischeiy Teshuvah 44:9 that a Mumar remains Jewish; Teshuvas Hageonim Shaareiy Tzedek 3 1:50 [regarding Mumar]; Meiri in Beis Habechira Avoda Zara 26 [regarding Mumar, however, regarding descendants-see below]; Rashbash 89; 368 [all generations]; Yachin Boaz 2:31 [all generations]; Igros Moshe E.H. 4:83 *"It is not possible for a Jew to become a non-Jew. The Mumrim and their children are complete Jews and one cannot join the opposing opinions even as a Safek. The Mahrashdam made a grave error by writing otherwise"*; See in great length [50 chapters] Divrei Yatziv Even Haezer 62; Radbaz 3:415; 4:12

Other opinions: Some Poskim rule that a Mumar is considered a gentile and his Kiddushin is invalid. [Opinion in Tur E.H. 44; Ittur Os Kuf 78a *"One who desecrates Shabbos in public is like a gentile and his Kiddushin is invalid"*; Rav Yehudaiy brought in Beis Yosef 157; Halachos Ketanos 2:240; See Teshuvas Riem ibid for a lengthy discussion on this subject; See Aruch Hashulchan E.H. 44:11; See Divrei Yatziv Even Haezer 62 who defends this approach] The Poskim ibid severely negate this approach and it cannot be used in Halacha for any leniency. [Beis Yosef ibid; Igros Moshe ibid]

The descendants of Mumarim: Some Poskim rule that although a Mumar and his/her descendants are Jewish, this only applies if the Mumar converted out of force. If, however, he/she converted out of his/her free will, then all the children born after the conversion are complete gentiles [even if both parents are Jewish]. [Teshuvas Reim ibid in name of Mahariy Chaviv; Rashdam E.H. 10; Kneses Hagedola 44 that from the grandchildren and onwards, this applies even according to Teshuvas Hareim; Beir Heiytiv E.H. 44:8; See Maharibal 2:45; Radab 6; Meiri in Beis Habechira Avoda Zara 26 rules that all the descendants of the Muamr are not Jewish] However, other Poskim vehemently negate this position, saying that a Jew remains a Jew even if his direct maternal ancestor willingly converted many generations ago. [Implication of Michaber ibid; Beis Yosef ibid severely negates the above position; Rashbash ibid; Aruch Hashulchan E.H. 44:11 *"There is no root for the above words of the Poskim ibid who negate the Judaism of the descendants, as how exactly does their Jewish identity disappear? So is explained in the Rambam and all Poskim, and so is Setimas Hamichaber in 44:9. The fact that the Rashdam ibid learnt his position from the Talmudic opinion revoking Jewish identity from the ten tribes has no basis, as there it is learned from a verse"* Igros Moshe E.H. 4:83 negates the above opinions from Halacha, saying they cannot be joined to any calculation of leniency]

158

Jewish or not. Use of such terms is inaccurate, and does not change the true definition of the person, just as calling an African person a Chinese, does not make him Chinese.]

Conversion:[57] A gentile who converts through a Halachically valid conversion is defined as a full-fledged Jew for all purposes. If the conversion was not valid according to Halacha, the individual remains a full-fledged gentile for all purposes.

The law of a questionable Jew: If one is unsure if his mother is Jewish, then he is considered a gentile, until proof is found of his mother's Jewish identity.[58] [Thus, there is no such concept as a questionable Jew, if he has question as to whether his mother was Jewish, as one is considered a gentile until he determines that his mother is Jewish.] However, the concept of a questionable Jew does apply in a case that a person claims to be Jewish [either due to having a Jewish mother, or due to conversion] but his claim contains suspicion, or requires Halachic proof according to the Poskim. Below we will discuss when we believe a person's claim of being Jewish and when we require proof of his claim.

B. If one says his mother is Jewish, is he to be believed?

Allowing him to marry a Jew: In general, if a person says he is Jewish [due to his mother being Jewish] then he is believed to be Jewish and is allowed to marry another Jew.[59] Some Poskim[60] rule that this applies even if the person came from a different country. Other Poskim[61] however rule that if an individual came from a different country then [in order to be allowed to marry a Jew[62]] he must prove his Jewishness, even if he acts like an observant Jew. [Practically, we no longer rely on the above Chazaka regarding Jews who come from areas where intermarriage is common, such as the USSR, and if the person desires to marry a Jew, they must proof their Jewishness, or convert.[63] This especially applies if there is a reason to place doubt into the person's claim of Jewishness. In Israel, the Rabbanut requires all foreigners to prove their Jewish identity and provide testimony from authorized Rabbis in the Diaspora in order to be allowed to marry or perform Aliyah.]

Other matters, such as Tefillin:[64] The above requirement for a Jew from out of country to bring proof of his Jewishness even if he acts like an observant Jew, only applies with regards to allowing him to marry a Jew. However, regarding all other matters of Judaism [such as Tefillin, Minyan etc], any person who states that he is Jewish [i.e. his mother is Jewish], is believed even without bringing proof.[65]

Murano's: The descendants of Murano Jews are considered to have converted out of duress [even though not all were threatened with their lives] and are considered Jewish according to all, so long as they did not intermarry with gentile women. [Teshvas Ream ibid; Rashbash 89; 368; Yachin Boaz 2:31]

[57] Shulchan Aruch Y.D. 268; Rambam Hilchos Issurei Biyah 12:17; 13;14; Bechoros 30b; Kerisus 9a; Yevamos 46a-b
[58] See Admur 329:2; Michaber Even Haezer 4:34
The reason: A person is assumed to be a gentile unless proven otherwise, as Kol Haporeish Merubo Poreish. [ibid]
[59] Michaber Even Haezer 2:2; Rashal Kesubos 2:40; Rabbeinu Tam in Yevamos 46b; Rashba; Ramban; Pischeiy Teshuvah 2:2; Aruch Hashulchan 2:12; ; Yabia Omer 7 E.H. 1
The reason: As people contain a Chezkas Kashrus, and majority of people who say they are Jewish are Jewish. [ibid] Vetzaruch Iyun regarding if the person is not observant, how this Chezkas Kashrus is maintained. See Meiri Yevamos 46a; Shut Maharit 1:149; Merkeves Hamishneh Issurei Biyah 13:10; Rav Akiva Eiger 1:121; Kiryat Chana David 2:3; Tiferes Yisrael Kesubois 2:46; Heichal Yitzchak 1:17; Chut Hameshulash 5; Chazon Ish Y.D. 158:8; Yibum 117:7; See the following Poskim who rule he does not need to be observant today: Kovetz Teshuvos E.H. 1:33; Igros Moshe E.H. 6
Other opinions: Some Poskim rule one is not believed to say he is Jewish unless he brings proof. [Rameh; Rashi, brought in Tur 2; Beis Shmuel 2:2 suspects for this opinion]
[60] Shach 268:21; Bach Yoreh Deah 268; Halef Lecha Shlomo Even Haezer 15; Yabia Omer 7 E.H. 1; See also Aruch Hashulchan 269:14 "Do we require proof from people who we don't know, and they claim to be Jewish"; See however Aruch Hashulchan in next footnote
[61] Beir Heiytiv Even Haezer 2:4 in name of Maharit 1:149 and Beis Hillel, and so rules Michaber Y.D. 268:10 regarding a gentile who says he converted; See however Aruch Hashulchan E.H. 2:13 that this only applies to an individual, while a family does not have to prove their Jewishness if they act like a Jew, as a family maintains a Chazaka. So is also implied from Beir Heiytiv ibid;
[62] See Michaber 268:10 that we are only stringent to require proof in order to marry the person
[63] So ruled many Dayanim and Gedolei Yisrael of today's generation, including Rav Moshe Feinstein, Rav Elyashiv; See Psak Din of Beit Din Rabbani Haifa case number 588549/1; Techumin 6:424; 12; Koveitz Darkei Horah 12; Yabia Omer 7 E.H. 1
[64] See Michaber 268:10 regarding a frum person who was known to be a gentile that we are only stringent to require proof of conversion in order to marry the person; See Aruch Hashulchan 269:14 "Do we require proof from people who we don't know and they claim to be Jewish";
[65] If he is not observant: Vetzaruch Iyun regarding if the person does not act as a Jew, and how to define this. See Meiri Yevamos 46a; Shut Maharit 1:149; Merkeves Hamishneh Issurei Biyah 13:10; Rav Akiva Eiger 1:121; Kiryat Chana David 2:3; Tiferes Yisrael Kesubois 2:46; Heichal Yitzchak 1:17; Chut Hameshulash 5; Chazon Ish Y.D. 158:8; Yibum 117:7; See the following Poskim who rule he does not need to be observant today: Kovetz Teshuvos E.H. 1:33; Igros Moshe E.H. 6

C. If one says he is Jewish because he converted, is he to be believed?[66]

Marrying a Jew: If a person who was known to be a gentile, claims that he went through a Kosher conversion and became Jewish, he is not believed to be allowed to marry a Jew unless he supplies witnesses [or other proof of his conversion], or reconverts. This applies even if this person now acts like an observant Jew. If, however, the person was always held to be Jewish, and now says that in truth he converted, then he is believed without witnesses.[67] Now, although some Poskim[68] argue that even such a person must bring witnesses, nevertheless, the custom is like the former opinion.[69] [In Israel, the Rabbanut requires all foreigners to prove their Jewish identity and provide authorized conversion papers, in order to be allowed to marry, or make Aliyah.]

Other matters, such as Tefillin:[70] The above requirement for a gentile to bring proof of his conversion even if he is now an observant Jew, only applies with regards to allowing him to marry a Jew. However, regarding all other matters of Judaism [such as Tefillin, Minyan etc], if he acts as an observant Jew he is believed to have converted even if he does not bring proof of his conversion.[71]

D. How to verify the claims of a person who says that his mother is Jewish:[72]

As explained in B, the custom today is to require proof of Jewishness for people who come from out of the country, from areas where assimilation was common, and in any case that there is reasonable doubt. The Batei Dinim have several ways of verifying a person's claim of Jewishness. Some Poskim[73] suggest the following criteria:

1) Checking the legal identification cards of the person or his mother, and seeing if it says that he or she is Jewish.
2) Verifying the Jewish names of the person and his family.
3) Knowledge of Yiddish, and acting like a Jew or knowledge of Jewish customs.

The person in question must fulfill at least two of the above three conditions to be considered a Jew, and there must not be any other reason to cast doubt on his Jewishness.[74] In today's times, one also heavily relies on the opinion of an investigator who is trained and experienced in verifying whether the person's claim is true or not. [So is done today in all Batei Dinim].

----------------*Childbirth*----------------

3. May one buy items for a child before he is born?

It is permitted to purchase items for the future child prior to birth.[75] Nevertheless, some have the custom to abstain from doing so due to Ayin Hara.[76] One who did not receive this tradition, is not required to follow this custom, and may choose to buy items and ignore the Ayin Hara.[77] However, those who received this tradition, are to try to abide by it.[78] Some are accustomed to have another person buy the item for them.[79] Others are accustomed to pick out the item, and only pay for it after the birth.

---

[66] Michaber Y.D. 268:10; Yevamos 46b
[67] Michaber ibid
[68] Rambam in Michaber ibid
[69] Shach 268:21 in name of Bach
[70] See Michaber 268:10 that we are only stringent to require proof in order to marry the person
[71] The reason: As an observant Jew maintains a Chezkas Kashrus.
[72] See Psak Din of Beit Din Rabbani Haifa case number 588549/1
[73] Opinion of Rav Moshe Feinstein, brought in Psak Din of Beit Din Rabbani Haifa case number 588549/1
[74] Opinion of Rav Moshe Feinstein
[75] There is no source for prohibiting this, and it is not considered an all encompassing practice of world Jewry that has the power of a set custom to obligate all Jewry to follow.
[76] Sheilas Rav 2:57 in reply of Rav Chaim Kanievsky
[77] Rav Eliyahu Landau wrote to me that that one may purchase without any worry, and that on this it states, "One who is not Makpid -Lo Kapdinan", and that so is the custom that he witnessed.
[78] This follows the famous ruling of the Rashba [See Rashba 1:9; Heishiv Moshe 13; Aryeh Dbei Ilai Y.D. 19] that the Minhag of women is holy and is to be abided. [Heard from Rav Leibel Groner who is of the opinion that one should guard this custom]
[79] Heard from Rav Leibel Groner

4. Doing ultrasounds/sonograms during pregnancy:[80]

There is no Halachic impediment that exists against performing an ultrasound and having a sonogram taken. Nonetheless, doing so at times broaches the subject of Jewish ethics, as well as poses a possible health concern, due to exposure to the waves. Ultrasounds, or the resultant sonograms, are done during pregnancy for various reasons, including: 1) Routine checkup on the health of the child, and to monitor the size and growth of the child; 2) To monitor the health of the birthing mother. 3) To determine the gender of the child; 4) To determine the due date.

The medical concerns involved in ultrasounds-Not to perform unnecessarily: An ultrasound transmits high-frequency sound waves through the uterus that bounce off the baby. While there is no current medical evidence which supports the idea that ultrasounds can have a negative effect on the health of the child, nonetheless, it is advised to avoid doing them unnecessarily. This was the Rebbe's philosophy and the advice that he gave others.[81] This is likewise the advice given by the ACOG [American Congress of Obstetricians and Gynecologists] *"Currently, there is no reliable evidence that ultrasound is harmful to a developing fetus. No links have been found between ultrasound and birth defects, childhood cancer, or developmental problems later in life. **However, it is possible that effects could be identified in the future. For this reason, it is recommended that ultrasound exams be performed only for medical reasons by qualified health care providers.**"* Accordingly, women should avoid doing ultrasounds simply for the fun of it, to enjoy viewing the baby. An additional reason for avoiding ultrasounds is that at times the ultrasound produces sonograms which are falsely read by the Doctor or technician, and cause the parents unnecessary worry or fear of an impending medical issue, which is later proven to be non-existent.

For routine checkup: Medical practitioners offer routine ultrasound checkups to verify the general health and size of the child, as well as the condition of the mother for giving birth. This is usually done during the second trimester, between weeks 18-23.[82] In general, the Rebbe is quoted to have been against routine ultrasound checkups, even if it is done to negate any medical issues, so long as there is no reason to suspect that those issues exist.[83] According to Rabbi Groner, the Rebbe's secretary, the Rebbe only agreed to the performance of an ultrasound if it was medically necessary and specific action can be taken as a result. Likewise, the Rebbe made the matter contingent on confirmation of a second medical opinion, that in truth the ultrasound is necessary. This is due to the possible medical consequences that the waves can have on the unborn child. In addition, ultrasounds at times produce sonograms which are falsely read by the Doctor or technician, as explained above. On the other hand, regarding the routine checkup which is customarily performed in the second trimester [between weeks 18-23] the Rebbe is quoted to have responded that if a woman desires it to be done, then she may do so.[84]

Due to actual medical concern: When an ultrasound is advised by a medical practitioner for the sake of checking the health of the mother or child due to an active medical issue, then the medical advice is to be followed. The Rebbe did not negate having in ultrasound performed under these circumstances, and on the contrary, encouraged it.[85]

To verify irreversible defects for purposes of abortion:[86] It is common for medical practitioners to perform an ultrasound for the sake of discovering if there are any irreversible birth defects in the child, and thus advise the mother of the option to perform an abortion. According to most Poskim, abortions may only be performed if the pregnancy poses a threat to the mother's life, and hence one is not to perform such checks without first discussing the matter with a Rav.

To verify the gender of the fetus: There is no Halachic issue involved with performing ultrasounds for the sake of discovering the gender of the child, although this certainly would fall under the unnecessary

---

[80] See Nishmas Avraham p. 160
[81] Heard from Rabbi Leibel Groner, printed in "Healthy in Body Mind and Spirit" Vol. 2; Hiskashrus
[82] See Nishmas Avraham p. 160 that this is usually done in the first trimester and again in the third trimester.
[83] Heard from Rabbi Leibel Groner, printed in "Healthy in Body Mind and Spirit" Vol. 2; Hiskashrus
[84] Quoted in article of Rabbi Ginsberg in Hiskashrus
[85] Recorded in Hiskashrus, by Rav Ginsberg, based on information received from Rabbi Groner
[86] Nishmas Avraham ibid

ultrasounds which are discouraged from a medical perspective. In addition, some[87] sources suggest that the gender of the child is to be left unknown until birth.

------------------Tzenius-Arayos----------------

5. May one extend greetings to a woman, such as saying Shalom, good morning, good evening, or how are you?[88]

One may not ask a woman at all as to her wellbeing.[89] This applies even if one does so indirectly, through a messenger. It is forbidden to send greetings even through the woman's husband. [This applies even to a woman who one does not know.[90] The above only applies towards phrases which contain affection and love, however, to say good morning and the like is permitted.[91] Furthermore, some Poskim[92] suggest that perhaps the entire prohibition is only against using the term Shalom while other terms are permitted to be used. The general ruling is that all greetings which contain absolutely no affection at all, and are a merely said as a common norm of society [i.e. Derech Eretz], are not considered under the prohibition against greeting a woman.[93] Practically, today, even to say the word Shalom without adding the word "Shalom **Alecha**", is permitted, and so is the custom of the world.[94] [One may certainly say Hello, good morning, good evening, or how are you.] Nonetheless, [if one is able to avoid doing so without risking offending the woman[95]] it is a holy act to be stringent not to recite even other greetings, such as good morning and the like.[96]

Asking other people as to the wellbeing of a woman: It is permitted to ask a husband as to the wellbeing of his wife.[97] Furthermore, some Poskim[98] rule it is permitted to ask any man as to the wellbeing of a woman. Other Poskim[99], however, rule it is forbidden to ask other men as to the wellbeing of a woman, and doing so is only permitted to the husband of the woman.

---

[87] Midrash Bereishis Raba 65:12 and Yifei Toar there; Koheles Raba 11:5, unlike Pesachim 54b; Nishmas Avraham Y.D. 189:3; Toras Hayoledet 57:1 footnote 2

[88] Michaber E.H. 21:6; Shmuel Kiddushin 70b

[89] The reason: As this can lead to them being acquainted with each other, which can lead towards an affectionate relationship. [Rashi ibid; Chelkas Mechokek 21:7; Aruch Hashulchan 21:8] Alternatively, the reason is because the voice of a woman is considered an Erva. [Kiddushin 70, brought in Ezer Mikodesh 21:6 and Aruch Hashulchan 21:8

[90] Betzeil Hachochmah 5:49

[91] Aruch Hashulchan 21:8; Ezer Mekodesh 21:6 that in the Talmud they were only particular against using the term Shalom; Betzeil Hachochmah 5:48-12

Other opinions: Some Poskim rule that ideally all phrases are included within this prohibition, although the custom is to be lenient even regarding Shalom, as the Rama allows doing so Lesheim Shamayim. [Maharam Shick E.H. 53]

[92] Ezer Mekodesh 21:6 based on Rama 385:1 regarding an Avel, that today we are lenient regarding Sheilas Shalom to an Avel as it's not similar to the Sheilas Shalom of previous times; Betzeil Hachochmah 5:49

[93] Aruch Hashulchan 21:8 in name of Ritva ibid; Pnei Yehoshua on Kiddushin ibid; Maharam Shick E.H. 53 that the world is accustomed like Shmuel [ruled in Rama 21:5] that whatever one does Lesheim Shamayim is permitted; Taharas Yisrael 21:6-16; Minchas Yitzchak 8:126

[94] Minchas Yitzchak 8:126; Betzeil Hachochmah 5:48-12; see Maharam Shick E.H. 53 that is Milameid Zechus on all forms of greetings of formality.

[95] See Betzeil Hachochmah ibid

[96] Maharam Shick E.H. 53; Betzeil Hachochmah ibid; Minchas Yitzchak ibid

[97] Michaber ibid; Bava Metzia 87a

[98] Bach 21; Shaiy Lemorah

[99] Beis Shmuel 21:13; Chelkas Mechokeik 21:7

Summary:
It is permitted to greet a woman with the phrase of good morning, Hello, or Shalom, when doing so out of Derech Eretz, and so is the custom. Nonetheless, those who are stringent against doing so, are performing a holy act [so long as this will not leave the woman offended], and so is the custom of many G-d fearing Jews.

Q&A

May one ask of a women's wellbeing during a telephone call?[100]
This follows the same ruling as one who tells a woman Shalom directly.

May one ask of the wellbeing of a female relative?[101]
Yes.[102]

May one ask of the wellbeing of a female child?[103]
The prohibition of saying Shalom does not apply to children who are below the age of Issur Yichud.

May a woman extend greetings and ask of the wellbeing of a man?[104]
This follows the same ruling as having a man tell Shalom to a woman.

May one wish a woman Mazal Tov by a Simcha?[105]
Yes.[106]

May one bless a woman?[107]
Yes.

If a woman asks as to one's well-being, may one reply?[108]
Yes.

May one ask a woman as to the wellbeing of her husband?[109]
Yes.

---

[100] Betzeil Hachochmah 5:49

[101] Aruch Hashulchan 21:8

[102] The reason: As all greetings which contain absolutely no affection, and are a merely said as a common gesture of society, are not considered under the prohibition against saying a greeting towards her. [ibid]

[103] Ezer Mikodesh 21:6

[104] Betzeil Hachochmah 5:49

[105] Ezer Mikodesh 21:6

[106] The reason: This is not considered like asking of her wellbeing, but simply blessing her. [ibid]

[107] Ezer Mikodesh 21:6

[108] Betzeil Hachochmah 5:48-11

[109] Aruch Hashulchan 21:8 in name of Maharsham Baba Metzia 87

6. Affectionate touch of relatives:

A. Hugging and kissing relatives:[110]

It is forbidden to hug or kiss any of one's relatives, including one's adult sister or aunt[111] [and uncle, niece, nephew, cousins[112]] and the like, with exception to a father/mother and daughter/son, as will be explained. This prohibition applies even though there is naturally no physical attraction towards the relative, and one receives absolutely no pleasure at all from the act of hugging or kissing them.[113] Hugging or kissing such relatives is a most deplorable act, and is a forbidden act[114], and is the doings of a foolish person, as one is not to bring himself in physical closeness with any relative of the opposite gender, whether she is an adult or a child.[115] [Relatives are not to hug or kiss children of the opposite gender beginning from nine years for a boy and three years for a girl, with exception to one's children, grandchildren, and siblings, as will be explained.[116] An uncle is thus not to hug or kiss his niece once she reaches three years of age[117] and an aunt is not to hug or kiss her nephew once he reaches nine years of

---

[110] Mi Michaber Even Haezer 21:7; Rambam Issureiy Biyah 21:6; Shabbos 13a "Ula stated that any closeness is forbidden as we say to the Nazir Sechor Sechor…"; Avoda Zara 17a; Bach in Kuntrus Achron 21; Chochmas Adam 125:1; Igros Moshe Y.D. 2:137; Nitei Gavriel Yichud 53:1; See Meil Tzedaka 19; Od Yosef Chaiy Parshas Shoftim p. 151

A Tzaddik: Although Ula himself made the above statement prohibiting any physical engagement between relatives, Ula himself would kiss his sisters by the hand or by the chest [Bei Chadaihu]. [Shabbos ibid] This is because Ula was a complete Tzaddik, and he knew that he would not be led to any immoral thoughts, as it was like kissing a wooden board. [Chelkas Mechokek 21:8; Beis Shmuel 21:14; Tosafos Shabbos 13a; Likkutei Sichos 6:415] Likewise, Ula would not come to do so with any other women, as he was a complete Tzaddik, and hence there is no reason to decree against him kissing his sister. Other people however may learn to hug other women if this were to be allowed. [Igros Moshe ibid] However, some explain that it is permitted to hug a relative if one has no affection, and the intent of Ula to prohibit hugging relative, is only if one has sexual pleasure from doing so. [Meil Tzedakah 19; Vetzaruch Iyun, as this contradicts the entire ruling of Michaber/Rambam ibid] Another example of the above allowance for Tzadikim can be found in scripture where Yaakov kissed Rachel. [See Meil Tzedaka 19; Od Yosef Chaiy Parshas Shoftim p. 151]

Yaakov kissing Rachel: The Torah [Bereishis 29:11] relates that Yaakov Avinu hugged and kissed Rachel, his first cousin, when he first met her. The Mefarshim and Poskim deal with why he did so, and how this does not contradict the above ruling. Some say that this was the accepted form of greeting in those times, and since they were cousins it would not be viewed by anyone as an erotic act. This is similar to a doctor touching a woman for medical reasons. [Midrash Raba Vayeitzei that it was a kiss of "Kirva"; Meil Tzedaka 19; Od Yosef Chaiy Shoftim p. 151] Others say that he kissed her on her forehead, or shoulder, and not on her lips. [Rabbeinu Bechayeh ibid] Alternatively, she was a small girl [and not an adult]. [Rabbeinu Bechayeh ibid] Others say that his was a mistake [See 2nd Pirush in Midrash Raba ibid] and Yaakov was in truth punished for doing so. See Tanya chapter 47; Torah Or Vayeitzei and other Chassidishe Sefarim where this matter is explained according to Penimiyus Hainyanim

[111] The Michaber ibid states one's father's sister, although obviously the same would apply to one's mother's sister.

[112] See Chochmas Adam ibid for a list of all the Arayos

[113] Michaber ibid; Rambam ibid; Bach in Kuntrus Achron 21

Other opinions: Some Poskim imply that there is never a prohibition to hug and kiss a relative [even of permissible marriage] if one is doing so without any sexual intent or pleasure, and is merely done out of Derech Eretz and the way of the world. [Implication of Meil Tzedaka 19 in his answer of Ula; Od Yosef Chaiy Parshas Shoftim p. 151 based on Midrash Raba Vayeitzei regarding Yaakov and Rachel and on Heter for a male doctor to have a female patient; Vetzaruch Iyun, as this contradicts the entire ruling of Michaber/Rambam ibid]

[114] Michaber ibid; See Beis Shmuel 21:14 who uses the term "forbidden" and not just a Davar Issur as writes Michaber; See Bach in Kuntrus Achron 21; Otzer Haposkim 21:51 in name of Batei Kehuna; See next footnote

[115] Michaber ibid; Rambam ibid; See Bach in Kuntrus Achron 21

Is this a Biblical or Rabbinical prohibition? Hugging, kissing, and other touch of relatives which is done for the sake of sexual pleasure, or from which one receives sexual pleasure, is a complete Biblical prohibition which is liable for lashes and is to be protested against. [Bach in Kuntrus Achron 21] Thus, hugging and kissing relatives who one can marry, such as a niece, or cousin, is a complete Biblical prohibition which is liable for lashes and is to be protested against. The reason for this is because one has benefit and pleasure from such contact, and is therefore include in the Biblical prohibition of touching an Erva in a form of Chiba [affection]. It is therefore Rabbinically forbidden even for a Tzaddik to hug and kiss such relatives, even though he has absolutely no erotic thoughts, as this appears as a forbidden act of affection. However, hugging and kissing other relatives with whom marriage is forbidden, and there is no natural attraction to them, such as a sister and aunt, is only a Rabbinical prohibition due to a decree that one may come to do so with other relatives. However, there is no Biblical prohibition involved, being that the Biblical prohibition only applies if one does so "Derech Chiba" in a way of pleasure. One is therefore not required to protest against one who does so, if one assumes that they will not listen. [Igros Moshe ibid; see Bach in Kuntrus Achron 21 that whenever one has a lust and pleasure for the touch of the relative, it is Biblically forbidden, even if one cannot marry them, and it is only when one has no feelings of lust and pleasure, which is usually the case, that this prohibition does not apply.]

[116] It does not state explicitly in Poskim the age from when hugging and kissing is forbidden. However, seemingly it would only apply by a child who has reached the age of Biyah, which is three years for a girl and nine years for a boy. [Implication of Beis Shmuel 21:9; Michaber 22:11 and Beis Shmuel 22:15 state regarding the start of the prohibition of Yichud that it begins from age nine for a boy and three for a girl and the same would seemingly [and certainly] apply towards affectionate touch; Beir Moshe 4:145; Nitei Gavriel 53:1]

[117] Rav SZ"A in Avnei Yashpei p. 189

Other opinions: Some Poskim rule an uncle may hug and kiss his niece until she becomes physically developed, which is usually not before age 11. [Beir Moshe ibid] The reason for this is because a niece which has not yet reached age of maturity is not an Ervah at all. Vetzaruch Iyun as the Sages prohibited Yichud with her from age three.

age. It is forbidden for a cousin to hug or kiss his cousin of the opposite gender, once he/she reaches the above age.]

Parents, Grandparents, children and grandchildren:[118] Kissing and hugging is permitted between parents and their children, even if they are of the opposite gender [and even if the children are now adults[119]]. Thus, a mother may hug and kiss her son [of any age] and a father may hug and kiss his daughter [of any age]. [See Q&A regarding if she is married!] Kissing and hugging is likewise permitted between grandparents and their grandchildren of the opposite gender.[120]

Brother/sister who are still children: It is permitted for one to hug or kiss his sibling of the opposite gender even if they have reached the age of nine years for a boy and three years for a girl. It is thus permitted for a brother to hug and kiss his three-year-old sister.[121] [It is likewise permitted for a sister to hug and kiss her nine-year-old brother.] This allowance applies until the child begins to become physically developed[122] which is approximately 11 years old for a girl and 12 years old for a boy.[123] [However, some[124] write that one is to be careful in this matter from age six.]

Q&A
May a parent/grandparent hug a married daughter/granddaughter?
Some Poskim[125] rule it is permitted for a father or grandfather to hug and kiss his daughter/granddaughter even if she is married. Other Poskim[126], however, rule it is forbidden for them to kiss or hug a married daughter/granddaughter. Practically, it is permitted to do so[127], although one who desires to be stringent upon himself is blessed.[128]

Relatives showing affection in public:[129]
It is permitted for a father/mother/grandfather/grandmother to engage in non-affectionate touch with their daughter/son/granddaughter/grandson even in public. [It is possible to learn in the Poskim that it is however forbidden for them to engage in affectionate touch in public, such as hugging and kissing.[130] On the other hand, one can argue that affectionate touch between such close relatives does not lead others to any immoral thoughts.[131] Practically, since in most situations it is not obvious to

---

[118] Michaber ibid; Kiddushin 80b; Kitzur SHU"A 159:10
[119] Perisha 21:7; Beis Shmuel 21:15; Beir Heiytiv 21:15; Taharas Yisrael 21:17; Chochmas Adam 125:6
If the daughter/granddaughter/mother/grandmother is a Niddah: The above allowance applies even if the relation is a Niddah. [Betzeil Hachochmah 3:12]
[120] Chelkas Mechokek 21:10 based on Kiddushin 81b; Beis Shmuel 21:14 [see there for a long discussion on this topic]; Pischeiy Teshuvah 21:5; Igros Moshe ibid
[121] Implication of Michaber 21:7 "older sister"; Chelkas Mechokek 21:9-11; Beis Shmuel 21:14; Chochmas Adam 124:6
The reason: As this is done simply Lesheim Shamayim for the sake of showing closeness to one's relative, and not for the sake of showing closeness of a marriage nature. [Chelkas Mechokek ibid]
[122] Based on Michaber 21:7 and Admur 73:3 who gives this age for parents with children in terms of sleeping together, and the Chelkas Mechokek 21:11 and Beis Shmuel 21:14 applies the same law to a younger sister, and certainly the same would apply to hugging and kissing [which is less severe than sleeping with each other unclothed, as brought in Beis Shmuel 21:15]
[123] Admur ibid; Chelkas Mechokek 21:12; Chochmas Adam ibid; Igros Moshe 2:144; Nitei Gavriel 53 footnote 10
[124] Nitei Gavriel 53 footnote 10
[125] Beis Shmuel 21:14 that when both are clothed there is no prohibition to sleep together even if she is an adult and is married; Pnei Moshe 21:5; Beir Heiytiv 21:14; Aruch Hashulchan 21:10; Taharas Yisrael 21:17; Nidchei Yisrael 24; Divrei Yatziv Even Haezer 36; Chochmas Adam 125:6 concludes with a Tzaruch Iyun; Betzeil Hachochmah 3:12
[126] Mishneh Lamelech on Rambam 21:6-7; Nesivos Shabbos 13a; Meiri Kiddushin 81b; See Betzeil Hachochmah ibid
[127] Betzeil Hachochmah 3:12 as rule majority of Poskim ibid
[128] Betzeil Hachochmah ibid; Beir Moshe 4:145; Igros Moshe Even Haezer 1:60 and 4:63; See also Od Yosef Chaiy Shoftim 21 that a Baal Nefesh is to be stringent on himself. [does not specifically stipulate regarding daughter who is married].
[129] See Beis Shmuel 21:12; Taz 21:1 that by the above relatives doing acts of non-affection acts in public [such as checking each other's hair] does not arouse immoral thoughts being that everyone understands that they do not share an incestuous relationship.
[130] As the above Poskim only permitted these relatives to check lice in public, which is not an affectionate touch, while by an affectionate touch, such as hugging and kissing, certainly it can arouse immoral thoughts in the onlooker.
[131] So is implied from the ruling of the Taz and Beis Shmuel ibid that there is no Zichron Tashmish by such relatives

others that the two are father/daughter etc one is to be stringent, and so rule some Rabbanim of today.[132] However for a parent/grandparent to hug their young child in public is certainly permitted.[133]]

May one shake hands with his/her sister/brother?
Some Poskim[134] write it is permitted to shake hands with one's sister that one has not seen for many years.[135]

If a parent sees a male relative hugging or kissing their daughter who is above age three, is he obligated to stop them from doing so?
One is not required to protest the relative[136], especially in a case that the relative may take this personally. However, one should explain to the relative and daughter the Halachas of touch, at an appropriate occasion.

The eradication of the Yetzer Hara of attraction for relatives:
The Talmud[137] states that in the times of Nechemia[138], after the destruction of the first Temple, the Sages prayed to G-d for the spiritual power in charge of the Yetzer Hara of idolatry to be given to them, so they can destroy it. After they were successful in suppressing it, seeing that it was an auspicious time, they prayed to also be given the inclination for sexual relations. This request too was granted, and they captured the spiritual force in charge of sexual lust. However, destroying this inclination would cause children to no longer be born. They kept it in captivity for three days and saw that in that three-day period, no eggs were layed. Instead then of destroying the spiritual force in charge of the inclination, they blinded it, and this diminished the lust and attraction that one has towards relatives.

B. Placing head of relative in one's arms:[139]
It is forbidden for even close relatives, such as a father, grandfather and brother, to place their heads on the laps or on the chest of their daughter, granddaughter or sister.[140] [The same applies vice versa.] Thus, if the above relatives need to check each other's hair for lice, they may only do so without having the head of the relative rest on their body.

C. Checking a relative's head for lice:[141]
It is permitted for close relatives, such as a father, grandfather and brother, to have their heads checked for lice by their daughter, granddaughter or sister. [The same applies vice versa.] This may be done even in public, in the face of others.[142] However, it is forbidden to place their heads on one's lap or chest while the hair is being checked, even in private. [It is forbidden for a daughter in-law to check her father-in-law's head for lice.[143]]

---

[132] So rules Hagaon HaRav Yaakov Yosef Zal, stating that those fathers who hug their older daughters in public are Amei Haretz and are causing others to stumble.

[133] Pashut, as people do not view this erotically.

[134] Rav Elyashiv in Koveitz Teshuvos 2:20; Mishneh Halachos 4:186

[135] The reason: As the Sages only forbade clear acts of affection, such as hugging and kissing, and not acts of respect such as shaking hands.

[136] See Igros Moshe Y.D. 2:137

[137] Yuma 69b

[138] The Talmudic statement is expounding the verse in Nechemia 9:4 which states "Vayitzaku El Hashem Bekol Gadol"

[139] Taz 21:10; Beis Shmuel 21:12

[140] The reason: As doing so involves too much affection. [ibid]

[141] Taz 21:10; Beis Shmuel 21:12

[142] The reason: As this is not an act of affection and will not cause others to have erotic thoughts of them. [ibid]

[143] Rav Akiva Eiger Y.D. 392 in name of Beis Yosef 135

D. Washing a relative's head:[144]

It is permitted for a daughter or daughter-in-law to wash her father's, or father in-law's head [i.e. Chafifa]. [However, it is best for a daughter in-law to be stringent not to do so.[145]]

Tznius

7. Public affection:

A. Couples showing affection in public:[146]

Some Poskim[147] rule it is forbidden for a husband and wife to affectionately touch each other in front of other people.[148] [Thus, a couple may not hold hands, dance, hug, or kiss in public. Practically, so is the final ruling[149], and so is the custom amongst all G-d fearing Jews.]

Checking lice in public and other acts that do not contain affection: A wife may not check her husband's hair for lice in public [even if his head is not resting on her chest[150]].[151] [The same applies vice versa.] [From here one can deduce that it is forbidden for a couple to touch in public even non-affectionately, if the touch extends for some period of time. However, one may momentarily share a non affectionate touch, such as to tap her on the shoulder and the like.]

B. Relatives showing affection in public:[152]

It is permitted for a father/mother/grandfather/grandmother to engage in non-affectionate touch with their daughter/son/granddaughter/grandson even in public. [It is possible to learn in the Poskim that it is however forbidden for them to engage in affectionate touch in public, such as hugging and kissing.[153] On the other hand, one can argue that affectionate touch between such close relatives does not lead others to any immoral thoughts.[154] Practically, since in most situations it is not obvious to others that the two are father/daughter etc one is to be stringent, and so rule some Rabbanim of today.[155] However, for a parent/grandparent to hug their young child in public, is certainly permitted.[156]]

Summary:
It is forbidden for a couple to touch in public. This applies even towards non-affectionate touch, [if the touch extends for some period of time]. It is permitted for father/mother/grandfather/grandmother to engage in **non-affectionate** touch with their daughter/son/granddaughter/grandson in public. However, they should not engage in affectionate touch in public, such as hugging and kissing, unless it is a young child.

---

[144] Michaber Y.D. 392:2
[145] Rav Akiva Eiger Y.D. 392 in name of Beis Yosef 135
[146] Rama Even Haezer 21:5
[147] Nemukei Yosef Bava Basra 186b, based on story of Rav Benah and Eliezer, brought in Baba Basra 58a
[148] The reason: As it is not modest for a couple to be engaged in affection in public. In addition, doing so will cause others to have erotic thoughts of them. [Taz 21:1]
[149] Kitzur SHU"A 152:11
[150] Beis Shmuel 21:12; Taz 21:1; Rashba 1188
Other opinions: Some Poskim rule it is permitted to check each other's hair for lice in public so long as the head does not rest on one's body. [Derisha, brought in Taz ibid]
[151] The reason: As although it is not considered an act of affection which is immodest to do in public. Nevertheless, doing so will cause others to have erotic thoughts of them, as it reminds them of their intimacy. [ibid]
[152] See Beis Shmuel 21:12; Taz 21:1 that by the above relatives doing acts of non-affection acts in public [such as checking each other's hair] does not arouse immoral thoughts being that everyone understands that they do not share an incestuous relationship.
[153] As the above Poskim only permitted these relatives to check lice in public, which is not an affectionate touch, while by an affectionate touch, such as hugging and kissing, certainly it can arouse immoral thoughts in the onlooker.
[154] So is implied from the ruling of the Taz and Beis Shmuel ibid that there is no Zichron Tashmish by such relatives
[155] So rules Hagaon HaRav Yaakov Yosef Zal, stating that those fathers who hug their older daughters in public are Amei Haaretz and are causing others to stumble.
[156] Pashut, as people do not view this erotically.

Q&A

Walking together in public:[157]
A couple must be careful to walk and talk in a modest fashion in public.

May a couple engage in affectionate touch [i.e. hugging, kissing, etc] in front of their children?
Halachic perspective:[158] Once one's child knows to talk, one is not to engage in affectionate touch in front of the children, just as is the law regarding any other person. It would thus be forbidden for the couple or parents to engage in open affection, such as hugging, kissing and holding hands in front of their children, just as it is forbidden to do so in public, and so is the custom of all G-d fearing Jews.
Educational perspective: Arguments pro and against showing affection in front of one's children have been given from an educational, and psychological, perspective. Some claim doing so is a positive thing that helps one's children know that the parents love each other, and introduce love to their lives. Others counter that doing so makes the child uncomfortable, as they are not interested in seeing a display of intimacy between their parents. It can also lead the child to have a heightened desire for his own intimacy for a partner, prior to marriage. One can educate one's children in showing love and teach them that their parents love each other, by performing acts of kindness to each other in their presence, and speaking respectfully to one another. Practically, as stated above, it is forbidden to show affectionate touch in front of others which would include one's children.

How to explain public intimacy that was witnessed by one's children?
If one's children witness other couples engaged in affectionate touch in public [i.e. hugging, kissing], there are several approaches one can take to explain this to the child. One can choose to ignore the issue and not bring it up, and not give a direct answer when asked. Alternatively, one can tell the child that what was done is wrong and disgusting and have them believe that kissing is an inappropriate act. Alternatively, one can tell the child that it is something done by married couples who love each other, although is only to be done in private and not in public. One can explain that the above couple hence did a permitted action in the wrong area, and that is immodest. Obviously, the answer given must remain appropriate for the age of the child.

May one touch in public in an area without Jews?
No.[159]

May one clean something from his wife's hair in public?
Seemingly, it is permitted to do so.[160]

---

[157] See Brachos 43b that one is not to speak with his wife, daughter, or sister in the marketplace; See Az Nidbaru 4:65 that the intent is that one must act in a modest manner; See Mishneh Halachos 10:217

[158] There is no unique Halacha that limits the showing of affection in front of children, or that excludes children from the above law that prohibits affectionate touch in front of others. Thus, seemingly, children are included in the above prohibition of showing affection in front of "others." Now, there are two reasons behind the prohibition against showing affection before others; 1) Tznius and 2) Hirhur. [See Taz ibid] Thus, it would be forbidden for the couple to engage in immodest affectionate touch in front of children who can speak [see below], while acts of touch that are not immodest necessarily would be permitted to perform in front of children until the child has reached an age to comprehend the concept of marital relations and thus may lead him to Hirhur. Vetzaruch Iyun from the Halacha that parents may be naked and sleep naked with their kids until the age of embarrassment, which is approximately 11-12 years of age. [Admur 73:3; Michaber E.H. 21:7] One must however conclude that there is a difference between being undressed in front of others and showing affection in front of others, as is seen from the fact that men may bathe together, and sleep under blankets, even though showing affection in front of them is forbidden due to Tznius.
The age from which the prohibition begins: It is forbidden to perform marital relations before any human being that has reached the age that they can speak. [Michaber 240:6] Seemingly, this same age would apply regarding showing affectionate touch in front of a child.

[159] The reason: As doing so is immodest and may lead gentiles to have immoral thoughts, and according to many Poskim, also gentiles have a prohibition of Zera Levatala. [Rashba in name of Ramban, brought in Mishneh Limelech Melachim 10/7 "Venachzor": "Although the gentiles are not commanded to have children they are nevertheless prohibited from destroying seed, as we see that they were all punished for doing so in the times of the Mabul." See Mishneh Lemelech ibid who concludes "I do not know where this is hinted to in the Torah"]

[160] As not all acts of touch are prohibited, as is seen from the fact one is not required to keep Harchakos in public, and we only find a prohibition mentioned regarding a touch of affection, or a touch of extended period of time, such as to check for lice.

------------------Covering hair----------------

8. Must a married [or once married] woman cover every strand of hair of her head?

It is forbidden for a married woman to reveal even a single hair of her head to the public, and hence all of the hair, must be covered.[161] It is for this reason that many of today's Poskim[162] rule one is to wear a wig [Sheitel] rather than a head Kerchief [Tichel], as the wig secures that all of the hair is covered, as opposed to a head kerchief. However, there is a minority opinion amongst today's Poskim[163] who novelized that according to Halacha, a woman is permitted to be lenient to uncover up to two finger-worth's [4 cm] of the top part of her hair. The Rebbe[164], as well as the vast majority of today's Poskim[165], negate this opinion, and state it has no place in Shulchan Aruch. Those women who uncover even more than 4 cm of their hair, are to be protested according to all. Furthermore, everyone agrees that according to the Zohar[166], it is a complete prohibition to reveal any hair of the head, and one who is not careful in this causes poverty and spiritual challenges for their children, as well as other Tzaros.

9. Must a married [or once married] woman cover her sideburns and others hair that protrude past the regular hair of the head?

Some Poskim[167] rule that a married woman is not required to cover the strands of hair that extend past her "Tzemasan" [which refers to a snood or other regular hair covering[168]]. [This allowance includes her sideburns[169] and any other hair that protrudes past the head, such as by the back of the neck and below the ear.[170] Some[171] write that all hair that does not grow as long as regular head hair, is considered as the "Tzemasan", which is not required to be covered. Some Poskim[172] suggest that perhaps even according to

---

[161] Tzemach Tzedek Even Haezer 139:2 from the fact he prohibits the sideburns; Chasam Sofer 36 "Any hair in any area of the head is an Erva"; See Mahariy Levi 9 who allows revealing some of the hair until the day after the Chuppah; Ashel Avraham Buchach "Proper to beware against even one hair"; Sdei Chemed; Dovev Meisharim 1:124; Teshuvos Vehanhagos 1:62; Beis Baruch on Chayeh Adam 4:10; Lehoros Nasan 5; Piskeiy Teshuvos 75:10; Chazon Ish in Dinim Vehanhagos 2:88-9 and in Teshuvos Vehanhagos 1:62; Rebbe Ben Tziyon Aba Shaul brought in Kuntrus Kisui Rosh Leisha; Rav Mashash in Tevuos Shemesh 137; Shemesh Umagen 2:15-17; Rav Yaakov Yosef, as heard in his Shiur; Az Nidbaru 12:41 that one should cover every hair; Rav Moshe Shternbuch in Daas Vehalacha 1; Rav Lefkovich in Kovetz Beis Hillel 9; Or Yitzchak 3; Nitei Gavriel in Kovetz Or Yisrael 36-37; Zohar Parshas Nasso p. 239, brought in M"A 75:4; Maharam Alshiker 35; Chasam Sofer ibid; M"B 75:14; See Sefer Tefila Lemoshe [Rav Moshe Levi] 5:50 for a lengthy discussion on this subject.

[162] Poskim ibid including: Chazon Ish ibid; Rebbe Ben Tziyon Aba Shaul ibid; Or Yitzchak 3 in name of Rav Moshe Feinstein; Letters of Rebbe printed in Shulchan Menachem 6:80-84

[163] Igros Moshe 4:112; Even Haezer 1:58 [However, see Or Yitzchak 3 in name of Rav Moshe Feinstein that even he agreed that initially one should wear a wig in order to cover every hair]; Rav Ovadia Yosef is quoted in Yalkut Yosef Otzer Dinim to be lenient Bedieved. Rav Yaakov Yosef, however, stated that the only Rav who was ever lenient in this matter was the Igros Moshe. The Teshuras Shaiy in a response initially tried to also learn this way in Maharam Alshiker, although he concluded stringently. In other Shiurim, however, he stated that Syrian women [Chalabi] were accustomed to be lenient in this, however, women who came from other Sephardic countries [Yemen, Egypt, Morocco, Iraq] were very strict.

The reason: As only a Tefach is considered an Erva by a woman [Igros Moshe ibid]; and less than a Tefach is only Rabbinical, and hence less than majority of a Tefach is allowed. [Rav Ovadia ibid]; See Sefer Tefila Lemoshe [Rav Moshe Levi] 5:50 for a lengthy discussion on this subject.

Opinion of Maharam Alashkar: Maharam Alshiker 35 based on Aruch rules that the sideburns, and other hair that protrudes from the corners of the head covering, is not required to be covered. Some have tried to use this ruling as a source to permit revealing up to a Tefach or two fingers worth of the head. This is not accurate. [See Teshuras Shaiy; Discussed by Rav Yaakov Yosef in Shiur in length]

[164] Igros Kodesh 9:325 [printed in Shulchan Menachem 6:81] "You want to wear a Sheitel that will leave two finger-worth's uncovered! Who are you trying to fool, not the world, but only yourself, and what is the purpose of fooling yourself? The rule is clear in Shulchan Aruch [that all the hair must be covered] and there is no room for question on this matter." See also Igros Kodesh 16:330 and other letters printed in Shulchan Menachem 6:80-84

[165] All Poskim brought in previous footnotes; So is also conclusion of Rav Yaakov Yosef and Rav Moshe Levi after bringing all the opinions on the subject

[166] Zohar Parshas Nasso p. 239, brought in M"A 75:4; Maharam Alshiker 35; Chasam Sofer ibid; M"B 75:14

[167] Admur 75:4 "So too, the hairs of women which regularly protrude past their Tzamatan in some lands, is permitted to learn Torah and Daven in its presence, as since the people are accustomed to see this area of hair revealed, it therefore does not lead to erotic thoughts."; Rama 75:2; Rashba Brachos 24a in name of Raavad; Maharam Alshiker 35 based on Aruch and others that such hair is not required to be covered; Biur Halacha 75:2 "Michutz" "This allowance applies to all women, unlike the Chasam Sofer who was stringent in this"; See Mahariy Levi 9

[168] A Tzematan is a knitted snood which is placed over the hair to gather it together in one bunch. The little bit of hair that cannot be gathered into the snood, and hence protrudes to the outside, is the hair referred to in this Halacha. [Chasam Sofer 36; M"B 75:14]

[169] Maharam Alshiker ibid "The hair between her ear and forehead"; See Chasam Sofer 36

[170] Shevet Halevi 5:207 that certainly from the letter of the law there is no need to cover the hair which grows on the actual neck, and those who choose to shave it off, seemingly do so due to Maaras Ayin.

[171] Piskeiy Teshuvos 75:10

[172] Maharam Alshiker ibid although he concludes that even if the Zohar prohibits even these hairs, we nevertheless rule like the Talmud against the Zohar

the Zohar, who is very stringent against a woman revealing even one hair, it is permitted for these areas of hair to be revealed.] Other Poskim[173], however, rule it is forbidden for any of the above hairs to be revealed, and it is thus required to be covered just like any other hair of the head. Furthermore, some Poskim[174] rule that even according to the lenient opinion, according to the Zohar[175] who prohibits to reveal any hair of the head, this hair is also included, and one who is not careful in this causes poverty and spiritual challenges for their children, as well as other Tzaros.[176] Practically, one is to be stringent in this matter.[177]

Areas where the custom is to be stringent:[178] In all areas, or communities, in which the custom is to be stringent to cover even hair that extends past the head, such as the sideburns and hair below the neck, it is forbidden according to all opinions for a woman in such a community to reveal these hairs.[179] This applies even if the woman is affiliated with another community or city which is accustomed to be lenient in this matter, nevertheless, when she is in a stringent community, she must be stringent.[180] In the case that a woman moved from a community which was stringent in this matter, to a community that is lenient, then according to the lenient opinion mentioned above, she may likewise be lenient if she intends to live in that new area.[181] According to the stringent opinion, it is forbidden in all cases.

In the privacy of her home, in front of her husband:[182] Even according to the stringent Halachic opinion mentioned above, it is permitted for a wife to uncover the sideburn areas and neck areas of her hair, when privately with her husband. This applies even at times that she is a Niddah. [However, some Poskim[183] rule that according to the Zohar who prohibits to reveal any hair of the head, this hair is also included, and it is not to be revealed even in the privacy of one's home.]

Summary:
It is disputed amongst Poskim as to whether a woman must cover the hair that extends past her head, such as the sideburns and hair that borders her neckline by her back. Practically, according to the implication of the Zohar, it is forbidden to reveal even these hairs, and every woman should be stringent in this matter. According to all Poskim, it is forbidden from the letter of the law to reveal these hairs in an area or community who is accustomed to be stringent in this matter.

Q&A

Does neck hair need to be covered?
Hair that borders the neckline of the back of the neck, and usually protrudes when wearing a snood, is

---

[173] Tzemach Tzedek Even Haezer 139:2 and Mishnayos Brachos 3:5-3 [The Tzemach Tzedek rules that the ruling of the above Poskim [Rashba, Rama and Admur ibid] was only said regarding a wife and husband and not regarding other people.]; Implication of Beis Yosef 75 in name of Rashba ibid that the allowance only applies to the husband; Chasam Sofer 36 that although according to the Talmud it is permitted, we rule like the Zohar, as is seen from the custom of Jewry to be stringent; Implication of Orchos Chaim Kerias Shema 36; Shevet Halevi 5:15 "One is to be stringent like their words."

[174] Chasam Sofer ibid; M"B 75:14; Kaf Hachaim 75:18; Possible way of learning M"A ibid; See Maharam Alshiker ibid who so implies in his conclusion

[175] Parshas Nasso

[176] Brought in Maharam Alshiker 35; Chasam Sofer ibid

[177] Shevet Halevi ibid

The Chabad ruling: Seemingly, the Chabad ruling should follow the stringent opinion, as we follow the rulings of the Tzemach Tzedek, at times even when it contradicts the ruling of Admur, and certainly in a case where the Tzemach Tzedek is more stringent. Vetzaruch Iyun. Nonetheless, in any event, based on the Zohar one is to certainly be stringent.

[178] M"A ibid in name of Mahram Alshiker ibid; See Admur ibid who writes "Who are accustomed to do so in some lands," thus implying like the M"A that this matter is dependent on Minhag, and is not a clear cut allowance to all areas. See Chasam Sofer ibid

[179] The reason: Seemingly, this is forbidden due to two reasons as a) If the custom is to be stringent to cover these areas, then uncovering it would transgress Daas Yehudis, and cause erotic thoughts to the men of that community who are not accustomed to seeing this hair uncovered. [See Admur ibid and Chasam Sofer ibid] b) It causes dispute when one is lenient in a community that is accustomed to be stringent. [See Admur 468:10]

[180] See Admur chapter 468 that she must be stringent like the stringencies of the new town even if visiting.

[181] M"A ibid in name of Mahram Alshiker ibid; See Admur 468:12-14, Vetzaruch Iyun regarding Admur's ruling to avoid doing the stringency in public due to Machlokes, and how that would apply in this case.

[182] Beis Yosef 75 in name of Rashba; Tzemach Tzedek ibid; Shalmas Chaim 64

[183] Chasam Sofer ibid; See Teshuvah Meahavah 48; Kevoda Bas Melech [Weiner] p. 51

relevant to the above dispute regarding whether it must be covered, of which the conclusion is to be stringent. However, those hairs which clearly grow on the neck, and are not part of the head at all, do not need to be covered, although some are accustomed to shave it off, seemingly due to Maras Ayin.[184]

How much of the sideburns must be covered?[185]
All hair that grows opposite the ear, must be covered according to the stringent opinion. All hair that grows below the ear, is not part of the sideburns, and is not required to be covered.

-----------------*Yichud*----------------

10. Baalah Bair-Yichud with a woman whose husband is in the city:[186]

A woman whose husband is in the city [i.e. Baalah Bair], does not contain a Yichud prohibition [to be alone with a man even at night[187]], being that the fear of her husband is upon her.[188] [Some Poskim[189] however rule it is Rabbinically[190] forbidden to have Yichud with a woman even if her husband is in the city.[191] Practically, the accepted custom is to be lenient[192], although one who is stringent is praised.[193]]

If one knows the woman:[194] If one is well acquainted with the wife [Libo Gas Ba], such as he grew up with her, or is a relative, or has/had a relationship with her, then it is forbidden for him to have Yichud with her, even though her husband is in the city.[195] [If, however, the husband is in a nearby room, Yichud is permitted even with a person who Libo Gas Ba.[196]]

---

[184] Shevet Halevi 5:207
[185] Shevet Halevi 5:15
[186] Michaber 21:8; Dvar Halacha chapter 7; Nitei Gavriel chapter 35
[187] Rabbeinu Yehonason of Lunil Kiddushin 81a; Nitei Gavriel 35:1
[188] Michaber 21:8; Raba Kiddushin 81a as interpreted by Tosafos ibid; Rambam Issur Biya 22; Semag 126; Tur; Kol Bo 75; Rabbeinu Yerucham 21:1; Rosh in Piskei Rosh; Radbaz 3:481; Rashal Kiddushin 22; Perisha 22:26; Taz 22:7; Levush 22:8; Chochmas Adam 126; Kitzur SHU"A 152:4; Poskim brought in Dvar Halacha 7:1; Nitei Gavriel 35
The reason: There are two reasons recorded in the Poskim behind the allowance of Yichud when the woman's husband is in the city:
   1.   Some Poskim rule that a woman has natural fear of her husband when he is in the city. [Rashbam; Implication of Michaber ibid; Imreiy Yosher 2:9; Chida in Birkeiy Yosef 22; Yosef Ometz 97:2; Dvar Halacha 7:2 in name of Chazon Ish; Divrei Yatziv Even Haezer 42; See Nishmas Kol Chaiy 2:15; Shevet Halevi 5:203] This fear is in innate feeling irrelevant of logic, and hence she fears doing an act of betrayal when he is in the city, even if she knows he will not be able to come home to catch her in the act, such as he is at work and it takes time for him to travel home.
   2.   Other Poskim however rule that a woman does not have an illogical inner fear of her husband when he is in the city, and rather she fears that he may come home and catch her in the act. [Rashi Kiddushin ibid as explained in Hamakneh Kiddushin 81a, brought in Igros Moshe E.H. 4:65-7; brought in Nitei Gavriel 35:4 and footnote 5] In the event that she knows he cannot come home within enough time to catch her in the act, then this allowance would not be relevant.
[189] Rashi Kiddushin ibid in interpretation of Raba in Kiddushin ibid, as understood by Tosafos ibid [However see Taz ibid who explains Rashi differently]; Ran ibid; Bach; brought in Beis Shmuel 22:12 and Chelkas Mechokeik 22:12 and Taz 22:7 and Aruch Hashulchan 22; Poskim brought in Dvar Halacha 7:1 footnote 1
[190] See Dvar Halacha ibid
[191] The reason: These Poskim rule that the intent of the Gemara is that there is only no Malkus given in the event of transgression, if her husband was in the city, although initially, it is forbidden to have Yichud with a woman even if her husband is in town. [Rashi and Poskim ibid]
[192] Dvar Halacha ibid that the Chazon Ish and Dovev Meisharim ruled that one may be lenient
[193] Some conclude that it is proper to suspect for the stringent opinion. [Chofetz Chaim of Rav Falagi 38:54]
[194] Michaber ibid; Gemara ibid; Or Zarua 1:615; Ravaya; Chochmas Adam 126:6; Kitzur SHU"A 152:4; Aruch Hashulchan 22:6
[195] The reason: As the Yetzer Hara is much greater when one is comfortable with the person, and hence it does not apply. [Shaar Yosef 3 of Chida] Alternatively, the reason is because in such a case the woman does not fear being seen in Yichud with the man, as the husband is aware of their relationship, and hence will dismiss their Yichud without suspicion. [Binas Adam 17]
[196] Meiri end of Kiddushin; Chida in Shaar Yosef 3, brought in Dvar Halacha 7:22; Nitei Gavriel 34:2; So is proven from the fact a wife is entrusted to guard her husband from Yichud with a woman who "Libo Gas Ba", and hence certainly he is trusted to guard his wife from a man who "Libo Gas Ba"

Q&A

Does the above allowance of Baalah Bair apply only when the wife is at home, or even if she came to the home of the man?

Some Poskim[197] rule that the allowance only applies when the wife is at home, however, when she is at the home of the man, then it does not apply, and Yichud is forbidden.

Does the above allowance of Baalah Bair apply if the wife is not at home and her husband does not know where she is?

Some Poskim[198] rule that if the wife is not at her home, and her husband does not know where she is, then the allowance does not apply, and Yichud is forbidden.

Does the above allowance of Baalah Bair apply if the city is very large and her husband is very far away in the city?

Some Poskim[199] rule that so long as the husband and wife are within the same city [municipality], it is valid to break the Yichud of his wife and another man, even if the city very large, such as New York city and London.[200] Other Poskim[201], however, rule that Yichud is not broken in the event that he is very far way within the city and it can take him considerable time to return home.[202] Some Rabbanim are accustomed to rule that distanced neighborhoods of a city are treated as two different cities, such as Ramot and Yerushalayim; Brooklyn and Manhattan; Stanford hill and Golders Green. Practically, one is to speak to a local Rav for a final ruling on this matter.

<u>Husband is at work</u>: See next!

Does the above allowance of Baalah Bair apply if the husband is at work and the wife knows that he will not return home for a while?

In the event that the husband is at work, far away in the city, and the wife is aware that he cannot return home for a while, then if the husband is an employee with set hours, some Poskim[203] rule that Yichud is if forbidden with his wife.[204] If, however, the husband is self-employed, and hence can come home as he wishes, then Yichud is broken.[205] Other Poskim[206] however are lenient even in a case that the husband is an employee with set hours and hence cannot come home as he pleases.

---

[197] Binas Adam 27 brought in Pischeiy Teshuvah 22:7

[198] Binas Adam 27 brought in Pischeiy Teshuvah 22:7

[199] Ezer Mikodesh 22:8 "The Sages did not make a differentiation in this matter, even if it is a city as large as Antioacha" [This follows the reason of Rashbam; However, see there that he concludes that if he let her know that he will be far away, it requires further clarification]; Igros Moshe E.H. 4:65-18 regarding N.Y. city, that so long as the husband can come back home that day by car, it is considered the same city in this regard [However see there 4:65-7 that according to Rashi it is only valid if the husband can return home un-expectantly at any time and the Igros Moshe concludes that "Knowing this matter is important for people"]; Nishmas Avraham E.H. 22:8 in name of Rav SZ"A; See Dvar Halacha 7:21 and in name of Chazon Ish that Bnei Brak and Ramat Gan are two different cities while the entire Tel Aviv is one city; This matter is not discussed in previous Poskim; See Nitei Gavriel 38:1

[200] <u>The reason</u>: As the husband can return home at any moment. [Ezer Mikodesh ibid]

[201] Shevet Halevi 4:180 regarding London and N.Y.; Arugas Habosem E.H. 18 says for this reason to be stringent like Rashi ibid; Nitei Gavriel 38:3 in his final conclusion

[202] <u>The reason</u>: This follows the reason of Rashi who requires the wife to fear that perhaps her husband will come home and find her in the act.

[203] Igros Moshe E.H. 4:65-7 following the reason of Rashi

[204] <u>The reason</u>: As he does not have permission to leave work early and come home as he pleases. The wife therefore does not fear him.

[205] Igros Moshe ibid; Nitei Gavriel 34:3

[206] So would seem according to reason of Rashbam, and Poskim who are lenient when the husband is far away within the city

May a man have Yichud with a gentile woman if her husband is in the city?[207]
If the husband is with her in the **same room**, then it is permitted to have Yichud with her.[208] If the husband is not in the same room, but is in the same city, then this matter requires further analysis.

Letting the man know that her husband is in the city and therefore Yichud is permitted:[209]
It is proper for a wife whose husband is in the city, and is alone with a man to tell the man that her husband is in the city, in order to prevent him from transgressing any sin.[210]

11. Ishto Bair-Permitting Yichud on the grounds that one's wife is in the city:[211]

Some Poskim[212] rule that having one's wife in the same city never permits a state of Yichud irrelevant of circumstance, and only when one's wife is in the **room** does it permit Yichud with another woman. Other Poskim[213], however, rule that a husband may be in a state of Yichud with a woman, even if his wife is not in the room, so long as she is in the same city.[214] This, however, only applies if he is in his house, or office which his wife often visits, and one's wife is able to arrive home at any moment, even if she does not have a key. If, however, one's wife is away at work, or is far away from home, or one is not at home or a known area, then Yichud if forbidden even if his wife in the same city, even according to the lenient opinion.[215] Practically, one may be lenient like the second opinion in a case of Rabbinical Yichud, such as one who is alone with two women.[216]

Wife has a key and may arrive at any moment:[217] If one's wife has a key to one's house or office [or the door is unlocked[218]] and is liable to arrive at any moment, it is permitted according to all for the husband to be in Yichud with a woman. If she does not have a key, then it falls under the dispute mentioned above.[219]

---

[207] Radal on Kiddushin 81a; Tzur Yaakov 16; Ezer Mikodesh 22; See Beshamayim Rosh 5, brought in Pischeiy Teshuvah E.H. 4:23; Dvar Halacha 7:23

[208] The reason: As a husband does not let his wife be promiscuous even if she is a gentile. [ibid] Now, although there are cases in which the gentile husband agrees for his wife to be promiscuous, this is not your normal situation that is needed to suspect for and prohibit Yichud as a result.

[209] Minchas Shlomo 35; Nitei Gavriel 35:17; See also Pela Yoeitz Halvah p. 50a regarding a loan

[210] The reason: As the man does not know that Yichud is broken if he is not told of it, and the Mishneh in Nazir 23a [brought in Rashi Matos 30:6] states that if a wife made a vow and her husband abolished it without her knowledge and she transgresses the vow, then she needs atonement ["Vahashem Yislach Lah"]. From here we learn that when one thinks he is doing a sin in his mind, it is considered that he has transgressed, even if in truth he did not transgress. Thus, if one intended to eat Treif and ate Kosher, he needs atonement. [Rebbe Akiva in Nazir ibid; See Minchas Shlomo 35 regarding Yichud]

[211] See Dvar Halacha 6:2-3

[212] Bnei Chayil [of Kneses Hagedola]; Maaseh Rokeiach on Rambam 2:4; Implication of Meiri Kiddushin 80b; Ezer Mekodesh 22:5 "She must be actually with him, and being in same city does not suffice"; Maharshan 4:148; Eretz Tzevi 22:29; Igros Moshe E.H. 4:65-6

[213] Beis Shmuel 22:22 based on Michaber 22:20 and Kesef Mishneh Talmud Torah 2:4 [however see Chelkas Mechokeik 22:21 who learns the Michaber to be referring to Giruiy and not Yichud]; Perisha Y.D. 245:20; Aruch Hashulchan 22:25; Imrei Yosher 2:9

[214] The reason: As his wife guards him from sin, as he fears that his wife may walk in on him at any moment. [Beis Shmuel ibid; Perisha ibid]

[215] See Dvar Halacha 6:4 footnote 4 for the proofs behind these conditions even according to the Beis Shmuel; Nitei Gavriel 41:2-3 based on Imrei Yosher ibid

[216] Doveiv Meishatim 5; Dvar Halacha 6:3; Nitei Gavriel 41:1

[217] Dvar Halacha 6:4 footnote 4

[218] Nitei Gavriel 41:1; Minchas Ish 9:3

[219] Even if she does not have a key, it helps according to the lenient opinion, as he will need to open the door for her as soon as she knocks. [Dvar Halacha 6 footnote 4]

Summary:

If one's wife is in the city and can arrive home, or to one's work, at any moment, then if she has a key to the house or the door is left unlocked, it is permitted for the husband to be in a state of Yichud with another woman. If the wife does not have a key to the house, and the door is locked, then if one's wife can arrive home, or to one's work, at any moment, the husband can be lenient regarding Rabbinical Yichud in the home or workplace. If one's wife is not expected to arrive in the near future, all forms of Yichud are forbidden.

Q&A

One's wife left the house momentarily [i.e. went to the neighbors; throw garbage] and there is a woman at home [i.e. maid, babysitter, relative, friend] may the husband remain home with the woman?

If she is expected to come home at any moment, it is permitted to do so if the wife has a key or the door is left unlocked.

One's wife left the home and will be gone for quite some time [i.e. went to work; shopping; school] and there is a woman at home [i.e. maid, baby sitter, relative, friend] may the husband remain home with the woman?
No.

One's wife left the home for work; shopping; school and is expected to return home at any moment and there is a woman at home [i.e. maid, baby sitter, relative, friend] may the husband remain home with the woman?

If one's wife has a key, or the door is left unlocked, then it is permitted to do so according to all opinions. One is not to leave the door locked if one's wife does not have a key, as according to some Poskim, Yichud is forbidden in this situation.

------------------Wedding----------------
12. Simcha-The Mitzvah of a Chasan to rejoice with the Kallah:[220]
A. Introduction-The obligation of Simcha:

The laws of Simcha refer to the obligation of the Chasan to rejoice his wife after the marriage takes place. This Mitzvah of rejoicing one's wife includes spending time with in festive meals, and not doing Melacha, or going to one's job or business throughout the Simcha period, in order so he is free to spend time with her and rejoice her. The amount of time in which the husband is obligated in these laws of Simcha differs between a Besula and Beula. The time period of Simcha is not connected to the time period of Sheva Brachos, and hence depending on whether the Kallah is a Besula or Beula will effect whether the obligation of Simcha extends for all seven days of Sheva Brachos [i.e. marries Besula], or ends after three days into the seven days of Sheva Brachos [i.e. Bachur who marries Beula according to one opinion], or ends after three days from the marriage, even though the Sheva Brachos only takes place on the first day by the first meal [i.e. Widower marries Beula]

B. How long is the couple to rejoice?

Besula:[221] If one married a Besula, the Chasan is obligated to rejoice with her for seven days [of Sheva Brachos after the wedding]. This applies whether the Chasan was never married before, or is a widower [or was divorced]

Beula:[222] If the Kallah is a Beula, the Chasan is obligated to rejoice with her for three days [after the wedding]. This applies whether the Chasan was never married before [and therefore recites Sheva

---

[220] Michaber 62:2 and 64:1-2
[221] Michaber 62:2 and 64:1; Kesubos 7b

Brachos for seven days[223]], or is a widower [or was divorced, and therefore recites Sheva Brachos for only the first meal[224]].[225] However, some Poskim[226] rule that a Chasan who was never married before, is to rejoice with his Kallah for seven days [after the wedding] even if she is a Beula, [and only in a case that he was previously married is he to rejoice with her for only three days].[227] [Practically, one is to be stringent to rejoice for seven days.[228]]

Summary:
If the Kallah is a Besula, the Chasan is obligated to rejoice with her for seven days after the wedding, even if he was previously married. If the Kallah is a Beula, and the Chasan was previously married, he is obligated to rejoice with her for three days after the wedding, even though Sheva Brachos is only said on the first day. If the Kallah is a Beula and the Chasan was never previously married, he is to be stringent to rejoice with her for seven days after the wedding.

Q&A

If the Kallah is a Beula, but was never previously married, and the Chasan was previously married, for how long must the Chasan rejoice with her?[229]
So long as the Kallah is a Beula, irrelevant of whether this occurred in wedlock or out of wedlock or even due to rape, the Chasan is only obligated to rejoice with her for three days, if he was previously married.

If the Chasan and Kallah had relations prior to the wedding, for how many days must the Chasan rejoice with her?
There are three opinions mentioned in this regarding Sheva Brachos, and the same would apply

---

[222] Michaber 62:2 and 64:2; Kesubos 7b

[223] Michaber 62:6; Chelkas Mechokeik 64:1

[224] Michaber 62:6

[225] Stam opinion in Michaber ibid
The reason: As the reciting of Sheva Brachos is not connected to the Mitzvah of Simcha, and thus although Sheva Brachos may be said for seven days, the obligation of Simcha is only for three days. The reason for this difference is as follows: The Sheva Brachos was instituted on behalf of the joy the Chasan or Kallah feel in their heart, and thus, so long as one of the couple were not yet previously married, they experience this joy which allows Sheva Brachos to be recited. Likewise, one who was previously married who now marries a Besula, experiences joy over the fact he was able to marry a Besula. However, the Mitzvah of Simcha, which includes festive meals and not doing Melacha, was instituted simply for the benefit of the Kallah, and the Sages established that a Besulah is to receive seven days while a Beula is to receive three days. The reason for this differentiation is because a Besula requires seven days of Simcha to be seduced to her new husband, while a Beula only requires three days of Simcha to be seduced. Thus, even a Bachur who marries a Beula is only obligated in Simcha for three days, even though the actual Sheva Brachos is said for seven days. [Chelkas Mechokek 64:1; Beis Shmuel 64:1 in name of Ran]

[226] 2nd opinion in Michaber ibid; Ran Kesubos ibid; Rashba

[227] The reason: As when a Bachur marries a Beula, they are to keep seven days of Sheva Brachos, and it is not logical to allow him to do work and continue life as normal after three days but continue to say Sheva Brachos for seven days out of expression of his Simcha. Rather, just as Sheva Brachos is said for seven days by a Bachur so too the Mitzvah of Simcha applies for the seven days. [Chelkas Mechokek 64:4 in name of Ran]

[228] Ran ibid writes that so is the custom; Nitei Gavriel 55:11 in name of Chasam Sofer E.H. 123 and Nesivos Hashalom Nesiv 19:3 that the main opinion is like the Ran; Kitzur SHU"A 149:12 records the stringent opinion and Misgeres Hashulchan 149:7 writes to be stringent unless she is Mochel. See however Chochmas Adam 129:11 who does not arbitrate this dispute.

[229] Shemesh Tzedaka 5:40 in name of Ginas Veradim 1:17, brought in Pischeiy Teshuvah 62:9; Poskim brought in Nitei Gavriel 110:8 footnote 17

regarding Simcha, according to the stringent approach: Some Poskim[230] rule they are to keep only three days of Simcha, even if neither were previously married.[231] Other Poskim[232] rule that if she was a Besula when she had relations with her Chasan, and did not have relations with anyone else, then they are to keep seven days of Simcha, even if the man was previously married. Other Poskim[233] rule that if he was previously married, then they only keep three days of Simcha, even if she was a Besula when she had relations with her Chasan and did not have relations with anyone else. If, however, he was not previously married, then they are to keep seven days of Simcha even if she was previously married, and he had relations with her before the wedding.

Is a woman who lost her Besulim due to an injury considered a Besula or Beula in the above regard?[234]
She is considered like a Besula.

If the Kallah was previously married, but is still a Besula, and the Chasan was previously married, for how long must the Chasan rejoice with her?[235]
If the Kallah is a Besula, irrelevant of whether she was never married, or was previously married and widowed [or divorced] prior to having relations with her husband, the Chasan is obligated to rejoice with her for seven days, even if the Chasan was previously married.

If one remarried his divorcee, for how long must the Chasan rejoice with her?
If one remarried his divorcee, some Poskim[236] rule that he is not obligated to rejoice her at all, not even for three days. Other Poskim[237] rule that the Chasan is to rejoice with her for three days.

	Sheva Brachos	Simcha
Besula	*Seven days*	*Seven days*
Beula with previously married Chasan	*First meal on first day*	*Three days*
Beula with non-previously married Chasan	*Seven days*	*Dispute-stringent seven days*

C. May the Kallah be Mochel [i.e. forgive] her Simcha?[238]

Some Poskim[239] rule that the Kallah may be Mochel [i.e. forgive] her Simcha [and thus allow the Chasan to do Melacha[240], and business, and not spend time with her in festive meals, within his obligatory days of Simcha].[241] Other Poskim[242], however, rule that she is unable to forgive her simcha, and thus the Chasan

---

[230] Noda Beyehuda Tinyana 61, brought in Pischeiy Teshuvah 62:9; Gloss on Shemesh Tzedaka 5:40 that so is implied from Teshuvah Devar Shmuel

[231] The reason: As they have already tasted the taste of relations and hence do not have as much Simcha to justify seven days of blessings. [ibid]

[232] Shemesh Tzedaka 5:40 in name of Ginas Veradim 1:17, brought in Pischeiy Teshuvah 62:9

[233] Chasam Sofer 123, brought in Pischeiy Teshuvah 62:9

[234] Shemesh Tzedaka 5:40 in name of Ginas Veradim 1:17, brought in Pischeiy Teshuvah 62:9; Poskim brought in Nitei Gavriel 110:10 footnote 19

[235] Chelkas Mechokek 64:3; Beis Shmuel 64:3 in name of Bach 64; Chida in Shiyurei Bracha 64:3 and Chaim Sheol 2:38-58; Chasam Sofer 123, brought in Pischeiy Teshuvah 62:9

[236] Radbaz 7:64 [863]; Mahrikash 63; Rav Akiva Eiger 62:1; Poskim brought in Nitei Gavriel 110:6 footnote 21

[237] Chida in Shiyurei Bracha 62:1; Chaim Sheol 2:38-56; Yifei Lalev 62:16; Nehar Mitzrayim; Ben Ish Chaiy Shotim 16; Kitzur SHU"A 149:8; Poskim brought in Nitei Gavriel 55:11 and 110:11 footnote 20

[238] See Nitei Gavriel Nissuin 55:12

[239] Simple implication of Rama 64:2; Rabbeinu Yerucham 22; Rashal in Yam Shel Shlomo Kesubos 1:12; Beis Shmuel 63:1 according to all Poskim who rule a Bochur does not keep seven days of Simcha; Chida in Shiyurei Bracha 64 and Chaim Sheol 2:38-Samech

[240] Simple implication of Rama ibid; Rashal ibid

[241] The reason: The entire reason that the Chasan must rejoice his wife is for her benefit. Hence, she may choose to forgive it. [Beis Shmuel 64:1; Chelkas Mechokeik 64:2]

[242] Implication of Ran and all Poskim who rule a Bochur always says Sheva Brachos for seven days [2nd opinion in Michaber ibid; Ran Kesubos ibid; Rashba], as understood by Beis Shmuel ibid; Tiv Keddushin 64:1; Merkavas Hamishneh 1; Eretz Tzevi E.H. 64; Daas Kedoshim 342:1

is prohibited from doing Melacha in all cases, and must rejoice with her in festive meals. Other Poskim[243] rule that while the Kallah may be Mochel on her Simcha of having the Chasan eat, drink and spend time with her, she cannot be Mochel to allow her Chasan to do Melacha. Other Poskim[244] rule that if the Kallah was a Beusla, she may not be Mochel on her Simcha, while if he was a Beula, then she may. Practically, the custom is to rejoice during these days, and not allow Mechila of the Kallah to absolve one of the obligation.[245] Some Poskim[246], however, are lenient to allow a Chasan to perform Melacha in the privacy of his home, if the Kallah is Mochel, even if she is a Besula.[247]

D. Rejoicing with the Kallah-Festive meals:[248]
The Chasan is obligated to rejoice with his wife, and eat and drink with her, for the above-mentioned time of Simcha [three or seven days depending on Besula/Beula as explained in A].

E. Melacha and Business:[249]
It is forbidden for the Chasan to do Melacha or business in the marketplace, throughout the period of Simcha [three or seven days depending on Besula/Beula as explained in A].[250]

Mechila/Receiving permission from Kallah to do Melacha:[251] The above prohibition applies even if the Kallah is Mochel on her Simcha, and allows the Chasan to do Melacha and go to work.[252] [However, some Poskim[253] rule that this applies only if the Kallah is a Besula, if however, the Kallah is a Beula, then she can forgive her honor and he may go to work.[254] See C! Likewise, some Poskim[255] are lenient to allow a Chasan to perform Melacha in the privacy of his home if the Kallah is Mochel, even if she is a Besula.[256]]

Haircut and laundry:[257] It is permitted for a Chasan [and Kallah] to cut his hair and launder/iron his clothing during Sheva Brachos.[258] This applies even if the Chasan [or Kallah] is in Aveilus.[259]

---

[243] Chelkas Mechokeik 64:2 in understanding of Rama 64:1; Implication of Beis Shmuel 64:2 in understanding of Rama 64:1; Aruch Hashulchan 64:5; Kitzur SHU"A 149:12 [regarding a Besula]; Poskim in Nitei Gavriel 56 footnote 2

[244] Hamakneh and Pischeiy Teshuvah 64:3, in his understanding of Rama; Chochmas Adam 129:11; Kitzur SHU"A 149:12; Aruch Hashulchan 64:5

[245] Nitei Gavriel ibid

[246] See Dovev Meisharim 3:47; Nitei Gavriel 56:2

[247] The reason: As a king is only forbidden from doing Melacha in public, and hence if the wife is Mochel, neither reason is relevant to prohibit the Chasan from doing Melacha in private. [ibid]

[248] Michaber 64:1

[249] Michaber and Rama 64:1

[250] The reason: As a) He is obligated to rejoice his wife. And b) A Chasan is like a king. [Chelkas Mechokek 64:2]

[251] Chelkas Mechokek 64:2 and Beis Shmuel 64:2 in explanation of the novelty of Rama ibid who repeats the same ruling of Michaber that a Chasan may not do Melacha; Hamakneh, brought in Pischeiy Teshuvah 64:3; Aruch Hashulchan 64:5; Kitzur SHU"A 149:12; Poskim in Nitei Gavriel 56 footnote 2
Other Poskim: Some Poskim rule it is permitted for the Kallah to be Mochel and have her Chasan do work. [Chida in Shiyurei Bracha 64 and Chaim Sheol 2:38-Samech]

[252] The reason: As a Chasan is like a king and hence may not do Melacha just like a King, irrelevant of the Kallah's permission. [Chelkas Mechokek 64:2]

[253] Hamakneh, brought in Pischeiy Teshuvah 64:3; Aruch Hashulchan ibid

[254] The reason: As only when one marries a Besula is he called a true Chasan in his own right that is similar to a king. [Pischeiy Teshuvah ibid]

[255] See Dovev Meisharim 3:47; Nitei Gavriel 56:2

[256] The reason: As a king is only forbidden from doing Melacha in public, and hence if the wife is Mochel, neither reason is relevant to prohibit the Chasan from doing Melacha in private. [ibid]

[257] Michaber Y.D. 342:1; Shach 342:11; Taz 342:5; Kneses Hagedila 342:1; Masas Binyamin 19; Tur 342; Ramban in Toras Hadam; Rabbeinu Yerucham 22:2; Rosh; Poskim brought in Nitei Gavriel 57 footnote 20; Yabia Omer E.H. 4:8
Other opinions: Some Poskim rule the Chasan is forbidden in getting a haircut or laundry during Sheva Brachos. [Maharibil 3:72 according to Raavad; Kerem Shlomo 64, brought in Pischei Teshuvah 64:1] The Shach ibid strongly negates his opinion, as it argues against all the above Rishonim and Poskim. See Nitei Gavriel ibid footnote 21

[258] The reason: As a king needs to look beautiful, and have a nicely trimmed haircut and laundered and ironed clothing. [Shach ibid; Taz ibid]

[259] Poskim ibid; See Michaber ibid and Taz ibid for the exact case scenario for which a Chasan/Kallah can get married and keep Sheva Brachos even if they are in Aveilus
Other opinions: Some Poskim rule the Chasan is forbidden in getting a haircut or laundry during Sheva Brachos if he is in Aveilus. [Bach Y.D. 342, brought in Shach ibid] The Shach ibid strongly negates his opinion, as it argues against all the above Rishonim and Poskim. See Nitei Gavriel ibid footnote 21

Summary:
A Chasan is forbidden to perform Melacha all seven days of Sheva Brachos if he married a Besula. If he married a Beula, it is only forbidden for three days. If the Kallah is Mochel on her Simcha, the Chasan may do Melacha in the privacy of his home, and if he married a Beula he may do Melacha even in public.

Q&A

May the Kallah perform Melacha during the Sheva Brachos?
Some Poskim[260] rule the Kallah is prohibited from performing Melacha, just as the Chasan. Other Poskim[261] however are lenient from the second day and onwards. She may certainly do Melacha in private with her husband's consent.[262]

May the Chasan/Kallah do Melacha to prevent monetary loss?[263]
Some Poskim[264] rule it is forbidden to do Melacha even in a case of loss. Other Poskim[265] rule it is permitted. Practically, the Chasan may do Melacha in private if his Kallah is Mochel.

Q&A on definition of Melacha
What form of Melacha is forbidden to be done by the Chasan/Kallah?[266]
All forms of work that are forbidden to be done on Chol Hamoed is likewise forbidden to be done by the Chasan/Kallah during their days of Simcha [with exception to getting a haircut and laundry[267]].[268] It is likewise forbidden to perform any Melacha that is troublesome, and prevents one from properly focusing on rejoicing his wife.[269] All Melachos that are food related, and are permitted to perform on Yom Tov, is likewise permitted to be performed by the Chasan/Kallah. Likewise, Simcha related Melachos are permitted.[270]

May a Chasan tie Tzitzis to his new Tallis during Sheva Brachos?[271]
Yes.

May a Chasan/Kallah write during Sheva Brachos?[272]
It is permitted for the Chasan/Kallah to briefly write during Sheva Brachos, although one may not engage in a long writing session, in order not to nullify the Mitzvah of rejoicing with his wife. It is certainly permitted to jot down Chidushei Torah.

May one's business partner run the business during Sheva Brachos?[273]
Yes.

---

[260] Nitei Gavriel 56:3 footnote 4 in name of Meiri Kesubos; Rashal Kesubos 12 and other Poskim
[261] Yifei Lalev 64:5; Meishiv Halacha 2:66; Sheol Umeishiv Mahdurah 5:91 See Rashi Kesubos 47a
[262] Nitei Gavriel ibid in name of Maharsham 3:206
[263] Nitei Gavriel 56:4
[264] Beis David Y.D. 177; Chaim Veshalom 2:27; Ben Ish Chaiy Shoftim 16; Kinyan Torah 3:32
[265] Daas Kedoshim 342:1; Dovev Meisharim 3:47; Chazon Ish E.H. 64:7; See Minchas Elazar 2:57
[266] Nitei Gavriel 56:5-6
[267] As explained above
[268] Levushei Mordechai E.H. Tinyana 56
[269] Chida in Shiyurei Bracha 64:1; Chaim Sheol 2:38; Chaim Falagi in Chaim Veshalom 2:57
[270] Sheilas Yaavetz 2:185
[271] Nitei Gavriel 56 footnote 12
[272] See Nitei Gavriel 56:7; Mishneh Halachos 9:223; Tzitz Eliezer 11:85
[273] Zekan Aaron 215; Perach Mateh Aaron 2:65, brought in Pischei Teshuvah 64:1 Chaim Sheol 2:38 Samech; Ben Ish Chaiy Shoftim 16; Aruch Hashulchan 64:3; Nitei Gavriel 64:8 footnote 17

> **May a Chasan who is a Shochet, Shecht during Sheva Brachos?**[274]
> Yes. He may even Shecht for the public, if other Shochtim are not available and it will lead to a shortage of meat.[275]
>
> **May a Chasan/Kallah cut nails during Sheva Brachos?**[276]
> Yes.

F. Haircut and freshly ironed clothing:[277]

A Chasan is compared to a king who must look beautiful and splendor and is hence to have freshly trimmed hair, and is to wear freshly ironed clothing, throughout the Sheva Brachos. The Chasan/Kallah may even get a haircut and launder/iron the clothing during Sheva Brachos, for this purpose.

13. The first year of marriage:

A. Rejoicing one's wife during the first year:

The verse[278] states that a husband is obligated to rejoice with his wife during the first year of marriage. Some Poskim[279] learn this to be a positive command, and part of the 613 Mitzvos. This does not mean that he should stay unemployed and spend time in wining and dining with his wife all year long. Rather, it means that he should fulfill her wishes in every way possible, to pleasure her.[280] He is to do for her all matters that make her happy. This command applies in all areas [and in all times] being it is a body dependent Mitzvah.[281] This Mitzvah applies for all new wives, whether a Besula or widow, although does not apply if one remarries his ex-wife.[282]

B. Traveling from home during the first year:[283]

The Torah[284] states that "When one marries a new wife he is not to go to the warfront or do other matters and is to be available to his house for one year and rejoice his wife that he took." From here we derive the Biblical command that a Chasan within the year of marriage may not go out to war.[285] Regarding if the Chasan may be away from home [i.e. his wife] for other purposes: Some Poskim[286] rule that the above command is only in reference to leaving his wife to go to war, however a Chasan during the first year, may travel away from home for business or other purposes, for his own benefit.[287] Other Poskim[288],

---

[274] See Levushei Mordechai Tinayna 56; Nitei Gavriel 57:10

[275] The reason: As even on Yom Tov it is permitted to perform Melacha of Ochel Nefesh.

[276] Michaber Y.D. 342:1 regarding a haircut and certainly this would apply regarding nails; Nitei Gavriel 64:11

[277] Michaber 342:1; Shach 342:11; Taz 342:5; Masas Binyamin 19; Tur 342; Ramban in Toras Hadam; Rabbeinu Yerucham 22:2; Rosh
Other opinions: Some Poskim rule the Chasan is forbidden in getting a haircut or laundry during Sheva Brachos. [Bach Y.D. 342, brought in Shach ibid] The Shach ibid strongly negates his opinion, as it argues against all the above Rishonim and Poskim

[278] Ki Seitzei Devarim 24:5

[279] Sefer Hachinuch Ki Seitzei Mitzvah 582; Yireim 190 [228]; Rambam Sefer Hamitzvos L.S. 311 lists the Mitzvah of not leaving the home during war, however, does not mention the matter of Simcha; See Tosafos Rieim on yireim ibid

[280] Aruch Hashulchan 64:4

[281] Yireim 190 [228]; See Aruch Hashulchan ibid who casts doubt as to whether this ruling of the Yireim is binding being that it is omitted by all the other Poskim

[282] Aruch Hashulchan ibid

[283] See Pischeiy Teshuvah 64:2; Rav Poalim 3 E.H. 9; Mishnas Yehoshua 31; Sdei Chemed Chasan Viklal 29; Shulchan Haezer E.H. 12:10; Otzer Haposkim E.H. 64; Tzitz Eliezer 19:41; Betzel Hachochma 4:72; Divrei Yatziv 2:274; Birur Halacha Telisa E.H. 64

[284] Ki Seitzei Devarim 24:5

[285] Rambam Sefer Hamitzvos L.S. 311 [According to one Nussach, However, see Radbaz ibid and Minchas Chinuch ibid that this is not the correct Nussach]; Sefer Hachinuch Ki Seitzei Mitzvah 58; Yireim ibid; Dvar Moshe E.H. 28; Nachal Kedumim Chida Ki Seitzei 24

[286] Radbaz 1:231 based on Semag and Rambam, brought in Pischeiy Teshuvah 64:2; Chaim Sheol 1:93 [unlike what he implied in his Sefer Nachal Kedumim Chida Ki Seitzei 24]; Minchas Chinuch 582; Chasam Sofer E.H. 2:155 "The Chinuch is a Daas Yachid in this matter and the Rambam did not rule this way"; Aruch Hashulchan 64:4 "Some want to say.. there is no source for such a thing"

[287] The reason: As the entire reason he is not to go to war is because his mind is preoccupied with his wife and he will not fight with all his heart. [See Chasam Sofer E.H. 2:155] Likewise, traveling for business is considered a Mitzvah. [Chasam Sofer ibid; See Admur 248]

[288] Rambam Sefer Hamitzvos L.S. 311 [According to one Nussach, However see Radbaz ibid and Minchas Chinuch ibid that this is not the correct Nussach]; Sefer Hachinuch Ki Seitzei Mitzvah 582; Likkutei Hapardes of Rashi; Dvar Moshe E.H. 28; Chochmas Adam 129:19 and Binas Adam 37, brought in Pischeiy Teshuvah 64:2; Kitzur SHU"A 149:13; China Vechisda Kesubos 2:230; Rav Poalim ibid [concludes like China Vechisda]; See Chasam Sofer E.H. 2:155; Tosafos Riem on Yireim ibid; Nachal Kedumim Chida Ki Seitzei 24

however, rule it is forbidden for the Chasan to leave his wife during the first year even for business purposes.[289] Some Poskim[290] rule. that even according to the latter opinion, that if one's wife is Mochel [i.e. forgives] for him to be away from home, one may travel away for business. Likewise, one may travel away from home for the sake of a Mitzvah.[291] [Practically, if it is necessary for one to be away from home, and his wife, during the first year, he should ask for her Mechila/permission. If she is not Mochel, then for a Mitzvah, he may travel even without her permission, otherwise a Rav is to be contacted.]

-----------------*Kesuba*----------------

14. How much money is the Kesuba worth?

A. Introduction:

A Kesuba is similar to a loan document or check, which obligates the husband, or his estate, to pay a certain sum of money to his wife. The Kesuba can only be actualized in the event of death of the husband or in case of a divorce. If a husband outlives his wife, the Kesuba document cannot be actualized. According to many Poskim[292], The Torah did not mandate the sum of money which the Chasan has to obligate towards his wife in the Kesuba, and the Kesuba document is not at all a Biblical obligation. Rather, it was the Sages who instituted for a certain sum of money to be obligated in the Kesuba, as will be explained. The evaluation of the monetary value of a Kesuba is complex due to several reasons: 1) There is a difference in value between the Kesuba of a Kallah who was a Besula versus a Beula? 2) There are several areas of dispute involved in how to calculate the value and currency recorded in the Kesuba. 3) It fluctuates based on the value of silver. 4) It is possible for a Chasan to obligate himself to more money than the bare minimum required in a Kesuba. The value of a Kesuba therefore varies from Kesuba to Kesuba and fluctuates from year to year, based on the value of silver, and every Kesuba requires the review of a Beis Din to determine its actual worth.

B. The ramifications:

The obvious ramification involved in knowing the value of the Kesuba, is knowing the sum that a husband must pay his wife in the event of divorce, or the amount that his estate must pay in the event of death. Nonetheless, in today's times, it is common in many divorce cases for the Beis Din to ignore the Kesuba value, as the monetary divorce agreements, splitting of assets, and alimony, set up between the couple, usually payout much more than the Kesuba is worth.[293] Nonetheless, in some instances, its value

---

[289] The reason: As the entire reason he is not to go to war, is in order to spend time with his wife and create a bond with her that will serve to solidify their relationship for all their future years and help build a Bayis Neman Beyisrael. The Torah desired that children be born to a family in where the husband and wife love each other, and this takes a year of development. [Chinuch ibid] Alternatively, just as Hashem stayed with Bnei Yisrael under Har Sinai for a full year after Matan Torah, so too, a husband is to act with his wife. [See Rabbeinu Bechayeh Ki Seitzei]

[290] Chochmas Adam ibid, brought in Pischeiy Teshuvah 64:2; Divrei Mordechai E.H. 3, brought in Rav Poalim 3:9; See China Vechisda Kesubos 2:230; Rav Poalim ibid

Other opinions: From some Poskim it is implied that it is forbidden to leave one's wife even with her permission. [See Divrei Mordechai ibid; Rav Poalim ibid; Chochmas Adam ibid]

[291] Chasam Sofer ibid

[292] See Kesubos 11a; 56b; 110b; Some rule the Kesuba is Rabbinical. [Chachamim in Kesubos ibid; Shita Mekubetzes Kesubos 10a; Ramban; Ritva; Rabbeinu Yona; Rambam; Geonim] Other Poskim rule it is Biblical. [Raban Shimon Ben Gamliel in Kesubos ibid; Rabbeinu Tam and Riy in Tosafos Kesubos 10a] Others rule that while the concept is Biblical, the amount is Rabbinical. [Mordechai Kesubos 312]

[293] Most countries contain laws regarding distribution of the estate and assets. In the USA there are nine Community Property States which consider both spouses as equal owners of all marital property (a 50-50 split is the rule). These are: Arizona, California, Idaho, Louisiana, Nevada, New Mexico, Texas, Washington and Wisconsin. This is likewise the law in Israel. The remaining 41 states in the USA are Equitable Distribution states. Settlements in Equitable Distribution States do not need to be equal, but they should be fair and equitable. In Equitable Distribution, several factors are taken into account, including the financial situation of each spouse when dividing assets. If a couple cannot come to a financial agreement on their own, then the courts give a verdict on the distribution.

The Kashrus of a divorce settlement: Being that due to the Takana of Rabbeinu Gershom, it is forbidden to divorce one's wife unwillingly, it therefore has become Halachically incumbent upon the husband to appease his wife financially in order for her to be willing to accept the Get. Accordingly, a divorce settlement outside of the Kesuba, while not mandated by Torah law, is at times a practical necessity even according to Torah. It is for this reason that in many cases today the collection of the Kesuba has become irrelevant, as the wife exits with a much larger sum, due to the divorce settlement. [See Mishpat Hakesuba 8:60]

is taken into account.[294] Another ramification involved is regarding the Chasan having proper knowledge of the amount of money that he is obligating himself to, during the wedding.[295]

C. The monetary obligations in the Kesuba:

A Kesuba contains two calculations of value. One is a standard required sum of obligation from the husband to the wife, and the second is a voluntary additional sum of obligation, which is given to the discretion of the Chasan, at the time that the Kesuba is written. The former is known as the Ikkur Kesuba while the latter is known as the Tosefes Kesuba. While the Ikkur Kesuba is a relatively a miniscule amount, the Tosefes Kesuba accounts for the big price tags usually seen on Kesubas today. Thus, the total value of a Kesuba is made up of the value of the Ikkur Kesuba, and the value of the Tosefes Kesuba. The following is the calculation of the Ikkur and Tosefes Kesuba:

D. The Ikkur Kesuba:[296]

Besula versus Beula:[297] The required sum of obligation, known as the Ikkur Kesuba, varies between a Besula and Beula. If one is marrying a Besula, then he must obligate himself to the sum of 200 Zuz. If he is marrying a Beula, he must obligate himself to the sum of 100 Zuz.

A Biblical versus Rabbinical Zuz: It is disputed amongst Poskim[298] as to whether the Zuz currency refers to the Biblical coin [Kesef Tzuri] or the Rabbinical coin [Kesef Medina]. The Biblical currency of the Zuz is worth 8 times more than the Rabbinical coin, as the Biblical coin was pure silver while the Rabbinical coin was 1/8 silver and 7/8 copper. Practically, the Sephardim follow the latter approach, as rules the Michaber, that the Zuz refers to the Rabbinical currency, while the Ashkenazim follow the former approach, as rules the Rama, that the Zuz refers the Biblical currency. Thus, the Ikkur Kesuba of an Ashkenazi Kesuba is worth 8 times more than that of a Sephardic Kesuba.[299]

The practical calculation for Ashkenazim: The value of a single Zuz for Ashkenazim is equivalent to 4.8 grams of silver. Accordingly, 200 Zuz is equivalent to 961.5 grams of silver.[300] Accordingly, the value of the Ikkur Kesuba fluctuates based on the current price of silver at the time of the Kesuba's actualization.[301] Based on the price of silver as of September 2017 [$0.57196 per gram], the worth of a single Zuz is $2.75. Accordingly, the 200 Zuz of the Kesuba of a Besula, which is equivalent to 961.5 grams of silver, is worth $550. The 100 Zuz of the Kesuba of a Beula, which is equivalent to 481 grams of silver, is worth $275.

The practical calculation for Sephardim: The value of a single Zuz for Sephardim is equivalent to .6 grams of silver. Accordingly, 200 Zuz is equivalent to 120 grams of silver.[302] Based on the price of silver as of September 2017 [$0.57196 per gram], the worth of a single Zuz is $.34. Accordingly, the 200 Zuz of the Kesuba of a Besula, which is equivalent to 120 grams of silver, is worth $69. The 100 Zuz of the Kesuba of a Beula, which is equivalent to 60 grams of silver, is worth $34.

Other opinions: Some of today's Poskim[303] suggest that in truth the value of the 200 Zuz of the Kesuba is not to be taken literally, and rather is a general value equivalent to one year's worth of living, and that the Kesuba is to be evaluated accordingly. Likewise, see Q&A regarding if we measure the exchange market's value of silver, or the current purchase value of silver in one's country.

---

[294] Such as in determining the proper division of property, or if the couple owned no property and assets, or if the Kesuba was an exorbitant amount, and cases of the like.
[295] See Piskei Dinim 13:308 of Rav Dechovsky; Article of Rav Eliyahu Bar Shalom, author of Mishpat Hakesuba; Hilchos Hagr"a Uminhagav 181 of Rav Shturnbuch
[296] See Mishpat Hakesuba 3:20
[297] Michaber 66:6; Mishneh Kesubos 51a
[298] Some Poskim rule it follows the Rabbinical coin, Kesef Medina. [Michaber E.H. 66:6; Rambam Ishus 10:8; Majority of Geonim and many Rishonim] Other Poskim rule it follows the Biblical coin. [Rama E.H. 66:6; Rabbeinu Tam Kesubos 11a; Rosh]
[299] Rama ibid
[300] Shiureiy Torah 3:44
[301] Shiureiy Torah 3:44
[302] Shiureiy Torah 3:44
[303] See Oraisa 18 for an article of Rav Eliyahu Bar Shalom based on the opinion of the Igros Moshe E.H. 4:92

E. The Tosefes Kesuba:[304]

Every Chasan has the option of adding to the minimal sum which he must obligate himself to, that is found in the Ikkur Kesuba established by the Sages. While, this is not obligatory, the custom is for the Chasan to do so. By Ashkenazim, there is a set customary amount that is added, while by Sephardim, every Chasan has the option of choosing his amount. The following is the details of the Ashkenazi and Sephardic customs:

Ashkenazim: The Ashkenazi custom is write a total sum of 200 Zekukim Kesef for the Tosefes Kesuba of a Besula and 100 Zekukim Kesef for the Tosefes Kesuba of as Beula.[305] This is known as the Kesuba of the Nachalas Shiva. The value of a Zakuk of silver is four times that of a Zuz.[306] Accordingly, the value of a single Zekukim Kesef is equivalent to 19.3 grams of silver, and 200 Zekukim Kesef is equivalent to 3846 grams of silver. Based on the price of silver as of September 2017 [$0.57196 per gram], the worth of a single Zekukim Kesef is $10.96. Accordingly, the 200 Zekukim Kesef of the Kesuba, which is equivalent to 3846 grams of silver, is worth $2,200.

Other opinions: Some Poskim[307] argue on the above and rule the 200 Zekukim Kesef is worth 57.6 Kilo [57,600 grams] of silver. Based on the price of silver as of September 2017 [$0.57196 per gram], the worth of the 200 Zekukim Kesef of the Kesuba according to this opinion, is $32,832. Other Poskim[308] rule the 200 Zekukim Kesef is worth 42 Kilo [42,000 grams] of silver. Based on the price of silver as of September 2017 [$0.57196 per gram], the worth of the 200 Zekukim Kesef of the Kesuba according to this opinion, is worth $24,000. [Practically, due to the rule of Hamotzi Michaveiro Alav Harayah, which places the burden of proof on the wife, the husband can claim that he holds of the previous mentioned lenient opinion, and therefore the Beis Din cannot obligate him to pay the larger amounts written by these other opinions.[309]]

Sephardim-Tosefes Kesuba: The Sephardim customarily do not record a set amount in the Tosefes Kesuba, and rather obligate themselves to whatever amount the Chasan agrees upon at the day of the wedding. [It is important to emphasize to the Chasan that the amount written by the Chasan, even if it is an exorbitant amount which he clearly cannot afford, may be accepted by the Beis Din as a true obligation, and therefore a Chasan should not quote a high sum simply for the sake of honor and show of love for his Kallah. Nonetheless, there are cases in which the Beis Din decides to abolish an exorbitant amount due to the claim of Asmachta.[310]]

[304] Michaber and Rama E.H. 66:7; See Mishpat Hakesuba 3:24; Seder Kiddushin Venissuin [Farkash] 2:8-10

[305] Kesubas Nachalas Shiva; Maharam Mintz 109; See Seder Kesuba Kehilchasa 1 footnote 13
The calculation: This amount is made up of 100 Zekukim for the Tosefes Kesuba, and 100 Zekukim in exchange for the Nedunya, for a total of 200 Zekukim. By a Beula the amount is 50 Zekukim for each matter.

[306] Nachalas Shiva 12:49 in name of Bach and Derisha; Shiurei Torah 3:44

[307] Chazon Ish Y.D. 182:19; E.H. 66:22; C.M. 16:30

[308] Igros Moshe E.H. 92-4.91

[309] Conclusion of Rav Eliyahu Bar Shalom in Mishpat Hakesuba; and so ruled Rav Ovadia Yosef in the Beis Din Rabbani [See Piskei Dinim 11:383]; Conclusion of Beit Din Rabbani Haifa; Conclusion of Rav Shlomo Dichovsky in Kovetz Kenes Hadayanim 5767; Rav Mordechai Eliyahu held of the stringent opinion

[310] See Techumin 18-19; Ruling of Rav Dechovski; Ruling of Beit Din Ezuri Haifa

Summary:
The worth of a Kesuba varies based on the following factors:

1. Is it a Kesuba of a Besula or Beula?
2. Is the husband Ashkenazi [i.e. Ashkenazi Kesuba] or Sephardi [i.e. Sephardic Kesuba].
3. What is the worth of the 200 Zekukim Kesef in grams of silver? This matter is debated amongst Poskim.
4. What is the current price of silver.
5. Do we follow the market value of silver or its purchase value? This matter is debated amongst Poskim. [see Q&A]
6. Was there any additional sum that the Chasan chose to obligate himself for in the section of Tosefes Kesuba [usually only found in Sephardic Kesubos, as opposed to Kesubos of Ashkenazim or Nachalas Shiva].

Practically: As of the price of silver in September 2017, the possible total minimal value of an Ashkenazi Kesuba for a Besula is approximately $2,750 while the possible maximum total value is approximately $33,382. If any other additional sums were obligated by the Chasan, as is common in Sephardic Kesubos, then that amount is also taken into account.

Q&A

Is the value of silver calculated based on world stock exchange rate [theoretical price] or based on its practical sale price in one's country?

The price for purchasing silver depends not only on the current market exchange rate, but also on the individual country that one is in. The reason for this is as follows: There is a general sales tax which is placed on the final purchase price in every country. If the silver must be shipped, one must also take into account various other costs involved, including tariffs levied by the importing country. Hence, the final price of silver as purchased by a consumer in a given country is higher than the value shown on the exchange market. Practically, it is disputed amongst the Poskim as to which value of silver we follow regarding evaluating the Kesuba; the market price, or the current sale price in one's country. Some Poskim[311] rule we follow the exchange market value. Other Poskim[312] rule we follow the current purchase price in one's area.

---

[311] Nachalas Shiva; Gr"a; Lechem Habikkurim; Chazon Ish, brought in Mishpat HaKesuba ibid [See Halichos Sadeh 60:20 that so ruled Rav Kanievsky and Elyashiv]

[312] Tumim; Smeh; Chasam Sofer; Chidushei Harim; Igros Moshe; brought in Mishpat HaKesuba ibid; Rav Mordechai Eliyahu was of the position that we follow the current sale price, which would include all tariffs and taxes.

Choshen Mishpat

--------------*Beis Din*----------------
1. Hearing the claims of each side in the presence of the other side:[1]

It is forbidden[2] for a judge to hear the claims of one side of the case [plaintiff or defendant] not in the presence of the other side.[3] This prohibition applies equally for the plaintiff/defendant, that they may not make a claim in front of the judge unless the other person is present.[4] [The Zohar states that one who hears one side without the other is considered as if he has accepted upon himself a foreign G-d.[5]]

Bedieved: In the event that a judge transgressed, and heard one side of the argument not in the presence of the other, some Poskim[6] rule he may still judge the case. Other Poskim[7], however, question this allowance.

If one does not plan on judging the case:[8] If one does not plan on judging the case, then it is permitted for him to hear one side of the case not in the presence of the other.[9] This applies even if there is a possibility that he may judge the case, but he does not know for certain that he will do so, he may nevertheless hear the claims of one not in front of the other, and then if he is asked to judge the case, he may do so with the consent of the other side, [after letting them know that he already heard the other side[10]]. If, however, one does plan on being the judge in the case, then he may not initially hear the testimony.[11]

Q&A
If the other side consents, may the judge hear the claim not in the presence of the other?[12]
If the both sides consent that the judge may hear the claim of one side without the other being present, then it seemingly is permitted to do so.

May a Rav hear a Shaala dealing with monetary claims from only one side?[13]
The Rav [if he is not also the Dayan] may hear the Shaala and tell the person whether he may go to Beis Din for his claim. However, he is not to give any advice or ruling to the individual, until the other side is present, and he hears his claims as well.

---

[1] Michaber 17:5; Sanhedrin 7b; Shavuos 31a
[2] Biblical or Rabbinical: Some Poskim rule it is a Biblical prohibition for the judge to hear one side without the other being present. [Kneses Hagedola 17:13, brought in Pischeiy Teshuvah 17:8] See Pischeiy Teshuvah ibid
[3] The reason: The verse states "Ushimoa Bein Acheichem Ushifatitem", which means that the judges must hear the claims of one side in front of the other side. [Smeh 17:10; Sanhedrin ibid] Alternatively, the reason is because the verse states "Lo Sisa Sheima Shav", and when one side makes a claim not in the presence of the other, he has no shame to make dubious claims and statements. [Smeh ibid; Beir Hagoleh ibid; Rav Kahana in Sanhedrin ibid] This then leads to fear in the other side, that the fictitious claims that were already heard were absorbed in the mind of the judge as true. [Smeh 17:11; Aruch Hashulchan 17:7]
[4] The reason: As the verse states "Lo Sisa Sheima Shav" and can be read as "Lo Sasi." [Smeh 17:12; Sanhedrin ibid]
[5] Zohar Vayeishev p. 149, brought in Pischeiy Teshuvah ibid; Aruch Hashulchan 17:7
[6] Shach 17:9; Implication of Smeh 17:11; Poskim brought in Kneses Hagedola 17:13 and Pischeiy Teshuvah 17:8; Vetzaruch Iyun from Rama ibid who implies that even Bedieved one may only hear the case if the defendant agrees, and so rules Bach 17
[7] Kneses Hagedola ibid
[8] Rama 17:5; Smeh 17:11
Writing a Teshuvah to a question from one side: See Kuntrus in Tzohar Hamishpat [Nachmaonson] in length on this subject
[9] May one advise one of the person's in the case as to the Psak? One may not give a potential ruling to the case until he hears both sides, even if he is not the judge and his rulings are not binding. [Rama ibid] Thus, while he may hear one side not in front of the other, if he does not plan on judging the case, he may not tell the person a ruling regarding it.
[10] Smeh 17:11
[11] The reason: As perhaps the other side does not feel comfortable being judged by a person who already heard the claim against him. [Smeh ibid]
[12] Clear implication of Rama and Smeh ibid; See Aruch Hashulchan ibid
[13] Rama ibid

2. May one take a gentile to a secular court?

The Biblical prohibition against going to secular courts applies even against taking a gentile to a secular court, and one who does so transgresses a negative command.[14] This applies even if the secular courts rule the same way as the Beis Din.[15] If one has a claim against a gentile, he is required to bring his claim to a Beis Din. However, in the event that the gentile does not desire to go to a Beis Din, one may take him to a secular court.[16] It is not necessary to receive Rabbinical permission for this matter.[17] Furthermore, if it is common knowledge that the gentile will not agree to appear before a Beis Din, then one may even initially take him to a secular court without even offering him the initiative of going to Beis Din.[18] Practically, based on this assumption, many are accustomed to take gentiles to secular court without attempting the option of a Beis Din.[19] If, however, one knows that the gentile will agree to go to a Beis Din, and certainly if the gentile has expressed his will to do so, then it is forbidden to take him to a secular court, just as it is forbidden by a claim against a Jew.[20] In such a case, if one went ahead and took the gentile to secular court, the money which was taken from the gentile is considered stolen, and he must return that money to him.[21]

3. Taking one's father, mother, or Rebbe to Beis Din:[22]

It is permitted to take one's father [or mother[23], or Rebbe[24]] to Beis Din, to file a monetary claim against them. For example, if one's father damaged one's item, one may take him to court to force him to pay for the damages. [However, some[25] learn it is a Midas Chassidus not to take one's father to Beis Din, in order not to cause him pain. Other Poskim[26], however, omit this act of piety.]

------------------Loans-----------------

4. Pressuring a borrower to pay back a loan:[27]

It is forbidden to pressure or confront [i.e. Nogeish] the debtor to pay back the loan in the event that one knows he does not have the means to pay. One who does so, transgresses the negative command of "Do not be like a debt collector.[28]"[29] One transgresses this command each time that he pressures the borrower, in the above circumstance that one knows that he cannot repay the loan.[30]

Who is considered to not have the means to pay?[31] The above prohibition only applies if one knows [for certain, based on his assessment[32]] that the debtor does not have the means to pay him, neither in cash nor assets [i.e. Mitaltilin, including belongings or land[33]].[34] If the debtor has belongings [or land], which

---

[14] Tashbatz 2:290; Tanchuma Shoftim and Yalkut Shimoni Tehilim 147: *From where do you know learn that if a Jew and gentile have claims against each other that it is forbidden for the Jew to tell the gentile "Lets go to your courts", this is learned from the verse of "Lo Asa Kein Lechol Goy Umishpatim Baal Yedaum" One who disobeys this law transgresses a negative command*; Bein Yisrael Lenachri p. 32

[15] Tashbatz ibid

[16] Tashbatz Chut Hameshulash Tur Hashelishi 6; Bein Yisrael Lenachri p. 32

[17] Rav Paltoit brought in Rosh; Bein Yisrael Lenachri p. 32

[18] Daas Kedoshim C.M. 26:2 even regarding a Jew

[19] Tashbatz Chut Hameshulash Tur Hashelishi 6; Rav Mordechai Gross of Chanichei Hayeshivos

[20] Tashbatz Chut Hameshulash Tur Hashelishi 6; Bein Yisrael Lenachri p. 32

[21] Tashbatz 2:290

[22] Rama Y.D. 240:8; Tur 240 in name of Rosh; Teshuvos Hageonim 206; Erechin 23a in story of Rav Huna

[23] See Shut Harif 22

[24] Kneses Hagedola 240, brought in Birkeiy Yosef 240

[25] Sefer Chassidim 584 based on a story he brings, brought in Birkeiy Yosef 240

[26] Omitted in Kneses Hagedola even though he normally records the teachings of Sefer Chassidim, brought in Birkeiy Yosef ibid

[27] Admur Halvah 2; Michaber C.M. 97:2; Bava Metzia 75b; See Beir Moshe 8:26-27 for a discussion on various points mentioned here

[28] Shemos 22:24

[29] Admur ibid; Smeh 97:2

The level of pressure that is forbidden: See Admur below that even showing one's face to the debtor is forbidden, and it is implied that doing so is included in the Biblical command. However, see Kesef Kedoshim 97:2 that seemingly only one who enters his house to take his belongings transgresses this command, while simply pressuring him is a Rabbinical injunction based on this command. He, however, then concludes that it is included in the Biblical command.

[30] Admur Halvah 5

[31] Admur Halvah 2 and 13

[32] Kesef Kedoshim 97:2

[33] Kesef Kedoshim 97:2; Admur ibid makes no mention of land

[34] Admur Halvah 2

excess the minimum amount that the Sages delegated for a debtor to keep, and hence can be collected by the Beis Din in exchange for the debt, then it is permitted to pressure him to sell his assets and find the means of paying the debt.[35] If, however, one knows that the debtor does not own any more than the basic assets allowed by the Sages to be owned by a debtor, then it is forbidden to pressure him as stated above.[36] This applies even if the debtor has ability to work [or borrow money] to pay off the loan.[37] [The above matter is to be determined by assessment of the lender, and if he asses that the debtor does not own more than this amount, the prohibition applies.[38]]

Appearing before the debtor without pressuring him:[39] It is forbidden for a lender to make an appearance to his debtor, at a time that he knows the debtor does not have the means to pay him. It is even forbidden to walk pass him.[40] [Some Poskim[41] learn that this applies even if the lender has no intent to pressure the debtor and is passing by to go about his own errands.[42] Vetzaruch Iyun.[43] It goes without saying that it applies if the lender intends to show up before him in order to antagonize the debtor for not paying the loan. However, after the passing of a lengthy period, when it can be assumed the debtor no longer feels remorse for his lack of payment, one may certainly pass by if one has no intent to antagonize him for the loan.[44]]

A convert:[45] One who pressures a convert to repay a loan, despite knowing that the convert does not have the means to pay it, transgresses three negative commands; 1) Do not pressure them, 2) Do not pressure a convert, 3) Do not be a debt collector. One is therefore required to be very careful in this matter.

A gentile: Some Poskim[46] rule it is a positive command to confront and apply means of pressure onto a gentile debtor [even if one knows that he does not currently have the means of how to pay].[47]

---

[35] Admur Halvah 13; Michaber 97:15; Kesef Kedoshim 97:2

The reason: (As the Torah only prohibited pressuring the debtor to pay when he does not have any means at all to pay.) [Admur ibid in parentheses; See Imrei Yaakov Biurim "Kdei"; Pischeiy Choshen 2:18]

How much pressure may one place on him: In a case that the debtor has assets to collect from, the debtor may even be hit until he agrees to pay back the loan, and doing so does not incorporate the prohibition of "Do not be like a Noshe". [Admur ibid; Michaber ibid; Kesubos 86a; See Michaber ibid that he may be hit until he dies! Now, although the above case is discussing the Shliach Beis Din and not the lender, and hence a lender may never enter the debtors house to collect a loan [Admur ibid], nevertheless, no distinction is made regarding hitting him. Vetzaruch Iyun.

[36] See Admur 5 for the list assets that the Sages allowed the debtor to keep for himself, and that he must even sell his house, Sefarim and Shabbos clothing of his children in order to pay the debt. Thus, in most cases today, people own enough assets to be able to sell and pay the loan.

[37] Admur Halvah 5; Michaber 97:15; However, see Beir Moshe 8:27 who says that while one may not pressure him to borrow, one may pressure him to go to work, Vetzaruch Iyun Gadol as it contradicts the above ruling

[38] Kesef Kedoshim 97:2

[39] Admur Halva 3; Michaber ibid; Baba Metzia 75b

Is this a Biblical or Rabbinical prohibition: From Admur ibid it is implied that doing so is included in the Biblical command. However, see Kesef Kedoshim 97:2 that possibly doing so is only a Rabbinical injunction based on this command. see Beir Moshe 8:26-27 where this matter is discussed in length

[40] The reason: As the debtor becomes ashamed when he sees the lender and he does not have the means to pay him. On this, the Torah hinted in the verse "Do not be like a debt collector", even though he is not actively pressuring to collect the loan. [Admur ibid; Michaber ibid]

[41] Aruch Hashulchan 97:2; See Beir Moshe 8:26-27 where this matter is discussed in length; Perhaps this is the entire novelty of Admur who wrote "and even to walk pass him"; Vetzaruch Iyun Gadol, as explained next

[42] As nevertheless, this causes the debtor to be ashamed, and causes him to be pressed about the loan, and hence the lender is like a debt collector, even though he has no intent to collect or pressure him.

[43] Tzaruch Iyun Gadol on the ruling of the Aruch Hashulchan, and possible implication of Admur, as accordingly, would it be forbidden to go to the same Shul as the debtor or go to a function that one knows the debtor is found by? Likewise, if one is in a store and sees the debtor there, must he leave the store? How far must one go to avoid causing another Jew pain if doing so infringes on his own lifestyle and he has no intent to harm the Jew? In my opinion one must say the entire prohibition is to intentionally appear before him with intents of pressuring him, and so is implied from the word "Leharoso" which implies an aggressive appearance. Perhaps, however, one can say that while one is not required to avoid going to Shul or to a function that he is in, nevertheless, if he sees him he may not pass or sit in front of him, and is to go through a different route. Hence, it prevents his debtor from the shame and does not infringe on his ability to do errands. Vetzaruch Iyun! See Beir Moshe 8:26-27 where this matter is discussed in length and he brings two different ways of explaining this Gemara, one like we said above and one like the Aruch Hashulchan ibid

[44] Aruch Hashulchan ibid

[45] Admur Onah 31

[46] Opinion in Admur Halva 2; Rambam Halvah 1:2; Sifri Devarim 15:3

[47] The reason: As the verse states "And the gentile you shall confront to pay", this is a positive command and not a mere voluntary suggestion. [Admur ibid]

Summary:

It is forbidden for a lender to pressure, or confront, a debtor to pay back the loan, in the event that one knows he does not have the means to pay, neither in cash nor assets [including belongings or land]. It is even forbidden for a lender to make an appearance to his debtor at a time that he knows the debtor does not have the means to pay him. It is even forbidden to walk pass him. [Some Poskim learn that this applies even if the lender has no intent to pressure the debtor, and is passing by to go about his own errands.] It is a positive command to confront and apply means of pressure onto a gentile debtor [even if one knows that he does not currently have the means of how to pay].

Q&A

Can one assume that a regular borrower has the means to pay back the loan even if he does not know for certain?[48]

Yes. Majority of people have the means and assets to pay off a debt, and hence one can assume that he has the ability to do so, even though one has not verified this. If, however, there is reason to suspect that perhaps the person does not have the means or assets to pay, then see next for a dispute in this matter. If, however, the person is a known pauper and a known G-d fearing Jew who would pay if he had the ability to do so, then according to all, it is forbidden to pressure him even though one does not have exact information as to his status.[49]

If one has reason to question whether the debtor has ability to pay back the loan, but does not know for certain, may he pressure the debtor to pay back?

Some Poskim[50] rule that if one is not certain that the debtor does not have the means to pay, even though it not certain that he has the means to pay, then the lender may pressure him to pay.[51] Furthermore, it is even encouraged for one to pressure him to pay and bring him to court so he fulfill his Mitzvah of paying back the loan.[52] Other Poskim[53], however, rule it is forbidden to pressure him to pay in a case of doubt of whether he has the means to pay, as Safek Deoraiysa Lechumra.

---

5. Pressuring an employer to pay one's salary, and pressuring a renter to pay rent:

Some Poskim[54] rule that the above prohibition against pressuring a person who owes one money, at a time that he does not have the ability to pay, only applies if the person borrowed the money. However, if one is owed money for other reasons that are not under the circumstances of a loan, then one may pressure them to pay him, even if the debtor currently does not have the means to pay. [The pressure will force the debtor to either borrow money to pay what he owes, or get a job.[55]] This allowance would include any of the following cases:

- One worked as an employee and his employer owes him a salary.
- Someone stole money from him, and he needs to pay him back.

---

[48] Kesef Kedoshim 97:2; Implication of Admur Halva 2 who says "Knows does not have the means to pay" thus implying that if one does not know this information, then there is no prohibition to pressure him, even though he also does not know for sure that he has the ability to pay; See also Michaber 99:4 and Smeh 99:13 who imply most people are able to pay, and can be pressured based on this assumption, and only one who is Muchzak to be a pauper does not have this Chazaka

[49] Michaber ibid

[50] Kesef Kedoshim 97:2; See also Michaber 99:4 and Smeh 99:13 who implies most people are able to pay and only one who is Muchzak to be a pauper does not have this Chazaka

[51] The reason: We do not apply the rule of Safek Deoraiysa Lechumra in such a case as the Torah explicitly states the prohibition only applies against an Ani Beamecha, which means that he is considered by all to be a pauper. [ibid]

[52] Kesef Kedoshim 97:2

[53] Pela Yoeitz

[54] Kesef Kedoshim 97:2 "A debt that is due to rent and the like, and not due to a loan, is not under the above prohibition" See Admur Halva 14 that regarding entering the home to take a Mashkon, that by a debt that is not due to a loan, it is permitted to do so. See Sefer Chevel Nachalaso 9:49 for a discussion on this matter, and that Rav Chaim Kanievsky is of the opinion that one does transgress the Biblical prohibition even by a debtor of a salary or rent.

[55] See Admur Halvah 5; Michaber 97:15

- One is owed money for rent of a property or item.

Nevertheless, even in the above cases of debt, it is proper not to pressure the person to pay if one knows he does not have the ability to do so.[56]

Zakfan Alav Bemilveh-The law if the debt became the status of a loan:[57] The above alowance to pressure the debtor only applies if the debt did not become the status of a loan. If, however, the debt was reinsured into a loan [i.e. Zakfan Alav Bemilveh] then from the letter of the law it follows the same laws as all debts due to loans, and it becomes forbidden for one to pressure him to pay if he truly has no means to do so, as stated above in Halacha 4. [Practically, as soon as the final due date arrives, and the employer or renter has still not paid his obligations, the owed money's become a debt.[58] Some say, however, that it becomes a debt as soon as one makes a calculation of the total amount he is owed.[59]]

6. May one forgive a loan without telling the borrower?

A. Introduction:

If one loaned someone money and has yet to be paid back, often the lender who sympathizes with the borrower's predicament, desires to simply forgive him the loan. The question however is raised whether the borrower must be made aware that his loan has been forgiven and he thus no longer needs to repay it. This touches on two Halachic aspects: 1) Since a borrower is required to repay a loan, perhaps he transgresses not repaying it so long as he is not made aware that the loan has been absolved, even if in truth it has been. 2) Perhaps in order for the pardoning of the loan to be legally valid, it must be done with the knowledge of the borrower. The following is the final ruling on this subject.

B. The law:

It is proper for one who forgives a loan to tell the borrower that the loan is forgiven, in order to prevent him from transgressing any sin.[60] Furthermore, some Poskim[61] rule that forgiving a loan is only legally binding if done with the knowledge of the borrower.

7. A person borrowed money as a child-Must he pay it back?[62]

If a child borrowed money for purposes of food or business, he is obligated to pay back the lender when he is older. [If, however, he was below six years of age, he is not liable.[63] However, some Poskim[64] rule that if he borrowed the money for food purposes, he is obligated to pay the debt even if he is below age six.]

---

[56] Kesef Kedoshim ibid

[57] See Admur Halva 14; Rambam Malveh 3:13; Braisa Bava Metzia 115a; Sifri 142

[58] Admur Halva 39; Rama 67:17; Aruch Hashulchan 67:8

[59] Admur ibid

[60] Pela Yoeitz Halvah p. 50a *"It does not suffice to forgive him the heart, as nevertheless the borrower is doing a sin, being that he is unaware that the loan was forgiven. Rather he must tell him not to worry that he can't pay back the loan, and I forgive it."*

The reason: As a borrower who does not pay back a loan, transgresses a prohibition, as brought in Admur Halva 4; Michaber C. M. 97:3. Now, the Mishneh in Nazir 23a [brought in Rashi Matos 30:6] states that if a wife made a vow and her husband abolished it without her knowledge, and she transgresses the vow, then she needs atonement ["Vahashem Yislach Lah"]. From here we learn that when one thinks he is doing a sin in his mind it is considered that he has transgressed even if in truth he did not transgress. Thus, if one intended to eat Treif and ate Kosher, he needs atonement. [Rebbe Akiva in Nazir ibid; See Minchas Shlomo 35 regarding Yichud] The same applies in Mitzvos of Bein Adam Lechaveiro, such as if a father is Mochel on his Kavod but does not tell his son, the son still needs atonement if he does not respect him. [Tosafos Kiddushin 32a; Ritva Kiddushin ibid; Chofetz Chaim Lashon Hara 4 regarding saying Lashon Hara Letoeles; However, see Sefer Chassidim 152 who allows a father to be Mochel without telling the son; See Or Hachaim Vayigash] This is aside for the fact that there are Poskim who rule a loan is not forgiven unless it is done in front of the borrower.

[61] See Erech Hashulchan Choshen Mishpat 12:5; Divrei Hageonim 57:1; Pischeiy Teshuvah C.M. 241:1 in name of Beis Meir E.H. 35; However, see Yabia Omer 3:2-5

[62] Michaber C.M. 235:15 and 96:3 [regarding business obligations of child]; Smeh 235:43

[63] Michaber 96:3 regarding business; Shach 235:7 that the same applies in 235:15 regarding loans

[64] Smeh 235:43; Nesivos Hamishpat 235:29; See Teshuvas Rebbe Akiva Eiger 147 [brought in Pischeiy Teshuvah 235:9]

-----------------Neighbors----------------
8. Entering another person's property without permission:
A. The prohibition:
It is forbidden to enter a person's property without their permission.[65] This applies whether the property is owned by a Jew or a gentile.[66] This applies even if the person is not currently living in that property.[67] This applies even if one is entering only momentarily, and will not cause any monetary loss to the property, such as to use it as a shortcut to pass to the other side, or to protect himself from the sun or the rain, and the like.[68] [It goes without saying that one may not make use of facilities within another's property without their permission, such as to use their swimming pool and the like. This applies whether to private property, such as a home, or to property of a business, which is owned by the business owners.[69] Accordingly, it is forbidden for non-guests to make use of hotel facilities, under the guise of a guest, such as to use the gym, swimming pool, partake in meals, and make use of any other amenity that is restricted only to guests. Likewise, it is forbidden to make use of a Mikveh without paying the due fee. It is forbidden to enter a bus or subway without paying the fare, and so on and so forth of all cases of the like.]

B. May one enter another person's property to retrieve an item that fell inside, such as a ball?
It is forbidden to enter another person's property to retrieve a lost object, such as a ball, without their permission, if the property is fenced or gated, or one knows that trespassing is forbidden.[70] If the property

---

[65] There are several sources which back this prohibition: **1)** So rule regarding a stolen home and seemingly the same would apply to using someone's property without their permission: Admur Hilchos Gezeila 11 "It is forbidden to enter the home for shade from the sun, or protection from the rain, or to pass through the field"; Michaber C.M. 369:2; Rambam Gezeila 5:3; **2)** So rule regarding the rule of Zeh Nehneh Vizeh Lo Chaser that we never force another to let someone else in their property: Rama 363:6 **3)** So rule regarding stealing with intent to return: Admur Gzeila Ugineiva 3; Michaber C.M. 348:1; Rambam Hilchos Gneiva 1:2; Learned from Braisa Bava Metzia 61b "Liminkat" regarding stealing in order to pay Keifel [See Kuntrus Achron ibid 1] **4)** By a private home or area, this is also forbidden due to Hezek Reiya: Admur Nizkei Mamon 11-13; Rama 154:3; Michaber 357:1 "Hezek Reiyah"; Tur 157; Rosh Baba Basra 1; Baba Basra 2b;
The reason: Entering another's property without permission is prohibited due to stealing, and if it is a private area, such as a private home, it is also forbidden due to Hezek Reiya. Vetzaruch Iyun in a case that Hezek Reiyah is not relevant if the prohibition is a Biblical transgression against stealing or not.
Other opinions: Some Poskim rule it is only forbidden to steal with intent to keep the item, however to steal temporarily is permitted, and so is done on a daily occurrence. [second Pirush, and conclusion, in Shita Mekubetzes on Bava Metzia 61b, brought in Pischeiy Teshuvah 348:2 and Ketzos Hachoshen 348:1; See Smeh ibid who seems to learn in Michaber that stealing for pain is to keep the item; Pischeiy Teshuvah 348:2 and Ketzos Hachoshen 348:1 conclude it is proper to be stringent] Seemingly, according to this opinion, the same would apply to entering someone's property without intent to steal. However, in truth, there are other prohibitions involved here, such as Hezek Reiya, and using facilities that are meant for payment, which certainly would apply even if one only enters temporarily.
[66] Admur Hilchos Gezeila 1 and 4
[67] Pashut, due to the stealing prohibition. See Admur Hilchos Gezeila 11
[68] Admur Hilchos Gezeila 11 regarding a stolen home "It is forbidden to enter the home for shade from the sun, or protection from the rain, or to pass through the field";
[69] Making use of facilities which are intended to be used by paying customers is considered stealing: See Michaber C.M. 363:6 regarding one who stays in a hotel without paying
[70] The prohibition to enter another's property: There are several sources which back this prohibition: **1)** So rule regarding a stolen home and seemingly the same would apply to using someone's property without their permission: Admur Hilchos Gezeila 11 "It is forbidden to enter the home for shade from the sun, or protection from the rain, or to pass through the field"; Michaber C.M. 369:2; Rambam Gezeila 5:3; **2)** So rule regarding the rule of Zeh Nehneh Vizeh Lo Chaser that we never force another to let someone else in their property: Rama 363:6 **3)** So rule regarding stealing with intent to return: Admur Gzeila Ugineiva 3; Michaber C.M. 348:1; Rambam Hilchos Gneiva 1:2; Learned from Braisa Bava Metzia 61b "Liminkat" regarding stealing in order to pay Keifel [See Kuntrus Achron ibid 1] **4)** By a private home or area, this is also forbidden due to Hezek Reiya: Admur Nizkei Mamon 11-13; Rama 154:3; Michaber 357:1 "Hezek Reiyah"; Tur 157; Rosh Baba Basra 1; Bava Basra 2b
The prohibition to enter another's property to retrieve an item: Entering another's property in order to retrieve an item falls under the law of "Adam Oseh Din Latzmo-Taking justice into his own hands", which is permitted to be done, since one is taking back an item that he knows belongs to him. [Admur Hilchos Gezeila Ugeneiva 28; Michaber 4:1; Bava Kama 27b] However, initially we rule that one may not enter the other persons property to retrieve the item, as it appears that he is stealing from him. [Admur Hilchos Gezeila Ugeneiva 28; Ben Bag Bag Bava Kama 27b] Furthermore, in this case one can say that it does not just look like one is stealing, but one is actually stealing, as the property owner did not have negligence involved in the fact the person's item fell on his property. Thus, it makes no sense to say that his property and privacy can be invaded without his permission for someone to retrieve an item, when he has done nothing wrong, and on the contrary, it's the negligence of the owner of the item, who allowed it to fall in his yard. Accordingly, while I have not found any direct source in Poskim for this case, it seems it would be considered actual stealing to enter the property without permission, and so is Lehavdil the state law.
The reason: Entering another's property without permission is prohibited due to stealing and if it is a private area, such as a private home, it is also forbidden due to Hezek Reiya. Vetzaruch Iyun if the prohibition is a Biblical transgression against stealing or not.
Other opinions: Some Poskim rule it is only forbidden to steal with intent to keep the item, however to steal temporarily is permitted, and so is done on a daily occurrence. [second Pirush, and conclusion, in Shita Mekubetzes on Gemara ibid, brought in Pischeiy Teshuvah 348:2 and

is open, such as the front lawn or the driveway in front of a home, it is permitted to do so.[71] Nonetheless, in all cases, the property owner is obligated to return the lost object to its rightful owner, and withholding it transgresses the command of Hashavas Aveida and Biblically transgresses the prohibition against stealing.[72] [This applies even according to state law, in many countries. It is illegal to withhold someone else's object, including a lost item that was found, and one who does so can be charged with larceny, or theft by conversion. This applies even if one is annoyed at how often the ball of his neighbor falls into his yard, nonetheless, according to Halacha and the law of the land, he must return it, and can face legal penalties if he does not do so.]

What is one to do if the owner cannot be found, or does not want to return the object?[73] In all cases that one is unable to receive the item back from the owner of the property [such as if the owner is out of town[74], or refuses to return it[75]], he is allowed to take matters into his own hands, and enter the property to retrieve his item.[76] [This may apply even according to state law.[77] It is advisable to first discuss the matter with an attorney.]

Business

Kosher business:[78]
A person must work for a living. However, he must make sure that his business is Kosher, following all the rules in Halacha, which include not lying, stealing, and cheating others. It is possible to achieve a good Parnasa without speaking lies and without doing untruthful matters. When one has a Kosher Parnasa, Hashem arranges that the income is used for only the basic expenses, without bringing any extra unexpected expenses to the person. This is similar to the Mun which was a heavenly bread that did not carry any Pesoles, any waste. If, however, one leads an untruthful business, cheats, and lies to others, the money will get swallowed by unnecessary and unexpected expenses, and in the end, not give anyone any gain.

Ketzos Hachoshen 348:1; See Smeh ibid who seems to learn in Michaber that stealing for pain is to keep the item; Pischeiy Teshuvah 348:2 and Ketzos Hachoshen 348:1 conclude it is proper to be stringent] Seemingly, according to this opinion, the same would apply to entering someone's property without intent to steal. However, in truth, there are other prohibitions involved here, such as Hezek Reiyah, which certainly would apply even if one only enters temporarily.

[71] The reason: As in such a case, the owner does not mind people walking on or through the area, such as when a person comes to knock on the door, and it thus not viewed as trespassing at all, to enter this area. Certainly then, one may retrieve an item from the front lawn or driveway without asking permission of the owner.

[72] Admur Hilchos Metzia Upikadon 1 and Michaber C.M. 259:1, and Rava Bava Metzia 26b that one who does not return a lost object transgresses the negative command of "Lo Sialeim" and also the negative command Lo Sigzol"; and nullifies the positive command of "Hashavas Aveida"

[73] Admur Hilchos Gezeila Ugeneiva 28; Bava Kama 27b and Tosafos there that even according to Ben Bag Bag, if there is a loss one may enter the property

[74] In such a case, the allowance to enter the property is not exactly clear from Admur ibid, as in that case it discusses a landowner who stole the person's item, and hence one can say that he forfeits his right against trespass if I come to retrieve my item. However, here, that the owner does not even know the item is in his property, perhaps the owner of the item would need to wait to get permission to enter, as the landowner did nothing wrong of his own. However, in truth, this is incorrect, as the entire idea of Adam Oseh Din Leatzmo is that he takes the place of a judge and Beis Din [See Sheim Derech Bava Kama 58], and a Beis Din has ability to retrieve an item from another, even if the other person does not know of it. Vetzaruch Iyun

[75] In such a case [i.e. withholding a lost item], the landlord is considered to be stealing [Admur Hilchos Metzia Upikadon 1] and is the exact case mentioned in Admur Hilchos Gezeila Ugeneiva 28 which permits one to enter the property to take his item if he cannot retrieve it otherwise.

[76] The reason: As this is a typical case of "Adam Oseh Din Leatzmo"

[77] See the following articles regarding State law: http:::www.dummies.com:education:law:property-rights-what-constitutes-a-trespass: ; https:::www.hg.org:article.asp?id=37066;https:::www.avvo.com:legal-answers:my-personal-property-is-on-someones-property-and-t-686190.html ; https:::en.wikipedia.org:wiki:Repossession; I was advised by a lawyer in Israel who specializes in Israeli property laws, that if one exhausted all options of retrieving his item, such as he knocked on the door went to neighbors, tried to call the property owner, and was still able to reach him, then he may enter the yard to retrieve an item that accidently fell inside. It is however a good idea to take a video of one's attempts to reach the owner, in order to defend himself from any legal suits that he may face for trespassing.

[78] Sefer Hasichos Toras Shalom p. 8

----------------*Business*----------------
9. How to legally validate a fine within a business transaction:[79]

A. The Ribis prohibition:[80]

It is permitted for one to legally obligate a buyer, employer, or renter at the time of the transaction, that if payments are not made on time, then a set fee will need to be paid in addition to the money's owed. However, this is only permitted if the total sum of the fee takes effect in one moment, immediately upon the passing of the due date for the payment of the owed money, and the fee hence does not grow together with the amount of time that the payment is delayed. However, to make the fine grow together with the delay of payment is Biblically forbidden due to Ribis. Likewise, every G-d fearing Jew is not to arrange with the debtor that so long as he pays the fine then the original payment may be delayed, and rather the original payment is to be paid by the due date irrelevant of whether he becomes liable to pay the fine or not. The above applies to all business transaction, with exception to a borrower. It is Rabbinically forbidden for one to stipulate with **a borrower** that if payments are not made on time then a set fee will need to be paid in addition to the money owed. This applies even if the fine will not grow together with the time of delay of payment.

B. How to legalize the fine:

In order for a fine to be legally valid in the parameters of Halacha, the person being fined must make a Kinyan Sudar at the time of the transaction, which solidifies that if he delays payment, then he agrees retroactively from now[81] to be liable to pay the agreed price, plus the fine, for the product or service he received. It does not suffice to make a mere documented agreement, and rather a Kinyan Sudar must be performed, as will be explained. (However, some Poskim[82] rule that a fine does not hold legal weight, even if it was solidified with a Kinyan Sudar, unless it was performed in the presence of a prestigious Beis Din.[83] Alternatively, he is to sign a contract which states that the fine was acquired through a prestigious Beis Din, in which case it suffices even if in truth there was no prestigious Beis Din there at all, so long as a Kinyan Sudar was performed by him in actuality. Practically, the main opinion follows this ruling.[84] One must warn the public who make a mistake in this matter and do not make a Kinyan Sudar at all, and illegally collect a fine based on a mere contract.)

Summary:
In order for a fine to legally be validated in the parameters of Halacha, the person being fined must make a Kinyan Sudar in the presence of a prestigious Beis Din, at the time of the transaction, solidifying that in the event that he delays payment he agrees to retroactively be liable to pay the agreed price, plus the fine, for the product or service he received. Alternatively, he is to perform a Kinyan Sudar, and sign a contract which states that the fine was acquired through a prestigious Beis Din.

---

[79] Admur Ribis 46; Michaber C.M. 207 that by an Asmachta a Kinyan must be made and "from now" must be said; Smeh 207:39 that a Stam Kinyan is Kinyan Sudar; Tosafos Baba Metzia 66a; See "Topics in practical Halacha" Vol. 1 Yoreh Deah Halacha 12

[80] See "Topics in practical Halacha" Vol. 1 Yoreh Deah Halacha 12 for the full discussion on this topic

[81] Meaning that he obligates himself to already be liable to pay from now the money of the fine. However, to agree that the fine will only take effect later on, is invalid, as a) It is considered a mere Asmachta [Michaber ibid] and because a Kinyan Sudar cannot take effect later on being the Sudar was already returned to the owner. [Smeh ibid; Tosafos ibid]

[82] Tosafos Baba Metzia 66a; Rosh 29

[83] The reason: As any fine is considered an Asmachta, even if acquired with a Kinyan Sudar. [ibid]

[84] Rama Choshen Mishpat 207:14

10. Mekach Taus-The Torah's Return policy on spoiled food products:

The Torah law: [The following law applies in all jurisdictions which do not contain consumer laws legislated on this issue:] One who purchased a food product and discovered that it was spoiled at the time of purchase, is entitled to receive a full cash refund for the product from the seller.[85] [According to Ashkenazim] this applies even if the seller is a merchant who himself purchased the product from the manufacturer, nevertheless, he is liable to personally refund the purchase from the buyer.[86] [Thus, the seller cannot tell the buyer to speak to the company manufacturer for a return. However, according to Sephardim, the seller has the right to refuse the refund, and send him to the original seller for his refund claim.[87]] This applies even if the store has a no return policy on foods, fruits or vegetables, and the buyer was made aware of this at the time of purchase.[88] This, however, only applies if the food was already spoiled at the time of purchase.[89] In a case where one is unsure, the burden of proof is on the one asking for the payment, which in a regular situation, is the consumer.[90] [In all cases that the seller is liable to accept a return, he must refund the buyer with money, and not with store credit, unless the seller does not have any money to give.[91]]

The State law:[92] The above Halacha is only in effect in an area that does not contain any consumer laws regarding the issue of returns on spoiled food products. If, however, the State in which the purchase took place, contains consumer laws and policies which are accepted upon that area, then the laws of returning a product follow all those laws and regulations for all purposes, unless explicitly stated otherwise by the buyer to the seller at the time of purchase. [Thus, if a certain State has a policy of no returns on food products, even if found to be spoiled from the time of purchase, then this policy overrides the Halacha, and the seller does not have to reimburse the buyer. Likewise, if the State law permits the seller to reimburse the buyer with store credit, then he may choose to do so.]

The store policy: As stated above, a store return policy that is not legally protected by State law, is not binding on the consumer, and he reserves the right to return a food product that was spoiled from the time of purchase and receive reimbursement.

Summary:

In all areas absent of consumer law and regulations regarding the return of spoiled food products, the buyer has the Halachic right to demand a cash refund for his food product, from the store, if it was spoiled at the time of purchase. If the buyer already paid for the product, the burden of proof regarding when the spoilage occurred falls on him. The personal policy of the store does not carry any legal Halachic weight in this regard. In jurisdictions with consumer policy laws regarding return of food products, all the laws are Halachically binding on the buyer and seller.

---

[85] Michaber C.M. 232:3 regarding general law; 230:7 regarding spoiled beer; 232:16 regarding spoiled cheese; 232:19 regarding bloody eggs

If only some of the item was spoiled: The above law only applies if the item is sold individually, such as one purchased a watermelon, and it was spoiled, or one purchased milk, and one of the cartons were spoiled. If, however, one purchased a bag of fruits, vegetables, and the like, and some of them were spoiled, then this matter is dependent on several factors, as explained in Michaber and Rama C.M. 229:1-2.

[86] Rama C.M. 232:18; Tur in name of Rosh; Aruch Hashulchan 232:30

Other opinions: Some Poskim rule the merchant may send the buyer to the original manufacturer for a refund. [Michaber 232:18] According to this ruling, all food chain stores may tell the buyer to speak to the food company for a return.

[87] See other opinions in previous footnote

[88] Michaber C.M. 232:7; Aruch Hashulchan 232:11

[89] See Michaber C.M. 232:11; Aruch Hashulchan 232:17

[90] Michaber ibid; Aruch Hashulchan ibid

[91] Aruch Hashulchan C.M. 232:37

[92] Michaber C.M. 232:6 that we follow the Minhag Hamedina regarding the definition of a Mum, and Michaber 232:19 that the Minhag is not to accept returns on eggs, and Minhag Mivatel Halacha! See Aruch Hashulchan 232:7 and 30

-----------------Hashavas Aveida----------------

11. What is one to do with a lost object that was found, and the owner cannot be located?[93]

The general law: Any item that must be returned to its owner [as explained in the laws of Hashavas Aveida], and the owner cannot be traced, is required to be held until the arrival of Eliyahu Hanavi, who will then reveal its rightful owner.[94] It is forbidden to make any use of the object, or sell it, until the owner is found.[95] Practically, many of the objects that we find [even without Simanim/signs] in Jewish majority areas[96], must be returned to its rightful owner, and fall under the above requirement, due to lack of knowledge if the owner gave up hope of retrieving the item, or had knowledge of its loss, prior to one finding it.[97] This raises the major question of what one is to do with all the lost objects that he finds, and why do we not see a closet of lost objects being kept in one's home, and eventually inherited from father to son? The following options are recorded in Poskim:

The options recorded in Poskim: Some[98] record that in truth one must store the lost object, and guard it for the rest of his life. Others[99] suggest that once one can assume that the rightful owner has passed away, he may then use the object for himself. Other Poskim[100] rule that after all required methods, and reasonable timeframe for finding the owner, have been exhausted, one may keep the object and do with it as he pleases. This applies both to items with and without Simanim [signs of ownership]. However, prior to making use of the item, he must record the value of the item, and any possible Simanim, in a file. Eventually, if the owner ever shows up, or when Eliyahu reveals the rightful owner, the finder will need to reimburse the owner with payment for the object, based on the assessment of worth that he wrote in his file.[101] Some Poskim[102] however limit this allowance only to objects that do not contain sentimental value and significance, and can be commonly purchased in stores. However, items that have sentimental value, or cannot be regularly purchased in stores, would in truth have to be held until the coming of Eliyahu, and cannot be used or sold. Practically, this is the common ruling followed today.[103]

---

[93] See Toras Haveida 6 p. 143

[94] Admur Hilchos Metzia Upikadon Halacha 22 [regarding all lost objects that must be returned] Halacha 2 [regarding object without Siman, which is a dispute and we are Machmir] and Halacha 3 [regarding object with Siman in which all agree] Halacha 8 and 15 [regarding if there is doubt if owner knew of its falling before it was found]; Michaber 267:15; Rambam Gezeila Veaveida 13:10; Mishneh Bava Metzia 29b

[95] Admur Hilchos Metzia Upikadon Halacha 22; Halacha 2 [regarding object without Siman, which is a dispute and we are Machmir] and Halacha 3 [regarding object with Siman in which all agree]; Rama 260:10

[96] See Admur ibid Halacha 17; Michaber 259:3

[97] See Admur Hilchos Metzia Upikadon Halacha 2 [regarding object without Siman, which is a dispute and we are Machmir] and Halacha 3 [regarding object with Siman in which all agree] Halacha 8 and 15 [regarding if there is doubt if owner knew of its falling before it was found]; Raavad and Tur, brought in Shach 260:26; Shach 260:26 [regarding if has Simanim] and 267:13

[98] Clear implication of Admur ibid; See Toras Haveida 6 p. 143

[99] Pischei Choshen 7 footnote 10 based on Nesivos Hamishpat 256 and Chasam Sofer C.M. 122

[100] Igros Moshe Choshen Mishpat 2:45

[101] The reason: The Igros Moshe ibid does not mention any reason behind this allowance. Vetzaruch Iyun.

[102] Toras Haveida ibid; Opinion of Rav Elyashiv; Based on Michaber 267:21 who omitted the wording of the Rambam, as brought in Smeh 267:30 [However Smeh ibid argues; See Chochmas Shlomo 267 ibid]

[103] Toras Haveida ibid

Summary:
All found objects that are required to be returned to their rightful owner, from the letter of the law must be stored until the coming of Eliyahu. However, the common practice is to rule that it may be kept and used by the finder if the following conditions are fulfilled:
1. The owner cannot be located,
2. The item is commonly available for purchase and is not of sentimental value.
3. One records the value and Simanim of the object in a file.

Example of items that one may keep/use/sell/discard [and mark their value in a file] if cannot find the owner:
- Common pen or pencil.
- Clothing
- Sefarim that are commonly available for purchase
- Phone [although the information is to be backed up and not erased]
- SD card [although the information is to be backed up and not erased]

12. Preventing monetary damage from occurring to a friend:[104]

If one is able to prevent his friend from incurring a possible monetary loss, he is obligated to exert as much effort possible, with all his bodily strength, to try to prevent the loss.[105] Doing so is a positive command, and is included in the Mitzvah of Hashavas Aveida.[106]

Example-Prevent flooding:[107] One who sees [a stream of] water threatening to flood the field of his friend, or to destroy his home/building, is obligated to build a fence in front of the water [to block it] on their behalf [if the friend is not around and is thus unable to do anything to prevent the damage].

Must one spend money to prevent the loss?[108] One is not obligated to spend money in order to help prevent monetary loss from his friend's property, unless he is certain that his friend will reimburse him for his expenses.

Must one help save his friends property if he is in middle of work:[109] If one is in middle of work and stopping to help save his friends property will cause him financial loss, or to lose a profit in business, then he is not obligated to do so.[110] Nevertheless, a person is to go beyond the letter of the law and not be so particular and say that my loss comes first. If one is always particular to precede his own potential loss, then he removes upon himself the yoke of Gemilus Chassadim, and in the end, will become in need of the public [for charity]. Nevertheless, if one has a certain and clear loss that will come as a result of saving the other's property, his loss comes first.[111]

A Mumar:[112] One is required to save one's friend's property, or item, from damage, even if one's friend is a Mumar Leteiavon, and a Baal Aveiros.[113] If, however, the Jew is an idol worshiper, or desecrates Shabbos in public, or is an Apikores who does not believe in the Torah and prophecy, then it is forbidden

---

[104] Admur Hilchos Metzia 33
[105] Admur Hilchos Metzia 33; Nizkei Mamon 5; Smeh 259:21; Bava Metzia 31a
The reason: As the verse states "Lechol Aveidas Achicha", this is coming to include a loss of land and any matter of the like. [Admur ibid; Smeh 259:21; Baba Metzia 31a]
[106] Admur Nizkei Mamaon 5
[107] Admur ibid; Michaber 259:9; Bava Metzia 31a
[108] Admur Hilchos Metzia 33; Nizkei Guf Vinefesh 8; See Michaber and Rama 265:1; Smeh 264:18 and 426:1; Sanhedrin 73a
[109] Admur Hilchos Metzia 33-34
[110] Admur Hilchos Metzia 33; Michaber and Rama 265:1; Smeh 264:18 and 426:1; Sanhedrin 73a
The reason: As one is not obligated to spend money on behalf of saving his friends property unless he knows his friend will reimburse him, and perhaps in this case his friend will not reimburse him for his lost income. [Admur ibid]
[111] Admur Hilchos Metzia 34; Michaber 264:1; Baba Metzia 33a
[112] Admur Hilchos Metzia 39; Nizkei Guf Vinefesh 8; Avoda Zara 26b
[113] The reason: As the verse states "Lechol Aveidas Achicha" and the Sages expounded that this is coming to include the items of a Mumar Liteiavon. [Admur ibid]

to help save his item.[114] [Seemingly, however, a Tinok Shenishba should be treated under the first category.[115]]

A gentile:[116] One is not required to help prevent damage from occurring to the property of a gentile, unless there will be a Chilul Hashem involved in not doing so.

Summary:

If one is able to prevent his friend from incurring a possible monetary loss, he is obligated to exert as much effort possible, with all his bodily strength, to try to prevent the loss. He however is not obligated to spend money to help prevent the monetary loss, unless he is certain that his friend will reimburse him for his expenses. One is not required to help prevent damage from occurring to the property of a gentile or a Mumar Lehachis and Apikores.

Q&A

If one saw a person shoplifting in a Jewish owned store, must he inform the owners?

Yes, as stated above! This applies even if the shoplifter is a Jew and is of young age and may be arrested for his actions.

-----------------*Yerusha*----------------

13. The double portion that a Bechor receives in inheritance:

Important note: All wills are to be written under the supervision of a lawyer, as well as an individual who is expert in this area of Jewish law, to ensure its legality. The following is background information about the inheritance of a Bechor according to Jewish law.

A. How much does a Bechor inherit?[117]

A firstborn son, who is Halachically defined as a Bechor[118], inherits a double share from amongst certain[119] assets of his father.[120] For example, if a father passed away leaving five sons, and one is a Halachically valid firstborn, the firstborn receives 1/3 [33%] of the assets, while each of the other four brothers receives a 1/6 [17%] of the assets. If the father left nine sons, the firstborn brother takes a 1/5 [20%] of the assets while each of the eight remaining sons takes a 1/10 [10%] of the assets. This method of distribution is to be followed in all cases.[121] [Accordingly, one splits the assets by one more than the current number of children, and the Halachic firstborn receives two of those portions. For example, if there are 5 children, one splits the assets into six portions, and the first born takes two out of the six portions.[122] So if the father left $100,000 of tangible assets for the five sons, the eldest son receives $33,000, while each of the 4 sons receive close to $16,500.]

Mother's assets:[123] A first born son only inherits a double portion from the assets of his father, and not from the assets of his mother.[124] This applies even if he is the firstborn son of his father and mother, nonetheless, he receives an equal portion from his mother's assets, just as all the other brothers.

---

[114] Admur Hilchos Metzia 39; Avoda Zara 26b

[115] However, Rav Yaakov Yosef z"l would rule in such a case that there is absolutely no obligation to help save his items from damage, as just like he would not save your item so too you not obligated to save his. Vetzaruch Iyun

[116] Admur Hilchos Metzia 38 regarding returning a lost object

[117] Michaber C.M. 277:1; Rambam Nechalos 2:1; Bava Basra 122b

[118] See 277 regarding who is defined as a Bechor and who is excluded.

[119] See 278 that only tangible assets that are currently in the hands of the father receive a double portion inheritance. A major exception of the above would be a bank account, which is excluded from the double portion being it is not tangible assets and is viewed as owed funds.

[120] The source: This is learned from the verse in Devarim 21:17 "The eldest son, the son of the hated wife, must be recognized to be given a double portion, as he is the firstborn and receives the judgment of the firstborn."

[121] The ruling here comes to negate an erroneous understanding of the "double portion", which interprets it to mean that the first born receives twice the amount of all the other sons put together. Rather, the first born is viewed as if he is two sons, and receives two portions, each one being equal to the single portion of each son, individually.

[122] Smeh 277:2

[123] Michaber C.M. 278:1; Bechoros 51b

B. May a father disinherit the firstborn, or give him an equal portion in the will?

A person is unable to change the laws of inheritance in the form of inheritance; to inherit to one who is not an heir, or to disinherit a rightful heir. This applies whether he is healthy or sick [Shechiv Meira], and whether he makes the change orally or puts it in writing [i.e. a will]. Thus, if a father stated that his son the firstborn will not inherit a double portion, his words are meaningless.[125] This applies whether he said that his firstborn son will inherit like a normal son, or he said the firstborn will not take or inherit a double portion, in all these cases, his words are meaningless.[126] [Likewise, if he said that the other sons will inherit a certain amount, which infringes on the double portion of the firstborn son, his words are meaningless.[127]] Even in an area where the custom is that the firstborn does not receive a double portion, one is to ignore the custom, as it contradicts the Biblical law.[128]

Legal ways of bypassing inheriting a double portion to the firstborn: The above inability to change the inheritance law of the Bechor, only applies if one stated the above disinheritance of the Bechor's double portion in a wording of "Yerusha/inheritance," such as one said "My firstborn will not inherit a double portion." If, however, the father made his statement in a way of a Kinyan and Matana[129], then he does have ability to change the order of inheritance and he may give the firstborn an equal portion of the Matana/Kinyan, or not give him anything at all, and instead give all the assets to the other brothers as a Matana/Kinyan.[130] [Likewise, one may use the method called Shtar Chatzi Zachar, which serves as an IOU addendum to the will, to force the Bechor to get an equal portion just like the other brothers.[131] Practically, this is the common method used today by estate planning attorneys who follow the guidelines of Halacha.] Nonetheless, the Sages were unhappy with one who uses a legally valid method to uproot the inheritance from a rightful heir.[132] Some Poskim[133], however, rule that this does not apply if one uses the legal method to simply equal the portion of the firstborn to that of the other brothers, and not to uproot it entirely.

------------------*Workers*-----------------

14. Severance pay-Pitzuyim:[134]
A. The letter of the law:[135]

There is no Torah requirement to give severance pay to a worker.[136] This applies even if the worker was fired. Nevertheless, according to Halacha, the conditions of payment for labor and employees follow the customs of the area, unless explicitly stated otherwise.[137] Hence, in countries that it is universally

---

124 The reason: This is learned from the verse which states "Ki Lo Mishpat Habechora," which means that the status of a Bechor applies to [the assets of] a man and not to [the assets of] a woman. [Smeh 278:1; Bechoros ibid]

125 Michaber 281:1; Rambam Nechalos 6:3; Mishneh Bava Basar 130a

126 Michaber 281:4; Rambam Nechalos 6:3
The reason: As the verse states "Lo Yuchal Levaker Es Ben Hahuva." [Michaber ibid]

127 Beir Hagoleh 281:9 that the ruling of Michaber 281:3 refers to a case that there is no Bechor

128 Rama 281:4; Maharik Shoresh 8

129 By a Shechiv Meira, simply saying the words is considered a Kinyan Matana, while by a Bari [healthy person] an actual Kinyan must be made. [See Aruch Hashulchan 281:1 and 5]

130 Michaber 281:7 regarding Shechiva Meira; Smeh 281:6 that the same applies for a Bari; Shach 281:4; Beir Hagoleh ibid; Aruch Hashulchan 281:5

131 See Rama C.M. 281:7; Kesef Hakedoshim 282; This serves as an IOU document, which enforce the heirs to comply by the secular will, otherwise they will have to pay the enormous debt written in the IOU. Thus, for example, the father can write that if his secular will is not abided by his heirs, which include an equal portion to all sons, and does not distribute a double portion to the firstborn, then all the sons will be owed an equal enormous amount, which surpasses the worth of the inheritance, and hence it will force the first born to only receive one share.

132 Michaber 282:1; Rambam Nechalos 10:11; Bava Basra 133b; See, however, Kesef Hakedoshim 282 that this issue does not apply when the share is given in a way of a present or as a Shtar Chatzi Zachar

133 See Kesef Hakedoshim 282; Kerem Shlomo 282 in name of Halachos Ketanos 2:30

134 See Chinuch 482; Minchas Yitzchak 6:167; Tzitz Eliezer 7:48-10; Likkutei Sichos 19:153 [printed in Shulchan Menachem 7:78-82]; Hayashar Vehatov 1:30; 9:191

135 Minchas Yitzchak 6:167; Tzitz Eliezer 7:48-10; Hayashar Vehatov 1:30; 9:191

136 There is no source in Torah, Talmud or Poskim to require an employer to give severance pay. The only obligation that exists regarding severance pay is from a master to his Jewish slave who is going free. [See Devarim 15:13-14; Chinuch ibid]

137 See Michaber C.M. 331:1; Bava Metzia 83a; See also Rama C.M. 356:7 and Shach 356:10 regarding Dina Demalchusa Dina
The reason: As whenever one hires another to do work for him all the accustomed work obligations and rights are assumed to have been agreed on and obligated on by the employer, and all business conditions set by two sides are Halachically binding. [See Michaber ibid] Accordingly, it is not the secular law that creates the Halachic obligation but rather the Minhag Hamedina. [Article of Rav Shpurn in Hayashar Vehatov ibid] Alternatively, the obligation is not due to the Minhag but due to the law, as Dina Demalchusa Dina. [See Rama and Shach ibid; Minchas Yitzchak ibid]

accepted to give severance pay, the employer must do so according to Halacha, unless he explicitly stipulated otherwise upon hiring the employee. However, in those countries that severance pay is not universally accustomed, there is no obligation upon the employer to do so, unless explicitly stated otherwise upon hiring. In all countries, the Halachic obligation is commensurate to the laws and customs of that country, and hence if severance pay is only awarded in certain cases and not in others, then the Halachic ruling follows likewise. The Beis Din must thus be knowledgeable in the severance laws of the country of the employer/employee to properly settle a claim brought before them.

Eretz Yisrael:[138] Practically, in Eretz Yisrael, the universal labor practice of many years, which later became legislated into law, is to give severance pay to employees, and hence the employer is bound by this requirement according to Halacha. If he refuses to do so, the employer can be taken to Beis Din, and be forced to make the payment. All Batei Dinim in Eretz Yisrael currently recognize the obligation of Israeli employers to pay severance pay.[139] The accustomed severance pay is the last month's salary per year of employment. [If, for example, a Judaic studies teacher received 5000 Shekel for his last month salary, and he worked for 15 years and was then laid off, he is to be give 75000 Shekel upon his leave.[140]] Nevertheless, as explained above, since the requirement is based on the custom of the country, in those circumstances that the custom in Eretz Yisrael is not to give severance pay, then the employer is not obligated to do so. Practically, in Eretz Yisrael, the custom is to give severance pay if the employee is fired or quits due to a worsening of working conditions, however, not when the employee quits under other circumstances. In all cases of doubt as to the definition of "worsening of conditions," the matter is to be brought before a Beis Din to adjudicate.

United States:[141] There is no universal custom, or law, regarding severance pay in the United States, and hence a USA employer is not obligated to pay severance pay to his employee, unless explicitly stated otherwise during hiring.

Chinuch institutions and Shuls: There exists a universal custom of Chinuch institutions and Synagogues to give severance pay to Judaic studies teachers, and Rabbi's, who are fired without due cause. Accordingly, the custom has created a Halachic obligation upon all learning Mosdos and Yeshivos to pay severance pay to terminated Judaic studies employees, unless explicitly stated otherwise in their contract at the time of hiring. The accustomed severance pay is one-month salary per year, or 8.333% per year of employment. [If, for example, a Judaic studies teacher received $5000 per month salary for 15 years and was then laid off, he is to be give $75000 upon his leave.]

B. The proper practice and Midas Chassidus:[142]

Even in areas in which there is no custom to give severance pay, it is nevertheless proper according to Torah, for an employer to give severance pay as a gesture of gratitude for the work he received.[143] It is

---

[138] Minchas Yitzchak 6:167; Tzitz Eliezer 7:48-10; Hayashar Vehatov 1:30; 9:191

If employee and employer are in two different countries: See Rama C.M. 331:1 that we follow the area that the workers were hired in.

[139] The giving of severance pay was in practice by some labor unions even prior to it being instated into law, however, at that time the Batei Dinim did not all agree to the obligation of severance pay by an employer. Once the law was passed and it became the universal practice in Israel, then all the Batei Dinim now enforce it. It is worthy to note as stated before, that it is not the secular law that creates the Halachic obligation but rather the Minhag Hamedina. [Article of Rav Shpurn in Hayashar Vehatov ibid]

[140] See here for the exact calculations of severance in Israel: https://www.prisha.co.il/article

[141] Hayashar Vehatov 9:191

[142] See Chinuch Mitzvah 482; Minchas Yitzchak 6:167; Likkutei Sichos 19:153 [printed in Shulchan Menachem 7:78-82]

[143] Chinuch Mitzvah 482 "Although the law of Hanakah is only in place by an Eved Ivri and in times of the Yovel, nevertheless, even today a wise man is to take lesson and give severance pay to one who worked for him"; Minchas Yitzchak 6:167; Likkutei Sichos 19:153 [printed in Shulchan Menachem 7:78-82] "Since it is possible that this ruling of the Chinuch applies according to all opinions it is therefore proper to publicize that one should abide by it"

The reason: This is learned from the Torah's obligation upon a master to give severance pay to his Jewish worker. Now, just as the Torah desired us to show gratitude to a slave who worked for us, so too we should show gratitude to an employee. [Chinuch ibid] This Mitzvah of Hanaka is a subcategory of the Mitzvah of charity. [Shach C.M. 86:3-3; Likkutei Sichos ibid] Alternatively, the Mitzvah of Hanaka is due to payment for the work. [See Likkutei Sichos ibid]

Other opinions: Some Poskim explain that the above "proper custom" mentioned by the Chinuch is only according to those Poskim who rule that Hanaka is given to all types of Eved Ivri [so rules Rebbe Eliezer Kiddushin 14b; Tosafos Kiddushin 15b] however according to those Poskim who rule that only a slave that was sold by Beis Din needs to be given Hanaka [so rules: Tana Kama Kiddushin ibid; Rambam Avadim 3:12; Majority of Poskim, brought in Encyclopedia Talmudis Hanaka p. 678] then there is no room to learn that all workers should receive severance pay, as the Torah was not teaching us a "proper custom" by commanding this law. [Minchas Chinuch ibid] Thus, according to the Minchas

appropriate to publicize this ruling, that according to Torah employers are to give severance pay as a good will gesture, and to abide by it [even though it is not obligatory from the letter of the law].[144]

In what circumstances does this apply: The above ruling applies irrelevant of the amount of time that the employee worked by the employer, whether it be a long time or a short time.[145] It applies irrelevant of whether one was satisfied with the work of his employee or not.[146] It applies even if he was a contracted employee for a limited amount of time and his contract expired. This applies even if the employee decided not to renew his contract, and certainly if the employer decided not to renew the contract. It certainly applies if the employee was fired before the end term of the contract. It, however, does not apply when the worker quits his job early.[147] Even if the employee agreed to forgo his severance pay, nevertheless, the employer is to pay him.[148]

How much to give: The employer is to give the employee severance pay commensurate to the amount of time he worked for him.[149] It is his decision as to how much to pay him, and does not follow the rule of one month's salary per year.[150] If the employer's business became successful due to the work of the employee, it is proper to give him a larger severance pay, in accordance to the benefit the business received.[151] Money's that are rightfully owed to the employee, due to salary bonuses and the like, are not to be deducted from the severance payment, and the severance payment is to be in addition to it.[152]

Summary:
Whenever an employee leaves his job, either due to being fired, end of contract, or quitting, the employer is obligated according to Halacha to follow the law and customs of his area of employment, regarding severance payment to the employee. The obligation of payment and amount due is decided solely based on that countries labor laws and customs. Even in a country that severance pay is not required to be given, it is a proper custom according to Torah for the employer to give the employee some severance payment, in accordance to the length of his employment, and success of the business that came as a result. The only circumstance that an employee does not deserve severance pay, even from a Torah perspective, is when he quit his job before expiry of contract for no justifiable reason. In all cases of doubt, debate or argument between employer/employee, the matter is to be before a Beis Din to settle.

Q&A

If the employer claims that it was agreed prior to hiring that he would not give severance pay, who is believed?[153]
In any case that the custom of the land is to give severance pay, then the burden of proof falls on the shoulders of the employer, and hence, if it's his word against the employee's, the employee is believed. [It is precisely for this reason that all such conditions must be recorded in a contract.]

Chinuch, the above ruling of the Chinuch is not Halachically binding [as we rule like Tana Kama ibid] and there is no need to give severance pay even as a good gesture. [Likkutei Sichos 19:153 footnote 4] The Minchas Chinuch concludes with a Tzaruch Iyun, as it is not usual for the Chinuch to swerve from the opinion of the Rambam. The Rebbe, however, in Likkutei Sichos ibid explains that if one learns that the reason for the Mitzvah of Hanakah is due to charity [as learns Shach ibid] then it is possible to learn that even according to the ruling that a self-sold slave is exempt, one can still learn this case to other cases, and it's just that the Torah makes a self-sold slave an exception to the rule. [Likkutei Sichos ibid]

[144] Likkutei Sichos ibid
[145] Chinuch ibid; Likkutei Sichos ibid
[146] Likkutei Sichos ibid
[147] Likkutei Sichos ibid, as a slave who ran away is not given Hanaka. [Kiddushin 16:b] However, see Minchas Yitzchak ibid regarding a case that the employer quit due to delayed pay, and that some severance pay should be given
[148] Igros Kodesh 14:404, printed in Shulchan Menachem 7:82
[149] Likkutei Sichos ibid
[150] Minchas Yitzchak ibid
[151] Chinuch ibid; Likkutei Sichos ibid
[152] Likkutei Sichos ibid
[153] Rav Akiva Eiger C.M. 331 based on Michaber 330:5

In a case where there is doubt as to whether according to the law/custom of the land, the employer must give severance pay, what is the ruling?[154]

In all cases of question in whether the employer is obligated to give severance pay to the employee, under the circumstances of his dismissal, or quitting of the job, the case is to be brought to a Beis Din. If the Beis Din is also left in question, then the ruling follows that the employer is exempt from the payment.

Maaseh Shehaya:[155]

The Rebbetzin passed away in 1988 and her house workers were no longer needed. That same day, the Rebbe directed that the workers be told that their job is terminated, and that they be given their salary in full together with severance pay. The Rebbe assured that the workers be paid in full prior to the funeral, and that doing so would be a merit for her soul.

-----------------*Stealing*----------------

15. One who accidently switched an item with another person:[156]

> If one attended an event, or participated in a Minyan or Shiur, and at the end of the event he accidently took the wrong coat, hat, umbrella, Tallis/Tefillin, or any other item, may he use that item until he finds the rightful owner?

> If one attended an event, or participated in a Minyan or Shiur, and at the end of the event he noticed that someone accidently took his coat, hat, umbrella, Tallis/Tefillin, or any other item, may he take that person's item and use it until he finds the rightful owner and makes the switch with him?

The law: One who [accidently] took the wrong item while at the house of a mourner, or while participating in a festive meal, may not use the item [that he accidently took]. Doing so is considered stealing. The same applies if one's item was accidently taken, and he then desires to take the item of the person who took his item, he may not use the item, and doing so is considered stealing. This prohibition applies even if one knows that the other person is [stealing and] using his item [without his permission], he may nevertheless not make use of his friend's item [unless he receives explicit permission from him].[157]

Returning the item:[158] Upon finding the rightful owner of the item, the person must return him the item even if his own item became lost [not due to the fault of the rightful owner].

Dry cleaners mistake:[159] If a gentile [or Jewish] dry cleaning company gave one the wrong shirt, it is forbidden for one to use it, and he must return it to the rightful owner even if his own shirt became lost.

---

[154] Michaber E.H. 118:6; Smeh C.M. 18:10; Minchas Yitzchak 6:167

[155] Yoman 1988, brought in Shulchan Menachem ibid

[156] Admur Gzeila Ugineiva 30; Michaber C.M.136:2; Bava Basra 46a

[157] The reason: As even if in truth his friend is using his item, if he were to use his friends item in exchange [without receiving his explicit permission] it is considered as if he is stealing from a stealer, and it is forbidden for one to place judgment alone without a Beis Din, as was explained above in Halacha 27. [Admur ibid; See however Aruch Hashulchan 136:2 who seems to learn that if one knows that the owner is using his item, then he may use the owners item even without his consent. Admur ibid clearly negates this approach.]

[158] Admur ibid; Rama ibid; Terumos Hadeshen 319

[159] Admur ibid; Rama ibid; Terumos Hadeshen 319

Q&A

What is the law if many days passed, and one has still not found the rightful owner?

Some Poskim[160] rule that if one knows that the rightful owner has given up hope in finding the item [Yiush], then he may use it. If many days passed, and one has not seen or heard from anyone looking for his item, then one can assume that he has given up hope in retrieving it.[161] Other Poskim[162], however, rule that one may not use the item, even after many days have passed [and he must hold on to it until Eliyahu Hanavi arrives and directs one to its rightful owner].[163]

What is the law in scenarios that it is very common for the items to be switched, and people are not particular in this matter?[164]

In any case that the custom of the world is not to be careful against having their item switched, and people constantly take their item while they constantly take other people's items, then one may use the item that he mistakenly took. This commonly occurred in previous times regarding shoes or slippers, as people would remove their shoes prior to entering the building and the shoes would become mixed up and each person would take whatever pair he finds. [Although this specific case is not common anymore, in the event that there is an item that is commonly switched, the above allowance would apply.]

What is one to do if he switched Talleisim or Tefillin with another person?[165]

One may use the Tallis [or Tefillin] as if it were his until he is able to switch it back with the person who took his Tallis [or Tefillin].[166] Upon being asked to switch back, one must comply.

---

16. Child who stole, and a person who stole as a child:[167]

If a child stole an object, then if the stolen object is still in existence, it is required to be returned to its owner. [This only applies if it is well known that the object in the child's possession was stolen by him.[168]] If the stolen object is no longer in existence, he is exempt from paying the owner for the object. This exemption remains in place even after the child reaches adulthood.[169] [If the child sold the object, and the money he received in exchange is still in existence, some Poskim[170] rule he is obligated to return the money to the owner.]

---

[160] Taz C.M. 136 based on Mordechai regarding a laundromat; Nesivos Hamishpat 136:2 records the opinion of Taz and explains in Mishpat Haurim 136:2 that perhaps even the Taz was only lenient in the case of a laundromat being that if the person did not give up hope, he would have heard about it from the laundromat; See Kesef Kedoshim for various answers on the questions of the Ketzos Hachoshen against the Taz.

[161] The reason: As the item has legally become his due to Yiush and Shinuiy Reshus. [See Taz ibid]

[162] Ketzos Hachoshen 136:2; Pischeiy Teshuvah 136:1; Nesivos Hamishpat in Mishpat Haurim 136:2 limits the allowance of the Taz ibid to that specific case, as explained in the previous footnote

[163] The reason: As even if the owner did give up hope in finding it, nevertheless, it does not help for one to give up hope after the item has already reached one's possession [Ketzos Hachoshen ibid], as brought in Admur Hilchos Metzia Upikadon 2. Furthermore, it does not even help to be allowed to use the item with intent to return when the rightful owner is found, as explained in the second opinion in Admur Halacha 2, and so is the main ruling. See however Kesef Kedoshim ibid for various answers on behalf of the Taz and why the above case is different than a case of a found object.

[164] Aruch Hashulchan 126:2; Kesef Kedoshim 126

[165] Birchas Habayis 37:10; See Kesef Kedoshim 126

[166] The reason: Although we rule that when one switched an article with another it is forbidden to use it due to stealing [Admur Gzeila Ugineiva 30; Michaber C.M.136:2] nevertheless, by a Tallis, we assume each person does not mind if the other uses his Tallis until they switch it back, as even in a case that the Talleisim were not switched, one may use his friends Tallis without permission under this basis, and thus certainly in this case it is permitted. [ibid]

[167] Michaber C.M. 349:3; see also Michaber 96:3; Rambam Gneiva 1; Mishneh Baba Kama 87a *"A child, getting into an altercation with them is bad, as if they damage they are exempt while if you damage them you are liable"*

[168] Smeh 349:7

[169] The reason: As a child does not have enough maturity of knowledge to be held accountable when he becomes an adult. [Smeh 349:6]

[170] Aruch Hashulchan C.M. 349:1; Piskeiy Teshuvos O.C. 343:14

If the child benefited from the stolen object: Some Poskim[171] rule that even if the object is no longer in existence, if the child benefited from the object, such as he stole food and ate it, then he is obligated to pay the full amount when he is older.

Doing repentance above the letter of the law:[172] Even if the object is no longer in existence, and he did not benefit from it, it is nevertheless proper when he gets older, to accept upon himself to do something for the sake of repentance and atonement, even though he had transgressed before becoming of punishable age.[173] [He should therefore pay the owner for the stolen object. He, however, is not required to pay for the entire worth of the object, but rather a symbolic amount.[174] Some[175], however, write that he should pay the owner for the entire amount, however, seemingly this is only a Midas Chassidus. Whatever amount the owner receives, he should be kind and merciful to forgive the person for his childhood sin.[176]]

Q&A

Is a child who stole that is below the age of Chinuch encouraged to perform a certain matter for the sake of repentance?

Some Poskim[177] rule that Teshuvah is only relevant for children who stole when they were of age to remember what they did. If, however, they were of very young age, and they don't remember the incident, they are not required to do Teshuvah at all.

Is the father of a child obligated to pay for the item his child stole?[178]
No.

---

[171] Shvus Yaakov 1:177 brought in Pischeiy Teshuvah C.M. 349:2; Based on Michaber 235:15 who requires a child to pay for a loan when he gets older if he borrowed the money for the sake of his food. Vetzaruch Iyun on Shvus Yaakov, as how a proof can be brought from the case of a loan which is a case of business, and by business we do make a child liable, being it is for his benefit, as brought in Michaber 96:3; Smeh 235:43; Nesivos Hamishpat 235:29, and the same would apply in a case of borrowing for one's food; However, here that we are discussing a stolen object, what benefit does making the child pay have for the child. Vetzaruch Iyun!

[172] Admur 343:11; Rama 343; Terumos Hadeshen 2:62; Bach 343; Shvus Yaakov 1:177 brought in Pischeiy Teshuvah C.M. 349:2; Based on story in Shabbos 56b; Baba Kama 98b, brought in Kaf Hachaim 343:32
Other opinions: Some Poskim rule that a child is not required to repent at all for his wrongdoing, even when he becomes older. [Beis Yaakov 3, brought in Shvus Yaakov ibid] Practically, we do not rule like his opinion. [Shvus Yaakov ibid; Kaf Hachaim ibid]

[173] The reason: The purpose of this repentance is not for the sake of removing Divine retribution, being that he is not liable for any punishment. However the forbidden act, despite not being punishable, leaves a damaging impact and spiritual stain on the soul of the child. It is for this reason that the child should do some act of repentance for the sake of cleansing his soul of any spiritual blemish. [Bach 343: The verse in Mishlei 19:2 states that "Even without knowledge, a soul is no good." This teaches us that even a child that transgresses a sin without knowledge causes impurity to his soul, it is thus proper for him to do Teshuvah"; Likkutei Sichos 14 p. 144 footnote 13; Sichos Kodesh Balak 5730; Shulchan Hamelech 343]
Other opinions: Some Poskim rule that a child who has reached the age of understanding what is a Mitzvah and Aveira, Onas Hapeutos, is punished for his sins. Veztaruch Iyun Gadol from all the above sources that imply he is not punished. [Noda Beyehuda Tinyana Y.D. 164, brought in Pischeiy Teshuvah Y.D. 376:3]

[174] Shvus Yaakov 1:177, brought in Pischeiy Teshuvah ibid; Kaf Hachaim ibid; Based on Admur an Rama ibid, based on Terumos Hadeshen 2:62

[175] Sefer Chassidim 692, brought in Shvus Yaakov ibid and Kaf Hachaim 343:35

[176] Shvus Yaakov ibid

[177] Sefer Chassidim ibid "However if he was very young when the action was committed and he does not remember, he does not need to pay"; Beis Yaakov 3; See Piskeiy Teshuvos 343:14; Lehoros Nasan 6:102

[178] See Pischeiy Choshen Nezikin 5 footnote 87; Piskeiy Teshuvos 343:14

17. Gambling:[179]
A. The prohibition:
Some Poskim[180] rule it is forbidden to gamble [with a Jew] due to a Rabbinical stealing prohibition.[181] Other Poskim[182] rule there is no stealing prohibition involved in gambling even with a Jew, just as is the law by a gentile [as explained next]. (Nevertheless, even according to this opinion, there is a prohibition involved in doing so.[183]) [Thus, practically, according to all opinions it is forbidden to gamble either on Shabbos or during the week, and the dispute is only regarding the severity of the prohibition. It is forbidden to gamble even on mere occasion, as a onetime occurrence, and not only when one does so as a hobby.[184] This prohibition is intensified if one does so as an occupation to support himself.[185]]

With a gentile:[186] There is no stealing prohibition involved in gambling with a gentile. Nevertheless, there remains a separate prohibition involved in spending time involved in matters of nonsense, as it is not befitting of a person to deal with such matters. Rather, throughout one's life, he is to be involved in matters of wisdom and matters that contribute towards civilization.

B. Definition of gambling:
Gambling is defined as any game in which two players stipulate that the winner will receive such and

---

[179] Admur Gzeila Ugineiva 31; Areas in Talmud and Shulchan Aruch that the Issur of gambling is discussed: Mishneh Rosh Hashanah 22a and Sanhedrin 24b; Orach Chaim 322:6; Choshen Mishpat 34:16 [laws of testimony]; Rama Choshen Mishpat 207:13 [laws of Asmachta]; 370:2-3 [laws of stealing]

Background:

The Mishneh states that one who gambles is invalid for testimony. [Mishneh Rosh Hashanah 22a and Sanhedrin 24b] The Gemara in Sanhedrin records a dispute as to the reason behind this invalidation. Rami Bar Chama says the reason is because it is similar to stealing, being that the loser never fully agreed to give him the money, being that he was planning on winning. The fact that he said he would give the money if he loses is a mere Asmachta, which is a not legally binding promise of words, being that he did not intend to truly relinquish his money but rather to use it to win. [Nonetheless, even according to this opinion, the winner is not considered a Biblical Gazlan/robber, being that he did not forcefully take the money from the loser. He is, however, considered a Rabbinical Gazlan. Rashi on Mishneh R.H. ibid; Machatzis Hashekel on M"A 422:8] Rav Sheishes, however, rules that the money is not considered stolen at all, being that it was not given as an Asmechta, but as an actual acquisition to the winner. Nevertheless, he is invalidated as a witness being that he is not involved in settling the world. The practical ramification between these opinions is regarding a gambler who has an occupation, in which case according to Rami Bar Chama he is still invalid, while according to Rav Sheshes he is valid. [Sanhedrin ibid] Practically, we rule like Rav Sheshes [Michaber 34:16; 370:3; Smeh 370:3; Machatzis Hashekel ibid; Rif; Rosh on Sanhedrin ibid] Nonetheless, even according to Rav Sheishes, it is disputed as to whether there is a Rabbinical stealing prohibition involved in gambling, with some ruling that it contains an actual Rabbinical prohibition due to Avak Gezel and others ruling that there is no Rabbinical prohibition involved. Admur, and other Achronim, novelize that according to all opinions there is some level of stealing involved in gambling and the dispute is only as to what level. The following is a summary of the opinions: 1) Actual Rabbinical Gezeila. [Rami Bar Chama] 2) Not actual Rabbinical Gezeila but Rabbinically prohibited due to Avak Gezel [Rav Sheshes as rules Michaber ibid] 3) No stealing at all even Rabbinically, although it is slightly forbidden. [Rav Sheshes as rules Admur and M"A in their understanding of Rama] 4) No stealing at all on any level. [Simple understanding of Rama ibid]

[180] First opinion in Admur ibid; Michaber Orach Chaim 322:6; Choshen Mishpat 34:16 [laws of testimony]; 370:2 [laws of stealing]; Rambam Gzeila 6:10; Rashi Rosh Hashanah 22a; Regarding opinion of Rambam: See Hilchos Gzeila 6; Eidus 10:4; Kesef Mishneh ibid

[181] The reason: This is considered Rabbinical Gzeila. [Michaber 370:2] Although the money is taken with the agreement of the loser, nonetheless, since the money was taken from his friend in a way of jest and fun, without him gaining anything in return, it is therefore Rabbinically forbidden. [Admur ibid; Perisha 34, brought in Smeh C.M. 40] This is considered "Avak Gezel" [Machatzis Hashekel on M"A 322:8]

[182] 2nd opinion in Admur ibid; Rama Choshen Mishpat 207:13 [laws of Asmachta] and 370:3 [regarding laws of stealing] "The custom is to gamble"; Tur Choshen Mishpat 34, 207, 370, brought in M"A 322:8; Rosh Sanhedrin 3:7; Tosafos Sanhedrin 25a

[183] Admur ibid in parentheses; M"A 322:8 "a slight prohibition"; Teshuvos Harivash 432; Machatzis Hashekel on M"A ibid; P"M 322 A"A 8; Rav Poalim Y.D. 2:30

Background: Admur ibid writes in parentheses that even according to the lenient opinion who rules it does not involve the stealing prohibition, it is nevertheless forbidden to do so; So also rules M"A 322:8 [see Machatzis Hashekel on ibid] that possibly one can learn this way from Michaber 322:6 that although there may not be a stealing prohibition involved there is still "a slight prohibition"; The P"M 322 A"A 8 interprets this to mean a Rabbinical "Avak Gezel", and so writes Machatzis Hashekel on M"A ibid; However, from Admur one can possibly learn that according to the lenient opinion there is no prohibition of even Avak Gezel, and the prohibition is simply due to "Yishuvo Shel Olam," as he writes regarding gambling with a gentile. Another reason for this prohibition can be learned from the Teshuvos Harivash ibid who writes "Even according to Rav Sheishes who states there is no stealing prohibition involved in gambling, nevertheless, this is a repulsive, revolting and immoral act. It has caused the lives of many people to be destroyed." Thus, in total we have three possible reasons for why there is a prohibition to gamble even according to the Rama 1) Avak Gezel 2) Yishuvo Shel Olam 3) putrid act.

Opinion of Rama: The Rama in 207:13 and 370:3 writes that the custom is to gamble. This implies that there is no prohibition involved at all, unlike Admur and the Poskim ibid. However, see Rav Poalim ibid, that even according to the Rama there is a prohibition involved.

[184] Smeh 34:40

[185] See Michaber Choshen Mishpat 34:16 that in such a case he is invalidated as a witness; See Smeh ibid

[186] Admur ibid; Michaber 370:3; Rambam Gzeila 6:11

Opinion of Rama: The Rama 370:3 writes that the custom is to gamble with gentiles. This implies that there is no prohibition involved at all, unlike Admur and the Poskim ibid. However, see Rav Poalim ibid that even according to the Rama there is a prohibition involved, and it is just that we are not accustomed to invalidating such a player for testimony.

such an item from the loser [whether it is money or an object].[187] Furthermore, it is considered gambling even if the items all belong to one person and he will distribute it to the winners of the game.[188] This applies even between family members.[189]

Betting:[190] Making bets with each other is considered like gambling, and is hence forbidden to be done. In the event that one transgressed and made a bet, he may withdraw from the bet, so long as the money has not yet been given to a third party. If, however, he promised to donate the money of his winnings to charity, then he may not retract from the bet.[191]

C. Invalidation for testimony/Eidus:[192]

One who transgresses the above prohibition and gambles, is Rabbinically invalid to serve as a witness in any Halachic matter that requires testimony. Such a person may not be used as an Eid/witness for a wedding, Kesuba, divorce, monetary dispute which is brought to Beis Din, and any matter of the like in which Kosher witnesses are required.

The type of gambling that invalidates: One is only invalidated for testimony if he gambles as his only set occupation, and supports himself from the proceeds of his winnings. If, however, he has another occupation from which he supports himself, then he is not invalidated if he gambles, even though it is forbidden to do so.[193] If he does not have an occupation, but lives off his savings without needing to support himself with the gambling money, it is disputed as to whether he is invalid to serve as a witness.[194] Likewise, if he has an occupation, but it does not suffice to fully support him, and he hence uses some of the gambling money's towards his livelihood, then it is disputed as to whether he is invalidated.[195]

---

[187] Admur ibid

[188] Michaber 322:6; Tur 322; Beis Yosef 322 that so rules Rif Shabbos 63b and Rosh 23:3; M"B 322:22

The reason: As this can lead to gambling with others and in a way that people lose and win. [M"B 322:22]

[189] 1st opinion in Michaber 322:6; Tur 322; Beis Yosef 322 that so rules Rif Shabbos 63b and Rosh 23:3; Bach 322 that so is the final ruling and so is implied to be the ruling of the Michaber ibid; M"B 322:22; Kaf Hachaim 322:31 that so is the final ruling

The reason: Although the father of the home owns all the items and it is not real gambling and worry of stealing, nonetheless it is forbidden as this can lead to gambling with others and in a way that people lose and win. [M"B 322:22]

Other Opinions: Some Poskim rule that it is permitted for a father to make a raffle for family members to see who receives which portion of food, even though the portions are different sizes, as they are not Makpid. [2nd opinion in Michaber 322:6; Rambam Shabbos 23:7; Taz 322:4] The reason for this is because gambling itself is only Rabbinically forbidden and hence there is no need to make an additional decree against this leading to one coming to gamble. [Maggid Mishneh on Rambam ibid; Olas Shabbos 322:10; Elya Raba 322:10; See Taz ibid for his alternative explanation]

[190] Admur ibid; Rama 207:13; Shabbos 31a

[191] The reason: As the mere words of promise towards charity is considered as if it was given [Amira Lagavoa Kemissirah Lehedyot]. [ibid]

[192] Michaber C.M. 34:16; Mishneh Rosh Hashanah 22a; Mishneh Sanhedrin 24b

[193] Michaber ibid; Sanhedrin ibid as rules Rav Sheishes

The reason: It is not enough to invalidate the person if he simply gambles for a hobby, as in such a case he is only performing Avak Gezel, which is only Rabbinically forbidden, and the Sages did not invalidate him in such a case. If, however, he also benefits from the proceeds, and uses it to support himself, then the Sages invalidated him as a witness due to worry that he may not be a reliable witness and may lie in his testimony. It is disputed amongst the Rishonim as to the reason we suspect the person will come to lie if he does not have an occupation. Some rule [Rambam] the reason is because he lives off the stolen money, and hence becomes an untrustworthy person. Others [Rashi/Tur] rule the reason is because he does not understand the worth of money and the stress involved in earning a living, and hence does not take lying under testimony as a serious offense. The practical ramification of this dispute of reasoning is found in the following two cases to be mentioned. [Smeh 34:40; 370:3]

[194] Smeh ibid; Michaber ibid and Rambam rule that he is valid; Rashi and Tur rule that he is invalid

The reason: According to the Rambam/Michaber, he is valid being that he does not live off the stolen money, however, according to Rashi and the Tur he is invalid being he does not know the worth of money and the stress involved in earning a living. [Smeh ibid]

[195] Smeh ibid; Michaber ibid and Rambam rule that he is invalid; Rashi and Tur rule that he is valid

The reason: According to the Rambam/Michaber, he is invalid being that he does partially live off the stolen money, however, according to Rashi and the Tur he is valid being he does know the worth of money and the stress involved in earning a living. [Smeh ibid]

Summary:
It is forbidden to gamble either on Shabbos or during the week, whether as a onetime occurrence, or on mere occasion, or as a continuous hobby, or as an occupation, and whether with a Jew or with a gentile. One who gambles on a constant basis, and does not have another occupation from which he lives off, is invalidated as a witness.

Q&A

May one play the lottery?[196]
Yes. Playing the lottery is not considered gambling and is permitted according to Halacha.[197]

May one play cards for money?
No. This is considered gambling

May one play Dreidel for the sake of money?
No. This is considered gambling.

----------------*Monetary damages*----------------

18. Liability for damages caused by one's items that were negligently left in a public area:

Not to place a potentially damaging object in a public area: It is an act of piety for a person to hide his sharp objects [nails/glass], and any other damaging item, in an area that will not cause any potential harm/damage, such as to throw them in the river or to burn them.[198] [This applies even if the potentially damaging object is in one owns property, and not in the public area, as it is still a potential harm for family, guests and visitors.[199]] It is forbidden to place a potentially damaging object in the public area[200], unless it is publicly accepted, or one has permission from the municipality to do so.[201]

Bodily injury:[202] If one placed a sharp object, such as a nail or glass, in a public area, and another person became injured from the object, then if the owner did not have permission to place the item there, he is liable to pay for the bodily damage of the victim.

Monetary damage:[203] If one placed a sharp object, such as a nail or glass, in a public area, and another person's item became damaged from the object, then the owner is exempt from liability, even if he did not have the right to place it there, and was negligent in placing it there, or even did so deliberately.[204] [Nevertheless, in areas that have set laws regarding these matters, it is possible to make the owner liable for monetary damages, despite the Biblical exemption.[205] One is to speak to a Beis Din for further information.]

---

[196] Rav Poalim Y.D. 2:30; Chavos Yair 61; Mishpitei Hatorah 1:28; Yaskil Avdi 8:5; Techumin 5:302-310
Other opinions: Some Poskim rule it is forbidden to purchase lottery tickets according to the opinion of the Rambam and Michaber. [Yabia Omer 7:106] The students of Harav Ovadia testify that practically, in his later years, he retracted from his ruling and permitted for one to purchase lottery tickets.

[197] The reason: a) As the company that holds the money it received from all the ticket buyers, is truly interested in giving it to the winner [unlike when one is playing versus another, in which case he owns the money until he loses]. B) As the tickets have a market value, and one hence purchased an actual item with the money, and is not like stealing at all. [Rav Poalim ibid]

[198] Michaber C.M. 415:3; Bava Kama 30a

[199] Pashut from Gemara ibid and from next Halacha which prohibits placing a hazardous object in the public area; Aruch Hashulchan 415:2

[200] Michaber C.M. 417:1; Bava Kama 50b

[201] Rama ibid; Beis Yosef 417 in name of Rashba

[202] Michaber C.M. 415:1 "One who hides his nails and glass in his property and it flew into the public area and damaged another person, he is liable"; Mishneh Baba Kama 30a; The above liability is only for bodily damage and not monetary damage, as brought in sources in next footnote

[203] A "Bur" is exempt from monetary damages of vessels: Michaber C.M. 410:21; 412:4; Tur 410; Rambam Nizkei Mamon 13:2; Mishneh Baba Kama 52a; Gemara ibid 53b and 28b; A nail or other object that damages has the same status as Bur: Michaber C.M. 411:1; 412:4-5; Rambam ibid

[204] The reason: As the Av Nezikin called Bor, as well as all its subcategories, is exempt from liability of monetary damage of vessels, and is only liable for damages of animals and man. [Michaber 410:21; Tur 410; Mishneh Bava Kama 52a; Gemara ibid 53b] This is learned from the verse which states the word "Shur" and comes to exclude vessels. [Baba Kama 53b]

[205] See the following regarding the ability of a community/country to enact stricter laws than the Torah and its Halachic binding: Rama C.M. 356:7 and Shach 356:10 regarding Dina Demalchusa Dina; Chevel Nachalaso 9:58; Baba Basra 8b; Meri ibid; Shut Harosh 7:1; Rashba 2:268

Summary:
Initially, one is to avoid placing a damaging object in an area that can cause damage, even in one's own property. If one was not careful to do so, and it caused damage to another person, one is liable for all bodily damage that it may cause, although is exempt from any monetary damage it causes.

Q&A
If one's clothing tore on a nail that was sticking out of someone's Sukkah, are they liable to pay for the clothing?
No. This applies even if the Sukkah was placed in public property without permission.

19. Child who caused damage:[206]

If a child caused bodily damage to another person, he is exempt from paying for damages even when he becomes older.[207]

Repenting above the letter of the law:[208] Although one is exempt from paying for damages he caused as a child, it is nevertheless proper for him to accept upon himself when he gets older to perform a certain matter for the sake of repentance and atonement, even though he had transgressed before he became of punishable age.[209] [He should therefore pay the owner for the stolen object. He, however, is not required to pay for the entire worth of the object, but rather a symbolic amount.[210] Some[211] however write that he should pay the owner for the entire amount, however, seemingly this is only a Midas Chassidus. Whatever amount the owner receives, he should be kind and merciful to forgive the person for his childhood sin.[212]]

Q&A
Is a child, who is below the age of Chinuch, caused damage, should he perform an act of repentance upon becoming older?
Some Poskim[213] rule that repentance is only relevant for children who caused damage when they were of age to remember what they did. If, however, the child was of very young age, and did not remember the incident, he is not required to do Teshuvah at all.

Is the father of a child obligated to pay for his son's damages?[214]
No. If, however, the father was negligent, and was the direct cause of the damage, then it is possible that he is liable to pay for damages

---

[206] Michaber 424:8; Mishneh Baba Kama 87a "A child, getting into an altercation with them is bad, as if they damage they are exempt while if you damage them you are liable"; See Igros Moshe Y.D. 2:10

[207] The reason: As at the time that the damage occurred, the person was not of responsible age. [Michaber ibid]

[208] Admur 343:11; Rama 343; Mahariy 62; Bach 343; Shvus Yaakov 1:177 brought in Pischeiy Teshuvah C.M. 349:2; Based on story in Shabbos 56b; Bava Kama 98b, brought in Kaf Hachaim 343:32; See Noda Beyehuda Tinyana Y.D. 164, brought in Pischeiy Teshuvah Y.D. 376/3 and Igros Moshe ibid

Other opinions: Some Poskim rule that a child is not required to repent at all for his wrongdoing, even when he becomes older. [Beis Yaakov 3, brought in Shvus Yaakov ibid] Practically, we do not rule like his opinion. [Shvus Yaakov ibid; Kaf Hachaim ibid]

[209] The reason: The purpose of this repentance is not for the sake of removing Divine retribution, being that he is not liable for any punishment. However, the forbidden act, despite not being punishable, leaves a damaging impact and spiritual stain on the soul of the child. It is for this reason that the child should do some act of repentance for the sake of cleansing his soul of any spiritual blemish. [Bach 343: The verse in Mishlei 19:2 states that "Even without knowledge, a soul is no good." This teaches us that even a child that transgresses a sin without knowledge causes impurity to his soul, it is thus proper for him to do Teshuvah"; Likkutei Sichos 14 p. 144 footnote 13; Sichos Kodesh Balak 5730; Shulchan Hamelech 343]

[210] Shvus Yaakov 1:177, brought in Pischeiy Teshuvah ibid; Kaf Hachaim ibid; Based on Admur an Rama ibid, based on Terumos Hadeshen 2:62

[211] Sefer Chassidim 692, brought in Shvus Yaakov ibid and Kaf Hachaim 343:35

[212] Shvus Yaakov ibid

[213] Sefer Chassidim ibid "However, if he was very young when the action was committed, and he does not remember, he does not need to pay"; Beis Yaakov 3; See Piskeiy Teshuvos 343:14; Lehoros Nasan 6:102

[214] See Michaber 424:8; Mishneh Baba Kama 87a "A child, getting into an altercation with them is bad, as if they damage they are exempt while if you damage them you are liable"; Pischeiy Choshen Nezikin 5 footnote 87; Piskeiy Teshuvos 343:14

Tzaar Baalei Chaim

20. Feeding street animals:

One is not obligated to feed his friends pets or street animals from his own food.[215] [This applies even if the animal is endangered and may die.[216] However, in such a case, one is obligated to place bodily effort to save the animal, if possible, such as to call a shelter, or give it food of Hefker, and the like.[217]] Nevertheless, it is proper to give a stray dog a small morsel of [even] food [that he owns] in order to emulate Hashem's ways of mercy.[218] One is to then hit the dog with a stick after throwing it the food in order to discourage it from returning back [and becoming a nuisance].[219] [Likewise, if one chooses, he may feed other animals as well, and it is considered an act of mercy to do so in a case that the animal is endangered.[220] This however only applies if the dog or animal is not a danger to the public, and does not bark or attack people. If, however, the animal is a nuisance, such as it barks or attacks people, or damages property, then it is forbidden to feed the dog or animal.[221] Likewise, in all cases, it is only permitted to feed the stray animal, animal fodder, or leftover foods that people will not eat, or non-Kosher food, however foods that are Kosher and fit for human consumption, are not to be given to stray animals.[222]]

Summary:
One is not Halachically required to feed stray animals from his own food/money, although it is proper to give some food to a dog on a one-time occasion, if the dog is not a danger to the public. In all cases, one is not to feed stray animals foods that are meant to be eaten by humans, and is rather to feed them animal foods, or leftovers that people do not eat.

Why does the Torah not obligate one to feed stray animals?
Various reasons can be attributed for why we do not find an obligation in this matter.

- Most stray animals have their own way of achieving a source of food, and by people feeding them it invites the animals into the neighborhood, and they can become a nuisance for others.
- The Torah does not command a person regarding all matters, and leaves certain areas to the judgment of man to decide. If one desires to be merciful, and feed the harmless stray animals, he certainly has the choice to do so.

---

[215] Admur Hilchos Ovrei Derachim 3; Bava Metzia 88b
The reason: As the Torah did not obligate due to Tzaar Baalei Chaim for one to spend his own money to help animals, and he is only obligated to place bodily effort in saving them. [Admur ibid]
[216] Admur in Kuntrus Achron 3; Vetzaruch Iyun as to why this is not included in the positive command [Mitzvah 611 in Chinuch] to follow the ways of Hashem and just as He is merciful, so too, you should be merciful"
[217] Admur Hilchos Ovrei Derachim Halacha 4
[218] Admur ibid; Admur 324:7 "Doing so contains a slight Mitzvah"; M"A 324:7; Shabbos 155b
How Hashem shows mercy to the dogs: Hashem shows mercy to dogs by having the food stay in their abdomen for 72 hours, being that its food is scarce. [Admur ibid and 324:7]
[219] Admur ibid; Shabbos ibid
[220] See regarding feeding birds on Erev Yom Kippur: Admur 605:6; Rama 605:1; Tur; Tashbatz 126; See regarding Shabbos Shira: Tosefes Shabbos 117; Minchas Shabbos; brought in Ketzos Hashulchan 131 footnote 5; Aruch Hashulchan 324:3; Nemukei Orach Chaim 324; Shaar Halacha Uminhag 1:149
[221] Olas Shabbos 324:19; Tosefes Shabbos 324; Daas Torah 324; M"B 324:31; Kaf Hachaim 324:45; See Maharsha Shabbos 155b; Admur Hilchos Shemiras Haguf Vihanefesh Halacha 3 that it is forbidden to own such a dog; Vetzaruch Iyun why M"A and Admur ibid omitted this ruling of the Olas Shabbos
[222] See Taanis 20; M"A 171:1; Machatzis Hashekel ibid; M"B 171:11; Ketzos Hashulchan 39:30; Piskeiy Teshuvos 171:8

Bodily Damages

21. Hitting one's children:[223]

It is permitted for one to hit his small children for disciplinary measures. This applies even to [non-biological] children that are part of one's household, such as an [adopted] orphan [or foster child].[224]

Until what age may one hit his child? It is forbidden for one to hit his adult children.[225] One who hits his adult children [in previous times] would be placed in excommunication, as he transgresses the prohibition of "Lifnei Iver Lo Sitein Michshol."[226] A child is considered an adult in this regard from age 24 years old.[227] The main time of educating a child is from age 16-24.[228] Prior to age 16 the child does not have enough maturity to fully receive reproof from his parent, and one is thus not to chastise him and give him too heavy of a punishment. After 24 years old, however, there is worry that perhaps the child will rebel and fight back.[229] [If, however, the child is already married, then he may no longer be hit by his father even if he is below the above age.[230] Likewise, if the child is already looked upon as an adult by society, he may no longer be hit, irrelevant of age.[231] Likewise, if the child is of age and/or of temperament that he would retaliate for being hit, such as by hitting his parent back or cursing him, then he is considered an adult in this matter and is forbidden to be hit.[232]]

For what reasons may one hit a child?[233] One's small children may be hit for their [i.e. the children's] personal benefit. For example, they may be hit for disciplinary measures to educate them in Torah and Mitzvos. They may also be hit in order to teach them Derech Eretz [proper manners and Middos, or for their personal safety].[234] Furthermore, if one's children are disobedient and do not listen to his instructions, he may hit them even for his own benefit, so they become obedient and listen to instructions.[235] If, however, the children are obedient and listen to his instructions, it is forbidden to hit them when it is not for their benefit, just as it is forbidden to hit any other person.[236] One who does so, transgresses a negative command of hitting a fellow Jew.[237] [One is to always first try to discipline the child through other methods prior to hitting him, and only if these methods do not work, may the child be hit.[238] There are many disciplinary philosophies in practice today which substitute hitting, for other more useful and harmless methods.[239] It is incumbent upon parents to train themselves to become effective disciplinarians so their children are disciplined, but not in an abusive manner.]

---

[223] Admur Hilchos Nizkei Guf Vanefesh 4; Michaber Y.D. 240:20; Rama Y.D. 233:1 regarding a child who makes vows; Kitzur Shulchan Aruch 143:18; 165:1; 184:2

[224] Admur Hilchos Nizkei Guf Vanefesh 4 in parentheses; Admur 156:9; Kitzur Shulchan Aruch 184:2

[225] Michaber Y.D. 240:20; Admur ibid "small children"; Moed Katan 17a

[226] Michaber ibid; Moed Katan ibid; Kitzur Shulchan Aruch 143:18

[227] Admur Hilchos Talmud Torah 1:6; second opinion in Rama 240:20 as explained in Shach 240:21; opinion in Beis Yosef 334
Other opinions: Some Poskim rule it is forbidden to hit a child from age 22. [Rama 240:20 says "22 or 24" and Shach 240:21 explains that this is a dispute in Poskim, some say 22 and some say 24; Rashal Kiddushin 68, brought in Pischeiy Teshuvah 240:16; Opinion in Kiddushin 30a and so rules Rashi ibid] Some Poskim rule the prohibition applies at age 22 although excommunication is only given from age 24. [Rashal ibid]

[228] Admur ibid based on merge of the two opinions in Kiddushin ibid; See Igros Kodesh 2:168

[229] Admur Hilchos Talmud Torah 1:6; Rashi Kiddushin ibid

[230] Rashal Kiddushin 68, brought in Pischeiy Teshuvah 240:16

[231] See Rashal ibid

[232] Ritva Moed Katan, brought in Birkeiy Yosef 240; Kitzur Shulchan Aruch 143:18; This does not contradict the Rama/Admur ibid as they mentioned the average age regarding this matter, although in truth the determining factor is whether the child will become obedient or retaliate back. [Ritva ibid]

[233] Admur Hilchos Nizkei Guf Vanefesh 4 in parentheses; Rambam Rotzeiach 5:5; Makos 8b

[234] The reason: As this kind of hitting is intended for their own benefit, and the parent is responsible in benefiting the children who are within his authority. [Admur ibid in parentheses]

[235] Admur Hilchos Nizkei Guf Vanefesh 4 in parentheses; Taz 240:1 based on Yerushalmi and Ramban that Beis Din may choose to hit children, so they perform the Mitzvah of Kibbud Av.
The reason: As it is permitted for a parent to force his children to listen to him, as is commanded of them [in the Torah "Honor your father and mother"]. [Admur ibid]
Other opinions: Some Poskim rule it is forbidden to hit a child so he perform the Mitzvah of Kibbud Av. [Smeh C.M. 107:2, based on Rama 240:1, brought in Taz ibid; Opinion of Rosh who argues on Ramban ibid]

[236] Admur Hilchos Nizkei Guf Vanefesh 4 in parentheses; Braisa Bava Kama 87b

[237] Admur Hilchos Talmud Torah 1:13 regarding Melameid who hits without Reshus

[238] Kitzur Shulchan Aruch 165:1; See Sefer Hasichos 5704 p. 15 that a Chassid never hits and rather uses other measures

[239] See https:::www.loveandlogic.com: for a wonderful disciplinary philosophy which is both harmless, and effective, and almost completely avoids the need to ever hit a child out of discipline.

How to hit: Even when a child needs to be hit for disciplinary reasons, he is not to be hit with cruelty, as do to the fools. Every parent must do so with wisdom.[240] When necessary, the child may be hit either with a hand, or with a belt or rod.[241]

Not to threaten a child by saying he will get hit later on:[242] If a child needs reprimanding, one is not to threaten the child that he will hit him later on, but is rather to either hit him immediately upon him doing the action, or is not to do anything at all.[243]

During the three weeks:[244] From the 17th of Tammuz until the 9th of Av one is to avoid hitting the students [or children[245]] during these days [even with a belt[246], and certainly not with a stick or rod[247].] [Some Poskim[248] however rule one may hit a child using hands. Other Poskim[249] rule that using one's hands to hit is also included in the prohibition. Some Poskim[250] rule that this restriction does not apply in a room with a Mezuzah. Some Poskim[251] rule that there is no restriction to hit on the outer limbs such as the hand and leg, and the restriction is only with regards to areas of the inner limbs. Some Poskim[252] rule that the above restriction only applies between the 4th and 9th hour [of the day]. Other Poskim[253] rule that one is to be stringent through the entire period.]

Summary:
It is Biblically forbidden to hit one's child for non-disciplinary reasons, or unjustifiably. Even hitting for disciplinary reasons, is only permitted when the child is still young enough to absorb the hit and become disciplined. Such a child may be hit to educate him in Torah, Mitzvos, Derech Eretz, safety, or obedience to parents. In all cases, one must first try to discipline the child in other measures, and may not use excessive force.

Q&A

May one hit a child out of anger?
It is Biblically forbidden to hit a child for non-disciplinary reasons. Thus, if one hits out of anger, simply in order to pain the child and quench one's fury, he transgresses a Biblical command. Even if one is also doing so in order to educate the child in one of the above-mentioned matters of which it is permitted for the child to be hit, nevertheless, it is not legally or Halachically advisable to hit one's child when angry. The reason for this is because it a) Leads to excessive use of force, beyond that necessary; b) Causes one to misjudge the child's guilt and the proper measure of discipline deserved by the child. Thus, one is to first calm down and only then cool headedly hand over the necessary measures of discipline. Many a times a parent is already agitated about other issues when he comes to hit the child, and in truth that hit contains previous anger and frustrations which are now being unjustifiably released on the child. Such a hit may carry a Biblical prohibition, even though its purpose is also for disciplinary measures. As a word of advice: Calm down, have a drink, eat something, set a time to think over the child's behavior, investigate the child's side of the story, and give a proper and effective disciplinary action. Don't hit just so you feel better, hit with a purpose that benefits the child.

[240] Kitzur Shulchan Aruch 165:1
[241] See Taz 551:18; M"B 551:103
[242] Kitzur Shulchan Aruch 165:7
[243] This is due to a story which occurred, that a child which was threatened to be hit went and committed suicide out of fear. [Kitzur SHU"A ibid]
[244] Michaber 551:18
[245] Levush 551; Kaf Hachayim 551:230
[246] Taz 551:18; M"B 551:103
[247] Piskeiy Teshuvos 551:57
[248] Ashel Avraham of Buchach 551
[249] Peri Megadim 551 M"Z 18
[250] Ashel Avraham of Buchach 551
[251] Ashel Avraham of Buchach 551
[252] Peri Megadim 551 M"Z 18; Levush 551; Siddur Yaavetz
[253] Tosefes Chaim Chayei Adam 133:17

Is it legal per secular law to hit your child?[254]

According to United States law in all 50 states, it is permitted to hit a child with reasonable force for disciplinary measures. Nevertheless, some states only allow hitting with a bare hand while others allow rod spanking and the like. In all states, it is illegal, and against Halacha, to hit a child out of anger or other non-disciplinary reasons, or with excessive force, and one who does so is liable to get arrested under counts of child abuse.

Is hot saucing a permitted and legal form of disciplinary action?

Halacha: According to Halacha, using hot sauce would seemingly have the same status as hitting a child, and may be used for disciplinary measures, although is forbidden to be used out of anger and without justifiable reasons. Nonetheless, its use must be measured in appropriation to the child's age, offense, and standing health of the child. Health concerns: Some pediatricians warn against the practice as it can cause an allergic reaction, swelling of the tongue and esophagus.

Secular law:[255] There is no law in the U.S.A. that prohibits hot saucing as a disciplinary measure, although in some jurisdictions it can be considered a call for concern.

What parents say:[256] Many parents strongly advocate against hot saucing while others claim it is a painful, but harmless and effective, disciplinary measure.

Sparks of Chassidus

A Chassid does not hit a child:[257]

The Rebbe Rayatz once related: A father who hits his child may be a Tzaddik, compassionate and righteous, although a Chassid he is not, as a Chasid does not hit.

Hitting one's child should bring him pain:

Even when one is forced into reprimanding his child through hitting him, this should cause him much pain to the point he feels like crying. A story is told of Rav Yitzchak Shaul, a dear colleague of Reb Baruch, the father of the Alter Rebbe, that his father wept bitterly after smiting his child for cruel behavior.[258]

The Torah requires one to be a loving disciplinarian:

The Sages[259] state that three matters are to be dealt with love of one's right hand and sternness with ones left hand:

1) The evil inclination; 2) Children; c) Women. This means that one must balance a proper measure of revealed love and care to a child together with discipline. If a child is only shown disciplinary measures from his parents, it can make him rebel. It can potentially damage his emotional health and relationship with the parent, and cause long term effects down the road of his life, such as in his relationships with his parents, siblings, spouse and own children. On the other hand, if the parent is not a disciplinarian, it teaches the child bad character traits, and can also lead to damaging effects down the road of his life. It is therefore incumbent on a parent to show a child both love and discipline in order to properly balance the child's emotional health with a good character. On this Chazal stated, use a right hand [i.e. love] and a left hand [i.e. discipline], but using just one is counterproductive and potentially damaging.

---

[254] See here: http://blogs.findlaw.com:blotter:2014:06:is-it-legal-to-hit-your-kids.html
[255] See here: http://www.washingtonpost.com:wp-dyn:articles:A52909-2004Aug9.html; and here https:::en.wikipedia.org:wiki:Hotsaucing
[256] See here: http://www.washingtonpost.com:wp-dyn:articles:A52899-2004Aug9.html
[257] Sefer Hasichos 5704 p. 15
[258] Memoirs Vol. 1 p. 334 [English edition]
[259] Sotah 47a; Kitzur Shulchan Aruch 165:7

Miscellaneous Topics

1. The constant Mitzvos:

The Poskim[1] enumerate a list of Mitzvos that one has the ability to constantly fulfill throughout the day being that they are not limited to any specific time, place or action. These are:

1. Belief in Hashem
2. Not to believe in the existence of any other G-d.
3. The unity of Hashem
4. Love of Hashem
5. Fear of Hashem
6. Not to swerve after one's heart and eyes.

2. How many Mitzvos, of the 613 Mitzvos, can be fulfilled during exile?[2]

Today in exile, it is possible to fulfill 369 Mitzvos out of the 613 total numbers of commands. Within this number, there are 99 commands which are only applicable in certain circumstances, and one may never come to fulfill them throughout his life. An example of such a command is the Mitzvah not to divorce one's wife if he was Motzi Shem Ra, or not to delay the payment of a worker. It is possible that throughout one's life he will never hire a worker or will never be Motzi Shem Ra on his wife. The total amount of Mitzvos applicable today which are a complete obligation upon all [men], and not dependent on circumstances, is 270 Mitzvos, which includes 48 positive commands and 222 negative commands. This total number of 270 is hinted to in the verse "Ani Yeshenah Velibi Er", as Er is spelled Reish Ayin which is 270.

3. Chatas offerings in the future:

A. In the future, will one need to bring a Chatas offering for the accidental sins he performed during Galus?

From certain sources in the Talmud[3] and Poskim[4] it is implied that those who sinned accidently during exile will be required to bring a Chatas offering for those sins, when Moshiach comes, if they merit for Moshiach to come during their lifetime. Some[5] deduce from these sources that in truth this is the final ruling. The Rebbe[6] however learns that one who sinned during exile is not obligated to bring a Chatas offering in the future.[7]

---

[1] Sefer Hachinuch in his introduction [brought in Biur Halacha 1]; Chayeh Adam Klal 1:5; The Sefer Chareidim [introduction] lists 6 constant positive commands and 7 constant negative commands

[2] Hakdama of the author to Sefer Hachinuch

[3] Rebbe Yishmael Shabbos 12b; Rebbe Elazar Yuma 80a; Yerushalmi Chagiga 1:2

Background:
The Gemara in Shabbos ibid records a dispute between the Tana Kama and Rebbe Yishmael Ben Elisha in regards to whether it is forbidden to learn near a candle on Shabbos lest one come to tilt the candle. Rebbe Yishmael was of the opinion that it is permitted to do so and he one time tilted the candle while reading, thus transgressing a Biblical command. Rebbe Yishmael then wrote on his booklet after Shabbos: I Yishmael Ben Elisha read near a candle and tilted it on Shabbos. When the Beis Hamikdash will be rebuilt I will bring a fat Chatas offering. Likewise, the Gemara in Yuma ibid and Yerushalmi Chagiga record that one who ate Cheilev in today's time is obligated to write down the amount of Cheilev one has eaten in order so he will know whether he must bring a Chatas offering when Moshiach comes and the Shiurim are adjusted by the Sanhedrin. From all the above sources we see that one is liable to bring a Chatas offering in the future if he sins during exile.

[4] M"A 334:33

[5] Riei Chaim of Rav Chaim Falagi Parshas Tazria; Encyclopedia Talmudit Chatas p. 503; Livyas Chen brought in Yalkut Geula Umoshiach Tzav 7:12

[6] Sichos Kodesh 1981 6th of Tishreiy; Likkutei Sichos 18 Maseiy footnote

[7] The reason: a) As the purpose of bringing a Chatas offering is for atonement purposes, and in today's times in which we do not have a Beis Hamikdash we can achieve complete atonement through Teshuvah, regret and resolution. Hence, when Moshiach comes, there will no longer be a need to bring a Karban Chatas for sins committed during exile. [Rebbe ibid] B) Alternatively, the reason is because during exile it is not possible to transgress a true Meizid, being that one cannot be given reliable Hasraah. Consequently, there is also no law of Shogeg today, as Shogeg can only exist in times that Meizid is possible. [Rebbe in Sichos Kodesh ibid]
How the Rebbe learns the above sources: The Rebbe learns that the entire concept of the above Tannaim and Amoraim recording their sin and necessity to bring a Chatas offering is not because they were truly obligated to do so, but because it is considered like a Nedava. This is why Rebbe Yishmael said he would bring a Chatas Shmeina, as this emphasizes the fact that he would bring a Karban Nedava as a Chatas. Vetzaruch Iyun as one cannot bring a Chatas as a Nedava. [Likkutei Sichos 18 Maseiy footnote 51]

B. Must one make note of a sin that he accidently transgressed if it carries a Chatas penalty?

From certain sources in the Talmud[8] and Poskim[9], it is implied that those who sinned accidently during exile, are required to write down the sin in order to remember to bring a Chatas offering when Moshiach comes. Some[10] deduce from these sources that in truth this is the final ruling. Practically, however, despite the above, one is not required to do so[11], and so is the widespread custom amongst majority of Jewry and Gedolei Yisrael.[12] The reason for this is because in truth one who sinned during exile is not obligated to bring a Karban Chatas and doing so is a mere voluntary act.[13]

4. Purchasing Life insurance:

Many Poskim[14] rule that it is permitted [and one is to be encouraged[15]] to purchase life insurance, and doing so is not a sign of lack of Bitachon and the like. Others[16] however take a more negative stance towards its purchase.[17] There is no clear directive of the Rebbe in either direction[18] although in one instance the Rebbe spoke negatively about the matter.[19]

---

[8] Rebbe Yishmael Shabbos 12b; Rebbe Elazar Yuma 80a; Yerushalmi Chagiga 1:2
Background:
The Gemara in Shabbos ibid records a dispute between the Tana Kama and Rebbe Yishmael Ben Elisha in regards to whether it is forbidden to learn near a candle on Shabbos lest one come to tilt the candle. Rebbe Yishmael was of the opinion that it is permitted to do so and he one time tilted the candle while reading, thus transgressing a Biblical command. Rebbe Yishmael then wrote on his booklet after Shabbos: I Yishmael Ben Elisha read near a candle and tilted it on Shabbos. When the Beis Hamikdash will be rebuilt I will bring a fat Chatas offering. Likewise, the Gemara in Yuma ibid and Yerushalmi Chagiga record that one who ate Cheilev in today's time is obligated to write down the amount of Cheilev one has eaten in order so he knows as to whether he must bring a Chatas offering when Moshiach comes and the Shiurim are adjusted by the Sanhedrin. From all the above sources we see that one is required to mark down the Chatas offerings that he becomes liable to bring when Moshiach comes.

[9] M"A 334:33 records the incident of Rebbe Yishmael

[10] Riei Chaim of Rav Chaim Falagi Parshas Tazria; Encyclopedia Talmudit Chatas p. 503; Livyas Chen brought in Yalkut Geula Umoshiach Tzav 7:12

[11] Implication of Admur 334:28 and all other Poskim who omit the ruling of the Gemara ibid and M"A 334:33; Implication of Shulchan Aruch and all Poskim who felt no need to record when one is obligated to bring a Chatas for a sin

[12] Sichos Kodesh 1981 6th of Tishreiy; Likkutei Sichos 18 Maseiy footnote 51

[13] Rebbe ibid, as explained in A!

[14] Lechem Shlomo Y.D. 2:67 [Shlomo Zalman Ehrinreich, Rav of Silvaniei 1863-1944]; Peri Hasadeh 2:44; Kochavei Yitzchak 1:22 in the name of the Shinaver Rav; Igros Moshe 2:111; 4:48; Beir Moshe 8:118; Cheshev Haeifod 3:50; Yabia Omer 3:85; Rav Elyashiv in Koveitz Teshuvos 1:19; Teshuvos Vehanhagos 4:325; Kaf Hachaim 26

[15] Rav Meir Shapiro, the *Rosh Yeshivah* of *Yeshivas Chachmei Lublin,* had a very large life insurance policy, even though he unfortunately had no children. His reason was that since fundraising for the yeshiva was completely on his shoulders, he was concerned that in the event of his premature death, the yeshiva would be forced to close. We see that he was not concerned with any of the above issues and felt that purchasing insurance was an appropriate course of action.

[16] Even Yisrael 9:161 writes he does not feel right to obligate people to buy life insurance, as perhaps the fact that one 's family is dependent on him monetarily is a reason in heaven to keep him alive. Likewise, it will remove the great Mitzvah and Zechus that Klal Yisrael has in providing for orphans and widows; See Teshuvos Vehanhagos ibid

[17] The reason: Several reasons and rebuttals are suggested for why one should not purchase life insurance.
1) The Gemara [Sota 48b] states that anyone who has money in his pocket and states "How will I live tomorrow" is amongst those that have little faith. From here it is possible to learn that one should not worry about what will happen after 120 years. On the other hand, the same way one is to continue working each day even though he has money in the bank to last him until tomorrow, so too he should make a life insurance policy. The Gemara's words mean to say that one should not worry about the issue, however certainly one is to place physical effort to achieve tomorrow's pay. [Igros Moshe ibid; Yabia Omer ibid]
2) One is not to open the mouth of the Satan and begin discussing matters of death. [See Brachos 19a and 60a; Kesubos 8b; M"A 239:7] Since the policies are based on the death of the policy holder, and it mentions his death in various places of the document, therefore one should not make a policy. On the other hand the Rivash 114 [based on Menachos 42a and Beis Yosef Yoreh Deah 339] rules that one may purchase a Kever while alive, and hence we see that doing matters that prepare for death is not considered that one is opening the mouth of the Satan. [Lechem Shlomo ibid]
3) Perhaps the fact that one's family is dependent on him monetarily is a reason in heaven to keep him alive. If one purchases a life insurance policy, then this merit will disappear. [Even Yisrael ibid] A counter claim to this is that to the contrary, having a life insurance is a Segula for long life being that the Mazal of life insurance companies is to be wealthy, and hence prevent them from losing money by having to pay out a policy in the event of death. [Kochavei Yitzchak ibid]

[18] In response to the authors query addressed to Rabbi Leibel Groner regarding the Rebbe's position on life insurance, and the rumors that the Rebbe encouraged it, he replied: *I have never heard that the Rebbe should encourage it.*

[19] In Sichas 13th Tammuz 1951 the Rebbe stated as follows: *"The concept of selling life insurance is a business from the side of Kelipa. Instead of going and announcing to people that they can purchase life, he announces on the contrary that one already now should arrange what will happen after 120 years, and therefore everyone should buy a policy through giving a small amount each year and thus being secure that when the time comes, they will take care of him monetarily. This job requires great effort and is contrary to logic: Why does one need to speak with others about what will happen after 120 years when he can speak to him about joyful matters. The Rebbe Rashab once told a Chassid who desired to write a will which included giving money to charity, that he should give the money now to charity and not wait for later."*

<u>A Kosher policy</u>: One who decides to purchase a life insurance policy must verify that the policy does not involve any Ribis prohibitions, if the policy is taking place through a Jewish owned company or agent. Likewise, some policies ask the owner to allow or provide an autopsy report in order to make a claim in the event of death. According to Halacha, it is forbidden to sign away the rights for autopsy on a Jewish corpse, due to it being desecration of the dead.

Our other Sefarim available on shulchanaruchharav.com, Amazon.com and selected book stores

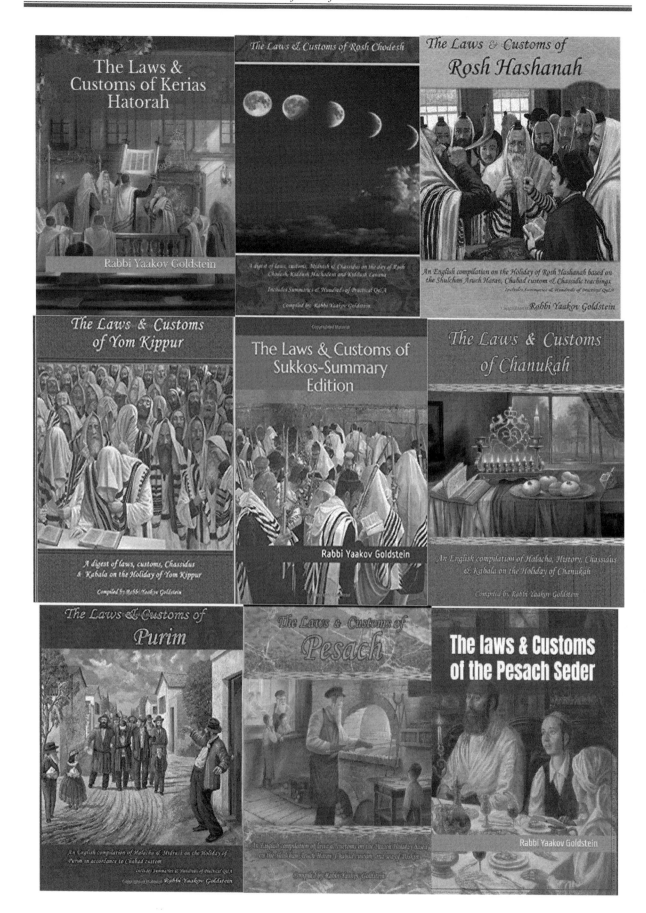

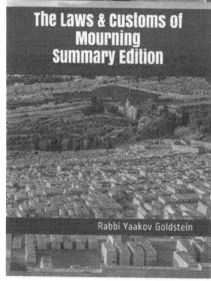

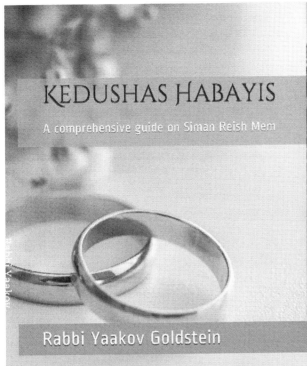

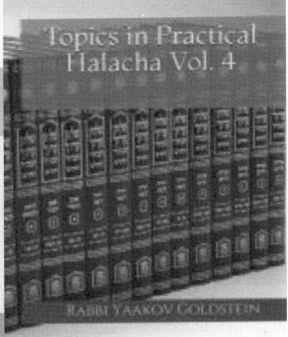

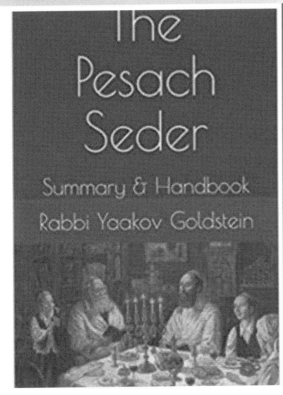

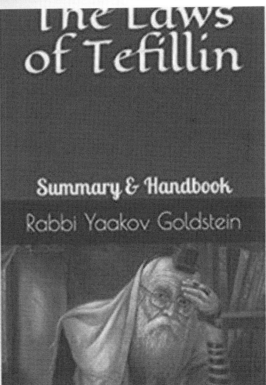

היה קורא   פרק שני   ברכות   יז.

ולא פריה ורביה ולא משא ומתן ולא קנאה ולא שנאה ולא תחרות אלא צדיקים יושבין ועטרותיהם
בראשיהם ונהנים מזיו השכינה שנאמר יויחזו את האלהים ויאכלו וישתו: גדולה הבטחה שהבטיחן
הקב"ה לנשים יותר מן האנשים שנא׳ ינשים שאננות קומנה שמענה קולי בנות בוטחות האזנה אמרתי
א"ל רב לר׳ חייא נשים במאי זכיין יבאקרויי בנייהו לבי כנישתא ובאתנויי גברייהו בי רבנן ונטרין לגברייהו
עד דאתו מבי רבנן. כי הוו מפטרי רבנן מבי ר׳ אמי ואמרי לה מבי ר׳ חנינא אמרי ליה הכי עולמך תראה בחייך
ואחריתך לחיי העולם הבא ותקותך לדור דורים הוגה לבך יהגה תבונה פיך ידבר חכמות ולשונך ירחיש רננות
עפעפיך יישירו נגדך עיניך יאירו במאור תורה ופניך יזהירו כזוהר הרקיע שפתותיך יביעו דעת וכליותיך

Rav said to Rav Chiya
"With what do women receive merit [of learning Torah]? Through
escorting their children to the Talmud Torah, and assisting their
husbands in learning Torah, and waiting for their husbands to return
from the Beis Midrash"

This Sefer is dedicated to my dear wife whose continuous support and
sharing of joint goals in spreading Torah and Judaism have allowed this
Sefer to become a reality.

May Hashem grant her and our children much
success and blessing in all their endeavors

שיינא שרה ליבא בת חיה ראשא
&
מושקא פריידא
שניאור זלמן
דבורה לאה
נחמה דינה
מנוחה רחל
חנה
שטערנא מרים
שלום דובער
חוה אסתר
בתשבע
יהודית שמחה

In memory of

Eliezer Goldstein

אליעזר בן יעקב ישראל ז"ל

May his soul be bound in the bonds of eternal life and his memory ever be for a blessing

ת.נ.צ.ב.ה

Dedicated by
Rabbi Yaakov Goldstein
The Author

In memory of

Gladys Szerer

שרה בת שלום ז"ל

May her soul be bound in the bonds of eternal life and her memory ever be for a blessing

ת.נ.צ.ב.ה

Dedicated by
Rabbi Roberto and Margie Szerer, New York

Dedicated by the Trestman Family in memory of

פריידל באשה בת חיים שלמה
Friedel Basha bas Chaim Shlomo

משה בן שלמה
Moshe ben Shlomo

May their souls be bound in the bonds of eternal life
ת.נ.צ.ב.ה

Dedicated by

Jeffrey Lee [Yaakov] Cohen

President of BECO Managements

In honor of his family, employees, & the Holy work of Shulchanaruchharav.com

In memory of

גדלי' בן שניאור זלמן ז"ל

שניאור זלמן בן זאב ז"ל

יאחא רייזל בת דוד ע"ה

נתנאל בן חיים הלוי ז"ל

טויבא בת ירוחם פישל ע"ה

May their souls be bound in the bonds of eternal life and their memory ever be for a blessing

ת.נ.צ.ב.ה

Dedicated by
Rabbi and Mrs. Jaffe, Manchester, England

Made in the USA
Monee, IL
19 April 2023